IT Skills for Accounting Stude

CW01477046

Ian T Robertson

BA (Hons), Msc, Cert Ed
Lecturer in Accounting and Information Technology,
University of Paisley

PITMAN
PUBLISHING

London · Hong Kong · Johannesburg · Melbourne · Singapore · Washington DC

PITMAN PUBLISHING
128 Long Acre, London WC2E 9AN
Tel: +44 (0)171 447 2000
Fax: +44 (0)171 240 5771

A Division of Pearson Professional Limited

First published in Great Britain in 1996

ISBN 0 273 61714 1

British Library Cataloguing in Publication Data
A CIP catalogue record for this book can be obtained from the British Library

10 9 8 7 6 5 4 3 2 1

Typeset by Land & Unwin (Data Sciences) Ltd
Printed and bound in Great Britain by Clays Ltd, St Ives plc

The Publishers' policy is to use paper manufactured from sustainable forests.

CONTENTS

PREFACE

The book is designed for accounting students or those students taking accounting as part of their course of study who wish to gain a knowledge of computerised accounting and spreadsheets. It is designed for self-study, thereby allowing students to take command of their own learning and progress at their own pace.

Part 1 deals with computerised accounting and aims to teach the student how to use the highly popular software package, Sage Sterling for Windows® Version 3.

The learning material is presented as a case study. The first few chapters deal with setting up the accounts for a new business, posting ledger transactions and the production of a set of Final Accounts. Later chapters cover Report Generation, Invoicing, Stock Control and Order Processing.

In computerised accounting, once transaction details have been entered, the postings to the ledger accounts are made automatically by the program and are therefore not immediately apparent to the user. For this reason the double entry recording which has taken place for each transaction is described and the reader is invited to view the entries made in the ledger accounts which have been affected.

There are four programs within the Sage Sterling for Windows range; Bookkeeper, Accountant, Accountant Plus and Financial Controller. The limit of progression through the material in Part 1 will be defined by the program which is being used. This is explained further in Material Structure and Program Requirements in Chapter 1.

Part 2 covers the use of spreadsheets and their application in the field of accounting and finance using Microsoft® Excel Version 5.

The essential features of worksheet building and formatting are described in the early chapters, followed by an introduction to the use of functions and the creation and formatting of charts and graphs including 'embedded' charts. The 3-D facilities are described in a chapter on Worksheet and Workbook Linking and this is taken a stage further in the coverage of Pivot Tables, a dynamic, multi-dimensional analysis and reporting tool. The techniques involved in building, sorting, maintaining and filtering a database are explained and finally some useful 'tools' such as Data Tables and Scenario Manager are described, and the procedure for transferring data files from Sage Sterling for Windows to Microsoft® Excel is given.

All features are described using accounting/finance-related examples and practice/consolidation exercises have been inserted where appropriate. Most of the worksheets created while using the learning material are maintained within one workbook, LearnXL, for tidiness and ease of access.

Chapter 24 consists of 20 exercises which are designed to emphasise the application of spreadsheets in the field of accounting and finance. For each exercise the student is asked to design a model which will not only answer the existing problem but can also be used for problems of a similar nature using different input data. This should test the understanding of both the problem area and the mechanics of spreadsheet modelling and allow the student to appreciate the usefulness of a well-designed model for sensitivity analysis.

The Appendix gives suggested solutions for each exercise except those marked with an asterisk which are provided in the Instructor's Manual. The model itself is shown on one worksheet and the underlying formulae are shown on a separate worksheet.

ACKNOWLEDGEMENTS

Many thanks to Peter Wilson, Neil McTaggart, Roger Graham and Pat Stevenson from the University of Paisley. Their patience and competent technical and secretarial support in the compilation of the book was invaluable and greatly appreciated.

I would also like to express my gratitude to Colin Bradshaw from the Sage Group plc, for supplying me with regular updates of 'beta' software and 'helpline' guidance while the book was being written.

PART 1

Computerised Accounting using Sage Sterling for Windows®: Version 3

CHAPTER 1

Introduction

Material Structure and Program Requirements · Sage Files · Loading the Program · The Desktop Window · Processing Windows · Help System · Exiting the Program

MATERIAL STRUCTURE AND PROGRAM REQUIREMENTS

In this training material the accounts are being kept for a wholesaler, Ascot Enterprises, which supplies kitchen equipment, TVs, hi-fi equipment and personal care items to the retail trade. The material covers a three-month period, January–March, and it is expected that students will work through the chapters sequentially, building up transaction histories in their accounts as they progress. The following is a summary of chapter contents and the Sage program required to cover the material in each chapter.

Chapters 1–4 (January)

- Setting up accounts in sales, purchases and nominal ledgers.
- Posting opening balances and transactions to these accounts.
- VAT return.
- Production of Profit and Loss Account and Balance Sheet at end of month.

Program

Any of the following: Bookkeeper (will not produce a Balance Sheet), Accountant, Accountant Plus, Financial Controller.

Chapters 5 and 6 (February)

- Bad debts, dishonoured cheques, contra entries, error correction.
- Automated routines for depreciation, recurring entries and accruals and prepayments.
- Production of Profit and Loss Account and Balance Sheet at end of month 2.
- Year-end procedure.
- Report Generator.

Program

Any of the following: Accountant, Accountant Plus, Financial Controller.

Chapter 7 (March)

- Stock control and Invoicing.

Program

Accountant Plus or Financial Controller.

Chapter 8 (March)

- Order processing.

Program

Financial Controller.

SAGE FILES

The material has been written on the assumption that the program is being run from a hard disc and that transactions data entered by the students will be saved to the data files also stored on hard disc.

LOADING THE PROGRAM

Sage Sterling for Windows® is a computerised accounting program which runs in the Windows® operating system.

Load the program. If a logon name and access password have been set up you will be prompted to enter them now. In a few seconds the **Desktop** window should be displayed.

THE DESKTOP WINDOW

The **Desktop** window showing the menu choices and Toolbar options should be similar to the following:

Control **Title** **Menu**   **Toolbar**   **Minimise**   **Maximise/**
button **bar** **bar**   **button**   **Restore**
                                            button

Sterling for Windows V3.01 - ASCOT ENTERPRISES

File   Edit   View   Options   Defaults   Data   Period End   Window   Help

Desktop area

Sterling for Windows V3.01   1st January 1996

Status bar   **Mouse pointer**

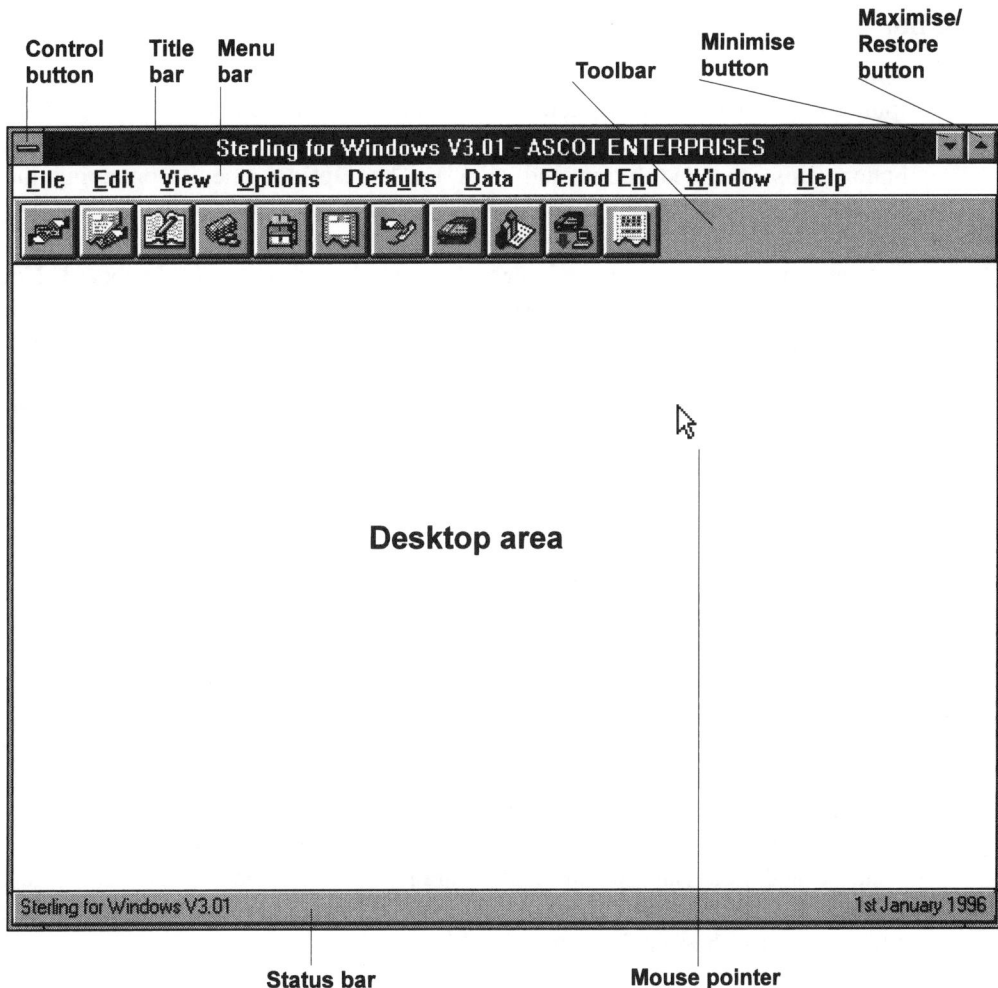

The Toolbar options will vary depending on the program you are using (Bookkeeper, Accountant, Accountant Plus or Financial Controller).

Mouse pointer

Windows® application programs such as Sage Sterling for Windows, Microsoft® Excel and Microsoft® Word are designed to be used with a mouse. Moving the mouse causes the arrow-shaped pointer (↖) on the screen to move also. This can be used to carry out certain functions such as opening a menu, selecting a command from a menu, activating a Toolbar button or selecting a text box for data entry. If the pointer is not visible on the screen move the mouse a little.

Title bar

Each window in this system has a Title bar in which the name of the window is displayed.

Menu bar

This displays a list of the menu choices – **File, Edit, View, Options,** etc. These are 'pull-down' menus which contain the Sage commands for carrying out specific functions. Move the mouse pointer over the word **Options** and click the left mouse button (this is called 'point and click'). The **Options** menu containing the list of associated commands should drop down. A command itself can be selected by pointing and clicking. Point and click anywhere outside the menu to close it.

Menu choices and commands can also be selected using the keyboard. Notice that each menu choice on the Menu bar has one of its letters underlined: **F**ile, **E**dit, **V**iew, **O**ptions, **Defa**ults, etc. To open a menu using the keyboard, hold down the [**Alt**] key and press the appropriate underlined letter. The corresponding menu should now drop down. Notice that each command on the menu also has one of its letters underlined. To activate one of the menu commands simply press the appropriate underlined letter or move the highlight bar over the command using one of the arrow keys and press [**Enter**]. Press the [**Alt**] or [**F10**] key to close the menu.

Toolbar

This consists of a row of buttons which give you access to the main processing areas within the program (**Customers, Suppliers, Nominal Ledger,** etc). If you allow the mouse pointer to hover over a button its name will appear next to the pointer. To select an option for processing move the mouse pointer over the appropriate Toolbar button and click. This will open a new processing window on the **Desktop**.

The options offered on the Toolbar can also be accessed from the **Options** pull-down menu. This means that the Toolbar can be removed from the **Desktop** window and you can operate the program entirely from the pull-down menus. To remove the Toolbar display open the **View** menu and select the **Toolbar** command. The display can be switched on and off in this manner.

PROCESSING WINDOWS

Move the mouse pointer over the **Customers** button on the Toolbar and click. The following **Customers** window should now open:

Control   Title   Click here to
button   bar   Toolbar   maximise the window

A/C	Name	Balance	Crd Limit	Contact

Criteria   Swap   Clear   Delete   Close

Click here to   Scroll
close the window   button

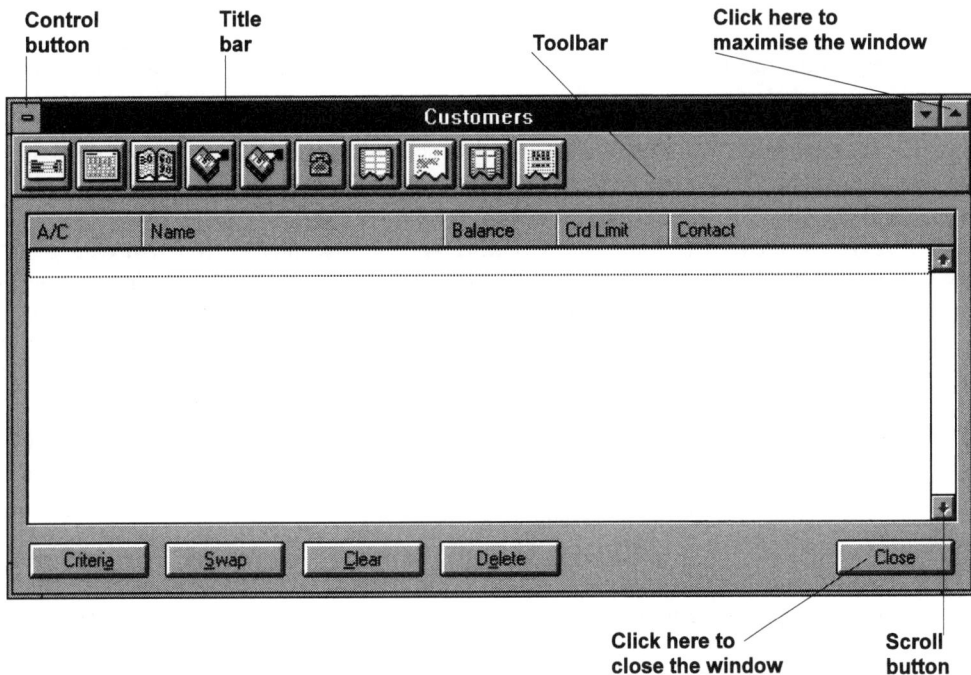

Notice that the **Customers** window also has a Toolbar and the buttons on this allow you access to further customer processing and reporting windows. The name of the button will appear when you position the mouse pointer over it. To select a Toolbar option in a processing window you can 'point and click' with the mouse or select the button using the **[Tab]** key on the keyboard and press **[Enter]**.

You can have several windows open simultaneously, each one overlaying the previous one, but only one can be active at a time. The **Window** menu will list the processing windows which are currently open and you can activate a window (bring it into the foreground for processing) by selecting from this list.

When you want to close a processing window there are several ways to do so:

(a) Click on the window's **Close** button.

(b) Press the **[Esc]** key. This will close one window at a time.

(c) Click on the window's 'control' button, ⊟ , at the extreme left of the Title bar, and select **Close** from the pull-down menu.
Be careful to click on the correct 'control' button. If more than one window is open, e.g. **Desktop** and **Customers**, a 'control' button will be visible for each window.

(d) Double-click on the window's 'control' button.

If you have several processing windows open you can close them all in one operation by selecting the **Close All** command from the **Window** menu.

Moving and sizing processing windows

Processing windows can be moved around on the **Desktop**. This is sometimes necessary if part of the window is obscured. The procedure is as follows:

♦ Point to the window's Title bar.

♦ While the mouse pointer is located over the Title bar click and hold down the left mouse button and drag the pointer in the direction you wish the window to move.

This operation is referred to as 'click and drag' and can also be used to reposition dialogue boxes.

Each window will have a maximise button, ▲, and a minimise button, ▼, at the extreme right of its Title bar. Clicking on the maximise button will enlarge the window to fill the **Desktop** and the minimise button will reduce the window to an icon on the **Desktop**. It is not advisable to use the minimise button unless you are familiar with the Windows® operating environment.

HELP SYSTEM

Assistance is constantly available from Sage's comprehensive 'Help' facility. This can be accessed by pressing the **[F1]** function key or by selecting the **Help** option from the Menu bar in the **Desktop** window. This assistance is context-sensitive, meaning that the help provided will relate to the part of the program you are currently working in.

♦ Ensure that the **Desktop** window is clear (i.e. all processing windows are closed).

♦ Click on the word **Help** on the Menu bar and the **Help** pull-down menu will appear.

♦ Click on the **Index** command on the **Help** menu and the following **Help Contents** window should open:

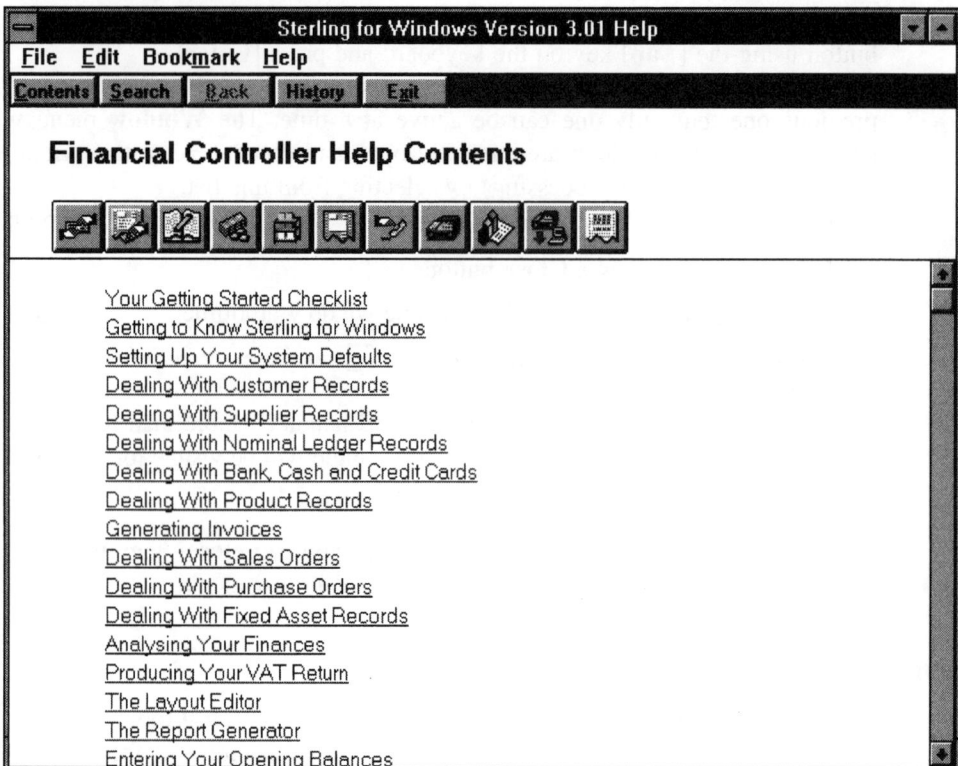

```
Sterling for Windows Version 3.01 Help
File   Edit   Bookmark   Help
Contents  Search  Back  History  Exit

Financial Controller Help Contents

  Your Getting Started Checklist
  Getting to Know Sterling for Windows
  Setting Up Your System Defaults
  Dealing With Customer Records
  Dealing With Supplier Records
  Dealing With Nominal Ledger Records
  Dealing With Bank, Cash and Credit Cards
  Dealing With Product Records
  Generating Invoices
  Dealing With Sales Orders
  Dealing With Purchase Orders
  Dealing With Fixed Asset Records
  Analysing Your Finances
  Producing Your VAT Return
  The Layout Editor
  The Report Generator
  Entering Your Opening Balances
```

The Toolbar buttons at the top of the **Help Contents** window are the same as those on the **Desktop** window and by selecting the appropriate button you can gain access to help on the different areas of the program (**Customers, Suppliers, Nominal Ledger**, etc.). If you move the mouse pointer slowly over the list of contents the pointer will change from an arrow to a hand shape as it passes over a topic. So for help on a particular topic move the mouse pointer to that topic and when it changes to a hand shape click the mouse button. A further **Help** window displaying contents on the selected topic should open and the selection procedure is similar (point and click). To close the **Help** window click the **Exit** button or open the **File** menu and select **Exit**. This should return you to the **Desktop** window.

Sage can also search for help on a particular topic entered by the user. This facility can be accessed by selecting the **Search for Help on..** option on the **Help** menu.

EXITING THE PROGRAM

The following is the exit procedure, although you are not required to do this at the moment.

♦ Open the **File** menu and select **Exit**.

A dialogue box will appear asking if you wish to Backup your Data.

♦ If you wish to backup the data files to floppy disc click the **Yes** button, otherwise click the **No** button.

CHAPTER 2

Data Files and Default Settings

Zero Data Files and set Financial Year Start Date · Training Procedure ·
Company Preferences · VAT Codes and Rates · Departments · Customer
Defaults · Supplier Defaults · Backup Data Files

ZERO DATA FILES AND SET FINANCIAL YEAR START DATE

The training material in this book assumes that the program is being run from the hard drive and that the data files are also stored on the hard disc. Before a student uses this material for the first time it will be necessary to ensure that these data files are blank.

The data files should be zeroed now using the following procedure:

♦ Open the **Data** menu and select **Disk Doctor**.

♦ When the **Disk Doctor** dialogue box opens click the **New Data** (or **Rebuild**) button and the following **Create New Data Files** (or **Rebuild Data Files**) dialogue box should appear:

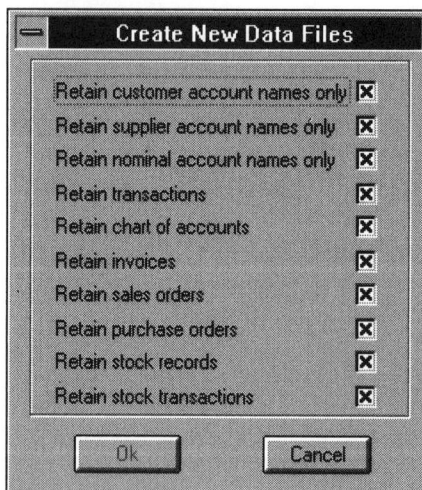

♦ Click on each one of the check boxes to deselect it (the cross will disappear). When the crosses have been removed from each check box click the **OK** button. You will now be asked to confirm that you want to rebuild your data files. Click the **Yes** button and the existing data files will be cleared. A **New nominal ledger** dialogue box should now open asking if you wish to use the default nominal structure. Click the **Yes** button.

Once the default nominal ledger structure has been set up the following **Financial Year** dialogue box should open:

```
┌─────────────────────────────────────────────────┐
│ ─            Financial Year                       │
│                                                   │
│ Financial Year Starts in   │January    │ ±│  │1996││
│                                                   │
│                      │   Ok   │   │ Cancel │      │
└─────────────────────────────────────────────────┘
```

The **Financial Year** dialogue box allows you to set your financial year start date. The material in the case study assumes that the financial year begins in January 1996. If January is not already displayed in the 'Month' box click the ⊞ button and select from the drop-down list. If the year 1996 is not displayed click in the 'Year' box, delete the existing entry using the **[Backspace]** or **[Delete]** key and type 1996.

♦ When you have set the start month and year properly select the **OK** button. If a **Confirm** dialogue box now opens, asking you to confirm that the financial year will start in January 1996, select the **Yes** button.

♦ **Close** the **Disk Doctor** dialogue box.

TRAINING PROCEDURE

It is highly likely in a training situation that several students will be inputting data to the same machine at different times. It is therefore necessary to have some procedure which ensures that each student is working with his/her own data. Sage's **Backup** and **Restore** routines can be used to good effect in this respect. The **Backup** routine can be used to copy the data files from the hard disc to a floppy disc and the **Restore** routine would copy these files back from the floppy disc to the hard disc. Both of these routines overwrite existing data files in the process.

The procedure during training sessions should therefore be as follows:

Training Session		*Operation*
1	Beginning	Zero data files.
	During	Enter transactions from training material.
	End	**Backup** data files to student's floppy disc.
2	Beginning	**Restore** data files from student's floppy to hard disc. (This will overwrite existing data on hard disc.)
	During	Enter further transactions from training material.
	End	**Backup** data files to floppy disc. (This will transfer updated files from hard to floppy disc overwriting the existing backup file.)
3	Subsequent sessions	As 2.

The **Backup** and **Restore** routines are described more fully at the end of this chapter in the section on Backup Data Files.

COMPANY PREFERENCES

The **Company Preferences** option which is accessed from the **Defaults** menu allows you to do the following:

(a) Enter or edit your company's name and address.

(b) Set up your system defaults, e.g. Access Rights, the VAT system you wish to use (Standard or VAT Cash Accounting), whether you wish to exclude deleted transactions from reports or include them, and others.

(c) Edit some of the text labels which appear next to the text boxes on the Customer, Supplier and Bank Record windows.

(d) Set up function keys to run other programs from within Sage Sterling for Windows and enter communication defaults for use with the telephone option.

We'll use the **Company Preferences** option to enter our company's name and address and check some of the other settings. However, due to the nature of the settings which can be made and edited using this option access to it may be denied.

♦ Open the **Defaults** menu and select **Company Preferences**. If this option does not appear on the menu you'll know that access has been denied and you'll have to accept the default settings. If **Company Preferences** is an option the dialogue box which appears should be similar to the following:

```
┌──────────────────────────────────────────────────────────────┐
│ ▭              Company Preferences                             │
├──────────────────────────────────────────────────────────────┤
│  ┌Details─┐┌Labels─┐┌System─┐┌Environment─┐                   │
│                                                                │
│   ┌Company Details──────────────────────────────────────┐     │
│       Name      │ASCOT ENTERPRISES                     │       │
│                                                                │
│       Street1   │Solway Business Park                  │       │
│                                                                │
│       Street2   │                                      │       │
│                                                                │
│       Town      │CARLISLE                              │       │
│                                                                │
│       County    │                                      │       │
│                                                                │
│       Post Code │CL10 5EU                              │       │
│   └──────────────────────────────────────────────────────┘    │
│                                                                │
│                                    ┌────Ok────┐ ┌──Cancel──┐   │
│                                    └──────────┘ └──────────┘   │
└──────────────────────────────────────────────────────────────┘
```

The dialogue box has several 'pages' which can be accessed using the index tab buttons arranged along the top: **Details, Labels, System** and **Environment**.

◆ Ensure that the **Details** 'page' is displayed as shown. If not, click on the **Details** tab button.

◆ Click in the **Name** field and the insertion cursor (a vertical bar) will begin 'flashing' there. Once you have positioned the insertion cursor in a field you can delete the contents of the field and type a new entry. Delete any existing entry in the **Name** field using the **[Backspace]** or **[Delete]** key and type in ASCOT ENTERPRISES. Click in or **[Tab]** to the **Street1** field, delete any existing entry and type in Solway Business Park.

◆ In a similar manner complete the **Details** 'page' with the following entries:

Street2   : −
Town   : CARLISLE
County   : −
Post Code : CL10 5EU

♦ Click on the **Labels** tab button and the **Labels** 'page', similar to the following, should be displayed:

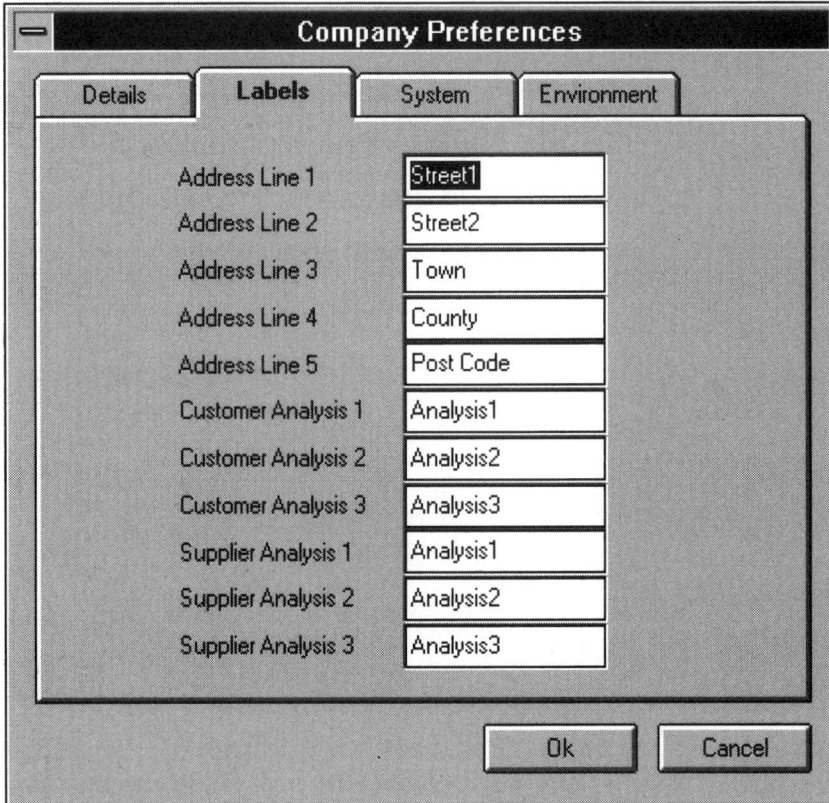

```
┌─────────────────────────────────────────────────────────┐
│ ▬            Company Preferences                          │
├─────────────────────────────────────────────────────────┤
│  ┌────────┬──────────┬────────────┬─────────────┐         │
│  │ Details│  Labels  │   System   │ Environment │         │
│  └────────┘          └────────────┴─────────────┘         │
│                                                           │
│           Address Line 1     [Street1          ]          │
│           Address Line 2     [Street2          ]          │
│           Address Line 3     [Town             ]          │
│           Address Line 4     [County           ]          │
│           Address Line 5     [Post Code        ]          │
│         Customer Analysis 1  [Analysis1        ]          │
│         Customer Analysis 2  [Analysis2        ]          │
│         Customer Analysis 3  [Analysis3        ]          │
│         Supplier Analysis 1  [Analysis1        ]          │
│         Supplier Analysis 2  [Analysis2        ]          │
│         Supplier Analysis 3  [Analysis3        ]          │
│                                                           │
│                              [    Ok    ]  [  Cancel  ]   │
└─────────────────────────────────────────────────────────┘
```

This 'page' allows you to amend the labels which appear alongside the address fields on the Customer, Supplier and Bank Records and the analysis fields on the Customer and Supplier Records.

♦ Check and alter where necessary the entries in the following fields:

Address Line 1	:	Street1
Address Line 2	:	Street2
Address Line 3	:	Town
Address Line 4	:	County
Address Line 5	:	Post Code
Customer Analysis 1	:	Analysis1
Customer Analysis 2	:	Analysis2
Customer Analysis 3	:	Analysis3
Supplier Analysis 1	:	Analysis1
Supplier Analysis 2	:	Analysis2
Supplier Analysis 3	:	Analysis3

♦ Click on the **System** tab button at the top of the dialogue box to display the **System** 'page'.

◆ Ensure that the **VAT Cash Accounting** check box is deselected. If a cross appears in the box click on the box to remove it. By deselecting this check box the VAT Return will be calculated on a Standard VAT Accounting basis, i.e. calculated from input and output VAT amounts you have invoices for, rather than amounts you actually receive and pay.

◆ Ensure that the **Exclude Deleted Transactions** check box is deselected (no cross). This means that if a transaction is amended and replaced with a new transaction using the **Disk Doctor** routine the original transaction will still be shown on reports and activity windows. This is explained more fully in Chapter 5 in the section on error correction.

◆ If you are using Version 3.10 of the program the **System** 'page' will allow you to select a **Non-Vatable Tax Code**, i.e. the tax code for transactions which do not involve VAT and are not included on the VAT Return. If this option is present set the code to **T9 0.00** by clicking the ⬇ button and selecting from the drop-down list.

There is also a **No Recurring Entries at Startup** check box in Version 3.10. If this option is present select the check box (a cross will appear when selected) and this will disable the reminder window which would otherwise appear each time you run the program if there are any recurring entries outstanding for posting.

◆ Select the **OK** button at the bottom of the dialogue box and your settings will be saved.

VAT CODES AND RATES

♦ Open the **Defaults** menu and select **Tax Codes**. The following **Tax Codes** dialogue box should appear displaying the current settings:

Code	Rate	In VAT ret	EC Sale	EC Purch
T0	0.00	Y	N	N
T1	17.50	Y	N	N
T2	0.00	Y	N	N
T3	0.00	Y	N	N
T4	0.00	Y	Y	N
T5	0.00	Y	N	N
T6	0.00	Y	N	N

Edit   Close

When entering transaction details to the ledger accounts VAT codes (T0, T1, T2, etc.) are used to identify to the program the appropriate rate of VAT to apply to the transaction. The rate applicable to each code can be set up or amended using the **Edit** button in the **Tax Codes** dialogue box. You can also specify which rates relate to transactions with EC countries so that these can be identified on the VAT Return form.

♦ Check that the following codes are set correctly:

Code	Rate	In VAT ret	
T0	0.00	Y	Use for zero-rated transactions.
T1	17.50	Y	Use for transactions which bear VAT at standard rate.
T2	0.00	Y	Use for exempt transactions.
T9	0.00	N	Use for non-VAT transactions.

You should not need to alter any of these rates but if you do, follow the amendment procedure described next.

Since VAT on fuel and power is 8% we'll allocate this rate to code **T3**.

♦ Select (highlight) code **T3** by pointing and clicking (or use the arrow key on the keyboard).

♦ Click on the **Edit** button at the bottom of the dialogue box and the following **Tax Code Setup** dialogue box should appear:

- ◆ Enter the **Rate** as 8 and ensure that the **Include in VAT return** check box is selected (it should have a cross in it). Ensure that the **EC Code** check box is de-selected (no cross).

- ◆ Click the **OK** button to return to the **Tax Codes** dialogue box where VAT code **T3** should now show the new rate of 8%.

These codes can now be used when recording the details of transactions in the ledgers. The appropriate VAT will be entered as a code and the program will apply the rate which corresponds to this code. For example:

- • When posting an invoice which bears the standard rate of VAT, code T1 would be used.

- • When recording the withdrawal of funds from the bank to pay salaries the code used would be T9 (non-VAT transaction).

- ◆ Click the **Close** button to return to the **Desktop** window.

DEPARTMENTS

It is possible to analyse transactions by department or division if your business is split in this way. The system can cope with up to 999 departments/divisions each of which is allocated a name and reference code number. This code number would then be entered when posting invoices, credit notes, bank and cash transactions and journal entries. This facility enables costs such as wages, stationery, etc. to be allocated to different departments and departmental cost analysis reports can then be produced with the aid of the Report Generator.

Let's assume that our wholesale business is to be split into three departments: Kitchen Equipment, TV/Hi-Fi and Personal Care. To set up these departments proceed as follows:

- ◆ Open the **Defaults** menu and select **Departments**. The following **Departments** dialogue box should now appear:

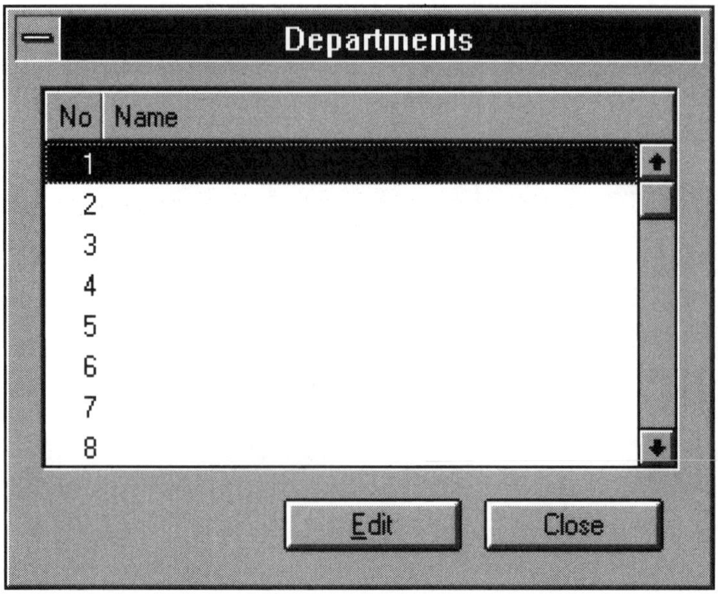
Departments
No
Name
1
2
3
4
5
6
7
8
Edit
Close

- Department **No 1** should be selected (highlighted) at the moment. If not, select it using the arrow key or by pointing and clicking and then click the **Edit** button.
- Enter the **Name** ADMINISTRATION to the small **Edit Departments** dialogue box which appears and select the **OK** button.

ADMINISTRATION should now appear in the **Departments** dialogue box against **No 1**.

If you want to remove a department name or if you make a mistake you can highlight the name in the **Departments** dialogue box and select the **Edit** button. When the small **Edit Departments** dialogue box appears you can clear the name by pressing the **[Delete]** or **[Backspace]** key.

- Complete the **Departments** dialogue box with the following names:

1	ADMINISTRATION	This will be used for costs which are general to the whole company rather than specific to a department.
2	KITCHEN EQUIPMENT	
3	TV/Hi-Fi	
4	PERSONAL CARE	

- When complete select the **Close** button in the **Departments** dialogue box.

CUSTOMER DEFAULTS

♦ Open the **Defaults** menu and select **Customer Defaults**. The **Customer Defaults** dialogue box, similar to the following, should now appear:

```
┌────────────────────────────────────────────────────────┐
│ ▬            Customer Defaults                           │
├────────────────────────────────────────────────────────┤
│ ┌─Defaults─┐ Statements    Periods     Discounts         │
│                                                          │
│  Department     [0                              ][±]      │
│  Credit Limit   [           0.00]                        │
│  Terms          [                                    ]    │
│  Pay Due Days   [0    ]                                   │
│  Sett. Due Days [0    ]                                   │
│  Sett.Discount  [           0.00]                        │
│  Def. N/C       [4000 ][Q]                               │
│  Def. Tax Code  [T1  17.50 ][±]                          │
│  Currency       [1   Pound Sterling][±]                  │
│  Disc. %        [           0.00]                        │
│  Additional Disc. [No additional       ][±]              │
│                                                          │
│                        [    Ok    ]   [  Cancel  ]       │
└────────────────────────────────────────────────────────┘
```

The dialogue box has several 'pages' which can be accessed using the index tab buttons arranged along the top: **Defaults, Statements, Periods, Discounts**.

♦ Ensure that the **Defaults** 'page' is displayed. If not, click the **Defaults** tab button at the top of the dialogue box.

When you set up your customer records you will be 'asked' for details such as credit limit, terms, discount allowed, etc. If these terms and conditions are similar for most customers you can create a set of default 'answers' which will appear automatically for each new customer record you create. This will save time when entering customer record details and these 'answers' can be altered on the customer record window if necessary.

♦ Check and alter where necessary the entries in the following fields. You can move the insertion cursor from field to field using the **[Tab]** key or by pointing and clicking in the field; existing entries can be deleted if necessary using the **[Delete]** or **[Backspace]** key.

Department	: 0	If this entry is not already displayed click the ⬇ button at the right side of the field and select from the drop-down list.
Credit Limit	: 0.00	The credit limit we give will vary from one customer to another so there is no point in entering a default figure here.
Terms	: –	
Pay Due Days	: 30	Usual credit terms, i.e. the number of days you give your customers to pay.
Sett. Due Days	: 0	
Sett. Discount	: 0.00	
Def. N/C	: 4000	If 4000 is not already displayed click in the field, delete the existing entry using the [**Backspace**] or [**Delete**] key and type in the correct entry.
Def. Tax Code	: T1 17.50	This entry will likely be displayed already, otherwise select from the drop-down list.
Currency	: 1 Pound Sterling	If this entry is not displayed select from the drop-down list.
Disc. %	: 0.00	
Additional Disc.	: No additional	

♦ Click on the **Statements** tab button at the top of the dialogue box.

The **Statements** 'page' can be used to specify whether to show on the customer statement individual invoices or the individual transaction items that make up each invoice. You can also elect to show only outstanding transactions on the statement. The text which will appear on the statement against each type of group transaction can also be defined here.

♦ Ensure that the entries on the **Statements** 'page' conform to the following, if not alter where necessary:

```
 ─                      Customer Defaults
┌─────────┬──────────────┬──────────┬───────────┐
│ Defaults │ Statements  │ Periods  │ Discounts │
└─────────┴──────────────┴──────────┴───────────┘

        ☐ Group transactions      ☒ Outstanding items only

    Invoice text       │Goods/Services                    │

    Credit note text   │Credit                            │

    Discount text      │Discount                          │

    Receipt text       │Payment                           │


                              ┌─────────┐   ┌─────────┐
                              │   Ok    │   │ Cancel  │
                              └─────────┘   └─────────┘
```

♦ Click on the **Periods** tab button at the top of the dialogue box. The **Periods** 'page' is used to set up the periods which will be used for your customers' aged balance reports. Ensure that the entries conform to the following, if not alter where necessary:

```
┌──────────────────────────────────────────────────────────┐
│ ═        Customer Defaults                                 │
├──────────────────────────────────────────────────────────┤
│  Defaults  │ Statements │ Periods │ Discounts │            │
│                                                            │
│                                                            │
│              ☐ Use calendar months                         │
│                                                            │
│   Aged Period 1 days outstanding from  [30]  up to  [59]   │
│                                                            │
│   Aged Period 2 days outstanding from  [60]  up to  [89]   │
│                                                            │
│   Aged Period 3 days outstanding from  [90]  up to  [119]  │
│                                                            │
│   Aged Period 4 days outstanding from  [120]  and older    │
│                                                            │
│                                                            │
│                              [    Ok    ]   [  Cancel  ]   │
└──────────────────────────────────────────────────────────┘
```

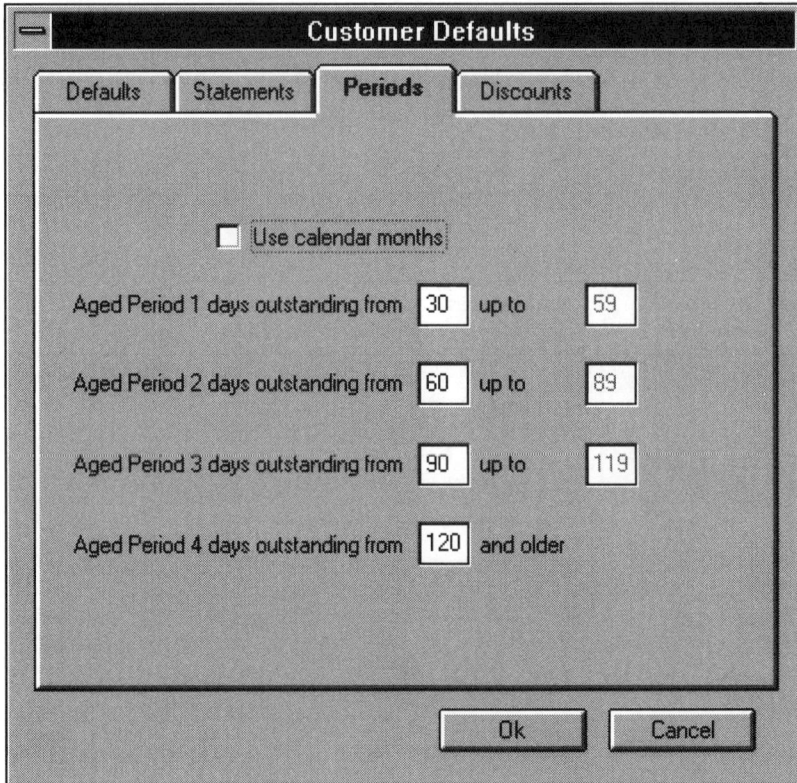

♦ Click the **Ok** button at the bottom of the dialogue box to save your settings.

SUPPLIER DEFAULTS

Open the **Defaults** menu and select **Supplier Defaults**. The **Supplier Defaults** dialogue box, similar to the following, should now appear:

```
┌─────────────────────────────────────────────────────────────┐
│ ⊟               Supplier Defaults                             │
│ ┌──────────┐                                                  │
│ │ Defaults │ Periods                                          │
│ └──────────┘                                                  │
│                                                               │
│   Department    [0                                       ↨]   │
│   Credit Limit  [                    0.00]                    │
│   Terms         [                                        ]    │
│   Pay Due Days  [0  ]                                         │
│   Sett. Due Days[0  ]                                         │
│   Sett. Disc.   [                    0.00]                    │
│   Def. N/C      [5000  Q]                                     │
│   Def. Tax Code [T1 17.5  ↨]                                  │
│   Currency      [1  Pound Sterling  ↨]                        │
│                                                               │
│                            [     Ok     ] [   Cancel   ]      │
└─────────────────────────────────────────────────────────────┘
```

♦ Ensure that the **Defaults** 'page' is displayed. If not, click the **Defaults** tab button at the top of the dialogue box. This 'page' allows you to set the defaults which will appear automatically on the Supplier Records which you create.

♦ Check and alter where necessary the entries in the following fields:

Department   : 0
Credit Limit   : 0.00
Terms   : –
Pay Due Days   : 30   The number of days you usually have to pay your suppliers.

Sett. Due Days : 0
Sett. Disc.   : 0.00
Def. N/C   : 5000
Def. Tax Code : T1 17.50
Currency   : 1 Pound Sterling

♦ Click on the **Periods** tab button at the top of the dialogue box.

♦ When the **Periods** 'page' appears ensure that the entries conform to the following, if not alter where necessary:

```
┌──────────────────────────────────────────────────────────┐
│  ▭                    Supplier Defaults                    │
│ ┌────────┐┌─────────┐                                      │
│ │Defaults││ Periods │                                      │
│ └────────┘└─────────┘────────────────────────────────────┐│
│ │                                                         ││
│ │                                                         ││
│ │            ☐ Use calendar months                        ││
│ │                                                         ││
│ │   Aged Period 1 days outstanding from  [30]  up to  [59]││
│ │                                                         ││
│ │   Aged Period 2 days outstanding from  [60]  up to  [89]││
│ │                                                         ││
│ │   Aged Period 3 days outstanding from  [90]  up to [119]││
│ │                                                         ││
│ │   Aged Period 4 days outstanding from [120]  to older   ││
│ │                                                         ││
│ │                                                         ││
│ │                            [   Ok   ]   [  Cancel  ]    ││
│ └─────────────────────────────────────────────────────────┘│
└──────────────────────────────────────────────────────────┘
```

♦ Click the **Ok** button at the bottom of the dialogue box to save your settings.

BACKUP DATA FILES

Sage Sterling for Windows data files are normally stored on the hard disc. However, there is a **Backup** and **Restore** routine within the program which allows you to transfer these files from the hard disc to a floppy disc and back again. Regular backing up should be standard practice in a commercial environment and several sets of backup discs should be kept in a secure place to safeguard against the possibility of hard disc failure/corruption. In a training situation this feature is particularly useful since students can backup to their own floppy disc at the end of one training session and restore to any machine which has the program files for the next session. Each **Backup** from hard to floppy disc will overwrite the existing backup file ensuring that the student's disc contains the same data files as the hard disc. Similarly, the **Restore** routine, which transfers data files from floppy to hard disc, will overwrite the existing data files on hard disc with those held on floppy.

Take a backup copy of your data files now:

♦ Insert a *blank* formatted disc in the floppy drive.

♦ Open the **Data** menu and select **Backup**. The following **Backup Data Files** dialogue box should now be displayed:

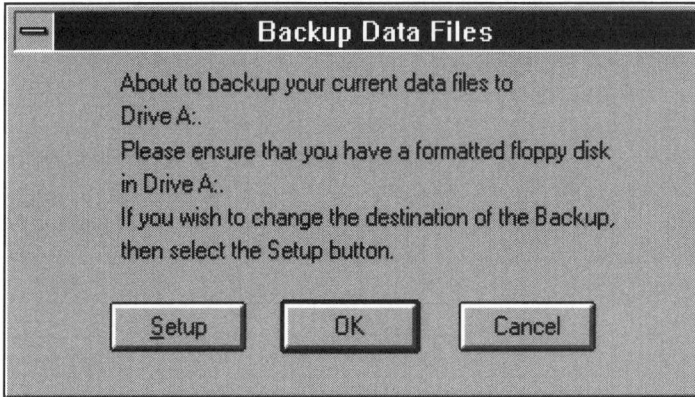

```
┌─────────────────────────────────────────┐
│ ═           Backup Data Files            │
├─────────────────────────────────────────┤
│  About to backup your current data files to │
│  Drive A:.                                │
│  Please ensure that you have a formatted floppy disk │
│  in Drive A:.                             │
│  If you wish to change the destination of the Backup, │
│  then select the Setup button.           │
│                                          │
│     [ Setup ]    [ OK ]    [ Cancel ]    │
└─────────────────────────────────────────┘
```

The dialogue box will indicate which floppy drive the data files will be copied to (the default is A:).

♦ If you wish to change the backup drive click the **Setup** button and the **Backup** dialogue box, similar to the following, will appear:

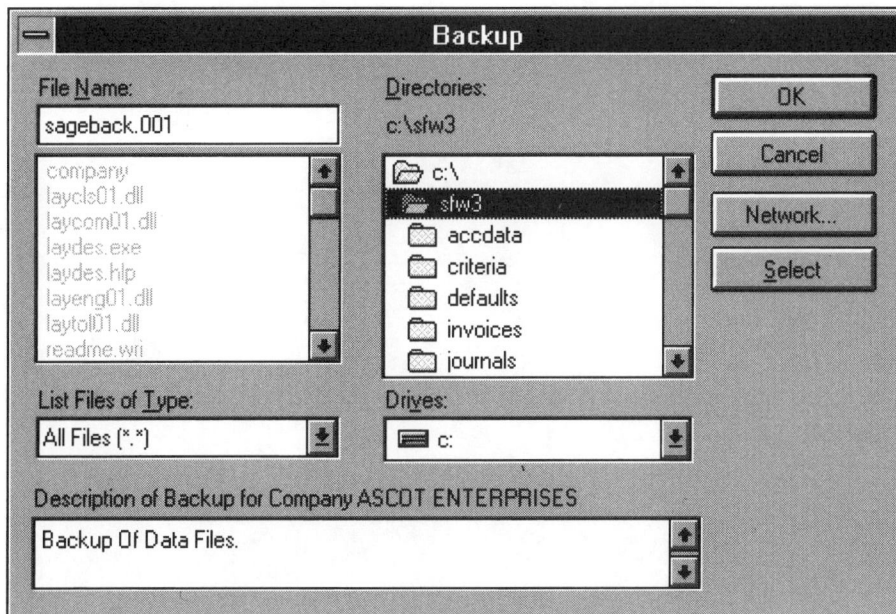

```
┌─────────────────────────────────────────────────────┐
│ ═                       Backup                        │
├─────────────────────────────────────────────────────┤
│ File Name:              Directories:        [ OK ]   │
│ sageback.001            c:\sfw3          [ Cancel ]   │
│ company        ▲   📁 c:\        ▲      [ Network... ]│
│ laycls01.dll       📁 sfw3              [ Select ]    │
│ laycom01.dll       📁 accdata                         │
│ laydes.exe         📁 criteria                        │
│ laydes.hlp         📁 defaults                        │
│ layeng01.dll       📁 invoices                        │
│ laytol01.dll       📁 journals  ▼                     │
│ readme.wri    ▼                                       │
│ List Files of Type:     Drives:                       │
│ All Files (*.*)    ▼    💾 c:        ▼                 │
│ Description of Backup for Company ASCOT ENTERPRISES   │
│ Backup Of Data Files.                          ▲▼     │
└─────────────────────────────────────────────────────┘
```

♦ Choose the drive you wish by clicking the ⊻ button in the **Drives** box and selecting from the drop-down list. When the correct drive letter appears in the **Drives** box click the **OK** button.

♦ Once the correct backup drive is shown in the **Backup Data Files** dialogue box click the **OK** button. A backup copy of your data files will now be made and you will be informed when the operation has been successfully completed.

♦ Click the **OK** button and you will be returned to the **Desktop** window.

You now have a duplicate copy of your data files (containing the default settings) which can be restored to any other machine which has the program files.

The **Restore** routine, also accessed from the **Data** menu, is similar to **Backup** but this time the data files are being transferred from the floppy disc to the hard disc and the existing data files on the hard disc are overwritten by those on the floppy.

CHAPTER 3

Setting up the Ledgers

Setting up Customer Records/Accounts · Setting up Supplier Records/ Accounts · Nominal Records/Accounts · Opening Nominal Account Balances · Program Date Change · Opening Trial Balance · Opening Balances on Customer and Supplier Accounts

SETTING UP CUSTOMER RECORDS/ACCOUNTS

One of the first jobs when computerising an accounting system is to set up your accounts in the Sales Ledger and enter details of your credit customers thereto.

♦ Select the **Customers** option in the **Desktop** window.

The **Customers** window, similar to the following, should now open:

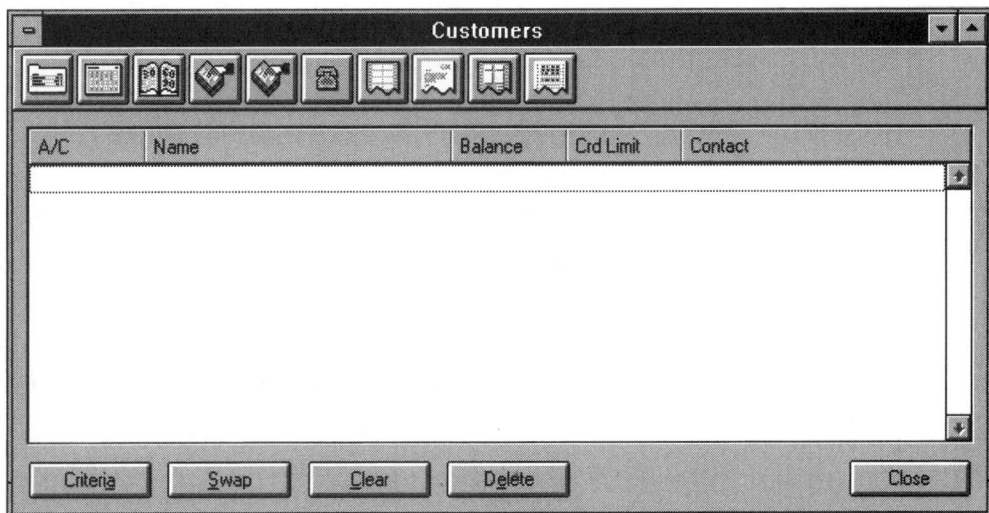

Most windows can be enlarged to fill the **Desktop** by clicking on the maximise button, ▲, at the top right corner of the window.

The **Customers** window should be blank since no customer records have been set up yet.

♦ Click on the **Customer Record** button at the top of the **Customers** window.

♦ The following **Customer Record** window should open to allow you to enter the details of your first customer.

```
┌──────────────────────────────────────────────────────────────────────┐
│ ▭                         Customer Record                     │▼│▲│  │
│┌──────┐ ┌────────┐ ┌──────┐ ┌──────┐ ┌────────┐ ┌──────┐                │
││Details│ │Defaults│ │ Sales│ │ Graph│ │Activity│ │ Memo │                │
│                                                                        │
│  A/C        [        |Q]              ☐ Account on Hold                 │
│  Name       [              ]     Delivery Address                      │
│                                                                        │
│  Street1   ┌──────────────┐      ┌──────────────┐                      │
│  Street2   │              │      │              │                      │
│  Town      │              │      │              │                      │
│  County    │              │      │              │                      │
│  Post Code └──────────────┘      └──────────────┘                      │
│                                                                        │
│  Contact Name ┌──────────────┐   ┌──────────────┐                      │
│  Telephone [☎]│              │   │              │                      │
│  Fax          └──────────────┘   └──────────────┘                      │
│                                                                        │
│  V.A.T. Reg. No [            ]   Customer Balance [0.00    ][%B]        │
│                                                                        │
│ ┌──────┐ ┌────────┐ ┌──────┐ ┌─┐ ┌─┐              ┌──────┐             │
│ │ Save │ │Abandon │ │Delete│ │<│ │>│              │Close │             │
│ └──────┘ └────────┘ └──────┘ └─┘ └─┘              └──────┘             │
└──────────────────────────────────────────────────────────────────────┘
```

Notice that the window has index tab buttons arranged along the top just below the Title bar – **Details, Defaults, Sales, Graph, Activity, Memo**. This means that the window has several 'pages' which can be used to enter details or display information relating to a particular customer.

♦ The **Details** 'page', as shown in the previous figure, should be displayed at the moment. If not, click on the **Details** tab button.

♦ The insertion cursor (a vertical bar) will be 'flashing' in the **A/C** field prompting for input. Enter the following details:

A/C   : ACORN   This is a short reference code for the customer. It can be eight characters long: alphabetic, numeric or a mixture.

♦ To move the insertion cursor to the next field press the **[Tab]** key on the keyboard (to move to a previous field use **[Shift]** + **[Tab]**). The cursor can also be moved by pointing to the appropriate field with the mouse and clicking (the shape of the mouse pointer will change to an 'I' beam when it covers an entry field). Complete the name and address as follows (remember you must move the cursor after each entry).

Name   : Acorn Electrics Ltd
Street1   : 42 Main Street
Street2   : –
Town   : St Albans
County   : –
Post Code : AB5 6BB

♦ Leave the other fields on the **Details** 'page' blank and click on the **Defaults** tab button. The Customer Record **Defaults** 'page', similar to the following, should now be displayed:

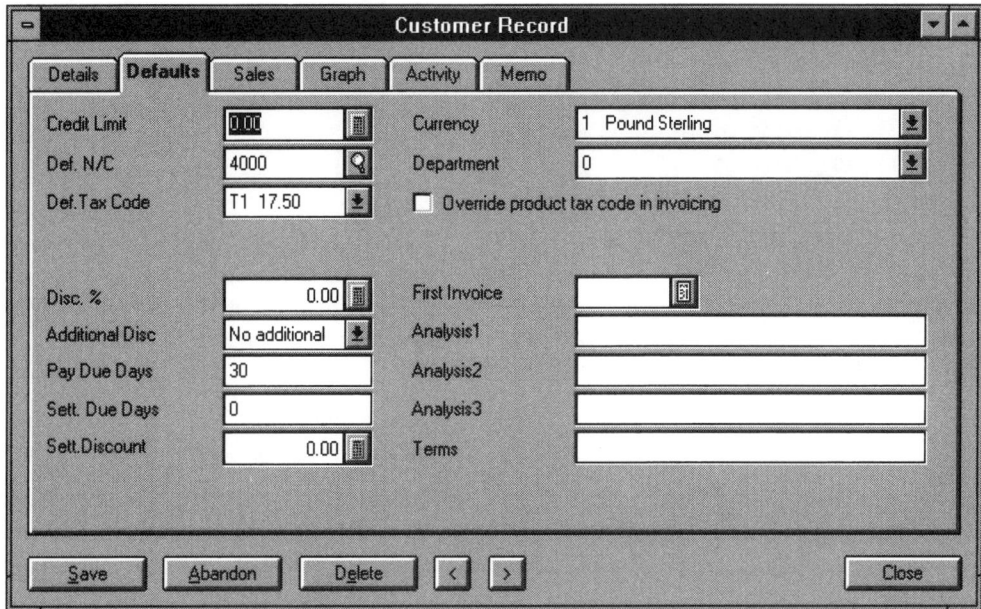

```
┌─────────────────────────────────────────────────────────────────┐
│ ─                       Customer Record                    ▼ ▲   │
│ ┌─────────────────────────────────────────────────────────────┐ │
│ │ Details │ Defaults │ Sales │ Graph │ Activity │ Memo         │ │
│ │                                                               │ │
│ │  Credit Limit    [0.00    ▦]   Currency   [1  Pound Sterling ±] │ │
│ │  Def. N/C        [4000   Q]    Department [0                 ±] │ │
│ │  Def.Tax Code    [T1 17.50 ±]  □ Override product tax code in invoicing │ │
│ │                                                               │ │
│ │  Disc. %         [  0.00 ▦]    First Invoice  [       ▦]      │ │
│ │  Additional Disc [No additional ±]  Analysis1 [          ]    │ │
│ │  Pay Due Days    [30    ]       Analysis2 [          ]        │ │
│ │  Sett. Due Days  [0     ]       Analysis3 [          ]        │ │
│ │  Sett.Discount   [  0.00 ▦]     Terms     [          ]        │ │
│ │                                                               │ │
│ │ [ Save ] [ Abandon ] [ Delete ] [<] [>]          [ Close ]    │ │
│ └─────────────────────────────────────────────────────────────┘ │
└─────────────────────────────────────────────────────────────────┘
```

Note: The layout of the **Defaults** 'page' will be slightly different if you are using Version 3.10 of the program.

♦ Check the entries in the following fields on the **Defaults** 'page' and amend where necessary:

Credit Limit : 3000 — This limit will be checked and a warning displayed if exceeded when invoices are raised or posted using the **Invoicing** routine and when orders are processed. Over-limit customers will also be identified in red on the **Customers** window.

Note that there is a calculator button at the right side of this field. If you click on this button a calculator will appear and enable you to enter the credit limit by clicking on the appropriate numbers with the mouse.

Def. N/C : 4000 — 4000 should already be displayed in this field. This is the default nominal code for the Sales account which will be offered for nominal analysis when invoices are being processed for this customer using the **Batch Invoices** routine. It can be overwritten at the time the transaction is processed. This default code was defined in the **Customer Defaults** dialogue box.

Def. Tax Code   : T1 17.50   If this code and rate are not already displayed click the ⬇ button at the right side of the field and select from the drop-down list. This is the default VAT code and rate which will be used when transactions are being processed for this customer although it can be overwritten at the time of processing.

Override product: Check –
tax code in   box should
invoicing   be blank.

Disc %   : 0.00   The percentage discount, if any, which you wish to give this customer should be entered here. This rate will then be applied automatically to all invoices raised for the customer.

Additional Disc   : No additional

Pay Due Days   : 30   Usual credit terms should be entered here, i.e. the number of days you give your customer to pay.

Sett. Due Days   : 0   If the customer pays within the number of days entered here he/she qualifies for an early settlement discount.

Sett. Discount   : 0.00   Early settlement discount percentage.

Currency   : 1 Pound   If this currency is not already displayed click the
   Sterling   ⬇ button at the right side of the field and select from the drop-down list.

Department   : 0   If this number is not already displayed click the ⬇ button at the right side of the field and select from the drop-down list. This field can be used when creating reports to analyse customers by department. Since our customers are not specific to a particular department we will not use this facility so ensure that 0 is displayed in this field.

First Invoice   : –   This field automatically displays the date of the first invoice sent to the customer. It is not available in Version 3.10 of the program.

Analysis1   : SOUTH   We will use this code in customer reports to analyse our customers/sales by area (South, Midlands, North, Scotland).

Analysis2   : Tom Smith   This code can be used to analyse customers/sales by sales representative.

Analysis3   : –

Terms   : –

The entries for the first customer record are now complete, check them for accuracy.

The **Customer Record** window gives access to additional features via the **Sales, Graph, Activity** and **Memo** tab buttons. We'll examine the **Sales, Graph** and **Activity** 'pages' later when we look at Sales Ledger reports. The **Memo** button enables you to attach a memorandum to the record. For example, you may wish to store conditions relating to sales made to this customer, such as 'No delivery without a signed order'.

Editing customer details

To delete the contents or part of the contents of a field:

(a) Point to the first character for deletion, hold down the mouse button and drag to highlight. Once highlighted or selected in this way the entry can be deleted using the [**Delete**] or [**Backspace**] key.

(b) Another way to delete the complete field entry is to [**Tab**] to or double-click on the appropriate field (contents should become highlighted) and press the [**Delete**] or [**Backspace**] key.

To delete a complete word:

• Select the word by pointing to it with the mouse pointer and double-clicking. This should highlight the word which can then be deleted using the [**Delete**] key.

To delete individual characters:

(a) Individual characters can be deleted by positioning the insertion cursor immediately to the right of the character (by pointing and clicking) and pressing the [**Backspace**] key.

(b) Alternatively, locate the insertion cursor immediately to the left of the character and press the [**Delete**] key.

To insert individual characters:

• Position the cursor at the point of insertion and type.

Note that you also have the option to abandon the complete record using the **Abandon** button at the bottom of the window. This will clear any data you have entered and allow you to start again.

♦ When you have checked the details of your first customer record select (click on) the **Save** button at the bottom of the window. The **Customer Record** window should now be cleared ready for entry of the next customer's details.

♦ In similar manner set up the following customer records (remember to **Save** each record). You need only enter details to the A/C, Name and Address, Credit Limit, Analysis1 and Analysis2 fields. All other fields should contain the default entries set up previously.

	A/C	Name and Address	Credit Limit	Analysis1	Analysis2
2	BOYD	Boyd Brothers 52 Southhouse Broadway Aberdeen AB10 4NE	3000	SCOTLAND	Dave White
3	ASHRAF	Ashraf Hi-Fi Ltd 131 High Street Coventry CN2 6DE	2000	MIDLANDS	Fred Jones
4	MACKAY	Mackay Electrical 24 Cornmarket Edinburgh EH14 2LE	2000	SCOTLAND	Dave White
5	CANON	Canon and Sons Ltd 12 Park Circus Plymouth PL5 6GG	1500	SOUTH	Tom Smith
6	IMRAN	Imran & Sons 14 Bridge Street Glasgow G22 4LN	2000	SCOTLAND	Dave White
7	SEDDON	Seddon Enterprises 122 The Esplanade Brighton BR10 2GL	2500	SOUTH	Tom Smith
8	DEACON	Deacon Showrooms Ltd 15 Station Road Cardiff CD14 2MN	1500	MIDLANDS	Fred Jones
9	BUDGET	Budget Electric 12 Old School Walk Newcastle NC5 6DF	1000	NORTH	Anne Roberts
10	SANDAR	Sandar Brothers Ltd 22 Columbus Centre Carlisle CL10 4CE	2500	NORTH	Anne Roberts
11	ABBEY	Abbey Brothers Ltd 55 Riverside Avenue Dover DN10 6NT	3000	SOUTH	Tom Smith
12	NAPIER	Napier Stores Plc Mall Shopping Precinct Torquay TQ4 6NL	2000	SOUTH	Tom Smith

♦ When you have saved the last customer record select the **Close** button at the bottom of the window. This should return you to the **Customers** window where the names, reference codes and credit limits for your 12 customers should be displayed in alphabetical order by code. You may have to scroll the window (click on the ⬇ button at the side) to see them all.

Updating customer details

If you wish to alter the details of a particular record, e.g. address change, you should select the customer (point and click to highlight the name) from the list in the **Customers** window and then select the **Customer Record** button from the same window. The selected customer record should now appear on the screen and you can amend as required.

If you wish to alter several customer records you should select all records for amendment in the **Customers** window. You can select and deselect by pointing to the name and clicking (clicking the **Clear** button at the bottom of the window will deselect all selected records). Then select the **Customer Record** button from the same window. The first selected customer record should now appear and you can move on to the next one using the ⊳ button at the bottom of the window. If you are amending remember to **Save** before you move on. You can move between the records in this way, using the ⊳ and ⊲ buttons. When you are finished select the **Close** button at the bottom of the **Customer Record** window.

Removing customer records

The **Delete** button on the **Customers** or **Customer Record** window can be used to delete a selected customer's record. However, you can only remove accounts which have a *nil* balance and no outstanding transactions.

Select the **Close** button at the bottom of the **Customers** window and you will be returned to the **Desktop** window.

Backup

You should now backup your data files once again following the procedure described earlier. If your floppy disc already contains a backup file (which yours should) you may be asked to confirm that this file is to be replaced. If so you should answer **Yes** to this prompt. The **Backup** routine will replace the existing file on floppy disc (containing the default settings) with an updated file containing the default settings and customer details.

SETTING UP SUPPLIER RECORDS/ACCOUNTS

The procedure for entering supplier details is almost identical to that for customers.

♦ Select the **Suppliers** option in the **Desktop** window. The **Suppliers** window should now open showing a very similar layout to that for **Customers**.

♦ Click on the **Supplier Record** button at the top of the **Suppliers** window and a **Supplier Record** window (again almost identical to the **Customer Record**) should open to allow you to enter the details of your first supplier.

This routine is used to set up accounts for suppliers of services as well as goods, so account details for the landlord who will send you a bill for rent and the power supplier who will send you electricity bills should be entered here.

♦ Ensure that the **Details** 'page' of the **Supplier Record** is displayed, if not click on the **Details** tab button at the top of the window.

♦ Enter the details of the following suppliers remembering to **Save** after each record is complete. As with customers the credit limits are entered on the **Defaults** 'page'.

	A/C	Name and Address	Credit Limit
1	DAVIS	Davis Manufacturing Plc 25 Derwent Road Doncaster DN10 5LN	3000
2	RANCO	Ranco Refrigeration Plc 15 Newton Street Portsmouth PS4 6TM	2500
3	HARRIS	Harris Supplies Plc Unit 12 Dawson Enterprise Park Preston PS6 4JJ	3500
4	BEAVER	Beaver Manufacturing Plc Unit 15 Larchfield Industrial Estate Dundee DD4 6DT	4000
5	CHEUNG	Cheung-Li Production Plc Unit 25 Beechgrove Industrial Estate Birmingham BR4 9GH	3000
6	BROOM	Broom Brothers 22 Pennymore Road Hastings HS2 5LE	2500
7	SOLENT	Solent Engineering Plc Unit 10 Ashdown Business Park Peterborough PB6 8GN	3000
8	KEENAN	Keenan & Sons 15 Hospital Road Southampton SH22 6DN	2500
9	ABDUL	Abdul Rahman & Sons Unit 16 Wilton Business Park Inverness IN6 9GL	3000
10	ALPHA	Alpha Autos Ltd 44 Riverside Kendal KN4 7BB	500

11 ROSS	Ross & Pollock	–
	Property Managers	
	22 Hope Street	
	Carlisle	
	CL7 3AB	
12 POWER	North West Electric	–
	55 High Street	
	Carlisle	
	CL2 4AD	

♦ When you have saved the last supplier record select the **Close** button at the bottom of the window. This should return you to the **Suppliers** window where the names, reference codes and credit limits for your 12 suppliers should be displayed in alphabetical order by code. You may have to scroll the window to see them all.

The procedures for updating supplier details and removing supplier accounts are similar to those described for customers.

♦ Select the **Close** button at the bottom of the **Suppliers** window and you will be returned to the **Desktop** window.

Backup

Backup your data files which should now contain the default settings and customer and supplier details.

NOMINAL RECORDS/ACCOUNTS

The Nominal Ledger contains the accounts for assets, liabilities, expenses and revenues. Since these accounts are fairly standard for most organisations (unlike customer and supplier accounts which are specific to each business) a comprehensive set of nominal accounts is supplied with the program. The following is a list of these accounts and they can be used as they stand or modified to suit your requirements.

Default set of nominal accounts

	Fixed Assets		*Current Assets*
0010	Freehold property	1001	Stock
0011	Leasehold property	1002	Work in progress
0020	Plant and machinery	1003	Finished goods
0021	Plant/machinery depreciation	1100	Debtors control
0030	Office equipment	1101	Sundry debtors
0031	Office equipment depreciation	1102	Other debtors
0040	Furniture and fixtures	1103	Prepayments
0041	Furniture/fixtures depreciation	1200	Bank current account
0050	Motor vehicles	1210	Bank deposit account
0051	Motor vehicles depreciation	1220	Building society account
		1230	Petty cash
		1240	Company credit card
		1250	Credit card receipts

	Current Liabilities		*Direct Expenses*
2100	Creditors control	6000	Productive labour
2101	Sundry creditors	6001	Cost of sales labour
2102	Other creditors	6002	Subcontractors
2109	Accruals	6100	Sales commission
2200	Sales tax control account	6200	Sales promotions
2201	Purchase tax control account	6201	Advertising
2202	VAT liability	6202	Gifts and samples
2210	PAYE	6203	PR (literature and brochures)
2211	National insurance	6900	Miscellaneous expenses
2220	Net wages		
2230	Pension fund		*Overheads*
2300	Loans	7000	Gross wages
2310	Hire purchase	7001	Directors' salaries
2320	Corporation tax	7002	Directors' remuneration
2330	Mortgages	7003	Staff salaries
		7004	Wages – regular
	Capital and Reserves	7005	Wages – casual
3000	Ordinary shares	7006	Employers' National Insurance
3010	Preference shares	7007	Employers' pensions
3100	Reserves	7008	Recruitment expenses
3101	Undistributed reserves	7009	Adjustments
3200	Retained profit and loss	7010	SSP reclaimed
		7011	SMP reclaimed
	Sales	7100	Rent
4000	Sales type A	7102	Water rates
4001	Sales type B	7103	General rates
4002	Sales type C	7104	Premises insurance
4009	Discounts allowed	7200	Electricity
4100	Sales type D	7201	Gas
4101	Sales type E	7202	Oil
4200	Sales of assets	7203	Other heating costs
4900	Miscellaneous income	7300	Fuel and oil
4901	Royalties received	7301	Repairs and servicing
4902	Commissions received	7302	Licences
4903	Insurance claims	7303	Vehicles insurance
4904	Rent income	7304	Miscellaneous motor expenses
4905	Distribution and carriage	7400	Travelling
		7401	Car hire
	Purchases	7402	Hotels
5000	Materials purchased	7403	UK entertainment
5001	Materials imported	7404	Overseas entertainment
5002	Miscellaneous purchases	7405	Overseas travelling
5003	Packaging	7406	Subsistence
5009	Discounts taken	7500	Printing
5100	Carriage	7501	Postage & carriage
5101	Import duty	7502	Telephone
5102	Transport insurance	7503	Telex/telegram/facsimile
5200	Opening stock	7504	Office stationery
5201	Closing stock	7505	Books
		7600	Legal fees

	Overheads (contd)		*Miscellaneous*
7601	Audit and accountancy fees	8000	Depreciation
7602	Consultancy fees	8001	Plant and machinery depreciation
7603	Professional fees	8002	Furniture/fittings depreciation
7700	Equipment hire	8003	Vehicle depreciation
7701	Office machines maintenance	8004	Office equipment depreciation
7800	Repairs and renewals	8100	Bad debt write off
7801	Cleaning	8102	Bad debt provision
7802	Laundry	8200	Donations
7803	Premises expenses	8201	Subscriptions
7900	Bank interest paid	8202	Clothing costs
7901	Bank charges	8203	Training costs
7902	Currency charges	8204	Insurance
7903	Loan interest paid	8205	Refreshments
7904	HP interest	9998	Suspense account
7905	Credit charges	9999	Mispostings account

As you can see the default set has been subdivided into groups of associated accounts and each account has a four-digit numeric reference code (minimum four digits, maximum eight digits). These groups can be categorised as follows:

Sales
Purchases
Direct expenses
Overheads

} Profit and Loss account categories

Fixed assets
Current assets
Current liabilities
Capital and reserves

} Balance Sheet categories

Fixed asset accounts use the codes 0001–0999 and sales/income accounts use the codes 4000–4999. When adding or modifying accounts this coding structure should be borne in mind since it has a bearing on the design of the Profit and Loss account and Balance Sheet.

You can examine these accounts by selecting the **Nominal Ledger** option in the **Desktop** window. The **Nominal Ledger** window should open and display the account names and reference codes. To see the entire list you will have to scroll the window.

The following is a possible Profit and Loss Account and Balance Sheet structure showing how the default nominal accounts would be categorised in these statements:

PROFIT AND LOSS STRUCTURE

SALES:	From	To
Product sales	4000	4099
Export sales	4100	4199
Sales of assets	4200	4299
Other	4900	4999
PURCHASES:		
Purchases	5000	5099
Purchase charges	5100	5199
Stock	5200	5299
DIRECT EXPENSES:		
Labour	6000	6099
Commissions	6100	6199
Sales promotion	6200	6299
Miscellaneous expenses	6900	6999
OVERHEADS:		
Salaries and wages	7000	7099
Rent, rates and insurance	7100	7199
Heat, light and power	7200	7299
Motor expenses	7300	7399
Travelling and entertainment	7400	7499
Printing and stationery	7500	7599
Professional fees	7600	7699
Equipment hire and rental	7700	7799
Maintenance	7800	7899
Bank charges and interest	7900	7999
Depreciation	8000	8099
Bad debts	8100	8199
General expenses	8200	8299

BALANCE SHEET STRUCTURE

FIXED ASSETS:	From	To
Property	0010	0019
Plant and machinery	0020	0029
Office equipment	0030	0039
Furniture and fixtures	0040	0049
Motor vehicles	0050	0059
CURRENT ASSETS:		
Stock	1000	1099
Debtors	1100	1199
Deposits and cash	1210	1299
Bank A/c	1200	1209
VAT liability	2200	2209

CURRENT LIABILITIES:

Creditors: short term	2100	2199
Taxation	2210	2299
Creditors: long term	2300	2399
Bank A/c	1200	1209
VAT liability	2200	2209

CAPITAL AND RESERVES:

Share capital	3000	3099
Reserves	3100	3299

Control accounts

Certain of the nominal accounts are classed as control accounts. These are essential nominal accounts for double-entry postings made by the program and are set up automatically although they can be changed if necessary. To examine these accounts open the **Defaults** menu and select **Control Accounts**.

The functions of the control accounts are explained below:

Account name		Code	Function
1	Debtors control	1100	This is a total Debtors account and is entered automatically whenever a transaction is posted to a customer's account.
2	Creditors control	2100	This is a total Creditors account and is entered automatically whenever a transaction is posted to a supplier's account.
3	Default bank	1200	This account is used by the program when bank transactions (receipts and payments) are being processed.
4 & 5	VAT on sales/purchases	2200 & 2201	The VAT element of all transactions bearing VAT will be posted automatically to one of these accounts.
6 & 7	Sales/purchase discount	4009 & 5009	Any discount allowed or received recorded through the Sales or Purchase ledgers is posted automatically to one of these accounts.
8	Retained earnings	3200	This account holds the accumulated net profit/loss. It is used by the program's **Year End** routine to post all Profit and Loss A/c items.

9	Default sales	4000	This is the default nominal account offered when sales invoices are entered. This can be overwritten at the time of invoice entry.
10	Accruals	2109	Used by the program when the **Month End/Post Accruals** routine is used.
11	Prepayments	1103	Used by the program when the **Month End/Post Prepayments** routine is used.
12	Bad debts	8100	The value of any bad debts written off in the Sales or Purchase ledgers is posted automatically to this account when the program's **Write Off** routine is used.
13	Mispostings	9999	Used by the program when error corrections are posted for incorrectly posted transactions, refunds or cancelled cheques, when you run the **Write Off, Refund, Return** option from the **Data** menu.
14	Suspense	9998	Used by the program's **Setup** routine when entering opening balances to accounts.

The program needs these control accounts in order to operate properly. They should be set up automatically but you should check their existence before proceeding. Do not alter them in any way.

If the **Control Accounts** dialogue box is open click the **Close** button.

Setting up/modifying Nominal Accounts

We will now modify the default set of accounts to suit our company. To set up nominal accounts or amend them proceed as follows:

♦ Select the **Nominal Ledger** option in the **Desktop** window.

♦ Click the **Record** button in the **Nominal Ledger** window and the following **Nominal Record** window should open:

♦ Ensure that the **Details** 'page' of the **Nominal Record** is displayed, if not click on the **Details** tab button at the top of the window.

♦ In the **N/C** field enter the reference code of 0040.

♦ Move (press the **[Tab]** key) to the **Name** field and Furniture and Fixtures should appear (indicating that this account is part of the default set and already exists).

♦ The **Balance** field is used to enter the opening balance to the account and is updated automatically by the program when transactions are entered. Do not enter anything in this field at the moment.

♦ Move the insertion cursor to the **Total** field at the bottom of the **Budgets** column (scroll the window to bring this field into view and the insertion cursor will move automatically).

♦ Enter the total budget for the year as 10000 (you can use the calculator button at the end of the field) and this will be spread evenly over the 12 months, or will be as soon as you move the insertion cursor to any other field. You can amend monthly budget figures if you wish.

The monthly **Actual** values are updated automatically as you enter transactions to the account and these will be compared with the **Budget** values when a Budget Report is produced.

♦ Check that the details are accurate. Remember, you can **Abandon** the entries completely and start again or edit if necessary.

♦ When the details are accurate select the **Save** button at the bottom of the window. The **Nominal Record** window should now be clear, ready for entry of the next account's details.

♦ In like manner set up the following nominal accounts. Some may already be set up, some may need modification only and some will have to be set up from scratch. Remember to **Save** each account.

N/C	Name	Yearly Budget (Total)
0041	Furniture/fixtures depreciation	–
0050	Motor vehicles	40000
0051	Motor vehicles depreciation	–
1001	Closing stock (balance sheet)	–
1230	Cash	–
2300	Bank loan	–
3000	Capital	–
4000	Sales – kitchen equipment	60000
4001	Sales – TV/hi-fi	100000
4002	Sales – personal care	10000
4500	Returns in – kitchen equip	–
4501	Returns in – TV/hi-fi	–
4502	Returns in – personal care	–
5000	Purchases – kitchen equipment	80000
5001	Purchases – TV/hi-fi	120000
5002	Purchases – personal care	12000
5200	Opening stock	–
5201	Closing stock (P&L A/c)	–
5500	Returns out – kitchen equip	–
5501	Returns out – TV/hi-fi	–
5502	Returns out – personal care	–
7003	Salaries	80000
7100	Rent	12000
7200	Electricity	1000
7305	Vehicle repairs	1000
7502	Telephone	800
7504	Office stationery	500
7801	Cleaning	600
8204	Insurance	1000

♦ When you have saved the last nominal account record select the **Close** button at the bottom of the window. This should return you to the **Nominal Ledger** window and the modified list of accounts should be displayed in numeric order. You will have to scroll the window to see them all.

♦ If you wish to alter the details of a particular nominal record select the account name from the list in the **Nominal Ledger** window and then select the **Record** button from the same window. The selected nominal account details should now appear on screen and you can amend as required.

♦ The **Delete** button on the **Nominal Ledger** or **Nominal Record** window can be used to delete a selected nominal account. However, you can only remove accounts which have a *nil* balance and no history of transactions. You cannot delete Control accounts.

♦ Select the **Close** button at the bottom of the **Nominal Ledger** window and you will be returned to the **Desktop** window.

Backup

Backup your data files once again. When you have done this the backup on your floppy disc will now hold the data relating to your default settings and customer, supplier and nominal account details.

OPENING NOMINAL ACCOUNT BALANCES

In this case study we are assuming that our wholesale business began operations on 1 January 1996. To avoid complications at this stage we will also assume that there are no opening balances on customer and supplier accounts. The procedure for dealing with these is described later. To enter your nominal account opening balances proceed as follows:

♦ Select the **Nominal Ledger** option in the **Desktop** window.

♦ Click on the **Record** button in the **Nominal Ledger** window.

♦ When the **Nominal Record** window opens ensure that the **Details** 'page' is displayed.

♦ Enter the nominal code (**N/C**) as 0040 and **[Tab]** to the **Name** field (Furniture and fixtures).

♦ Now click on the opening balance button, %, at the end of the **Balance** field and an **Opening Balance Setup** dialogue box should open similar to the following:

Ref	Date	Debit	Credit
O/BAL	01/01/96	0.00	0.00

Save   Cancel

♦ Enter the following details (remember, to move from one field to the next or previous, use the **[Tab]** or **[Shift]** + **[Tab]** keys or select the field by pointing and clicking with the mouse).

Ref	: O/BAL	This should be displayed already.
Date	: 010196	
Debit	: 6000	
Credit	: 0.00	

♦ Now save your entry by clicking the **Save** button and you will be returned to the **Nominal Record** for Furniture and fixtures which should now show an entry of 6000.00 in the **Balance** field.

♦ The opening balance of 6000 should also appear in the **Actuals** field for the month of January.

♦ Move back to the **N/C** field and delete 0040 so that you can enter the code for your next nominal account. In similar manner enter the following opening balances as at 01/01/96:

N/C	Name	Debit	Credit
0050	Motor Vehicles	25000	0
5200	Opening Stock	44000	0
1200	Bank Current Account	4800	0
1230	Cash	200	0
3000	Capital	0	80000

♦ Once the last entry has been made select the **Close** button in the **Nominal Record** window and you will be returned to the **Nominal Ledger** window. The relevant accounts in this window should now display their opening balances.

♦ Click the **Close** button in the **Nominal Ledger** window.

PROGRAM DATE CHANGE

For many of its reports and automatic posting routines Sage Sterling for Windows uses the current system date, i.e. the date on the computer's clock. We are about to print the opening Trial Balance so we want the program to 'think' that the current date is sometime in January 1996 irrespective of what the actual system date is. To achieve this we will use the program's **Change Program Date** facility to set the program date to 1 January 1996.

♦ Open the **Defaults** menu and select **Change Program Date**.

♦ The following **Change Program Date** dialogue box should appear:

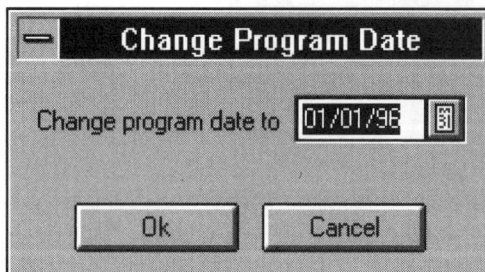

♦ Enter the date, 010196, in the **Change Program Date** field and click the **Ok** button.

OPENING TRIAL BALANCE

♦ To view the opening Trial Balance select the **Financials** option in the **Desktop** window and the following **Financials** window should open displaying the Audit Trail.

No	Tp	Account	Nominal	Dep	Details	Date	Ref
4	JC		9998	0	Opening Balance	01/01/96	O/BAL
5	JD		5200	0	Opening Balance	01/01/96	O/BAL
6	JC		9998	0	Opening Balance	01/01/96	O/BAL
7	JD		1200	0	Opening Balance	01/01/96	O/BAL
8	JC		9998	0	Opening Balance	01/01/96	O/BAL
9	JD		1230	0	Opening Balance	01/01/96	O/BAL
10	JC		9998	0	Opening Balance	01/01/96	O/BAL
11	JC		3000	0	Opening Balance	01/01/96	O/BAL
12	JD		9998	0	Opening Balance	01/01/96	O/BAL

Financials window — Close

♦ Select the **Trial Balance** button in the **Financials** window and the following **Trial Balance Report** dialogue box should appear:

Trial Balance Report

Accounting Range
- ● Current
- ○ Period

Period Range
To   January 1996 Mth 1

Output
- ○ Printer
- ● Preview
- ○ File

Run   Cancel

You have the option to view the current Trial Balance or one for a specified period.

You can view the Trial Balance on screen, print a hard copy or save it to a file by making the appropriate selection in the **Output** panel.

♦ Select the **Current** option button in the **Accounting Range** panel.

♦ **January 1996 Mth1** should already be displayed in the **Period Range** panel.

♦ Select the **Printer** option button in the **Output** panel then click the **Run** button. The following **Print** dialogue box should now open:

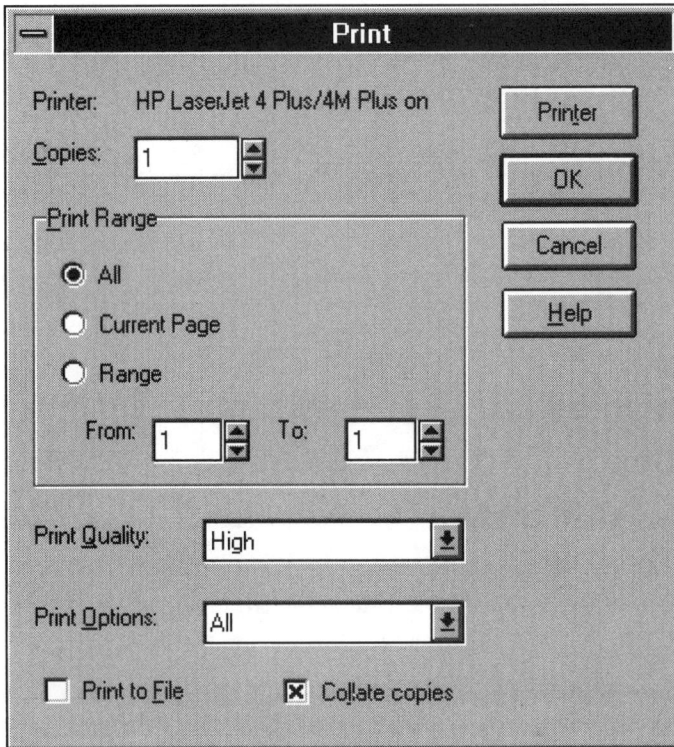

```
┌─────────────────────────────────────────────────────────┐
│ ─          Print                                          │
├─────────────────────────────────────────────────────────┤
│                                                            │
│  Printer:   HP LaserJet 4 Plus/4M Plus on    ┌─────────┐ │
│                                               │ Printer │ │
│  Copies:   [1    ]  ▲▼                        └─────────┘ │
│                                               ┌─────────┐ │
│  ┌─Print Range──────────────────────────┐    │   OK    │ │
│  │                                        │    └─────────┘ │
│  │   ⦿ All                                │    ┌─────────┐ │
│  │                                        │    │ Cancel  │ │
│  │   ○ Current Page                       │    └─────────┘ │
│  │                                        │    ┌─────────┐ │
│  │   ○ Range                              │    │  Help   │ │
│  │                                        │    └─────────┘ │
│  │      From: [1  ] ▲▼   To: [1  ] ▲▼    │               │
│  │                                        │               │
│  └────────────────────────────────────────┘               │
│                                                            │
│  Print Quality:  [High              ▼]                     │
│                                                            │
│  Print Options:  [All               ▼]                     │
│                                                            │
│  □ Print to File          ☒ Collate copies                │
└─────────────────────────────────────────────────────────┘
```

♦ Ensure that your printer is switched on then click the **OK** button.

♦ The following Trial Balance report should now be printed:

Date: 01/01/96   **ASCOT ENTERPRISES**

Current Trial Balance

N/C	Name	Debit	Credit
0040	Furniture and fixtures	6000.00	
0050	Motor vehicles	25000.00	
1200	Bank current account	4800.00	
1230	Cash	200.00	
3000	Capital		80000.00
5200	Opening stock	44000.00	
	Totals:	80000.00	80000.00

♦ Select the **Close** button in the **Financials** window.

♦ If your Trial Balance is not accurate **Restore** your last backup file and re-enter the opening balances.

Backup

Backup your data files which should now contain the default settings, customer, supplier and nominal records plus nominal account opening balances.

OPENING BALANCES ON CUSTOMER AND SUPPLIER ACCOUNTS

When moving from a manual to a computerised accounting system it will usually be necessary to enter opening balances to customer and supplier accounts. The opening balance can be entered as one figure, i.e. the outstanding balance on the account at that date. Alternatively the individual outstanding transactions which make up the balance can be entered separately using their original dates. The latter method will provide a detailed account history in the new accounts and allow you to age the transactions accurately.

The following procedures are given for reference only since we are assuming in our case study that there are no customer and supplier opening balances.

Procedure for entering an opening balance to a customer's account with the standard VAT scheme

♦ Select the **Customers** option in the **Desktop** window.

♦ Click on the **Customer Record** button in the **Customers** window.

♦ When the **Customer Record** window opens ensure that the **Details** 'page' is displayed.

♦ Click the magnifying glass button in the **A/C** field, select the customer's name from the drop-down list and click **OK**.

♦ Click on the opening balance button, %, at the end of the **Customer Balance** field and the following **Opening Balance Setup** dialogue box should appear:

Ref	Date	Invoice	Credit
		0.00	0.00

Opening Balance Setup

Save   Cancel

For example, to post an opening debit balance of £500 to AVIS's account the following entries would be made in the dialogue box:

Ref	: 0/BAL	If individual outstanding invoices are being entered this field can be used for the invoice number.	
Date	: xx/xx/xx	Setup date or date of original invoice or credit note.	
Invoice	: 500		
Credit	: –	A credit balance would be entered here.	

If the £500 balance represented three outstanding invoices they could be entered on three separate lines. This is useful for ageing purposes and if you wish to allocate receipts from these customers against particular invoices later.

When the completed dialogue box is saved the following entries would be made to the ledger accounts:

AVIS's A/c in the Sales (Customers) Ledger	DR	500
Suspense A/c (9998) in the Nominal Ledger	CR	500
Debtors Control A/c (1100) in the Nominal Ledger	DR	500

Procedure for entering an opening balance to a supplier's account with the standard VAT scheme

To enter an opening balance to a supplier's account the procedure is very similar to that for customers. This time you would use the setup button in the appropriate **Supplier Record** window.

For example, to post an opening credit balance of £200 to BACONS's A/c the following entries would be made in the **Opening Balance Setup** dialogue box:

Ref	: 0/BAL	
Date	: xx/xx/xx	
Invoice	: 200	
Credit	: –	A debit balance would be entered here.

When these details are saved the following entries would be made to the ledger accounts:

BACONS's A/c in the Purchase (Suppliers) Ledger	CR	200
Suspense A/c (9998) in the Nominal Ledger	DR	200
Creditors Control A/c (2100) in the Nominal Ledger	CR	200

Once these postings have been made the nominal ledger will contain balances which must be zeroed *before* the opening Trial Balance figures are entered. This would be done using the **Journals** option from the **Nominal Ledger** window. Using the previous two examples the following entries in the Journal would be necessary to zero the nominal accounts:

Ref	: Zero TB	
Date	: 010196	

N/C	Name	Dept	Details	Tc	Debit	Credit
1100	Debtors control	0	Zeroing	T9		500
2100	Creditors control	0	Zeroing	T9	200	
9998	Suspense	0	Zeroing	T9	300	

Once this has been done you can then go ahead and enter the opening nominal ledger balances. So the procedure for entering opening balances should be:

♦ Enter opening balances to Customer and Supplier accounts.

♦ Zero Nominal Ledger balances (Suspense, Debtors Control and Creditors Control accounts).

♦ Enter Nominal account opening balances.

CHAPTER 4

Ledger Transactions and Reports

Transactions with Customers · Sales Ledger (Customer) Reports · Transactions with Suppliers · Purchase Ledger (Supplier) Reports · Nominal Ledger Bank Transactions · Nominal Ledger Journal Entries · Nominal Ledger Cash Transactions · Nominal Ledger Reports · Audit Trail · VAT Return Analysis and Reconciliation · Final Accounts

TRANSACTIONS WITH CUSTOMERS

Transactions with customers will cover, at this stage, the posting of sales invoices and credit notes which have been produced manually and cheque receipts from credit customers. Some of the programs in the Sage Sterling for Windows series also have an additional **Invoicing** routine which will generate and print invoices and credit notes and post the details to the ledgers. This is covered separately in Chapter 7.

Sales invoices

We will post the details from a batch of copy invoices which represent sales made to credit customers during the month of January. In a manual system of bookkeeping copy sales invoices would first of all be entered to the Sales Day Book and to the customer's personal account in the Sales Ledger. At the end of the month the total from the Sales Day Book would be posted to the Sales and VAT accounts in the Nominal Ledger thereby completing the double entry. The Sales Day Book total would also be entered in the Debtor's Control account in the Nominal Ledger.

With the computerised system the details of the invoice are entered once using the **Batch Invoices** routine and posting to the relevant accounts in the ledgers is carried out automatically by the program.

To enter the details from your sales invoices proceed as follows:

♦ Select the **Customers** option in the **Desktop** window.

♦ Click the **Batch Invoices** button in the **Customers** window and the following **Batch Customer Invoices** window should open:

```
┌──────────────────────────────────────────────────────────────────────┐
│ ▭                        Batch Customer Invoices              ▼  ▲     │
├──────────────────────────────────────────────────────────────────────┤
│ ┌─────────┐                                                            │
│ │Invoices │                                                            │
│ ├─────────┴──────────────────────────────────────────────────────────┤
│                                                                        │
│   A/C Name  ┌──────────────────────────┐     Tax Rate   ┌──────0.00┐  │
│   N/C Name  ┌──────────────────────────┐     Batch Total┌──────0.00┐  │
│                                                                        │
│  ┌──────┬───────┬─────┬──────┬────┬────────┬──────┬───┬────────┐      │
│  │ A/C  │ Date  │ Ref │ N/C  │Dept│ Details│ Net  │Tc │ Tax    │      │
│  ├──────┼───────┼─────┼──────┼────┼────────┼──────┼───┼────────┤      │
│  │   🔍 │       │     │      │  0 │        │ 0.00 │   │  0.00 ▲│      │
│  ├──────┼───────┼─────┼──────┼────┼────────┼──────┼───┼────────┤      │
│  │      │       │     │      │    │        │      │   │        │      │
│  ├──────┼───────┼─────┼──────┼────┼────────┼──────┼───┼────────┤      │
│  │      │       │     │      │    │        │      │   │        │      │
│  ├──────┼───────┼─────┼──────┼────┼────────┼──────┼───┼────────┤      │
│  │      │       │     │      │    │        │      │   │        │      │
│  ├──────┼───────┼─────┼──────┼────┼────────┼──────┼───┼──────▼─┤      │
│  │      │       │     │      │    │        │  0.00│   │  0.00  │      │
│  └──────┴───────┴─────┴──────┴────┴────────┴──────┴───┴────────┘      │
│                                                                        │
│  ┌──────┐  ┌─────────┐  ┌────────────┐          ┌───────┐             │
│  │ Save │  │ Abandon │  │Calculate Net│         │ Close │             │
│  └──────┘  └─────────┘  └────────────┘          └───────┘             │
└──────────────────────────────────────────────────────────────────────┘
```

On the **Batch Customer Invoices** data entry window you can complete one line for each invoice or for each item on the invoice. If you intend to analyse the items on the invoice to more than one nominal account, tax code or departmental code you will have to list each item separately.

♦ Enter the following details for your first invoice:

A/C   You will be prompted initially to make an entry in the **A/C** field. This is the account reference for your customer. At the right side of the **A/C** field you will see a magnifying glass button (the 'Finder'). Select this (click on it) and a Customer Accounts selection box should open listing all your customers. Select **ACORN** and then select the **Ok** button. The selection box should close, ACORN should appear in the **A/C** field on the Invoice entry window and the full name, Acorn Electrics Ltd, should appear in the **A/C Name** field at the top.

If you wish you can type the account reference directly into this field. If you make a spelling mistake when typing in the reference the Customer Accounts selection box will open allowing you to select the accurate reference code.

Date   030196   You can use the Calendar button at the end of the **Date** field to enter the date using the mouse.

Ref   1200   Invoice number.

N/C   This field is used to identify the nominal ledger account code to which the sale will be credited. You can enter the reference directly or use the 'Finder' (magnifying glass button) again. The correct nominal account code in this case is 4000 (Kitchen Equipment Sales) and it may already appear in the field.

Dept	The department number to which the sale relates should be entered here. In this case enter 2 (Kitchen Equipment).
Details	4 Washing Machines
Net	The *net* amount of the invoice is normally entered here. Enter 1200. If you wish you can use the calculator button at the end of the field to make the entry with the mouse.
Tc (Tax code)	The tax code for the standard rate of VAT (T1) should be entered here. This code may already appear in the field in which case simply [**Tab**] to the next field.
Tax	This field shows the VAT applicable. It will be calculated automatically depending on the tax code entered in the **Tc** field. It should be 210.00.

The invoice details can still be edited at this point. If you notice that you have made a mistake you can click on or [**Tab**] to the field for amendment, clear the field ([**Delete**] or [**Backspace**] key) and re-enter or simply overtype.

If you wish to remove a complete line on the invoice locate the insertion cursor in any field on that line and press [**F8**].

The entries to this window can also be cleared completely using the **Abandon** button and nothing will be posted to the ledger accounts.

♦ Ensure that the insertion cursor is in the **A/C** field on the second line of the window and enter the details of the following 10 sales invoices. The window will scroll to accommodate all the entries. Note that you will have to enter the **Tax** for invoice 1205 manually.

A/C	Date	Ref	N/C	Dept	Details	Net	Tc	Tax
BOYD	110196	1201	4001	3	8 TVs	2180	T1	381.50
ABBEY	110196	1202	4000	2	6 Refrigerators	1340	T1	234.50
ACORN	120196	1203	4001	3	6 Videos	2150	T1	376.25
NAPIER	150196	1204	4000	2	4 Dishwashers	1090	T1	190.75
ASHRAF	160196	1205	4001	3	6 Hi-fi Systems	2400	T1	378.00*
ABBEY	160196	1206	4002	4	24 Hair dryers	224	T1	39.20
CANON	190196	1207	4002	4	12 Electric shavers	186	T1	32.55
DEACON	250196	1208	4000	2	12 Food processors	380	T1	66.50
IMRAN	260196	1209	4000	2	4 Chest freezers	1660	T1	290.50
SANDAR	280196	1210	4002	4	12 Hair stylers	76	T1	13.30

*Ashraf Hi-Fi Ltd (invoice No. 1205) have been offered a 10 per cent discount for payment within one month. It has been assumed that they will take advantage of this and the VAT has been adjusted accordingly. You will have to overwrite the VAT amount calculated by the program since this will be based on 17.5 per cent of 2400 rather then 17.5 per cent of 2160.

♦ When you have entered the details of all invoices check that the entries are correct. The **Batch Total** should be 15099.05. Once you post these details to the ledger accounts you cannot remove them. If a mistake is discovered after posting, a compensating entry is necessary to cancel it.

♦ When you are sure the entries are accurate click the **Save** button. The details will be posted to the appropriate ledger accounts and the **Batch Customer Invoices** window will clear.

♦ Click the **Close** button and you will be returned to the **Customers** window where the account balance should now be displayed against each customer's name. For those customers who have exceeded their credit limit the entry will appear in red (if you have a colour monitor).

Accounting entries

When a sales invoice is posted to the ledgers the accounts are updated in the following way:

DEBIT   Customer's A/c in Sales Ledger with *gross* invoice value (net + tax).
DEBIT   Debtors Control A/c in Nominal Ledger with *gross* invoice value (net + tax).
CREDIT   Sales A/c in Nominal Ledger with *net* invoice value.
CREDIT   Sales Tax Control A/c in Nominal Ledger with VAT amount.

In addition the invoice details are entered in the Sales Day Book and on the Audit Trail, which is a list of all ledger transactions.

For example, when invoice 1200 to ACORN was posted the following entries would be made to the accounts:

Ledger	A/c Name and Code		£
Sales (Customers) Ledger	Acorn Electric's A/c (ACORN)	DR	1410.00
Nominal Ledger	Debtors Control A/c (1100)	DR	1410.00
Nominal Ledger	Kitchen Equipment Sales A/c (4000)	CR	1200.00
Nominal Ledger	Sales Tax Control A/c (2200)	CR	210.00

You can confirm that these entries have been made by examining the accounts themselves. When you wish to examine a customer's account or several customers' accounts you should select (highlight) their name(s) first of all in the **Customers** window. You will then be allowed to view the account details for the selected customer(s) only. If you wish to examine all the accounts make no selections in the **Customers** window and the program will assume that you wish to work with all the records. You can select a customer's name by pointing and clicking and deselect by pointing and clicking again. The **Clear** button at the bottom of the window will deselect any customer names which are highlighted.

♦ Select ACORN in the **Customers** window and ensure that all other names are deselected.

♦ Click the **Activity** button.

♦ When the **Defaults** dialogue box opens prompting for a **Transaction Range** and a **Date Range** do not make any changes, just click the **OK** button.

The **Activity** window should now open displaying the details of the entries made to ACORN's account. Note that the gross value of invoice 1200 (£1410) is shown as a debit entry in the account. We will examine the details shown in the **Activity** window later in the Sales Ledger Reports section.

♦ Select the **Close** button at the bottom of the **Activity** window and you will be returned to the **Customers** window.

♦ Select the **Close** button in the **Customers** window.

To view the nominal ledger accounts select the **Nominal Ledger** option in the **Desktop** window.

♦ When the **Nominal Ledger** window opens select the following three accounts: Debtors Control A/c (1100), Sales Tax Control A/c (2200) and the Kitchen Equipment Sales A/c (4000). You will have to scroll the window to make the selections.

♦ Click the **Activity** button in the **Nominal Ledger** window and when the **Defaults** dialogue box opens click the **OK** button.

Details of the entries made to the Debtors Control A/c should now be displayed in the **Nominal Ledger Activity** window. Note that the gross amount of invoice 1200 (£1410) has been debited to the account.

♦ Click the ⟩ button at the bottom of the **Activity** window and the next account selected – Sales Tax Control A/c – should be displayed. Note the credit entry for £210 – the tax amount on invoice 1200.

♦ Click the ⟩ button again and the third account selected – Kitchen Equipment Sales A/c – should be displayed. Note the credit entry for £1200 – the net value of invoice 1200.

The ⟨ and ⟩ buttons will move you backwards and forwards through the selected accounts.

♦ Click the **Close** button in the **Nominal Ledger Activity** window.

♦ **Close** the **Nominal Ledger** window.

So details of an invoice are entered to the Customer's account in the Sales Ledger and the Nominal Ledger accounts are updated automatically by the program. This feature is known as integration of ledgers.

Sales credit notes

The routine for entering sales credit notes operates in a very similar way to the invoice entry routine.

Assume that one of the washing machines we supplied to Acorn Electrics Ltd is discovered to be faulty. They advise us of this and we send them a credit note. To enter the details of the credit note proceed as follows:

♦ Select the **Customers** option in the **Desktop** window.

♦ Click the **Batch Credits** button in the **Customers** window and the following **Batch Customer Credits** window should open:

```
┌─────────────────────────────────────────────────────────────────┐
│ ▭                    Batch Customer Credits                  ▼ ▲ │
│ ┌──────┐                                                         │
│ │Credits│                                                        │
│                                                                  │
│  A/C Name  [                    ]        Tax Rate  [    0.00]    │
│  N/C Name  [                    ]        Batch Total[    0.00]   │
│  ┌────┬──────┬────┬────┬────┬───────┬──────┬──┬────┐            │
│  │A/C │ Date │Ref │N/C │Dept│Details│ Net  │Tc│Tax │            │
│  │  [Q]│      │    │    │  0 │       │ 0.00 │  │0.00│▲           │
│  │    │      │    │    │    │       │      │  │    │            │
│  │    │      │    │    │    │       │      │  │    │            │
│  │    │      │    │    │    │       │      │  │    │            │
│  │    │      │    │    │    │       │      │  │    │            │
│  │    │      │    │    │    │       │      │  │    │▼           │
│  └────┴──────┴────┴────┴────┴───────┴──────┴──┴────┘            │
│                                          [ 0.00] [ 0.00]        │
│                                                                  │
│  [ Save ]  [ Abandon ]  [ Calculate Net ]          [ Close ]    │
└─────────────────────────────────────────────────────────────────┘
```

As with invoices you can complete one line for each credit note or for each item on the credit note. If you intend to analyse the items on the credit note to more than one nominal account, tax code or departmental code you will have to list each item separately.

♦ Enter the following details:

A/C	Date	Ref	N/C	Dept	Details	Net	Tc	Tax
ACORN	210196	C2000	4500	2	Faulty washing machine	300	T1	52.50

Note that the nominal code (**N/C**) this time is 4500, being the reference code for the Kitchen Equipment Returns Inwards account.

♦ When you have entered and checked the details select **Save** to post to the ledgers then select the **Close** button to return to the **Customers** window.

♦ **Close** the **Customers** window.

Accounting entries

When the credit note was posted to the ledgers the accounts would be updated as follows:

Ledger	A/c Name and code		£
Sales (Customers) Ledger	Acorn Electric's A/c (ACORN)	CR	352.50
Nominal Ledger	Debtors Control A/c (1100)	CR	352.50
Nominal Ledger	Returns-In (kitchen equipment) A/c (4500)	DR	300.00
Nominal Ledger	Sales Tax Control A/c (2200)	DR	52.50

You can confirm that these entries have been made by examining the appropriate accounts in the Sales and Nominal Ledgers.

Receipts from credit customers

We shall now enter some cheque receipts from customers made against previously issued invoices. We have three customer cheques to enter: one from Boyd Brothers, one from Abbey Brothers Ltd and a third from Ashraf Hi-Fi Ltd.

Proceed as follows:

♦ Select the **Bank** option in the **Desktop** window and the following **Bank Accounts** window should open:

The account names displayed in the **Bank Accounts** window represent the default accounts which have been set up to record the receipt and payment of money. The **Bank Record** button can be used to record the details of these accounts (e.g. bank name, address, account no. and sort code) and to set up new accounts to record receipts and payments.

♦ Ensure that **Bank Current Account**, nominal code 1200, is selected (highlighted) and click the **Bank Record** button.

♦ When the **Bank Record – Bank Current Account** window opens click the **Bank Details** tab button at the top and the following 'page' should be displayed:

♦ Make the following entries to the **Bank Details** 'page':

Bank Name	:	Downtown Bank PLC
Street1	:	Main Street
Street2	:	–
Town	:	Carlisle
County	:	–
Post Code	:	CL2 1BB
Account Name	:	Ascot Enterprises
Account Number	:	00558127
Sort Code	:	85-27-29

♦ Click the **Save** button at the bottom of the window then **Close** the **Bank Record** window.

♦ In the **Bank Accounts** window ensure that **Bank Current Account,** nominal code 1200, is selected and then click the **Customer Receipt** button. A **Customer Receipt – Bank Current Account** window, similar to the following, should now open:

```
┌─────────────────────────────────────────────────────────────────┐
│         Customer Receipt · Bank Current Account        ▼  ▲       │
│  ┌─A/C──┐ ┌───Name────┐ ┌──Date──┐ ┌──Ref──┐ ┌─Amount─┐          │
│  │    🔍│ │           │ │31/01/96│ │       │ │  0.00 🔢│          │
│  ┌──┬─────┬─────┬────────┬──┬───────┬───────┬────────┐            │
│  │Tp│Date │Ref  │Details │Tc│Amount │Receipt│Discount│            │
│  │  │     │     │        │  │       │       │        │▲           │
│  │  │     │     │        │  │       │       │        │            │
│  │  │     │     │        │  │       │       │        │            │
│  │  │     │     │        │  │       │       │        │            │
│  │  │     │     │        │  │       │       │        │▼           │
│  Bank Balance │ 4800.00 │          Analysis Total │  0.00 │        │
│  [Save] [Abandon] [Pay in Full] [Wizard] [Automatic]    [Close]   │
└─────────────────────────────────────────────────────────────────┘
```

♦ The first receipt we are going to process is a cheque for £2561.50 from Boyd Brothers. Enter the following details:

A/C   : Boyd   You can use the 'Finder' here. Note that the outstanding transaction for Boyd has now appeared.
Date   : 230196   Cheque date.
Ref   : 000731   Cheque number.
Amount : 2561.50   Notice that the **Bank Balance** shown at the bottom of the window is increased by this amount when you [Tab] to the next field.

♦ When you have entered these details the insertion cursor should be 'flashing' in the **Receipt** field for invoice 1201. We will use this cheque to pay off invoice No. 1201 in full so click the **Pay in Full** button at the bottom of the window.

♦ The **Receipt** field will now show the amount of the cheque and the **Analysis Total** will be increased by the same amount. Check that the entry is correct. Alterations can still be made or the complete entry abandoned, using the **Abandon** button, if necessary.

♦ If the entries are correct click the **Save** button. The transaction will be posted to the ledger accounts and the window will refresh, ready to receive details of the next cheque.

♦ The next cheque is from Abbey Brothers Ltd and the value is £1600. Enter the following details:

A/C   : ABBEY   Outstanding transactions for Abbey should now appear.
Date   : 260196
Ref   : 008866
Amount : 1600

We will allocate £1336.80 against invoice 1202 leaving a balance of £263.20 which we will use to fully pay invoice 1206.

♦ When the insertion cursor is in the **Receipt** field for invoice 1202 enter 1336.80 (you can use the calculator button if you wish). [**Tab**] to or click in the **Receipt** field for invoice 1206 and click the **Pay in Full** button.

♦ The **Analysis Total** should now agree with the **Amount** (1600) and the **Bank Balance** should have increased to 8961.50. Examine your entries carefully. Remember at this stage you can still edit or **Abandon**. If your entries are accurate select the **Save** button to post to the ledger accounts.

♦ The third cheque is from Ashraf Hi-Fi Ltd for £2538. Remember we offered them a discount of 10 per cent for prompt payment which they have accepted. Enter the following details:

A/C	:	ASHRAF
Date	:	270196
Ref	:	936392
Amount	:	2538

This cheque will fully pay invoice 1205 since the discount allowed amounts to £240.

♦ When the insertion cursor is in the **Receipt** field for invoice 1205 enter 2538 and [**Tab**] to the **Discount** field.

♦ Enter 240 in the **Discount** field and press the [**Tab**] key again.

The **Receipt** and **Analysis Total** fields should now show 2538. The **Discount** field should show 240 and the **Bank Balance** should have increased to 11499.50.

♦ When your entries are accurate select **Save**.

♦ Select **Close** on the next blank **Customer Receipt** window.

♦ **Close** the **Bank Accounts** window and you will be returned to the **Desktop** window.

Payment on Account

You can choose to post (**Save**) a receipt before the full cheque balance has been allocated against available invoices. If you select the **Save** button when the **Analysis Total** is less than the cheque **Amount** you will be asked to confirm that you wish to post the unallocated balance as a Payment on Account. This balance can be allocated against an invoice at a later date.

Customer Receipts Wizard

There is a **Wizard** button in the **Customer Receipt** window which activates the **Customer Receipts Wizard** tool. This is a series of dialogue boxes which lead you, in a step-by-step manner, through the process of posting cheques or payments on account.

Cash receipts from customers

If a customer pays in cash this would be recorded by selecting the **Cash** Account, nominal code 1230, in the **Bank Accounts** window then clicking the **Customer Receipt** button. Details of the cash receipt would then be entered to the **Customer Receipt – Cash** window and when saved the details would be debited to the Cash Account.

Accounting entries

When cheque receipts are posted to the ledgers the accounts are updated as follows:

CREDIT   Customers A/c in Sales Ledger with cheque amount.
CREDIT   Debtors Control A/c in Nominal Ledger with cheque amount.
DEBIT   Bank A/c in Nominal Ledger with cheque amount.

If discount has been allowed the entries would be as follows:

CREDIT   Customers A/c in Sales Ledger with cheque amount.
CREDIT   Customers A/c in Sales Ledger with discount amount.
CREDIT   Debtors Control A/c in Nominal Ledger with total amount (cheque + discount).
DEBIT   Bank A/c in Nominal Ledger with cheque amount.
DEBIT   Discount Allowed A/c in Nominal Ledger with discount amount.

For example the cheque receipt from ASHRAF would be posted to the ledgers in the following way:

Ledger	A/c Name and Code	£	
Sales (Customers) Ledger	Ashraf Hi-Fi Ltd A/c (ASHRAF)	CR	2538
Sales (Customers) Ledger	Ashraf Hi-Fi Ltd A/c (ASHRAF)	CR	240
Nominal Ledger	Debtors Control A/c (1100)	CR	2538
Nominal Ledger	Debtors Control A/c (1100)	CR	240
Nominal Ledger	Bank A/c (1200)	DR	2538
Nominal Ledger	Discounts Allowed A/c (4009)	DR	240

You can confirm that these entries have been made by examining the appropriate accounts in the Sales and Nominal Ledgers.

SALES LEDGER (CUSTOMER) REPORTS

A variety of fixed-format and user-designed reports which provide important information on customers can be produced with ease and speed from Sales Ledger data. The following four option buttons in the **Customers** window give you access to some of these reports:

- **Activity**   Allows you to view transaction details recorded in a customer's account.

- **Aged Balances** Provides an aged analysis of customer balances.

- **Statements**   Allows you to view and print customer statements and to design a new layout for statements.

- **Reports**   Allows you to view and print a variety of pre-designed reports and to design new reports. The pre-designed reports include the following:
  – Aged Debtors Analysis;
  – Customer Day Books;
  – Customer List;
  – Customer Activity (same as Activity report previously mentioned).

Additional information relating to customers can be accessed from the **Customer Record** window using the following 'page' tab buttons:

- **Sales**   This 'page' displays an analysis of transactions with the selected customer showing monthly totals for invoices, credit notes and sales receipts over the period of a year.

- **Graph**   This 'page' can be used to provide transaction information for a selected customer in graphical format. Various types of graphs/charts can be produced almost instantaneously showing monthly totals for invoices, credit notes and customer balances over the period of a year.

- **Activity**   Similar to the Activity report accessed from the **Customers** window the report allows you to view transaction details recorded in a customer's account.

We will examine each of these reports but first of all we'll take a closer look at the information provided in the **Customers** window itself.

♦ Select the **Customers** option in the **Desktop** window.

The **Customers** window displays useful information in addition to the customer name. The short reference code, balance and credit limit are shown for each customer and over-limit customers are identified in red (on a colour monitor).

   The column headings (**A/C, Name, Balance, Crd Limit, Contact**) are also sort buttons which allow you to sort the customer list on the basis of the heading chosen. For example, if you click the **Name** button the list will be sorted in ascending alphabetical order (A–Z) by name. Clicking the **Name** button while holding down the **[Shift]** key will sort the list in descending alphabetical order (Z–A) by name. If the column of data is numerical, such as account balances, selecting the sort button will arrange the values in ascending order and selecting the button while holding down the **[Shift]** key will arrange the values in descending order.

♦ Ensure that your list is sorted in ascending alphabetical order by **Name**.

The **Criteria** button at the bottom of the window allows you to select customers who meet specified conditions and only those customers who meet the defined criteria will then be displayed in the **Customers** window. To illustrate this feature we'll restrict the window display to those customers who are located in sales area SOUTH.

♦ Select the **Criteria** button and the **Customer List Criteria** dialogue box should appear.

♦ Ensure that the **Details** tab button at the top of the dialogue box is selected.

♦ You must first select the field you wish the criteria to be applied to. In the **Field** column select the **Analysis1** check box (a cross will appear in it when selected).

♦ You must now set the criteria to be applied to that field. Ensure that **equals** is displayed in the **Criteria** box for the **Analysis1** field, if not, click the ⬇ button and select from the drop-down list. **[Tab]** to or click in the first **Values** box for the **Analysis1** field (next one on the right) and enter SOUTH.

The completed **Customer List Criteria** dialogue box should now be similar to the following:

Customer List Criteria			
Details	**Amounts**		
Field	Criteria	Values	
A/C	☐	equals ⬇	
Name	☐	equals ⬇	
Street1	☐	equals ⬇	
Street2	☐	equals ⬇	
Town	☐	equals ⬇	
County	☐	equals ⬇	
Post Code	☐	equals ⬇	
Telephone No.	☐	equals ⬇	
Fax No.	☐	equals ⬇	
Department	☐	equals ⬇	0 ⬇
Analysis1	☒	equals ⬇	SOUTH
Analysis2	☐	equals ⬇	
Analysis3	☐	equals ⬇	
Account on hold	☐	equals ⬇	
Criteria On ☐	Save	Load	Abandon	Delete	Close

♦ Select the **Criteria On** check box at the bottom of the dialogue box (a cross should appear when selected) then select the **Close** button. You will be returned to the **Customers** window where only the five SOUTH area customers should now be listed; ABBEY, ACORN, CANON, NAPIER and SEDDON.

We'll now further restrict the list to SOUTH area customers whose balance is greater than £1000.

♦ Select the **Criteria** button and when the **Customer List Criteria** dialogue box appears select the **Amounts** tab button at the top of the box.

♦ When the **Amounts** 'page' appears select the **Balance** check box in the **Field** column. Click the ⬇ button in the **Balance** field's **Criteria** box and select **greater than** from the drop-down list. **[Tab]** to or click in the first **Values** box for the **Balance** field and enter 1000.

♦ Ensure that the **Criteria On** check box is still selected then click the **Close** button.

The **Customers** window should now display only the two SOUTH area customers whose balance is greater than £1000; ACORN and NAPIER.

We'll now switch the criteria off so that we can return to a full display in this window.

♦ Select the **Criteria** button again.

♦ When the **Customer List Criteria** dialogue box opens click the **Abandon** button to reset the selections.

♦ Ensure that the **Criteria On** button is deselected (no cross) then **Close** the **Customer List Criteria** dialogue box and you will be returned to the **Customers** window with the full list restored.

We'll now examine the details contained in each of the reports listed at the beginning of this section.

Activity

♦ Ensure that the **Customers** window is open with the full customer list displayed.

♦ Click the **Clear** button at the bottom of the window to ensure that no customer names are selected then select the **Activity** button.

♦ A small **Defaults** dialogue box should appear enabling you to restrict the report to specified transaction and date ranges. Make no changes in this dialogue box, simply click the **OK** button.

♦ An **Activity** window, similar to the one overleaf, should now open showing details of the entries made to your first customer's (ABBEY's) account.

The entry in the **Balance** field at the top right of the window is the balance outstanding on the customer's account and an aged analysis of this is shown at the bottom of the window. However, the Activity report uses the current system date (the date on the computer's clock) to calculate the age of this balance. This could result in an inaccurate analysis if the system date is later than January 1996. An accurate reading will be provided when we look at the Aged Balances report next.

The **Turnover YTD** field shows the net sales (sales – returns) before tax made to the customer.

Invoices which are partly paid (invoice no. 1202 in ABBEY's case) are marked in the account with the letter p and the amount outstanding shown in the **O/S** column. Any invoices which are outstanding (none in ABBEY's case) are marked with an asterisk (*).

The entry in the **No** column of the account is the Audit Trail number and the entry in the **Tp** column indicates the type of transaction (e.g. SI = sales invoice, SR = sales receipt).

Each line of transaction details in the **Activity** window represents a single invoice, credit note, receipt or payment on account. If an invoice consists of several items the invoice total will be shown as one line in the **Activity** window but individual item details can be displayed by double clicking on that transaction line. The **Tidy List** button can be used to clear all sub-items from view.

You can move through the list of accounts in alphabetic sequence using the ⟩ and ⟨ buttons at the bottom of the window or you can move to a specific account using the 'Finder' button in the **A/C** field.

Select the **Close** button at the bottom of the **Activity** window and you will be returned to the **Customers** window.

If you wish to print an Activity report for one or several customers this can be done using the **Reports** routine described later in this section.

Aged Balances

You can produce an **Aged Balances** report for customers which you have selected in the **Customers** window or a report which includes all customers. We will produce a report for all our customers.

♦ Click the **Clear** button at the bottom of the **Customers** window to ensure that no customer names are selected then select the **Aged Balances** button.

♦ When the **Defaults** dialogue box opens enter the **Date of Report** as 310196 (if you are using Version 3.10 of the program also enter the **Include Payments Up To** date as 310196) then click the **OK** button.

An **Aged Balances** window, similar to the following, should now open giving an aged analysis of all customer balances (you will have to scroll the window to view them all).

A/C	YTD	Credit Limit	Balance	Future	Current	30 Days	60 Days
ABBEY	1564.00	3000.00	237.70		237.70		
ACORN	3050.00	3000.00	3583.75		3583.75		
ASHRAF	2400.00	2500.00					
BOYD	2180.00	3000.00					
BUDGET	0.00	1000.00					
CANON	186.00	1500.00	218.55		218.55		
DEACON	380.00	1500.00	446.50		446.50		
IMRAN	1660.00	2000.00	1950.50		1950.50		
MACKAY	0.00	2000.00					

Aged Balances as of 31st January 1996

Future	Current	30 Days	60 Days	90 Days	Older	Total	Debtors
0.00	7807.05	0.00	0.00	0.00	0.00	7807.05	7807.05

The report shows debts which are current (0–29 days old) and those aged over 30–59, 60–89, 90–119 days or older. Since we entered the date of the report as 31/01/96 all the balances should be current.

♦ **Close** the **Aged Balances** window and you will be returned to the **Customers** window.

♦ Select the **Aged Balances** button again and when the **Defaults** dialogue box opens enter the **Date of Report** this time as 290296 (if you are using Version 3.10 of the program also enter the **Include Payments Up To** date as 290296) and click **OK**.

The **Aged Balances** report should now show the customer balances as being over 30 days old.

♦ Select ACORN in the **Aged Balances** window and click the **Detailed** button at the bottom. The **Detailed Aged Analysis** window provides an aged analysis for each outstanding invoice.

♦ **Close** the **Detailed Aged Analysis** window then **Close** the **Aged Balances** window.

If you wish to print the Aged Balances report this can be done using the **Reports** routine described later in this section. An Aged Debtors Analysis is one of the pre-designed reports contained within this routine.

Statements

Let's say we want to send a statement to any customer who has exceeded their credit limit. If the list of customers was large the selection could be made quickly using the **Criteria** button. However, our list of customers is small and only one has exceeded their credit limit.

♦ Select ACORN in the **Customers** window and ensure that all other customer names are deselected.

♦ Now select the **Statements** button in the **Customers** window and the following **Customer Statements** window should open:

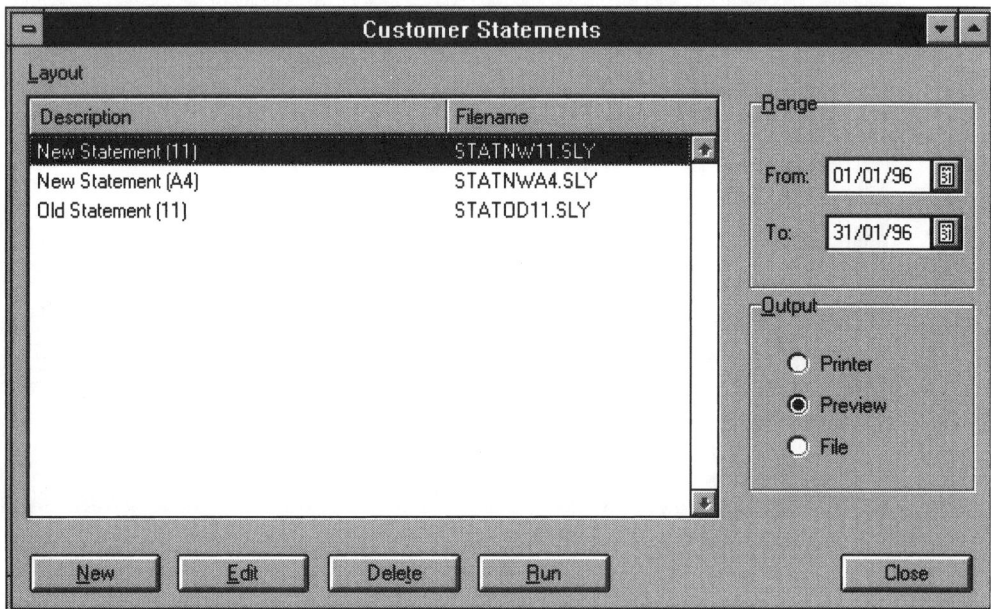

The files listed in the **Layout** panel are the default layout template files which match the Sage pre-printed statement stationery. The file descriptions and filenames may vary depending on which version of the program you are using. The **New** button at the bottom of the window allows you to design your own layout file.

♦ Select the file **New Statement (A4)** in the **Layout** panel (the file description is **A4 Statement with Tear Off Remit Advice** in Version 3.10 of the program); this is one of the standard statement layout files supplied by Sage and is designed for A4 paper.

♦ In the **Range** panel set the **From** date to 010196 and the **To** date to 310196.

♦ Select the **Printer** option button in the **Output** panel and then click the **Run** button.

♦ When the **Print** dialogue box opens click the **OK** button and Acorn's statement should be printed.

♦ **Close** the **Customer Statements** window.

Reports

The **Reports** option enables you to view, print and save to file a variety of pre-designed reports on all customers or those previously selected in the **Customers** window. You can also design and print new reports on all or selected customers.

♦ Click the **Clear** button in the **Customers** window to ensure that no customer names are selected.

♦ Select the **Reports** button in the **Customers** window and the following **Customer Reports** window should open:

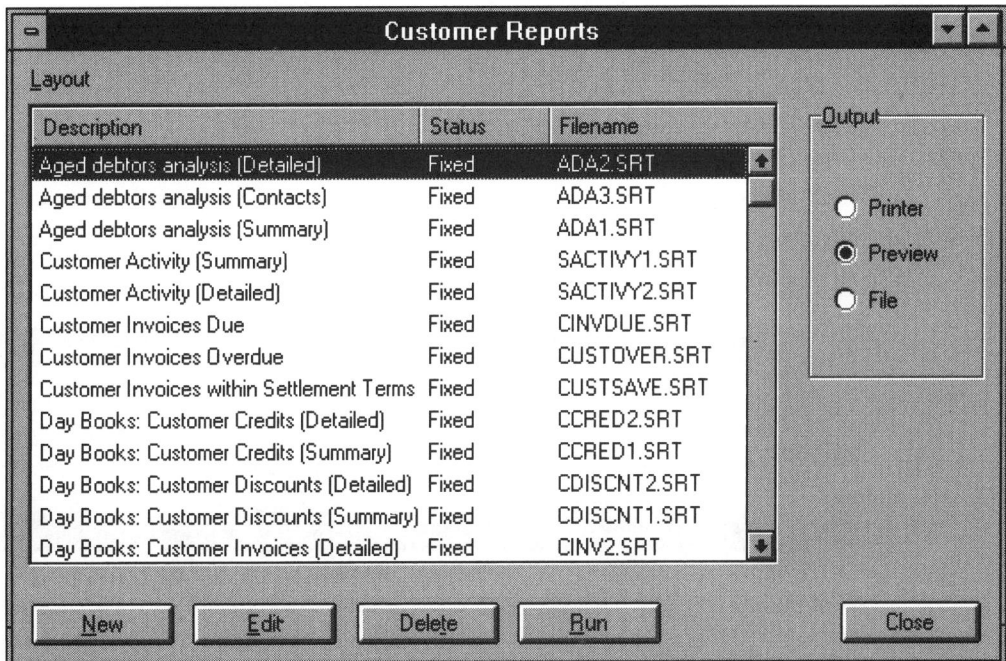

The **Layout** panel in the window lists the pre-designed reports. If you wish to examine one of these reports you have the option of displaying it on screen or printing a copy by making the appropriate selection (**Preview** or **Printer**) in the **Output** panel. You can also save the report to a file for printing later by selecting the **File** option in the **Output** panel.

The contents of the reports should be obvious from the **Description**. Note that **Aged debtors analysis** and **Customer Activity** reports can be viewed or printed for all or selected customers using this routine.

♦ Select the **Day Books: Customer Invoices (Summary)** report in the **Layout** panel, click the **Printer** button in the **Output** panel and select the **Run** button.

♦ When the **Additional Report Filter** dialogue box opens click the **OK** button and when the **Print** dialogue box opens click the **OK** button.

The Customer Invoices Day Book report should now be printed giving details of your 11 invoices.

Any of the pre-designed reports can be printed in this way. Alternatively they can be viewed on screen or saved to file by making the appropriate selection in the **Output** panel.

You can also design new reports on your customers using the **New** button in the **Customer Reports** window. This gives you access to **Layout Wizard** and then to **Layout Editor**. These 'tools' allow you to select data fields for inclusion in the report and to design the report layout. The procedure for creating new reports is described in Chapter 6 on the Report Generator.

♦ **Close** the **Customer Reports** window.

Sales

♦ In the **Customers** window click the **Clear** button to ensure that no customer names are selected then click the **Customer Record** button.

♦ When the **Customer Record** window opens click the 'Finder' button in the **A/C** field, select ABBEY from the small selection box which opens then click **OK**.

♦ Select the **Sales** 'page' tab button at the top of the window and the following 'page' of information should be displayed:

	Customer - Abbey Brothers Ltd			
Details	Defaults	**Sales**	Graph	Activity	Memo

Last Invoice	Last Payment		M.T.D.	Y.T.D.	Prior Y.T.D.
16/01/96	26/01/96		1564.00	1564.00	0.00

Month	Invoices	Credits	Sales Balance	Receipts
B/F	0.00	0.00	0.00	0.00
January	1837.70	0.00	1837.70	1600.00
February	0.00	0.00	0.00	0.00
March	0.00	0.00	0.00	0.00
April	0.00	0.00	0.00	0.00
May	0.00	0.00	0.00	0.00
June	0.00	0.00	0.00	0.00
July	0.00	0.00	0.00	0.00

| Save | Abandon | Delete | < | > | | Close |

The **Sales** 'page' shows monthly totals for invoices and credit notes. These totals include VAT. Amounts received from the customer are also shown as monthly totals. Month-to-date (**M.T.D.**) and year-to-date (**Y.T.D.**) totals are shown at the top and these represent net sales (invoices – credit notes) before tax.

If you wish to see the individual transactions that make up any of the monthly total values double-click on the required value and an Activity dialogue box will open displaying these transaction details.

Graph

♦ Select the **Graph** tab button at the top of the **Customer Record** window to display the transactions data in graphical format. The display can show monthly totals for invoices, credit notes or net balance, or any combination of these three, by making the appropriate selection(s) in the **Display** panel. The format of the display can be altered by selecting from the drop-down list in the **Graph Type** field.

Activity

♦ Select the **Activity** tab button at the top of the **Customer Record** window. When the **Activity** 'page' is displayed you will note that the information shown is the same as that in the **Activity** report accessed directly from the **Customers** window.

You can move through your customer records and check the information displayed on the **Sales, Graph** and **Activity** 'pages' using the ⊳ and ⊲ buttons at the bottom of the window. As you move from one record to the next a small **Record has been modified** dialogue box may open asking if you wish to save it. If this happens click the **No** button.

♦ When you have finished viewing the records **Close** the **Customer Record** window. If a small **Confirm** dialogue box opens at this point asking if you are sure you wish to exit click the **Yes** button.

♦ **Close** the **Customers** window.

TRANSACTIONS WITH SUPPLIERS

Transactions with suppliers will cover, at this stage, the posting of purchase invoices, credit notes and cheque payments.

Purchase invoices

We will post the details from a batch of invoices which represent credit purchases of goods for resale and bills for services which we have received. In a manual system of bookkeeping purchase invoices would first of all be entered to the Purchase Day Book and to the supplier's personal account in the Purchase Ledger. At the end of the month the total from the Purchase Day Book would be posted to the Purchases and VAT accounts in the Nominal Ledger thereby completing the double entry. The Purchase Day Book total would also be entered in the Creditors Control account in the Nominal Ledger.

With the computerised system the details of the invoice are entered once using the **Batch Invoices** routine and posting to the relevant accounts in the ledgers is carried out automatically by the program.

To enter the details from your purchase invoices proceed as follows:

♦ Select the **Suppliers** option in the **Desktop** window.

♦ Click the **Batch Invoices** button in the **Suppliers** window and the following **Batch Supplier Invoices** window should open:

```
┌──────────────────────────────────────────────────────────────────────┐
│ ▬                     Batch Supplier Invoices                    ▼│▲ │
│ ┌────────┐                                                           │
│ │Invoices│                                                           │
│ ├────────┘                                                           │
│  A/C Name  ┌──────────────────────────┐     Tax Rate  ┌────────┐    │
│            └──────────────────────────┘               │   0.00 │    │
│  N/C Name  ┌──────────────────────────┐    Batch Total┌────────┐    │
│            └──────────────────────────┘               │   0.00 │    │
│  ┌──────┬────────┬─────┬─────┬────┬───────┬───────┬───┬──────┐      │
│  │ A/C  │ Date   │ Ref │ N/C │Dept│Details│  Net  │Tc │ Tax  │      │
│  ├──────┼────────┼─────┼─────┼────┼───────┼───────┼───┼──────┤▲    │
│  │     🔍│        │     │     │  0 │       │  0.00 │   │ 0.00 │      │
│  ├──────┼────────┼─────┼─────┼────┼───────┼───────┼───┼──────┤      │
│  │      │        │     │     │    │       │       │   │      │      │
│  ├──────┼────────┼─────┼─────┼────┼───────┼───────┼───┼──────┤      │
│  │      │        │     │     │    │       │       │   │      │      │
│  ├──────┼────────┼─────┼─────┼────┼───────┼───────┼───┼──────┤      │
│  │      │        │     │     │    │       │       │   │      │      │
│  ├──────┼────────┼─────┼─────┼────┼───────┼───────┼───┼──────┤▼    │
│  │      │        │     │     │    │       │ 0.00  │   │ 0.00 │      │
│  └──────┴────────┴─────┴─────┴────┴───────┴───────┴───┴──────┘      │
│  ┌─────┐  ┌───────┐  ┌─────────────┐              ┌───────┐         │
│  │Save │  │Abandon│  │Calculate Net│              │ Close │         │
│  └─────┘  └───────┘  └─────────────┘              └───────┘         │
└──────────────────────────────────────────────────────────────────────┘
```

The **Batch Supplier Invoices** window is similar to that for customer invoices. As with customer invoices you can complete one line on the data entry window for each supplier invoice or for each item on the invoice. If you intend to analyse the items on the invoice to more than one nominal account, tax code or departmental code you will have to list each item separately.

♦ Enter the details of the following purchase invoices. Be careful to enter the correct tax codes for electricity and rent and note that you will have to enter the **Tax** for invoice 414141 manually.

A/C	Date	Ref	N/C	Dept	Details	Net	Tc	Tax
DAVIS	050196	984134	5000	2	6 Washing machines	1500	T1	262.50
RANCO	070196	414141	5000	2	5 Refrigerators	1000	T1	157.50*
CHEUNG	070196	997765	5001	3	12 TVs	2400	T1	420.00
BROOM	080196	444891	5002	4	18 Hairdryers	210	T1	36.75
SOLENT	090196	754218	5000	2	36 Food processors	760	T1	133.00
KEENAN	090196	321789	5001	3	10 Hi-fi systems	1500	T1	262.50
ABDUL	100196	418101	5002	4	24 Electric shavers	280	T1	49.00
POWER	270196	–	7200	1	Electricity	75	T3	6.00
ALPHA	280196	905628	7305	1	Repair to vehicle	102	T1	17.85
ROSS	310196	011223	7100	1	Rent	1000	T2	0.00
DAVIS	310196	765764	5000	2	4 Tumble dryers	1040	T1	182.00

*Ranco Refrigeration PLC (invoice No. 414141) have offered us an early settlement discount of 10 per cent for payment within one month. They have assumed that we will take advantage of this and the VAT has been adjusted accordingly. You will have to overwrite the VAT amount calculated by the program since this will be based on 17.5 per cent of 1000 rather than 17.5 per cent of 900.

Notice that some of the invoices are for expenses: rent, vehicle repairs and electricity. Remember that any purchase or expense invoice from a supplier with a personal account must be entered using the **Suppliers** routine. Any other expense for which you have no supplier account is entered directly into the Nominal Ledger.

♦ When you have entered the details of all invoices check that the entries are correct. The **Batch Total** should be 11394.10. Remember that the invoice details can still be edited at this point and if necessary all the entries to the window can be cleared using the **Abandon** button and you can start again.

♦ When you are sure the entries are accurate click the **Save** button. The details will be posted to the appropriate ledger accounts and the **Batch Supplier Invoices** window will clear.

♦ Click the **Close** button and you will be returned to the **Suppliers** window where the account balance should now be displayed against each supplier's name.

♦ **Close** the **Suppliers** window.

Accounting entries

When a purchase invoice is posted to the ledgers the accounts are updated in the following way:

CREDIT   Supplier's A/c in Purchase Ledger with *gross* invoice value (net + tax).
CREDIT   Creditors Control A/c in Nominal Ledger with *gross* invoice value (net + tax).
DEBIT   Purchases A/c (or Expense A/c) in Nominal Ledger with *net* invoice value.
DEBIT   Purchase Tax Control A/c in Nominal Ledger with VAT amount.

In addition the invoice details are entered in the Purchase Day Book and on the Audit Trail.

For example, when invoice no. 984134 from DAVIS was posted the following entries would be made to the accounts:

Ledger	A/c Name and Code		£
Purchase (Suppliers) Ledger	Davis Manufacturing A/c (DAVIS)	CR	1762.50
Nominal Ledger	Creditors Control A/c (2100)	CR	1762.50
Nominal Ledger	Kitchen Equipment Purchases A/c (5000)	DR	1500.00
Nominal Ledger	Purchase Tax Control A/c (2201)	DR	262.50

You can confirm that these entries have been made by examining the accounts themselves following the procedure described in the Transactions with Customers section.

Return to the **Desktop** window after looking at the accounts.

Purchase credit notes

The routine for entering credit notes operates in a very similar way to the invoice entry routine.

Assume that one of the TVs we purchased from Cheung-Li Production Plc was damaged. We advise them of this and they send us a credit note. To enter the details of the credit note proceed as follows:

♦ Select the **Suppliers** option in the **Desktop** window.

♦ Click the **Batch Credits** button in the **Suppliers** window and the following **Batch Supplier Credits** window should open:

```
┌──────────────────────────────────────────────────────────────────────┐
│ ▫              Batch Supplier Credits                           ▾ ▴   │
│ ┌───────┐                                                             │
│ │Credits│                                                             │
│ └───────┘                                                             │
│  A/C Name  ┌─────────────────────────┐    Tax Rate  ┌──────── 0.00 ┐ │
│  N/C Name  └─────────────────────────┘    Batch Total└──────── 0.00 ┘ │
│                                                                        │
│  ┌────────┬──────┬─────┬──────┬────┬────────┬──────────┬───┬────────┐ │
│  │ A/C    │ Date │ Ref │ N/C  │Dept│ Details│   Net    │Tc │ Tax    │ │
│  │      🔍│      │     │      │  0 │        │    0.00  │   │  0.00 ▲│ │
│  │        │      │     │      │    │        │          │   │        │ │
│  │        │      │     │      │    │        │          │   │        │ │
│  │        │      │     │      │    │        │          │   │        │ │
│  │        │      │     │      │    │        │          │   │        │ │
│  │        │      │     │      │    │        │          │   │       ▼│ │
│  └────────┴──────┴─────┴──────┴────┴────────┴──────────┴───┴────────┘ │
│                                          ┌── 0.00 ┐      ┌── 0.00 ┐   │
│                                          └────────┘      └────────┘   │
│  ┌──────┐   ┌─────────┐  ┌─────────────┐              ┌───────┐      │
│  │ Save │   │ Abandon │  │Calculate Net│              │ Close │      │
│  └──────┘   └─────────┘  └─────────────┘              └───────┘      │
└──────────────────────────────────────────────────────────────────────┘
```

♦ Enter the following details:

A/C	Date	Ref	N/C	Dept	Details	Net	Tc	Tax
CHEUNG	210196	003344	5501	3	Damaged TV	200	T1	35.00

Note that the nominal code (**N/C**) this time is 5501, being the reference code for the TV/Hi-Fi Returns Outwards account.

♦ Check the details then click the **Save** button.

♦ Select the **Close** button to return to the **Suppliers** window.

♦ **Close** the **Suppliers** window.

Accounting entries

When the credit note was posted to the ledgers the accounts would be updated as follows:

Ledger	A/c Name and Code		£
Purchase (Suppliers) Ledger	Cheung-Li Production Plc A/c (CHEUNG)	DR	235.00
Nominal Ledger	Creditors Control A/c (2100)	DR	235.00
Nominal Ledger	Returns Out (TV/Hi-Fi) A/c (5501)	CR	200.00
Nominal Ledger	Purchase Tax Control A/c (2201)	CR	35.00

You can confirm that these entries have been made by examining the appropriate accounts in the Purchase and Nominal Ledgers.

Payments to suppliers

We have made three cheque payments to suppliers during the month to Broom Brothers, Solent Engineering and Ranco Refrigeration. The entry procedure is similar to cheque receipts from customers. Proceed as follows:

♦ Select the **Bank** option in the **Desktop** window.

♦ In the **Bank Accounts** window ensure that the **Bank Current Account**, nominal code 1200, is selected (highlighted) and then click the **Supplier Payment** button. A **Supplier Payment – Bank Current Account** window similar to the following should now open:

In the top half of the window a representation of a page from a cheque book is shown and the bottom half is used to list outstanding supplier transactions.

The first payment we are going to process is a cheque for £246.75 payable to Broom Brothers.

♦ Enter the following details:

Payee	: BROOM	You can use the 'Finder' here. Note that the outstanding transaction for Broom has now appeared.
Date	: 270196	Cheque date.
Chq. No.	: 249182	
£ (cheque amount)	: 246.75	Notice that the **Bank Balance** shown at the bottom of the window is decreased by this amount when you [Tab] to the next field.

♦ When you have entered these details the insertion cursor should be 'flashing' in the **Payment** field for invoice 444891. We will use this cheque to pay off invoice 444891 in full so select the **Pay in Full** button at the bottom of the window.

The **Payment** and **Analysis Total** fields will now show the amount of the cheque.

♦ Check your entries. Alterations can still be made or all entries abandoned completely if necessary.

♦ If the entries are correct select the **Save** button to post the transaction to the ledgers.

The next cheque payment is to Solent Engineering PLC for £500.

♦ Enter the following details:

Payee	:	SOLENT Outstanding transaction for Solent should now appear.
Date	:	270196
Chq. No.	:	249183
£ (cheque amount)	:	500.00

♦ The insertion cursor should be 'flashing' in the **Payment** field for invoice 754218. We are obviously going to use the cheque to make a part payment towards this invoice so enter 500 in the **Payment** field. Check your entries.

This time we'll print a Remittance Advice Note to accompany our cheque payment to SOLENT.

♦ Select the **Remittance** button from the bottom of the window and a **Bank Remittance** window should open.

♦ Select the file **New Remittance Advice (A4)** in the **Layout** panel (the file description is **A4 Remittance Advice** in Version 3.10 of the program); this is one of the standard remittance advice layout files supplied by Sage and is designed for A4 paper.

♦ Select the **Output** medium as **Printer** and click the **Run** button.

♦ Click the **OK** button in the **Print** dialogue box and a remittance advice note for SOLENT should be printed.

♦ **Close** the **Bank Remittance** window.

♦ In the **Supplier Payment** window select the **Save** button and the details of the payment to SOLENT will be posted to the ledgers.

The third cheque payment is to Ranco Refrigeration PLC for £1057.50. They offered us an early settlement discount of 10 per cent for prompt payment and we are taking advantage of this.

♦ Enter the following details:

Payee	:	RANCO
Date	:	270196
Chq. No.	:	249184
£ (cheque amount)	:	1057.50

This cheque will fully pay invoice 414141 since the discount received amounts to £100.

♦ When the insertion cursor is in the **Payment** field for invoice 414141 enter 1057.50 and [**Tab**] to the **Discount** field.

♦ Enter 100 in the **Discount** field and press the [**Tab**] key again.

♦ The **Payment** and **Analysis Total** fields should now show 1057.50. The **Discount** field should show 100 and the **Bank Balance** should have reduced to 9695.25.

♦ Check your entries and select the **Save** button to post to the ledgers.

♦ **Close** the **Supplier Payment** window then **Close** the **Bank Accounts** window.

Payment on Account

You can choose to post (**Save**) a payment before the full cheque balance has been allocated against available invoices. If you select the **Save** button when the **Analysis Total** is less than the cheque amount you will be asked to confirm that you wish to post the unallocated balance as a Payment on Account. This balance can be allocated against an invoice at a later date.

Supplier Payment Wizard

There is a **Wizard** button in the **Supplier Payment** window which activates the **Supplier Payment Wizard** tool. This is a series of dialogue boxes, similar to the Customer Receipt Wizard, which lead you through the process of posting cheques or payments on account.

Cash payments to suppliers

If you pay a supplier in cash this would be recorded by selecting the **Cash** Account, nominal code 1230, in the **Bank Accounts** window then clicking the **Supplier Payment** button. Details of the cash payment would then be entered to the **Supplier Payment – Cash** window and when saved the details would be credited to the Cash Account.

Accounting entries

When cheque payments are posted to the ledgers the accounts are updated as follows:

DEBIT   Suppliers A/c in Purchase Ledger with cheque amount.
DEBIT   Creditors Control A/c in Nominal Ledger with cheque amount.
CREDIT   Bank A/c in Nominal Ledger with cheque amount.

If discount has been received the entries would be as follows:

DEBIT   Suppliers A/c in Purchase Ledger with cheque amount.
DEBIT   Suppliers A/c in Purchase Ledger with discount amount.
DEBIT   Creditors Control A/c in Nominal Ledger with total amount
         (cheque + discount).
CREDIT   Bank A/c in Nominal Ledger with cheque amount.
CREDIT   Discount Received A/c in Nominal Ledger with discount amount.

For example the cheque payment to RANCO would be posted to the ledgers in the following way:

Ledger	A/c Name and Code		£
Purchase (Suppliers) Ledger	Ranco Refrigeration PLC A/c (RANCO)	DR	1057.50
Purchase (Suppliers) Ledger	Ranco Refrigeration PLC A/c (RANCO)	DR	100.00
Nominal Ledger	Creditors Control A/c (2100)	DR	1057.50
Nominal Ledger	Creditors Control A/c (2100)	DR	100.00
Nominal Ledger	Bank A/c (1200)	CR	1057.50
Nominal Ledger	Discounts Taken A/c (5009)	CR	100.00

PURCHASE LEDGER (SUPPLIER) REPORTS

Supplier reports which are produced from Purchase Ledger data are very similar to the Sales Ledger reports described previously. The following three option buttons in the **Suppliers** window give you access to some of these reports:

- **Activity**

  Allows you to view transaction details recorded in a supplier's account.

- **Aged Balances**

  Provides an aged analysis of supplier balances in detailed or summary form.

- **Reports**

  Allows you to view and print a variety of pre-designed reports and to design new reports. Included in the pre-designed reports are the following:
  – Aged Creditors Analysis;
  – Supplier Day Books;
  – Supplier List;
  – Supplier Activity (same as Activity report previously mentioned).
  The procedure for viewing or printing any of these reports is the same as that described in the Sales Ledger Reports section earlier in this chapter. The procedure for designing a new report is described in Chapter 6 on the Report Generator.

Additional information relating to suppliers can be accessed from the **Supplier Record** window using the following 'page' tab buttons:

- **Purchases**

  This 'page' displays an analysis of transactions with the selected supplier showing monthly totals for invoices, credit notes and purchase payments over the period of a year.

- **Graph**

  This 'page' can be used to provide transaction information for a selected supplier in graphical format. Various types of graphs/charts can be produced almost instantaneously showing monthly totals for invoices, credit notes and supplier balances over the period of a year.

- **Activity**

  Similar to the Activity report accessed from the **Suppliers** window the report allows you to view transaction details recorded in a supplier's account.

NOMINAL LEDGER BANK TRANSACTIONS

This section deals with bank transactions (payments and receipts) for nominal ledger analysis only, i.e. no entries are required to supplier or customer accounts.

Bank payments

Cheque payments were made in respect of the following transactions during the month of January:

(a) Jan. 27   Bought 2 office chairs paying by cheque, No. 249181. The chairs cost £329 *including VAT*.

(b) Jan. 28   £2600 withdrawn from bank to pay office salaries in cash, cheque No. 249185.

To enter these transactions proceed as follows:

♦ Select the **Bank** option in the **Desktop** window.

♦ In the **Bank Accounts** window ensure that the **Bank Current Account**, nominal code 1200, is selected (highlighted) and then click the **Payment** button.

♦ The following **Bank Payment – Bank Current Account** data entry window should now open:

```
┌──────────────────────────────────────────────────────────────────┐
│ ▬              Bank Payment - Bank Current Account          ▼ ▲   │
├──────────────────────────────────────────────────────────────────┤
│  Bank Current Account        Date:  31/01/96  ▦   Chq.No. _____ │
│                                                                    │
│  Payee:  _____                 │
│          _____  £      0.00    │
│          _____ ASCOT ENTERPRISES            │
│                                                                    │
│  N/C   Name         Dept Details        Net    Tc  Tax            │
│  ┌──────────────────────────────────────────────────────┐        │
│  │                                                        │        │
│  └──────────────────────────────────────────────────────┘        │
│  Bank Balance   9695.25          Analysis Total      0.00         │
│  [ Save ]  [ Abandon ]  [ Calc. Net ]              [ Close ]      │
└──────────────────────────────────────────────────────────────────┘
```

♦ Enter the following details for the purchase of the office chairs:

Date	: 270196	
Chq. No.	: 249181	
Payee	: Monarch Furnishings	It is not necessary to complete this field.
£ (cheque amount)	: 329	Note that the **Bank Balance** decreases after you press the [**Tab**] key.
N/C	: 0040	Nominal code for Furniture and fixtures, debit entry will be made to this A/c.
Dept	: 1	
Details	: 2 Office Chairs	

Read carefully before proceeding. The £329 was the *gross* amount, including VAT, paid for the chairs. The program can calculate the net amount and the VAT for you if you use the **Calc. Net** button at the bottom of the window.

♦ Enter 329 in the **Net** field, ensure that T1 is displayed in the **Tc** field, then click the **Calc. Net** button. If you do this correctly 280 should appear in the **Net** field and 49 in the **Tax** field.

♦ Ensure that the entry in the **Analysis Total** box is the same as that in the **£** (cheque amount) box otherwise you will not be allowed to save these details.

♦ When your entries are correct click the **Save** button to post to the ledger and the **Bank Payment** window will clear.

Note: If your cheque payment is for several items which you wish to analyse to separate nominal, departmental or tax codes you can complete one line in this window for each item.

♦ Enter the following details for the payment of salaries:

Date	: 280196	
Chq. No.	: 249185	
Payee	: Ascot Enterprises	
£ (cheque amount)	: 2600	
N/C	: 7003	Nominal code for salaries, debit entry will be made to this account.
Dept	: 1	
Details	: Office salaries for January	
Net	: 2600	
Tc	: T9	This is a non-VAT transaction.
Tax	: 0.00	

Note that there is no VAT on the last transaction so the tax code used is T9.

♦ Check that your entries are correct and select the **Save** button to post to the ledger.

♦ **Close** the **Bank Payment** window.

Accounting entries

The following entries will have been made in the accounts:

Transaction (a) – Purchase of office chairs:

DEBIT   Furniture and Fixtures A/c (0040) in the Nominal Ledger with net amount, £280.
DEBIT   Purchase Tax Control A/c (2201) in the Nominal Ledger with tax amount, £49.
CREDIT   Bank A/c (1200) in the Nominal Ledger with gross amount, £329.

Transaction (b) – Payment of office salaries:

DEBIT   Salaries A/c (7003) in the Nominal Ledger with gross amount, £2600.
CREDIT   Bank A/c (1200) in the Nominal Ledger with gross amount, £2600.

You can confirm that these entries have been made by examining the appropriate accounts using the **Activity** button in the **Nominal Ledger** window.

Bank receipts

Let's say we negotiate a bank loan of £4000 and the funds are transferred into our account on 29 January. To record this transaction proceed as follows:

♦ In the **Bank Accounts** window ensure that the **Bank Current Account**, nominal code 1200, is selected and then click the **Receipt** button. The following **Bank Receipt – Bank Current Account** data entry window should now open:

```
┌─────────────────────────────────────────────────────────────────────┐
│ ─ │         Bank Receipt - Bank Current Account           │ ▼ │ ▲ │
├─────────────────────────────────────────────────────────────────────┤
│   ┌──── Ref ────┐      ┌──── Date ────┐         ┌── Amount ──┐        │
│   │             │      │ 31/01/96  📅 │         │    0.00  ▦ │        │
│   └─────────────┘      └──────────────┘         └────────────┘        │
│  ┌──────┬───────────┬─────┬──────────┬────────┬────┬─────────┐        │
│  │ N/C  │ Name      │ Dept│ Details  │  Net   │ Tc │ Tax     │ ▲      │
│  ├──────┼───────────┼─────┼──────────┼────────┼────┼─────────┤        │
│  │      │           │     │          │        │    │         │        │
│  │      │           │     │          │        │    │         │        │
│  │      │           │     │          │        │    │         │        │
│  │      │           │     │          │        │    │         │        │
│  │      │           │     │          │        │    │         │        │
│  │      │           │     │          │        │    │         │        │
│  │      │           │     │          │        │    │         │        │
│  │      │           │     │          │        │    │         │ ▼      │
│  └──────┴───────────┴─────┴──────────┴────────┴────┴─────────┘        │
│   Bank Balance ┌──────────┐         Analysis Total ┌──────────┐       │
│                │  6766.25 │                         │     0.00 │       │
│                └──────────┘                         └──────────┘       │
│   ┌───────┐ ┌─────────┐ ┌─────────────┐            ┌───────┐          │
│   │ Save  │ │ Abandon │ │ Calculate Net│           │ Close │          │
│   └───────┘ └─────────┘ └─────────────┘            └───────┘          │
└─────────────────────────────────────────────────────────────────────┘
```

♦ Enter the following details of the loan receipt:

Ref	:	727173	Ref. No. for posting, e.g. pay-in slip no.
Date	:	290196	
Amount	:	4000	
N/C	:	2300	Nominal code for Bank Loan; credit entry will be made to this account.
Dept	:	1	
Details	:	Bank Loan	
Net	:	4000	
Tc	:	T9	This is a non-VAT transaction.
Tax	:	0.00	

Again, this is a non-VAT transaction so the tax code used is T9.

♦ Check your entries then select **Save** to post to the ledger.

Note: If your cheque receipt is for several items which you wish to analyse to separate nominal, departmental or tax codes you can complete one line in this window for each item.

♦ **Close** the **Bank Receipt** window then **Close** the **Bank Accounts** window.

Accounting entries

The following entries will have been made in the accounts:

DEBIT   Bank A/c (1200) in the Nominal Ledger with amount of loan, £4000.
CREDIT   Loan A/c (2300) in the Nominal Ledger with amount of loan, £4000.

NOMINAL LEDGER JOURNAL ENTRIES

The journal entries routine can be used for the following types of transaction:

1   entering opening balances to the nominal ledger accounts (there is also a setup button in the **Nominal Ledger Record** window which can be used to carry out this operation);

2   entering closing stock figures to the stock accounts in the nominal ledger;

3   recording depreciation, accruals and prepayments at a period-end if the automated routines for these functions are not being used.

In fact the Journal can be used where double-entry postings need to be made to any accounts within the nominal ledger, including control accounts. However, when using the Journal you must make a minimum of two entries – a debit posting and a corresponding credit posting. You will not be allowed to save your journal entries until total debits equal total credits.

Since we usually make several petty cash payments at the end of the month, we are going to transfer £100 from our Bank Account into our Cash Account.

There is a **Transfer** option in the **Bank Accounts** window which allows you to transfer funds between any of your Bank and Cash accounts but we will use the **Journals** routine in the **Nominal Ledger**.

◆ Select the **Nominal Ledger** option in the **Desktop** window.

◆ Click the **Journals** button in the **Nominal Ledger** window. A **Nominal Ledger Journal Entry** window similar to the following should now open:

♦ Enter the following details:

Ref	:	P/Cash	
Date	:	270196	
N/C	:	1200	Bank Current Account.
Dept	:	1	
Details	:	Transfer to Petty Cash	
Tc	:	T9	Non-VAT transaction.
Debit	:	0.00	
Credit	:	100	

♦ Move the insertion cursor to the **N/C** field on the second line and enter the other 'half' of the transaction as follows:

N/C	:	1230	Cash Account.
Dept	:	1	
Details	:	Transfer from Bank	
Tc	:	T9	
Debit	:	100	
Credit	:	0.00	

♦ Check that your entries are accurate. The **Balance** field at the top of the window should be zero, indicating that debit entries equal credit entries.

♦ Select the **Save** button to post to the ledger.

♦ **Close** the **Journal Entry** window, then **Close** the **Nominal Ledger** window.

Accounting entries

The following entries will have been made in the accounts:

DEBIT   Cash A/c (1230) in the Nominal Ledger, £100.
CREDIT   Bank A/c (1200) in the Nominal Ledger, £100.

NOMINAL LEDGER CASH TRANSACTIONS

This section deals with cash transactions (payments and receipts) for Nominal Ledger analysis only, i.e. no entries are required to supplier or customer accounts. The **Payment** routine, accessed from the **Bank Accounts** window, can be used to record cash payment transactions involving another nominal ledger account, e.g. cleaning or stationery. The **Receipt** routine in the same window can be used to record cash receipt transactions involving another nominal ledger account, e.g. cash sales, where the funds are received in cash and not banked.

Cash payments

Cash payments were made in respect of the following transactions during the month of January:

1 Jan. 28 Bought office stationery for cash. The price was £51.70 *including VAT* (petty cash voucher No. PC21).

2 Jan. 29 Paid £35 cash for office cleaning (voucher No. PC22). This is a non-VAT transaction.

To enter these transactions proceed as follows:

♦ Select the **Bank** option in the **Desktop** window.

♦ In the **Bank Accounts** window ensure that the **Cash** Account, nominal code 1230, is selected (highlighted) and then click the **Payment** button. The following **Cash Payments** data entry window should now open:

Ref			Date				Amount		
			31/01/96				0.00		

N/C	Name	Dept	Details	Net	Tc	Tax

Cash Balance   300.00   Analysis Total   0.00

[Save] [Abandon] [Calculate Net]   [Close]

♦ Enter the following details for the purchase of stationery:

Ref   : PC21   Petty cash voucher no.
Date   : 280196
Amount : 51.70
N/C   : 7504   Nominal code for Office Stationery; debit entry will be made to this account.
Dept   : 1
Details : Stationery
Net   : 51.70   Ensure that T1 is displayed in the **Tc** field, then click on the **Calculate Net** button to extract the VAT element (**Net** becomes 44.00 and **Tax** becomes 7.70).

♦ When your entries are accurate click the **Save** button to post the transaction to the ledger and the **Cash Payments** window will clear.

♦ Enter the following details to record the cash payment for Office Cleaning:

Ref	: PC22	
Date	: 290196	
Amount	: 35	
N/C	: 7801	Nominal code for office cleaning; debit entry will be made to this account.
Dept	: 1	
Details	: Office cleaning	
Net	: 35	
Tc	: T9	Non-VAT transaction.
Tax	: 0.00	

♦ Click the **Save** button to post these details to the ledger accounts.

♦ **Close** the **Cash Payments** window.

Accounting entries

The following entries will have been made to the accounts:

Transaction (a)

DEBIT   Stationery A/c (7504) in the Nominal Ledger with net amount, £44.00.
DEBIT   Purchase Tax Control A/c (2201) in the Nominal Ledger with tax, £7.70.
CREDIT   Cash A/c (1230) in the Nominal Ledger with gross amount, £51.70.

Transaction (b)

DEBIT   Cleaning A/c (7801) in the Nominal Ledger, £35.00.
CREDIT   Cash A/c (1230) in the Nominal Ledger, £35.00.

Cash receipts

On 30 January we sold a hair dryer (£10 + VAT) and a food processor (£30 + VAT) to a member of staff for cash. Since this is a cash sale (two cash sales in fact) there is no need to enter it through the Sales Ledger (**Customers**) routine. Proceed as follows:

♦ In the **Bank Accounts** window ensure that the **Cash Account**, nominal code 1230, is selected (highlighted) and then click the **Receipt** button. The following **Cash Receipts** data entry window should now open:

```
┌──────────────────────────────────────────────────────────────────────┐
│ ─                         Cash Receipts                         ▼  ▲   │
│  ┌───────────┐            ┌─────────────┐            ┌──────────────┐  │
│  │    Ref    │            │    Date     │            │   Amount     │  │
│  │           │            │ 31/01/96 📅 │            │    0.00 🖩   │  │
│  ├───────┬────────┬──────┬─────────┬─────────┬─────┬───────┐          │
│  │ N/C   │ Name   │ Dept │ Details │  Net    │ Tc  │  Tax  │ ▲        │
│  │       │        │      │         │         │     │       │          │
│  │       │        │      │         │         │     │       │          │
│  │       │        │      │         │         │     │       │          │
│  │       │        │      │         │         │     │       │          │
│  │       │        │      │         │         │     │       │ ▼        │
│  └───────┴────────┴──────┴─────────┴─────────┴─────┴───────┘          │
│                                                                        │
│  Cash Balance  ┌──────────┐      Analysis Total   ┌──────────┐         │
│                │  213.30  │                       │    0.00  │         │
│  ┌────────┐  ┌──────────┐  ┌──────────────┐         ┌────────┐        │
│  │  Save  │  │ Abandon  │  │ Calculate Net│         │ Close  │        │
│  └────────┘  └──────────┘  └──────────────┘         └────────┘        │
└──────────────────────────────────────────────────────────────────────┘
```

♦ Enter the following details for the cash sales:

Ref	: 1211	Invoice No.
Date	: 300196	
Amount	: 47	
N/C	: 4002	Nominal code for Personal Care Sales, credit entry for hair dryer sale will be made to this account.
Dept	: 4	
Details	: Staff sale	
Net	: 10.00	
Tc	: T1	
Tax	: 1.75	

♦ Move the insertion cursor to the **N/C** field on the second line and enter the following details for the food processor sale:

N/C	: 4000	Nominal code for Kitchen Equipment Sales, credit entry for food processor sale will be made to this account.
Dept	: 2	
Details	: Staff sale	
Net	: 30	
Tc	: T1	
Tax	: 5.25	

♦ When your entries are accurate select the **Save** button to post the details to the ledger accounts.

♦ **Close** the **Cash Receipts** window then **Close** the **Bank Accounts** window.

Accounting entries

The following entries should have been made to the accounts:

DEBIT   Cash A/c (1230) in the Nominal Ledger with gross amount, £47.00.

CREDIT   Personal Care Sales A/c (4002) in the Nominal Ledger with net amount, £10.00.

CREDIT   Kitchen Equipment Sales A/c (4000) in the Nominal Ledger with net amount, £30.00.

CREDIT   Sales Tax Control A/c (2200) in the Nominal Ledger with tax, £7.00.

NOMINAL LEDGER REPORTS

As with the Sales and Purchase Ledgers, Nominal Ledger data can be used to produce a variety of pre-designed and user-designed reports relating to nominal accounts. The following two option buttons in the **Nominal Ledger** window give you access to some of these reports:

- **Activity**   Allows you to view transaction details recorded in a nominal account. This is similar to the Activity reports produced in the Sales and Purchase Ledgers.

- **Reports**   Allows you to view and print a variety of pre-designed reports and to design new reports. Included in the pre-designed reports are the Nominal Ledger Day Books and a Nominal Activity report providing a transaction history for all or selected nominal accounts.

        The procedure for viewing or printing any of these reports is the same as that described in the Sales Ledger Reports section earlier in this chapter. The procedure for designing a new report is described in Chapter 6 on the Report Generator.

Additional information relating to nominal accounts can be accessed from the **Nominal Record** window using the following 'page' tab buttons:

- **Details**   This 'page' displays the actual and budgeted figures for each month of the financial year for the account concerned.

- **Graph**   This 'page' can be used to produce almost instantaneously various types of graphs and charts which display and compare actual and budgeted monthly totals for the selected account over the period of a year.

- **Activity**   Similar to the Activity report accessed from the **Nominal Ledger** window this report allows you to view transaction details recorded in a nominal account.

AUDIT TRAIL

The Audit Trail is a list of all transactions which have been posted to the ledgers. The transactions are numbered consecutively and added to the Audit Trail in entry order (rather than transaction date order).

To display or print the Audit Trail proceed as follows:

♦ Select the **Financials** option in the **Desktop** window. When the **Financials** window opens, the Audit Trail, similar to the following, should be displayed:

No		Tp	Account	Nominal	Dep	Details	Date	Ref
	45	BP	1200	0040	1	2 Office Chairs	27/01/96	249181
	46	BP	1200	7003	1	Office salaries for January	28/01/96	249185
	47	BR	1200	2300	1	Bank Loan	29/01/96	727173
	48	JC		1200	1	Transfer to Petty Cash	27/01/96	P/Cash
	49	JD		1230	1	Transfer from Bank	27/01/96	P/Cash
	50	CP	1230	7504	1	Stationery	28/01/96	PC21
	51	CP	1230	7801	1	Office cleaning	29/01/96	PC22
	52	CR	1230	4002	4	Staff sale	30/01/96	1211
	53	CR	1230	4000	2	Staff sale	30/01/96	1211

Financials — Close

The display shows the bottom of the list, i.e. the most recent transactions. To view all the transactions from the beginning of January scroll the window vertically. To view all the columns scroll the window horizontally.

Printing the Audit Trail

There is no need for you to do this at the moment but the procedure is as follows:

♦ Click the **Audit Trail** button in the **Financials** window.

♦ When the **Audit Trail Report** dialogue box opens, select either **Brief, Summary** or **Detailed** (these show increasing amounts of detail) in the **Audit Trail Type** panel. Select **Printer** in the **Output** panel and click the **Run** button.

♦ When the **Additional Report Filter** dialogue box opens you can use any or all of the range boxes to limit the transactions you want listed. If you wish all transactions to be listed in the Audit Trail report make no changes in the **Additional Report Filter** dialogue box, simply click the **OK** button.

♦ Click **OK** in the **Print** dialogue box and the Audit Trail report will be printed.

♦ **Close** the **Financials** window.

VAT RETURN ANALYSIS AND RECONCILIATION

Before looking at the VAT Return, check and note the balances on the Sales Tax Control A/c (2200) and the Purchase Tax Control A/c (2201), both in the Nominal Ledger. Calculate the difference between the two balances.

Sales VAT is the output tax which you have charged your customers. Purchase VAT is the input tax which you have paid to your suppliers. If output tax is greater than input tax the difference is due to the Customs and Excise Department and this would appear as a liability in your Balance Sheet until it is paid. If input tax is greater than output tax then the difference can be reclaimed from Customs and Excise and this would appear as an asset in the Balance Sheet.

VAT Return

♦ Select the **Financials** option in the **Desktop** window.

♦ Click the **VAT Return** button in the **Financials** window. A representation of the VAT Return form, similar to the following, should now be displayed:

♦ At the top right of the form enter the **For the period** date as 010196 and the **to** date as 310196.

♦ Now select the **Calculate** button at the bottom of the form (window) and the program will analyse the VAT for the month of January and display the number of transactions found in a small **VAT Return** dialogue box. Click the **OK** button in this box and the results will be entered to the appropriate boxes on the form.

♦ When the analysis is complete, box 5 on the **Value Added Tax Return** will display net VAT to be paid to Customs and Excise or reclaimed by you. This figure should agree with the net balance you have just calculated from the Sales and Purchase Tax Control accounts in the Nominal Ledger.

Note: An analysis of the figures in the boxes can be obtained by clicking on the appropriate box (except 3 and 5). This will produce a **VAT Breakdown** by transaction type and tax code. In the **VAT Breakdown** dialogue box you can produce complete listings for invoices, credits, receipts/payments, etc. for a selected tax code by double clicking the appropriate field.

♦ When you have inspected these return to the **Value Added Tax Return** window.

Standard VAT accounting and VAT cash accounting

The VAT Return can be calculated on a standard VAT accounting basis or on a VAT cash accounting basis. The former method will produce figures based on input and output VAT amounts you have invoices for, whereas the latter method will calculate the VAT figures from amounts you have actually received and paid. The method used will depend on whether the **VAT Cash Accounting** check box in the **Company Preferences** dialogue box (accessed from the **Defaults** menu) is selected or deselected. The default setting (check box is deselected) will produce the VAT Return on a standard VAT accounting basis and this is the method you should be using.

Reconciling the VAT transactions

Reconciliation 'flags' the VAT transactions used to calculate the latest VAT Return. These 'flagged' transactions can then be excluded from subsequent VAT Returns.

The **Reconcile** button at the bottom of the **Value Added Tax Return** window is used for this purpose and reconciliation would normally be carried out at the end of a VAT period. You should not carry out the reconciliation procedure at the moment.

Printing the VAT Return analysis

The VAT Return analysis can be printed, or saved to file in detailed or summary form. The procedure is as follows:

♦ In the **Value Added Tax Return** window select the **Print** button and this will open a small **Print VAT Return** dialogue box. This dialogue box allows you to choose the **Output** medium and to select whether you want a **Detailed** or **Summary** report. Selecting the **VAT Return** option in this box will produce a copy of the report in the same format as that shown on the screen (i.e. like the VAT Return form).

♦ If the **Print VAT Return** dialogue box is open at the moment close it by selecting the **Cancel** button.

♦ **Close** the **Value Added Tax Return** window then **Close** the **Financials** window.

FINAL ACCOUNTS

We are going to produce a Profit and Loss Account and Balance Sheet at the end of January. Before we do this we will set up a new account to hold our Cost of Goods Sold and print a Trial Balance.

Cost of Goods Sold

♦ Select the **Nominal Ledger** option in the **Desktop** window.

♦ Click the **Record** button in the **Nominal Ledger** window.

♦ Enter the following details to the **Nominal Record** data entry window:

N/C   :   5300
Name :   Cost of Goods Sold

♦ Once these details are entered click the **Save** button. **Close** the **Nominal Record** window.

We will now enter our Opening and Closing Stock, Purchases and Returns Out figures to the new account to allow us to calculate the Cost of Goods Sold for the period to date. The Opening Stock, Purchases and Returns Out figures can be obtained from the ledger accounts themselves, the Trial Balance or the **Nominal Ledger** window and should be as follows:

A/c Name and Code No.	Balance	
	Dr	*Cr*
Opening Stock (5200)	44000	
Purchases – Kitchen Equipment (5000)	4300	
Purchases – TV/Hi-Fi (5001)	3900	
Purchases – Personal Care (5002)	490	
Returns Out – TV/Hi-Fi (5501)		200

Assume that after a stock check the Closing Stock (at the end of January) is valued at £46200. We'll now enter these figures to the Cost of Goods Sold Account (5300) using the **Journals** routine.

♦ Click the **Journals** button in the **Nominal Ledger** window.

♦ Enter the following details to the **Journal Entry** window (the window will scroll to accommodate your entries):

N/C	Dept	Details	Tc	Debit	Credit
Ref	:	COGS			
Date	:	310196			
5200	0	Transfer to COGS	T9	0	44000
5300	0	Stock at 1 January	T9	44000	0
5000	0	Transfer to COGS	T9	0	4300
5001	0	Transfer to COGS	T9	0	3900
5002	0	Transfer to COGS	T9	0	490
5300	0	Purchases for January	T9	8690	0
5501	0	Transfer to COGS	T9	200	0
5300	0	Returns Out for January	T9	0	200
1001	0	Stock at 31 January	T9	46200	0
5300	0	Stock at 31 January	T9	0	46200

♦ Check your entries carefully. Ensure that the **Balance** field at the top of the window displays 0.00 (meaning that debits equal credits) then select the **Save** button to post the entries to the ledger accounts.

♦ **Close** the **Journal Entry** window then **Close** the **Nominal Ledger** window.

The entries may look complex but all you have done is to transfer the balances on the Opening Stock, Purchases and Returns Out Accounts to a new account for Cost of Goods Sold. You have also entered the value of closing stock to this account and to a Closing Stock Account. The latter will be used in the Balance Sheet.

Cost of Goods Sold is calculated as follows: Opening Stock + (Purchases – Returns Out) – Closing Stock. This calculation can be shown on the face of the Profit and Loss Account or separately as we have done in a Cost of Goods Sold Account. If the latter method is used one entry only will be necessary in the Profit and Loss Account (the balance on the Cost of Goods Sold Account) and it will facilitate the production of accurate monthly Profit and Loss Accounts in the future.

Print Trial Balance

We now require a printout of the current Trial Balance to enable us to design the Final Accounts accurately. Before we do this we'll set the program date to 31 January 1996.

♦ Open the **Defaults** menu and select **Change Program Date**.

♦ When the **Change Program Date** dialogue box opens change the date to 310196 and click the **OK** button.

♦ Now select the **Financials** option in the **Desktop** window and when the **Financials** window opens click the **Trial Balance** button.

♦ When the **Trial Balance Report** dialogue box appears ensure that the **Current** option button is selected in the **Accounting Range** panel. **January 1996 Mth1** should already be displayed in the **Period Range** panel. Select the **Printer** option button in the **Output** panel then click the **Run** button.

♦ When the **Print** dialogue box appears click the **OK** button and the current Trial Balance should be printed.

The Trial Balance should be similar to the following:

ASCOT ENTERPRISES
Current Trial Balance

N/C	Name	Debit	Credit
0040	Furniture and fixtures	6280.00	
0050	Motor vehicles	25000.00	
1001	Closing stock (Bal. Sheet)	46200.00	
1100	Debtors control account	7807.05	
1200	Bank current account	10666.25	
1230	Cash	260.30	
2100	Creditors control account		9254.85
2200	Sales tax control account		2167.55
2201	Purchase tax control account	1548.80	
2300	Bank loan		4000.00
3000	Capital		80000.00
4000	Sales – kitchen equipment		5700.00
4001	Sales – TV/Hi-Fi		6730.00
4002	Sales – personal care		496.00
4009	Discounts allowed	240.00	
4500	Returns In – kitchen equipment	300.00	
5009	Discounts taken		100.00
5300	Cost of goods sold	6290.00	
7003	Salaries	2600.00	
7100	Rent	1000.00	
7200	Electricity	75.00	
7305	Vehicle repairs	102.00	
7504	Office stationery	44.00	
7801	Cleaning	35.00	
		108448.40	108448.40

♦ When you have obtained the print out **Close** the **Financials** window.

Design Final Accounts

The program can produce a Profit and Loss Account and Balance Sheet from the account balances in the Nominal Ledger.

♦ Select the **Nominal Ledger** option in the **Desktop** window.

♦ Click the **Chart of Accounts** button in the **Nominal Ledger** window.

♦ When the **Chart of Accounts** window opens, ensure that **Default Layout of Accounts** is selected (highlighted) in the **Description** panel then click the **Edit** button.

♦ The **Chart of Accounts** dialogue box should now open and display the following default layout for the Final Accounts supplied with the program.

The Profit and Loss Account is divided into four sections (categories) and these are shown in the **Category Type** column:

1 **Sales**;

2 **Purchases**;

3 **Direct Expenses**;

4 **Overheads**.

The entries in the **Description** column are the default titles for these categories. These titles will appear in the Profit and Loss Account report and they can be altered to suit your requirements. Appropriate nominal ledger accounts have been allocated to each of these categories and these are displayed in the **Category Account** panel. The program calculates the gross and net profits as follows:

> **Gross Profit=Sales – (Purchases + Direct Expenses)**
> **Net Profit=Gross Profit – Overheads**

Similarly the Balance Sheet is divided into the following four sections (categories):

1 **Fixed Assets**;

2 **Current Assets**;

3 **Current Liabilities**;

4 **Capital & Reserves**.

The default titles for these categories are shown in the **Description** column. These are the titles which will appear in the Balance Sheet report and again they can be edited if need be. Appropriate nominal ledger accounts have been allocated to each of these categories.

Clicking on one of the **Category Type** buttons (or in the **Description** field) will display in the **Category Account** panel a list of nominal account names and codes which have been allocated to the selected category.

The existing default layout can be used as it is or modified or a new layout can be designed. We'll design a new layout based on the nominal accounts in our Trial Balance.

♦ Select the **Close** button at the bottom of the **Chart of Accounts** dialogue box and you will be returned to the **Chart of Accounts** window which should be similar to the following:

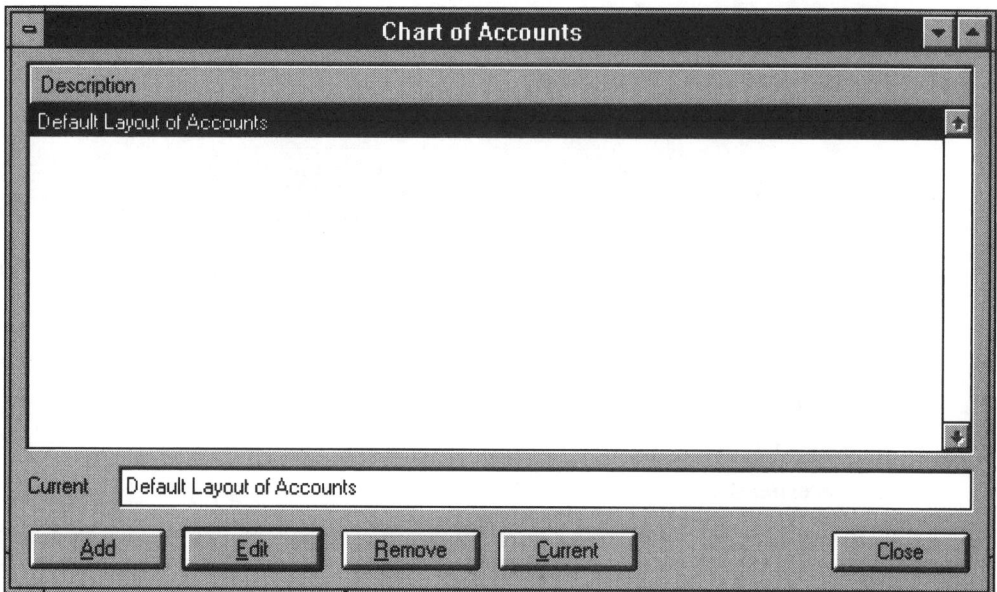

```
┌─────────────────────────────────────────────────────────────────┐
│ ─                    Chart of Accounts                     ▼ ▲ │
├─────────────────────────────────────────────────────────────────┤
│  Description                                                      │
│  Default Layout of Accounts                                   ↑  │
│                                                                  │
│                                                                  │
│                                                                  │
│                                                                  │
│                                                                  │
│                                                                  │
│                                                              ↓  │
│  Current   Default Layout of Accounts                           │
│  ┌─────┐  ┌─────┐  ┌────────┐  ┌─────────┐       ┌─────┐        │
│  │ Add │  │ Edit│  │ Remove │  │ Current │       │Close│        │
│  └─────┘  └─────┘  └────────┘  └─────────┘       └─────┘        │
└─────────────────────────────────────────────────────────────────┘
```

♦ Select the **Add** button and a small **Add New Chart** dialogue box should appear prompting for a name for the new layout.

♦ Enter the **Name** as Layout2 and click the **OK** button. The following **Chart of Accounts** dialogue box for Layout2 should now open allowing you to design your new layout.

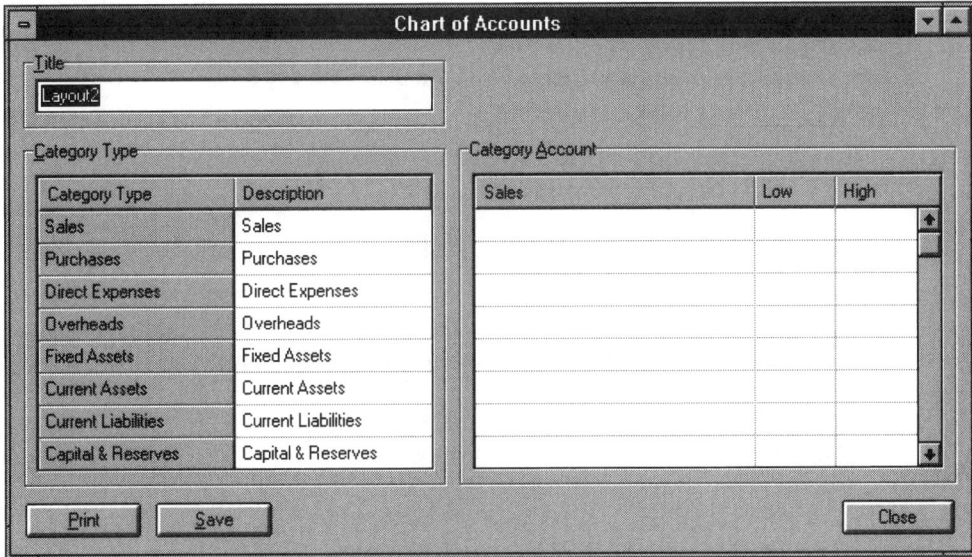

First of all we'll modify the category titles slightly.

♦ Select (click in) the **Sales** field in the **Description** column and change the title to Turnover. Similarly, click in or **[Tab]** to the **Purchases** field in the **Description** column and change the title to Cost of Sales.

The next task is to allocate nominal ledger accounts to each category. From the Trial Balance you will see that we have three types of Sales: Kitchen Equipment, TV/Hi-Fi and Personal Care, the codes running from 4000–4002. We want one figure for Sales in our Final Accounts so we will group them together.

♦ In the **Category Type** column click the **Sales** button to select this category.

♦ Now select (click) the **Sales** button in the **Category Account** panel on the right and this should locate the insertion cursor in the first account name field.

♦ You can move from field to field in the **Category Account** panel using the **[Tab]** key or by pointing and clicking, and you can delete entries, once they have been selected (highlighted), using the **[Delete]** key. Enter the following account names and codes to the first two lines in the **Category Account** panel:

Sales	**Low**	**High**
Sales	4000	4002
less Returns-in	4500	4502

The entries in the **Sales** column are what will appear in the Profit and Loss Account printout. The **Low** and **High** fields relate to nominal codes and identify to the program where to find the account balances for the corresponding entry in the **Sales** column. Note that although we have three Sales accounts they have been grouped together. The program will add the balances on accounts 4000, 4001 and 4002 and enter the total against Sales in the Profit and Loss Account.

An entry for each type of sale could be made on the Profit and Loss Account if required in which case each account name would be listed in the **Sales** column and the **Low** and **High** fields would have the same nominal code.

♦ Once you have designed the **Sales** category click on the **Purchases** button in the **Category Type** column and enter the following account name and codes to the first line in the **Category Account** panel:

Purchases	Low	High
Cost of goods sold	5300	5300

♦ We have no direct expenses so now select the **Overheads** category button and enter the following names and codes to the **Category Account** panel:

Overheads	Low	High
Discount allowed	4009	4009
Salaries	7003	7003
Rent	7100	7100
Electricity	7200	7200
Vehicle repairs	7305	7305
Office stationery	7504	7504
Cleaning	7801	7801
less Discount received	5009	5009

That's the Profit and Loss Account designed so we can now continue with the design of the Balance Sheet.

♦ Select the **Fixed Assets** category and enter the following account names and codes to the first two lines in the **Category Account** panel:

Fixed Assets	Low	High
Furniture and fixtures	0040	0040
Motor vehicles	0050	0050

♦ Select the **Current Assets** category and enter the following details on the first three lines of the **Category Account** panel:

Current Assets	Low	High
Stock	1001	1001
Debtors	1100	1100
Cash	1230	1230

Read the next part carefully before you do any more.

The Bank A/c can appear in the Balance Sheet as either an asset or a liability depending on whether it has a debit or a credit balance. Similarly, if Sales Tax is greater than Purchase Tax the net figure is the amount due to Customs and Excise and should appear as a liability in the Balance Sheet. However, if the balance on the Purchase Tax A/c is greater than the balance on the Sales Tax A/c the net figure is reclaimable from Customs and Excise and should appear as an asset in the Balance Sheet.

So, the Bank and VAT accounts should be entered as both assets and liabilities in the Chart of Accounts layout and the program will decide which category to allocate each account to depending on their balance or net balance.

For the program to be able to do this *the accounts must be entered as one of the last five account names in the* **Category Account** *panel*. There are a total of 50 lines in the **Category Account** panel so:

♦ Enter the following details on *lines 46 and 47* (you will have to scroll the box):

Current Assets	Low	High
Bank	1200	1200
VAT reclaimable	2200	2201

♦ Select the **Current Liabilities** category and enter the following details on the first two lines of the **Category Account** panel:

Current Liabilities	Low	High
Creditors	2100	2100
Bank loan	2300	2300

♦ Now enter the following details on *lines 46 and 47*:

Current Liabilities	Low	High
Bank overdraft	1200	1200
VAT liability	2200	2201

When the Balance Sheet is printed the program will check the balance on the Bank A/c (1200) and enter it as an asset if it is debit or a liability if it is credit.

Similarly, the net balance on the two VAT accounts (2200 and 2201) will be entered as an asset if it is debit or a liability if it is credit.

♦ Select the **Capital & Reserves** category and enter the following on the first line of the **Category Account** panel:

Capital & Reserves	Low	High
Capital	3000	3000

That's your Chart of Accounts layout complete, but before you leave this dialogue box you should check the account names and code numbers which you have allocated to each **Category Type**.

♦ When you are satisfied with your layout select the **Save** button then select the **Close** button. If a small **Confirm** dialogue box appears asking if you are sure that you wish to exit click the **Yes** button.

♦ The **Chart of Accounts** window should now list both layouts (Default Layout and Layout2) in the **Description** panel. Ensure that **Layout2** is selected (highlighted) and click the **Current** button at the bottom of the window. **Layout2** should now appear in the **Current** box indicating that this is the layout which will be used when the Profit and Loss Account and Balance Sheet are printed.

Your **Chart of Accounts** window should be similar to the following:

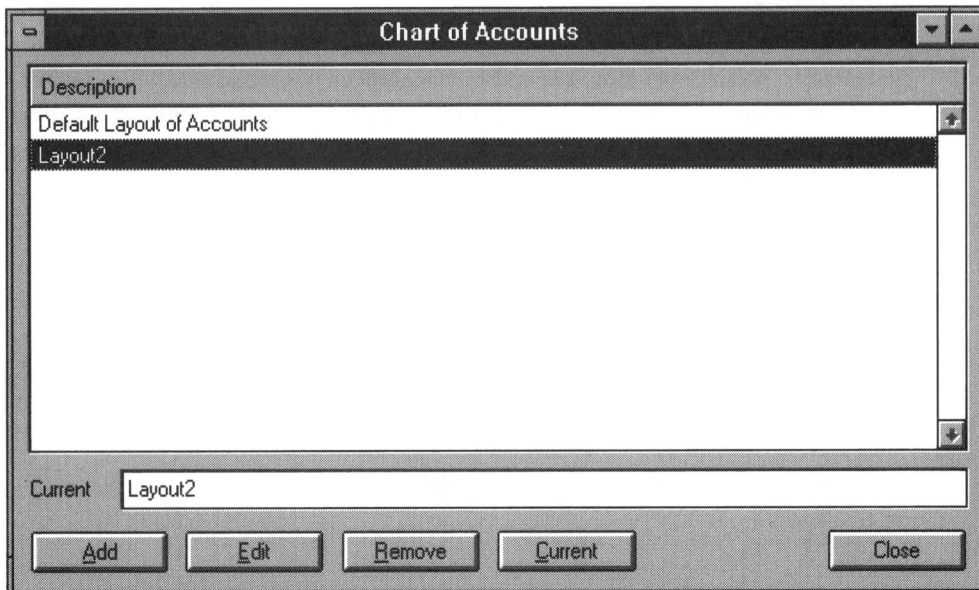

♦ **Close** the **Chart of Accounts** window then **Close** the **Nominal Ledger** window.

Print Chart of Accounts layout

If you wish to check the layout before printing the Final Accounts the procedure is as follows:

♦ In the **Chart of Accounts** window select the layout you wish to check then click the **Edit** button.

♦ When the Chart of Accounts dialogue box opens click the **Print** button and the following **Print Chart of Accounts** dialogue box should appear:

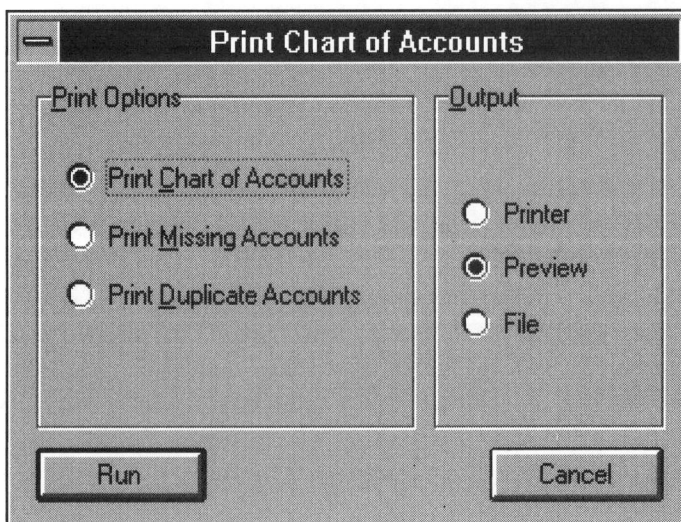

♦ Select **Printer** in the **Output** panel and **Print Chart of Accounts** in the **Print Options** panel. Note that you also have the options to **Print Missing Accounts** and **Print Duplicate Accounts** to check whether you've missed any nominal accounts from your Chart of Accounts layout or put any in twice.

♦ Click the **Run** button and when the **Print** dialogue box appears click the **OK** button. The Chart of Accounts layout should now be printed.

Delete Chart of Accounts layout

The procedure is as follows:

♦ In the **Chart of Accounts** window select the layout you wish to delete and click the **Remove** button.

♦ When the **Delete Layout** dialogue box appears asking you to confirm that you wish to remove this layout click the **Yes** button.

Note: You cannot remove the **Current** layout.

Print Profit and Loss Account for January 1996

♦ Set the program date to 310196 using the **Change Program Date** option on the **Defaults** menu.

♦ Select the **Financials** option in the **Desktop** window.

♦ Click the **Profit & Loss** button in the **Financials** window and the following **Profit & Loss** dialogue box should appear:

♦ **January 1996 Mth1** should already be displayed in the **Period Range** boxes. Ensure that the **Current** option button is selected in the **Accounting Range** panel and **Printer** in the **Output** panel. **Layout2** should be displayed in the **Layout** panel, if not select it from the drop-down list.

♦ Click the **Run** button and when the **Print** dialogue box opens click the **OK** button. The Profit and Loss Account for January 1996 should now be printed showing figures for This Month and the Year-To-Date (both should be the same in this case).

Print Balance Sheet at 31 January 1996

♦ Ensure that the program date is set to 310196.

♦ Select the **Financials** option in the **Desktop** window.

♦ Click the **Balance Sheet** button in the **Financials** window and the **Balance Sheet** dialogue box, similar to that for Profit & Loss should appear. Check the following settings:

Accounting Range panel	: **Current** should be selected.
Period Range panel	: **January 1996 Mth1** should be displayed.
Output panel	: **Printer** should be selected.
Layout panel	: **Layout2** should be displayed.

♦ Click the **Run** button and when the **Print** dialogue box opens click the **OK** button. The Balance Sheet as at 31 January 1996 should now be printed.

If your Balance Sheet does not balance check your Chart of Accounts layout to ensure that all items in the Trial Balance have been included and check the nominal account code numbers. The Print Missing Accounts and Print Duplicate Accounts reports mentioned earlier in the section on Print a Chart of Accounts Layout may help to identify any errors.

Print Budget Analysis for January 1996

♦ Ensure that the program date is set to 310196.

♦ Select the **Financials** option in the **Desktop** window.

♦ Click the **Budget Analysis** button in the **Financials** window and the **Budget Analysis** dialogue box, similar to that for Profit & Loss and Balance Sheet, should appear. Ensure that the settings in the **Budget Analysis** dialogue box are the same as those in the **Balance Sheet** dialogue box.

♦ Click the **Run** button and when the **Print** dialogue box opens click the **OK** button.

The Budget Analysis report, which has the same format and contents as the Profit and Loss Account, shows the actual performance against budget and produces a variance for each item.

♦ **Close** the **Financials** window.

CHAPTER 5

Additional Ledger Posting Facilities

**Second Month's Transactions · Error Correction · Contra Entries · Refunds ·
Returned Cheques · Bad Debt Write Off · Recurring Entries · Depreciation and
Fixed Asset Records · Prepayments and Accruals · VAT Return Analysis ·
Final Accounts · Year-End Procedure**

SECOND MONTH'S TRANSACTIONS

We are now going to process the transactions for the second month of our financial
year (February) and describe some of the additional features of the program.

Sales invoices

Enter the details of the following invoices which were sent out to customers during the
month of February:

A/C	Date	Ref	N/C	Dept	Details	Net	Tc	Tax
MACKAY	010296	1212	4000	2	6 Refrigerators	1410	T1	246.75
SEDDON	020296	1213	4001	3	8 TVs	2080	T1	364.00
BUDGET	020296	1214	4002	4	24 Hair stylers	340	T1	59.50
ABBEY	040296	1215	4001	3	6 Videos	1860	T1	325.50
ACORN	040296	1217	4002	4	12 Electric shavers	182	T1	31.85
NAPIER	050296	1218	4001	3	4 Portable TVs	520	T1	91.00
CANON	070296	1219	4000	2	4 Dishwashers	1040	T1	182.00
DEACON	070296	1220	4001	3	3 Hi-fi systems	890	T1	155.75
ASHRAF	080296	1221	4000	2	12 Food processors	420	T1	73.50
SANDAR	080296	1222	4000	2	5 Washing machines	1550	T1	271.25

♦ Check the entries (the **Batch Total** should be 12093.10) then **Save** the invoice
details.

♦ **Close** the **Batch Customer Invoices** window then **Close** the **Customers** window.

Purchase invoices

In similar manner enter the details of the following invoices which were received from
suppliers during the month of February. Be careful to enter the correct tax codes for
electricity and rent.

A/C	Date	Ref	N/C	Dept	Details	Net	Tc	Tax
HARRIS	070296	537156	5000	2	8 Washing machines	1960	T1	343.00
BEAVER	070296	649532	5001	3	8 TVs	1660	T1	290.50
RANCO	090296	414171	5000	2	6 Refrigerators	1240	T1	217.00
CHEUNG	090296	997789	5001	3	4 Portable TVs	560	T1	98.00
SOLENT	100296	754226	5000	2	24 Food processors	540	T1	94.50
KEENAN	110296	321801	5001	3	4 Hi-fi systems	600	T1	105.00
ABDUL	110296	418120	5002	4	36 Electric shavers	440	T1	77.00
BROOM	120296	444901	5002	4	12 Hair dryers	180	T1	31.50
POWER	270296	–	7200	1	Electricity	90	T3	7.20
ROSS	270296	011257	7100	1	Rent	1000	T2	0.00

♦ Check the entries (the **Batch Total** should be 9533.70) then **Save** the invoice details.

♦ **Close** the **Batch Supplier Invoices** window then **Close** the **Suppliers** window.

Receipts from customers

♦ Select the **Bank** option in the **Desktop** window.

♦ In the **Bank Accounts** window ensure that the **Bank Current Account**, nominal code 1200, is selected (highlighted) and then click the **Customer Receipt** button.

♦ Enter the details of the following three cheque receipts:

1 **A/C**   : BUDGET
   Date   : 100296
   Ref   : 000551
   Amount : 399.50

   ♦ When the insertion cursor is in the **Receipt** field for invoice 1214 select the **Pay in Full** button and the invoice will be paid off in full.

   ♦ Select **Save** to post the entry to the ledgers.

2 **A/C**   : ACORN
   Date   : 110296
   Ref   : 004982
   Amount : 2000

   ♦ When the insertion cursor is in the **Receipt** field of the first transaction (invoice No. 1200) select the **Pay in Full** button.

   ♦ [**Tab**] to or click in the **Receipt** field for the second transaction (invoice No. 1203) and enter a part-payment of 590.

   ♦ Check your entries and select the **Save** button to post to the ledgers.

3 **A/C**   : IMRAN
   Date   : 120296
   Ref   : 003965
   Amount : 2000

♦ When the insertion cursor is in the **Receipt** field for invoice 1209 select the **Pay in Full** button and this invoice will be paid off.

♦ Select the **Save** button and you will be informed that there is an unallocated cheque balance of £49.50. Click on the **Yes** button and this will be posted as a Payment on Account. Payments on Account can be selected for allocation at a later date.

♦ **Close** the **Customer Receipt** window.

Payments to suppliers

♦ In the **Bank Accounts** window ensure that the **Bank Current Account**, nominal code 1200, is selected and then click the **Supplier Payment** button. Enter the details of the following four cheque payments.

1   **Payee**   : DAVIS
    Date   : 140296
    Chq. No.   : 249186
    £ (cheque amount) : 2000

♦ Use this cheque to pay off invoice No. 984134 in full and use the balance to part-pay invoice No. 765764.

♦ Check your entries (the **Analysis Total** should be 2000) and select the **Save** button.

2   **Payee**   : CHEUNG
    Date   : 140296
    Chq. No.   : 249187
    £ (cheque amount) : 3000

♦ Click the **Automatic** button and the payment will be allocated to the invoices in the order they are shown on the screen. Invoice 997765 will be paid in full and invoice 997789 part-paid.

♦ Check your entries and select **Save**.

3   **Payee**   : KEENAN
    Date   : 140296
    Chq. No.   : 249188
    £ (cheque amount) : 1500

♦ Use this cheque to part-pay invoice No. 321789.

♦ Check your entry and select **Save**.

4   **Payee**   : BROOM
    Date   : 140296
    Chq. No.   : 249189
    £ (cheque amount) : 211.50

♦ Use this cheque to pay off invoice No. 444901 in full.

♦ Select **Save** to post your entry to the ledgers then **Close** the **Supplier Payment** window.

Nominal bank payment

♦ Ensure that the **Bank Current Account**, nominal code 1200, is selected in the **Bank Accounts** window then click the **Payment** button.

♦ Record the following bank payment:

Date	: 250296	
Chq. No.	: 249189	
Payee	: Ascot Enterprises	
£ (cheque amount)	: 2750	
N/C	: 7003	Nominal code for salaries.
Dept	: 1	
Details	: Office salaries for February	
Net	: 2750	
Tc	: T9	
Tax	: 0.00	

♦ Check your entries, select the **Save** button then **Close** the **Bank Payment** window.

Cash payments

♦ In the **Bank Accounts** window select (highlight) the **Cash** Account, nominal code 1230, then click the **Payment** button.

♦ Record the following two payments in the **Cash Payments** window:

(a) Bought office stationery for cash on 26 February (petty cash voucher No. PC23). The price was £47.00 *including VAT*. The nominal code for Office Stationery is 7504 and the expense should be allocated against department No.1. The **Calculate Net** button can be used to calculate the net and tax figures from the gross price (**Net** should be 40.00 and **Tax** should be 7.00).

♦ When you have entered these details accurately click the **Save** button.

(b) Paid £42 for office cleaning on 26 February (petty cash voucher No. PC24). The nominal code for cleaning is 7801 and the expense should be allocated against department No. 1. This is a non-VAT transaction so the tax code used should be T9.

♦ When you have entered these details accurately click the **Save** button then **Close** the **Cash Payments** window.

♦ **Close** the **Bank Accounts** window.

Ledger reports

You should now have a look at the updated reports in the Sales and Purchase Ledgers (**Customer** and **Supplier** options in the **Desktop** window), and those in the **Nominal Ledger**.

ERROR CORRECTION

If a mistake is noticed before the transaction is posted to the ledgers it can be corrected by selecting the error field, deleting the existing entry and re-entering the correct details. However, if the transaction has already been posted to the ledger accounts it is necessary to use one of the **Disk Doctor** routines.

Let's say we discover that the following two mistakes have been made:

1   Credit sale to ASHRAF on 8 February, invoice No. 1221. The net amount was entered and posted as 420 and it should have been 440.

2   Withdrawal of £2750 from bank on 25 February to pay for office salaries. Cheque No. entered and posted was 249189 and it should have been 249190.

To correct the first mistake proceed as follows:

◆ Open the **Data** menu and select **Disk Doctor**.

◆ When the **Disk Doctor** dialogue box opens click the **Correct** button.

◆ The following **Posting Error Corrections** dialogue box should now appear listing all transactions made since the beginning of the year.

Posting Error Corrections

No	Tp	Date	Account	Bank/N/C	Ref	Details	Net	Tax
83	PI	270296	ROSS		011257	Rent	1000.00	0.00
84	SR	100296	BUDGET	1200	000551	Sales Receipt	399.50	0.00
85	SR	110296	ACORN	1200	004982	Sales Receipt	2000.00	0.00
86	SR	120296	IMRAN	1200	003965	Sales Receipt	1950.50	0.00
87	SA	120296	IMRAN	1200	003965	Payment on Account	49.50	0.00
88	PP	140296	DAVIS	1200	249186	Purchase Payment	2000.00	0.00
89	PP	140296	CHEUNG	1200	249187	Purchase Payment	3000.00	0.00
90	PP	140296	KEENAN	1200	249188	Purchase Payment	1500.00	0.00
91	PP	140296	BROOM	1200	249189	Purchase Payment	211.50	0.00
92	BP	250296		1200	249189	Ascot Enterprises	2750.00	0.00
93	CP	260296		1230	PC23	Office stationery	40.00	7.00
94	CP	260296		1230	PC24	Office cleaning	42.00	0.00

Edit   Close

◆ Scroll the dialogue box until transaction No. 72 (the credit sale to ASHRAF) is visible.

◆ Select (highlight) this transaction by pointing and clicking, then select the **Edit** button.

◆ An **Edit Transaction Header Record** dialogue box, similar to the following, should now open showing posting details for the credit sale:

◆ Click the **Edit** button at the bottom of the dialogue box and an **Edit Transaction Split Record** dialogue box, similar to the following, should open:

```
┌─────────────────────────────────────────────────────────────────────┐
│ ▬                      Edit Transaction Split Record                   │
│ ┌─Details──────────────────────────────────────────────────────────┐ │
│ │  Number      ┌──────────┐                                         │ │
│ │              │ 72       │                                         │ │
│ │  Type        │ Sales Invoice                                   │   │ │
│ │  N/C         │ 4000    │ Q                                       │ │
│ │  Details     │ 12 Food Processors                             │   │ │
│ │  Date        │ 08/02/96 │                                        │ │
│ │  Department  │ 2 KITCHEN EQUIPMENT              │ ▼ │            │ │
│ └───────────────────────────────────────────────────────────────────┘ │
│ ┌─Amounts──────────────────────────────────────────────────────────┐ │
│ │  Net  │     420.00│ Tax │      73.50│ T/C │T1 17.50│▼│ Paid │  0.00│ │
│ └───────────────────────────────────────────────────────────────────┘ │
│ ┌─Flags──────────────────────────────┐ ┌─Links───────────────────────┐ │
│ │  □ Paid in full   □ VAT Reconciled │ │  No Of Alloc  │ 0 │         │ │
│ └────────────────────────────────────┘ └─────────────────────────────┘ │
│ ┌─Allocations──────────────────────────────────────────────────────┐ │
│ │  Tp │ Date    │ Ref   │ Details        │        Amount    │      │ │
│ │                                                            │ ▲   │ │
│ │                                                            │     │ │
│ │                                                            │ ▼   │ │
│ └───────────────────────────────────────────────────────────────────┘ │
│      ┌──────────────┐                          ┌──────────────┐        │
│      │     Edit     │                          │    Close     │        │
│      └──────────────┘                          └──────────────┘        │
└─────────────────────────────────────────────────────────────────────┘
```

♦ Click in the **Net** field in the **Amounts** panel, delete the existing entry and replace it with 440.

♦ **[Tab]** to or click in the **Tax** field in the **Amounts** panel, delete the existing entry and replace it with 77.

♦ Select the **Close** button at the bottom of the dialogue box.

When you return to the **Edit Transaction Header Record** dialogue box the new figures should be shown in the **Amounts** panel and in the **Splits** panel.

♦ Click the **Save** button. A small **Confirm** dialogue box should now appear asking if you wish to post these changes. Click the **Yes** button and you will be returned to the **Posting Error Corrections** dialogue box.

The **Net** and **Tax** figures for transaction No. 72 should now be correct.

The original transaction details may now be visible as the last entry in the dialogue box. This is explained in the following Accounting Entries section.

♦ To correct the second mistake select transaction No. 92 (February salaries cheque) in the **Posting Error Corrections** dialogue box then click the **Edit** button.

The **Edit Transaction Header Record** dialogue box should open again showing the posting details for the salaries withdrawal.

♦ [Tab] to or click in the **Reference** field, delete the existing entry and replace it with 249190.

♦ Click the **Save** button and select **Yes** in the **Confirm** dialogue box.

The **Ref** field for transaction No. 92 in the **Posting Error Corrections** dialogue box should now show the correct cheque No. (249190).

♦ **Close** the **Posting Error Corrections** dialogue box then **Close** the **Disk Doctor** dialogue box.

Accounting entries

Correction 1

The accounting entries which should have been made in the ledger accounts to record the correction are as follows:

DEBIT   Ashraf Hi-Fi Ltd A/c in the Sales (Customers) Ledger with the gross amount   517.00
CREDIT   Kitchen Equipment Sales A/c in the Nominal Ledger with the net amount   440.00
CREDIT   Sales Tax Control A/c in the Nominal Ledger with the tax amount   77.00
DEBIT   Debtors Control A/c in the Nominal Ledger with the gross amount   517.00

Check that these entries have been made by examining the transaction details for each of the accounts affected:

• Ashraf Hi-Fi Ltd A/c (ASHRAF);

• Kitchen Equipment Sales A/c (4000);

• Sales Tax Control A/c (2200);

• Debtors Control A/c (1100).

The original transaction details will have been retained and may or may not be shown in the ledger accounts. If the **Exclude Deleted Transactions** check box in the **Company Preferences** dialogue box (**System** 'page') is selected deleted transactions will *not* be shown, otherwise they will. However, although the original transaction can be displayed in the accounts it does not affect the balance and is merely there for auditing purposes. You cannot exclude Disk Doctor transactions from the Audit Trail; they will appear there automatically in red (if you have a colour monitor).

Note: Choosing the **Delete** button in the **Edit Transaction Header Record** dialogue box retains the original transaction but marks it as 'deleted'. A new transaction is not generated in this case.

Correction 2

To check that the correction has been carried out in this case, examine the transaction details of the following two accounts in the Nominal Ledger:

• Bank (1200);

• Salaries (7003).

CONTRA ENTRIES

This routine allows you to offset a debit balance in a Sales Ledger (Customer) account against a credit balance in a Purchase Ledger (Supplier) account.

To demonstrate this we will create accounts for Mr BuyandSell as a customer and a supplier and enter some transactions to them. Proceed as follows:

♦ Select the **Customers** option in the **Desktop** window.

♦ Click the **Batch Invoices** button in the **Customers** window.

♦ The **Batch Customer Invoices** data entry window should now open and prompt you for an account reference (**A/C**).

Enter the reference as BAS and press the [**Tab**] key.

Since this account has not been set up yet a small Customer Accounts selection box should open displaying your list of customers.

♦ Select the **New** button at the bottom of the Customer Accounts selection box and a **Customer Record** window should open allowing you to enter the details of your new customer.

♦ Enter the following details:

A/C	: BAS
Name & Address	: James BuyandSell
	Knightswood
	St Annes
Analysis1 (**Defaults** 'page')	: NORTH

♦ **Save** your entry and you will be returned to the Customer Accounts selection box where your new customer, BAS, should be listed. You have just experienced the 'live' account creation facility. Highlight BAS in the selection box and click the **OK** button to return to the **Batch Customer Invoices** window.

♦ Enter the details of the following two invoices.

A/C	Date	Ref	N/C	Dept	Details	Net	Tc	Tax
BAS	150296	1223	4000	2	2 Refrigerators	400	T1	70.00
BAS	170296	1224	4000	2	4 Washing machines	1200	T1	210.00

♦ **Save** the details of these invoices then **Close** the **Batch Customer Invoices** window.

♦ **Close** the **Customers** window.

We will now carry out a similar operation in the Purchase (Supplier) Ledger.

♦ Select the **Suppliers** option in the **Desktop** window.

♦ Click the **Batch Invoices** button in the **Suppliers** window.

♦ The **Batch Supplier Invoices** data entry window should now open and prompt you for an account reference (**A/C**).

Enter the reference as BAS and press the [**Tab**] key. Since this is a new account the small Supplier Accounts selection box should appear.

♦ Once again you will have to set this account up in the Purchase (Supplier) Ledger and the procedure is exactly the same as it was in the Sales (Customer) Ledger.

♦ Enter the same **A/C, Name & Address**.

♦ Once the account has been set up and **Saved** return to the **Batch Supplier Invoices** window and enter the details of the following invoice:

A/C	Date	Ref	N/C	Dept	Details	Net	Tc	Tax
BAS	100296	009977	5001	3	36 Radios	400	T1	70.00

♦ **Save** these details, **Close** the **Batch Supplier Invoices** window then **Close** the **Suppliers** window.

The Contra Entries routine involves an automatic posting where the date on the computer's clock is used as the transaction date so set the program date to 290296 using the **Change Program Date** option on the **Defaults** menu.

♦ When you have set the date open the **Data** menu and select **Contra Entries**.

♦ A **Contra Entries** window should now appear similar to the following:

♦ Respond to the prompts as follows:

Sales A/C : BAS
Purchase A/C : BAS

The sales invoices for BAS should now be listed in the left panel and purchase invoice in the right. This window allows you to select the invoice(s) from each ledger which are to be paid off as part of the contra entry.

Selection and deselection of invoices is made by pointing and clicking (a selected invoice will be highlighted).

♦ Select sales invoice 1223 and purchase invoice 009977.
The **Total** field at the bottom of each panel should now show 470.00. Remember you can deselect invoices if you make a mistake.

♦ When your entries are accurate click the **OK** button and the set-off will take place. If a **Warning** dialogue box appears indicating that there are no transactions outstanding on the account click the **OK** button.

Accounting entries

The accounting entries made to the ledgers to record the contra will be as follows:

CREDIT	James BuyandSell's A/c in the Sales Ledger	470
DEBIT	James BuyandSell's A/c in the Purchase Ledger	470
CREDIT	Debtors Control A/c in the Nominal Ledger	470
DEBIT	Creditors Control A/c in the Nominal Ledger	470

The program also makes entries in the Bank A/c but the effect on the balance is *nil*. Check that these entries have been made by examining the transaction details of each of the following accounts noting that the posting date is 29/02/96 in each case:

• James BuyandSell's A/c (BAS) in the Sales Ledger (**Customers**);

• James BuyandSell's A/c (BAS) in the Purchase Ledger (**Suppliers**);

• Debtors Control A/c (1100) in the **Nominal Ledger**;

• Creditors Control A/c (2100) in the **Nominal Ledger**.

REFUNDS

The Refunds routine permits you to process a refund for a fully paid invoice. The routine can be used on either customer or supplier accounts. If the invoice has not been refunded in full it will be necessary to process the transaction 'manually' using the Journal Entry routine in the Nominal Ledger.

On 12 February we purchased 12 hair dryers from Broom for £180 + £31.50 VAT (invoice No. 444901). We paid for these in full on 14 February. On closer inspection we found that all the dryers were damaged. We informed Broom about this and they sent us a full refund by cheque on 28 February. We'll now process this transaction but before proceeding:

♦ Set the program date to 29/02/96.

Then carry on as follows:

♦ Open the **Data** menu and select the **Write Off, Refund, Return** option.

♦ The **Write off, refund, return Wizard** tool will now be activated. This is a series of dialogue boxes which lead you through the process of data amendment in easy-to-follow steps.

Step 1

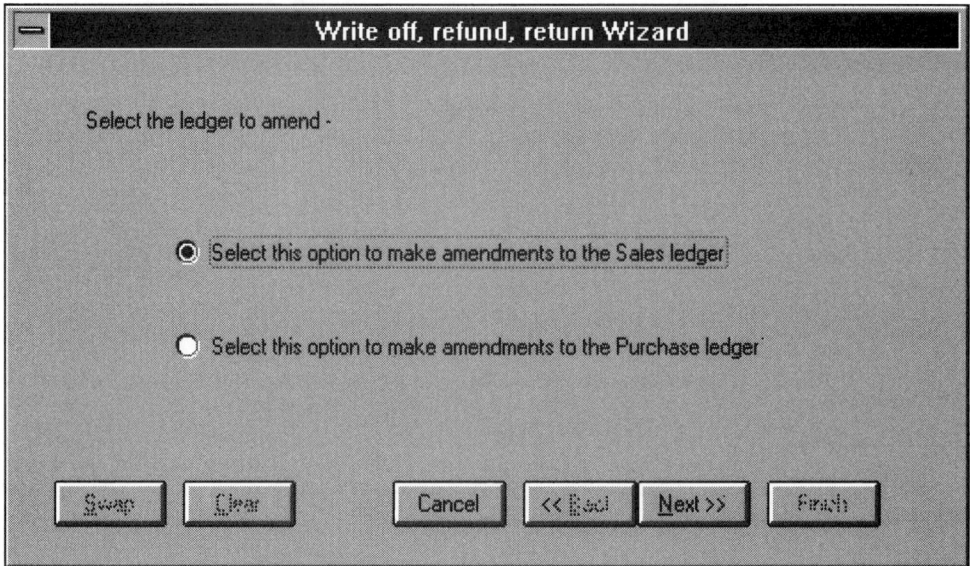

The Step 1 dialogue box which should be displayed at the moment allows you to select the ledger you wish to amend.

♦ Ensure that the Purchase Ledger amendment button is selected then click the **Next** button to move on to the next dialogue box.

Step 2

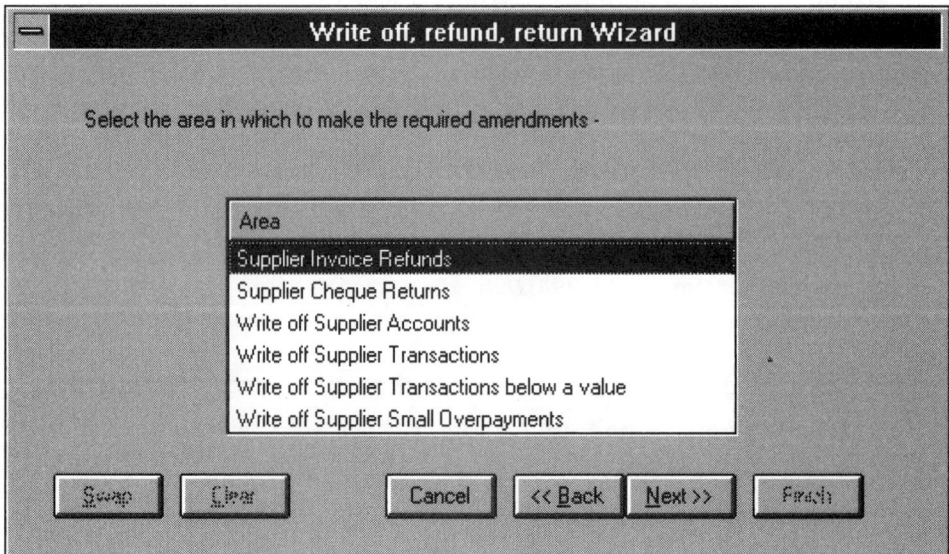

The Step 2 dialogue box allows you to select the **Area** for amendment.

♦ Select **Supplier Invoice Refunds** and click the **Next** button. You can move backwards and forwards through the dialogue boxes using the **Back** and **Next** buttons.

Step 3

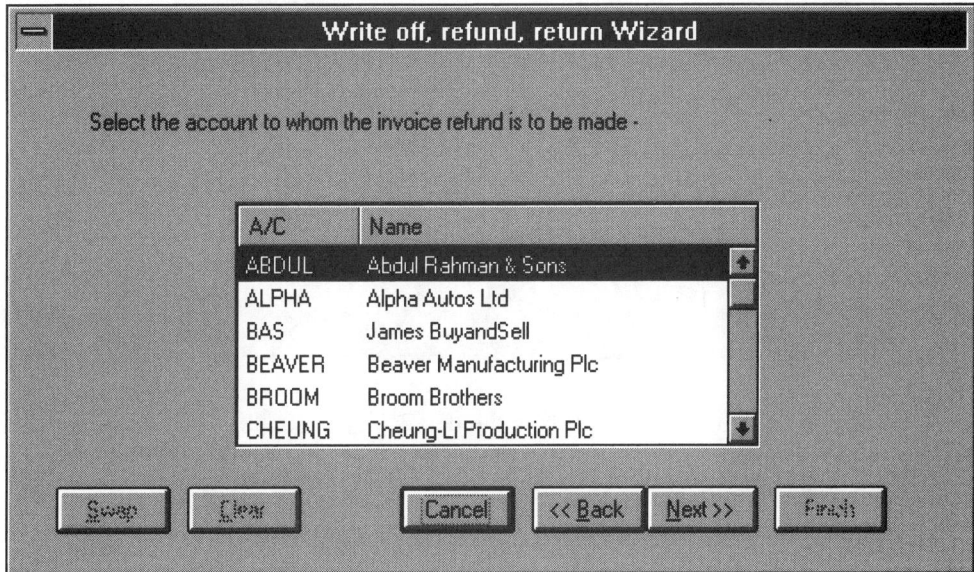

♦ In the Step 3 dialogue box select the account reference BROOM and click **Next**.

Step 4

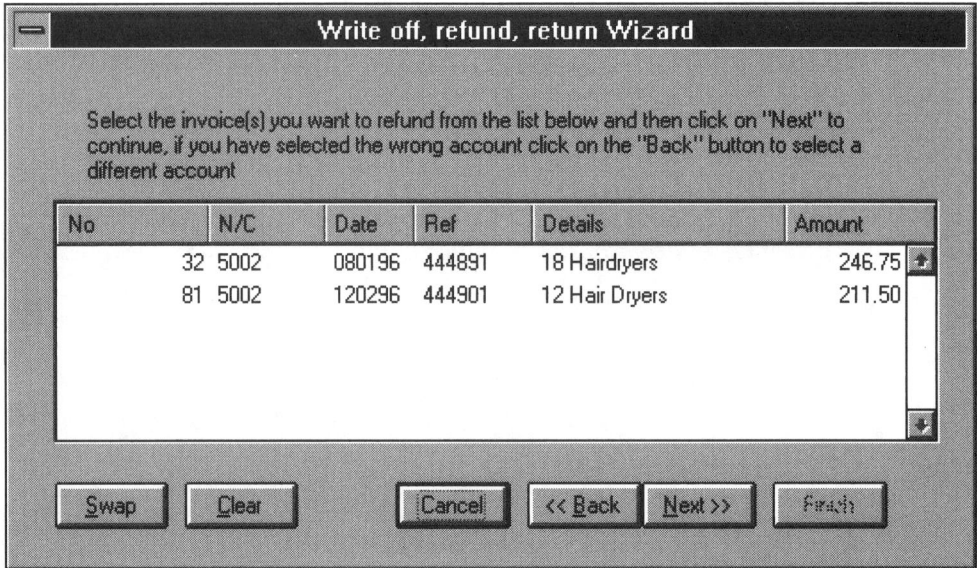

The Step 4 dialogue box displays the details of the supplier's invoice(s) and allows you to select one or more for refund. Selections and deselections are made by pointing and clicking.

♦ Select invoice No. 444901 and click the **Next** button.

Step 5

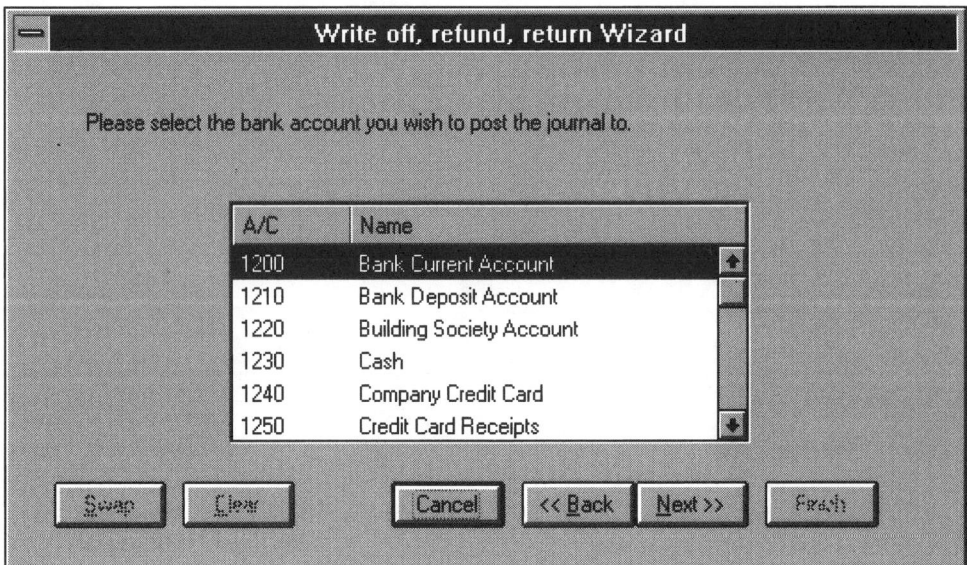

The Step 5 dialogue box allows you to select the bank account you wish to post the refund to.

♦ Ensure that **Bank Current Account**, nominal code **1200**, is selected and click the **Next** button.

Step 6

The **Wizard** now has all the information necessary to process the refund but before proceeding it displays in the Step 6 dialogue box the **Account** name and the **Total** amount to be refunded. If this information is not accurate you can move back through the dialogue boxes using the **Back** button and make the necessary alterations.

♦ When the information displayed is correct click the **Finish** button and the refund details will be posted to the appropriate ledger accounts.

Accounting entries

The accounting entries made to the ledgers to record the refund will be as follows:

DEBIT   Bank A/c in the Nominal Ledger with the gross amount   211.50
CREDIT   Purchases A/c in the Nominal Ledger with the net amount   180.00
CREDIT   Purchase Tax Control A/c in the Nominal Ledger with the tax element 31.50

The program also makes entries in the Suppliers A/c (BROOM) and the Creditors Control A/c but the effect on the balances of these two accounts is *nil*.

Check that these entries have been made by examining the transaction details of each of the following accounts, noting that the posting date is 29/02/96 in each case:

- Bank A/c (1200) in **Nominal Ledger**;
- Personal Care Purchases A/c (5002) in **Nominal Ledger**;
- Purchase Tax Control A/c (2201) in **Nominal Ledger**;
- Creditors Control A/c (2100) in **Nominal Ledger**;
- Broom Brothers A/c (BROOM) in Purchase Ledger (**Suppliers**).

RETURNED CHEQUES

The **Return** routine allows you to process cheques which have been dishonoured and are 'referred to drawer'. The routine can be used on either customer or supplier accounts. Let's assume that cheque No. 000551 for £399.50 which we received from Budget Electric on 10 February has been dishonoured; it has been returned to us by our bank marked 'REFER TO DRAWER'.

We'll now process this transaction but before proceeding:

♦ Set the program date to 29/02/96.

Then carry on as follows:

♦ Open the **Data** menu and select the **Write Off, Refund, Return** option.

♦ When the **Write off, refund, return Wizard** Step 1 dialogue box appears ensure that the Sales Ledger amendment button is selected, then click the **Next** button.

♦ In the Step 2 dialogue box select the **Area** for amendment as **Customer Cheque Returns**, then click **Next**.

♦ In the Step 3 dialogue box select the account reference BUDGET and click **Next**.

♦ All cheque receipts from the customer should now be displayed in the Step 4 dialogue box and you can select the receipt which is to be cancelled. In our case there has been only one receipt and you should select this by pointing and clicking. When the receipt details are highlighted click the **Next** button.

♦ The **Account** name and the cheque **Total** should now be displayed in the Step 5 dialogue box. Check these details and, if accurate, click the **Finish** button and the ledger accounts will be updated.

Accounting entries

The entries made to the ledger accounts to record the dishonoured cheque will be as follows:

DEBIT	Budget Electric's A/c in the Sales Ledger	399.50
CREDIT	Bank A/c in the Nominal Ledger	399.50
DEBIT	Debtors Control A/c in the Nominal Ledger	399.50

You can confirm these entries by examining the transaction details of each of the following accounts in turn, noting that the posting date is 29/02/96 in each case:

- Budget Electric's A/c (BUDGET) in the Sales Ledger (**Customers**);

- Bank A/c (1200) in the **Nominal Ledger**;
- Debtors Control A/c (1100) in the **Nominal Ledger**.

BAD DEBT WRITE OFF

Let's say that on 28 February we are informed that Budget Electric have gone into liquidation and it is unlikely that they will be able to pay any of their outstanding debts. We decide to write off the outstanding balance on their account.

Before proceeding:

♦ Set the program date to 29/02/96.

Then carry on as follows:

♦ Open the **Data** menu and select the **Write Off, Refund, Return** option.

♦ When the **Write off, refund, return Wizard** Step 1 dialogue box appears ensure that the Sales Ledger amendment button is selected then click the **Next** button.

In the Step 2 dialogue box four 'Write off' options should be displayed:

1   **Write off Customer Accounts**   This allows you to write off the full outstanding balance on an account.

2   **Write off Customer Transactions**   This allows you to write off a specific transaction on a customer's account over which there may be some dispute.

3   **Write off Customer Transactions below a value**   This allows you to write off small values from several accounts. For example, you may have several customer accounts with small outstanding balances which are not worth pursuing. These small values can be written off as a bad debt using this option. When you choose this option you will be prompted for a maximum write off value.

4   **Write off Customer Small Overpayments** This allows you to write off overpayments which have resulted from receipts or credit notes which are greater than the original invoice value.

These write off routines can be used in either the Sales or the Purchase Ledger depending on the selection made in the Wizard's Step 1 dialogue box.

♦ We intend to write off the full outstanding balance on the account so select **Write off Customer Accounts** and click **Next**.

♦ In the Step 3 dialogue box select the account reference BUDGET and click **Next**.

♦ All transactions which can be written off should now be displayed in the Step 4 dialogue box.

♦ Click the **Next** button.

♦ The Step 5 dialogue box should display the **Account** name and the **Total** for write off: £399.50. Check these details and, if accurate, click the **Finish** button and the relevant postings will be made to the ledger accounts.

Accounting entries

The accounting entries made to the ledgers to record the bad debt write-off will be as follows:

DEBIT   Bad Debts A/c in the Nominal Ledger   399.50
CREDIT   Budget Electric's A/c in the Sales Ledger   399.50
CREDIT   Debtors Control A/c in the Nominal Ledger   399.50

Check that these entries have been made by examining the transaction details of each of the accounts affected noting that the posting date in each case is 29/02/96:

- Bad Debts A/c (8100) in the **Nominal Ledger**;

- Debtors Control A/c (1100) in the **Nominal Ledger**;

- Budget Electric's A/c (BUDGET) in the Sales Ledger (**Customers**).

Important note

The program does not compensate for any VAT liability that you may have as a result of raising the original invoice(s) which have now been written-off. In special cases where you may be able to claim back VAT or reduce VAT liability as a result of a bad debt, then you should not use the **Write-Off Customer Accounts** routine just described. Instead you should enter the bad debt 'manually' by raising a credit note for the amount, enter this to the customer's account using the **Batch Credits** routine (tax code T1) but enter the nominal code as *8100 (Bad Debts)* instead of the code for Sales Returns.

If the bad debt was recorded in this way the following entries would be made in the ledger accounts:

CREDIT Customers A/c in the Sales Ledger with the gross amount of credit note.
CREDIT Debtors Control A/c in the Nominal Ledger with the gross amount of credit note.
DEBIT Bad Debts A/c in the Nominal Ledger with the net amount of credit note.
DEBIT Sales Tax Control A/c in the Nominal Ledger with the tax element of credit note.

RECURRING ENTRIES

Most businesses have a list of transactions which must be posted on a regular basis each month, the value of the transaction each month being the same, e.g. standing orders and direct debits. These regular payments can be set up as recurring entries and posted automatically.

The following types of transaction can be set up as recurring entries:

(a) Payments: Bank Payments (BP), Cash Payments (CP), Credit Card Payments (VP);

(b) Receipts: Bank Receipts (BR), Cash Receipts (CR), Credit Card Receipts (VR);

(c) Journal Debits (JD);

(d) Journal Credits (JC).

Note: When setting up a recurring entry a journal debit must be matched with a journal credit (and vice versa) otherwise you will not be allowed to post the entry.

Setting up recurring entries

Let's say that we pay our buildings insurance and our rates on a regular monthly basis by standing order through our bank and that we pay our gardener £75 cash each month. Before setting these up as recurring entries you should create a new nominal account for Rates with a code of 7103 and a yearly budget of 1800 and one for Gardening Expenses with a code of 7850 and a yearly budget of 1000.

To set up the recurring entries proceed as follows:

◆ Select the **Bank** option in the **Desktop** window.

◆ In the **Bank Accounts** window click the **Recurring Entries** button.

A **Recurring Entries** window, similar to the following, should now open:

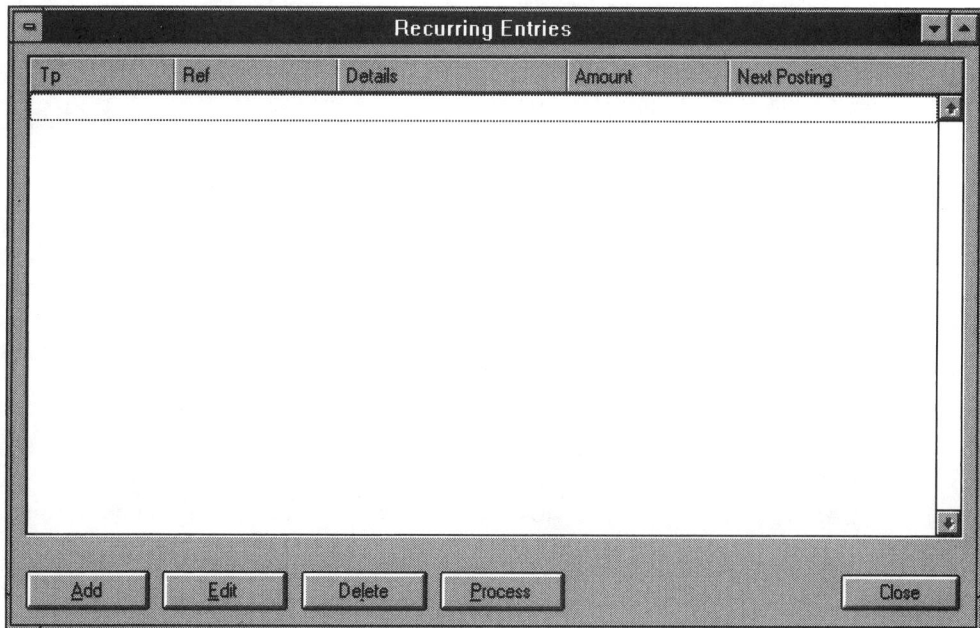

◆ Select the **Add** button at the bottom of the window and an **Add/Edit Recurring Entry** dialogue box, similar to the following, should appear:

```
┌─────────────────────────────────────────────────────────────┐
│ ─ ▐            Add / Edit Recurring Entry                     │
├─────────────────────────────────────────────────────────────┤
│                                                               │
│  Trans. Type   │Payment            │ ▼│                       │
│                                                               │
│  Bank A/C      │         │🔍│ │                         │     │
│  Nominal Code  │         │🔍│ │                         │     │
│                                                               │
│  Ref           │DDR/STO  │  Details │                  │     │
│  Department    │0                             │ ▼│            │
│                                                               │
│  Day to post   │0  │                                          │
│  Last Posted   │         │    ☐ Suspend Posting               │
│                                                               │
│  ─────────────────────────────────────────────────────────   │
│                                                               │
│  Net Amount   │  0.00 🔢│  Tax Code │T1 17.50│▼│ VAT │ 0.00🔢│ │
│  ─────────────────────────────────────────────────────────   │
│                                                               │
│                              │   Ok   │    │  Cancel  │       │
└─────────────────────────────────────────────────────────────┘
```

♦ Enter the following details in the dialogue box:

Trans. Type	:	Payment	If this is not already displayed click the ⊡ button and select from the drop-down list.
Bank A/C	:	1200	Bank Current A/c. You can use 'Finder' here to select.
Nominal Code	:	8204	Insurance A/c.
Ref	:	RCR001	
Details	:	Buildings insurance	
Department	:	1 ADMINISTRATION	Click the ⊡ button and select from the drop-down list.
Day to post	:	28	
Last Posted	:	Date entered auto- matically by program	
Suspend Posting	:	Check box should be deselected (no cross)	Useful if you want to post a batch of recurring entries together but exclude this one.
Net Amount	:	48	
Tax Code	:	T2 0.00	Click the ⊡ button and select from the drop-down list.
VAT	:	0.00	

♦ Check your entries and when they are accurate click the **OK** button. The **Recurring Entries** window should now display summary details of the recurring entry for Buildings Insurance.

It is important to realise that no entries in the accounts are made as a result of saving these details. You have merely set up a Recurring Entries file. Postings to the relevant accounts are only made when the **Process** button in the **Recurring Entries** window is selected. Do not select this button yet.

● The Recurring Entries file can be edited by selecting (highlighting) the recurring entry for amendment in the **Recurring Entries** window then clicking the **Edit** button.

● The **Add/Edit Recurring Entry** dialogue box will open and you can make the necessary alterations.

● To remove a recurring entry select the one for removal in the **Recurring Entries** window and click the **Delete** button.

We'll now set up the recurring entry for our monthly Rates payment.

♦ Select the **Add** button in the **Recurring Entries** window and when the **Add/Edit Recurring Entry** dialogue box opens enter the following details for the Rates standing order:

Trans. Type	: Payment	
Bank A/C	: 1200	
Nominal Code	: 7103	Rates A/c.
Ref	: RCR002	
Details	: Business rates	
Department	: 1 ADMINISTRATION	
Day to post	: 28	
Suspend Posting	: Check box should be deselected (no cross)	
Net Amount	: 150	
Tax Code	: T2 0.00	
VAT	: 0.00	

♦ Check your entries then click the **OK** button. The **Recurring Entries** window should now display summary details for both standing orders.

The cash payment for gardening expenses can now be set up as a recurring entry.

♦ Click the **Add** button in the **Recurring Entries** window and record the following details in the **Add/Edit Recurring Entries** dialogue box:

Trans. Type	: Payment	
Bank A/C	: 1230	Cash A/c.
Nominal Code	: 7850	Gardening Expenses A/c.
Ref	: RCR003	
Details	: Gardening expenses	
Department	: 1 ADMINISTRATION	
Day to post	: 28	

Suspend Posting	:	Check box should be deselected (no cross)
Net Amount	:	75
Tax Code	:	T9 0.00
VAT	:	0.00

◆ Check your entries then click the **OK** button. The **Recurring Entries** window should now display summary details for all three recurring entries.

◆ **Close** the **Recurring Entries** window then **Close** the **Bank Accounts** window.

Posting recurring entries

Before proceeding:

◆ Set the program date to 29/02/96.

Then carry on as follows:

◆ Select the **Bank** option in the **Desktop** window, then from the **Bank Accounts** window click the **Recurring Entries** button.

◆ When the **Recurring Entries** window opens select the **Process** button and the **Process Recurring Entries** dialogue box, similar to the following, should appear:

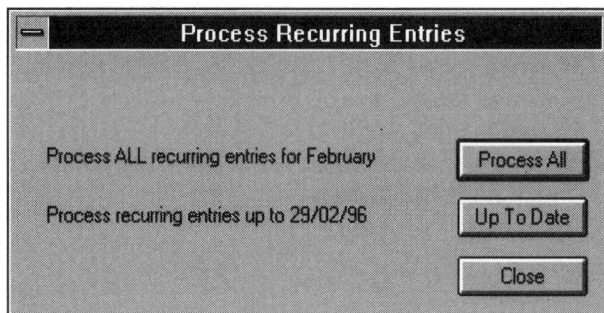

The **Process All** button can be used to process all recurring entry transactions for the month displayed in the dialogue box. The **Up To Date** button will post only those transactions which have posting day numbers which are the same as or earlier than the program date.

◆ Select the **Process All** button.

The **Recurring Entries** window should now show the **Next Posting** date as 28/03/96 for each recurring entry. You will not be allowed to post the recurring entries again for this period.

You can process your recurring entries as many times as you like because entries will only be processed once in each month.

◆ **Close** the **Recurring Entries** window then **Close** the **Bank Accounts** window.

Note: If there are any recurring entries outstanding, each time you run the program a window apears informing you of the transaction(s) that need posting. This situation could occur when using the case study if the system date (the date on the computer's 'clock') is later than the **Next Posting** date for your recurring entries, i.e. 28/03/96. If you are using Version 3.10 of the program this feature can be 'turned off' by selecting the disable check box in the reminder window or on the **System** 'page' of the **Company Preferences** dialogue box. If you cannot disable the reminder window you can remove it from the screen by selecting the **No** check box in response to the prompt **Post Recurring Entries**.

Accounting entries

The entries made to the ledger accounts to record the recurring entries will be as follows:

DEBIT	Insurance A/c in Nominal Ledger	48.00
CREDIT	Bank A/c in Nominal Ledger	48.00
DEBIT	Rates A/c in Nominal Ledger	150.00
CREDIT	Bank A/c in Nominal Ledger	150.00
DEBIT	Gardening expenses A/c in Nominal Ledger	75.00
CREDIT	Cash A/c in Nominal Ledger	75.00

Check that these entries have been made by examining the transaction details of each of the accounts affected and note that the posting date in each case is 28/02/96:

- Insurance A/c   (8204)
- Rates A/c   (7103)
- Gardening Expenses A/c   (7850)
- Bank A/c   (1200)
- Cash A/c   (1230)

DEPRECIATION AND FIXED ASSET RECORDS

Depreciation

The program accommodates three methods of depreciation for fixed assets:

Straight line

Here the annual rate of depreciation is applied to the original cost and the result is divided by 12 to give the monthly depreciation figure. For example:

Original cost	2400
Depreciation rate	10 per cent
Annual depreciation	240
Monthly depreciation	20

Reducing balance

In this case the annual depreciation rate is applied to the net book value to arrive at the depreciation charge for the year. For example:

Original cost   2400
Depreciation rate   10 per cent
Depreciation – Year 1   240 (10 per cent of 2400)
Depreciation – Year 2   216 (10 per cent of (2400 – 240))

When the program is calculating monthly depreciation figures using this method the figures will reduce month by month but they will total 240 in year 1, and 216 in year 2.

Write off

Here, the whole of the current value is written off as depreciation.

Nominal accounts required

The nominal accounts needed to record depreciation are as follows:

1. An accumulated depreciation account for each category of fixed asset. These accounts accumulate the depreciation which has been written off the asset category concerned from the date of purchase. The balances on these accounts at the end of a financial period are subtracted from the original cost of the asset category concerned to give the net book value in the Balance Sheet.

2. A depreciation expense account for each category of fixed asset. The period depreciation charge for each asset is posted to the appropriate depreciation expense account. The balances on these accounts at the end of a financial period will therefore represent the total depreciation written off that category of asset during the period and these balances should appear in the Overheads section of the Profit and Loss account.

The accounting entries to record depreciation are:

DEBIT   Depreciation Expense A/c (for category of asset concerned).
CREDIT Accumulated Depreciation A/c (for category of asset concerned).

The assets which you are going to depreciate are Furniture and Fixtures and Delivery Vehicles. Check the Nominal Ledger accounts list and ensure that the following accounts have been set up. If not do so now.

Furniture/Fixtures Depreciation   0041
Motor Vehicles Depreciation   0051
Furniture/Fittings Depreciation   8002
Vehicle Depreciation   8003

The first two accounts will be used to record the accumulated depreciation of the asset category concerned and the balances will be entered in the Balance Sheet at the end of the financial period. The last two accounts will be used as expense accounts to record the period's depreciation charge for each asset category and the balances will be transferred to the Profit and Loss account at the end of the financial period.

Fixed Asset records

Fixed Assets should first of all be categorised then the identification, cost and depreciation details for each one entered on a record.

♦ Open the **Defaults** menu and select **Fixed Asset Categories**.

The following **Fixed Asset Categories** dialogue box should appear:

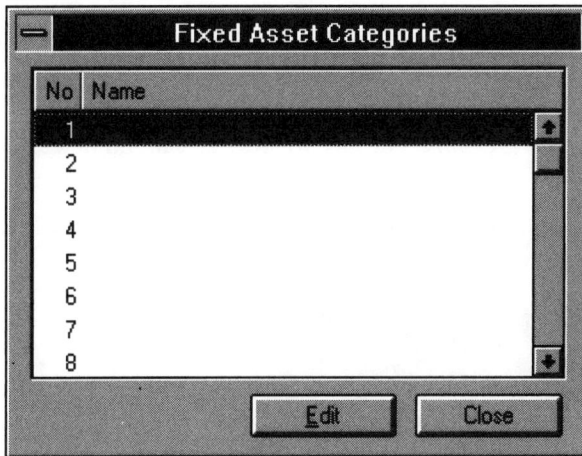

♦ Select (highlight) category **No 1** and click the **Edit** button.

♦ Enter the **Name** Furniture and Fittings to the small **Edit Asset Categories** dialogue box which appears and select the **OK** button.

♦ Furniture and Fittings should now appear in the **Fixed Asset Categories** dialogue box against **No 1**.

If you want to remove a category name or if you make a mistake you can select the name in the **Fixed Asset Categories** dialogue box and click the **Edit** button. When the small **Edit Asset Categories** dialogue box appears you can clear the name by pressing the **[Delete]** key.

♦ Select (highlight) category **No 2**, click the **Edit** button, enter the **Name** Vehicles and click the **OK** button.

♦ When the two category names are displayed in the **Fixed Asset Categories** dialogue box select the **Close** button.

♦ Select the **Fixed Assets** option in the **Desktop** window and the following **Fixed Assets** window should open:

♦ Click the **Record** button in the **Fixed Assets** window and the following **Fixed Asset Record** window should open:

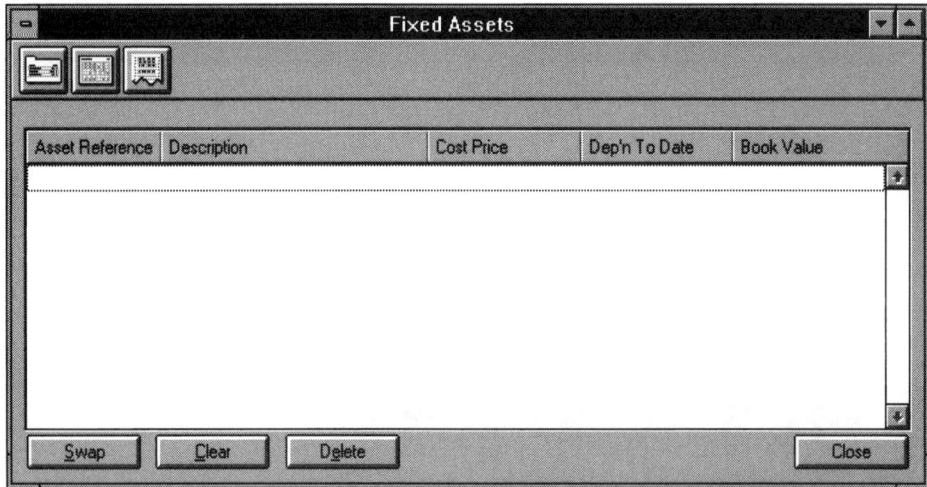

If the details of any fixed assets are shown in this window select and delete them using the **Delete** button.

♦ Click the **Record** button in the **Fixed Assets** window and the following **Fixed Asset Record** window should open:

♦ Make the following entries on the **Details** 'page':

Asset Reference	: F-CH-01	
Description	: Office chair	
Serial Number	: –	
Location/Emp'ee	: –	
Date Purchased	: 150196	
Supplier A/C	: –	
Asset Category	: 1 Furniture and Fittings	Select from the drop-down list here.

◆ Now click the **Posting** tab button at the top of the **Record** window and make the following entries on the **Posting** 'page'.

Department	: 1 ADMINISTRATION	Select from the drop-down list.
Dep'n B.S. N/C	: 0041	Depreciation will be credited to this account.
Dep'n P&L N/C	: 8002	Depreciation will be debited to this account.
Dep'n Method	: Straight	Select from the drop-down list.
Dep'n Rate	: 20	
Cost Price	: 140	
Book Value	: 140	Entered automatically by the program.

◆ Check your entries and click the **Save** button at the bottom of the **Fixed Asset Record** window. The window should now refresh and prompt for details of the next asset.

◆ Enter the details of the following fixed assets and remember to **Save** each record.

2 **Asset Reference** : F-CH-02
  Description : Office chair
  Date Purchased : 150196
  Asset Category : 1 Furniture and fittings
  Department : 1 ADMINISTRATION
  Dep'n B.S. N/C : 0041
  Dep'n P&L N/C : 8002
  Dep'n Method : Straight
  Dep'n Rate : 20
  Cost Price : 140

3 **Asset Reference** : F-DSK-01
  Description : Office desk
  Date Purchased : 010196
  Asset Category : 1 Furniture and fittings
  Department : 1 ADMINISTRATION
  Dep'n B.S. N/C : 0041
  Dep'n P&L N/C : 8002
  Dep'n Method : Straight
  Dep'n Rate : 20
  Cost Price : 700

4 **Asset Reference** : F-DSK-02
  Description : Office desk
  Date Purchased : 010196
  Asset Category : 1 Furniture and fittings
  Department : 1 ADMINISTRATION
  Dep'n B.S. N/C : 0041
  Dep'n P&L N/C : 8002
  Dep'n Method : Straight
  Dep'n Rate : 20
  Cost Price : 700

5 **Asset Reference** : F-CAB-01
  Description : Filing cabinet
  Date Purchased : 010196
  Asset Category : 1 Furniture and fittings
  Department : 1 ADMINISTRATION
  Dep'n B.S. N/C : 0041
  Dep'n P&L N/C : 8002
  Dep'n Method : Straight
  Dep'n Rate : 20
  Cost Price : 500

6 **Asset Reference** : F-CAB-02
  Description : Filing cabinet
  Date Purchased : 010196
  Asset Category : 1 Furniture and fittings
  Department : 1 ADMINISTRATION
  Dep'n B.S. N/C : 0041
  Dep'n P&L N/C : 8002
  Dep'n Method : Straight
  Dep'n Rate : 20
  Cost Price : 500

7 **Asset Reference** : F-RACK-1
  Description : Storage racking
  Date Purchased : 010196
  Asset Category : 1 Furniture and fittings
  Department : 0
  Dep'n B.S. N/C : 0041
  Dep'n P&L N/C : 8002
  Dep'n Method : Straight
  Dep'n Rate : 20
  Cost Price : 2100

8 **Asset Reference** : F-RACK-2
  Description : Storage racking
  Date Purchased : 010196
  Asset Category : 1 Furniture and fittings
  Department : 0
  Dep'n B.S. N/C : 0041
  Dep'n P&L N/C : 8002
  Dep'n Method : Straight
  Dep'n Rate : 20
  Cost Price : 1500

9	**Asset Reference**	:	L725-MUS
	Description	:	Volvo truck
	Date Purchased	:	010196
	Asset Category	:	2 Vehicles
	Department	:	0
	Dep'n B.S. N/C	:	0051
	Dep'n P&L N/C	:	8003
	Dep'n Method	:	Reducing
	Dep'n Rate	:	25
	Cost Price	:	10000
10	**Asset Reference**	:	L666-WSU
	Description	:	Mercedes van
	Date Purchased	:	010196
	Asset Category	:	2 Vehicles
	Department	:	0
	Dep'n B.S. N/C	:	0051
	Dep'n P&L N/C	:	8003
	Dep'n Method	:	Reducing
	Dep'n Rate	:	25
	Cost Price	:	15000

♦ When the last record has been saved **Close** the **Fixed Asset Record** window. The **Fixed Assets** window should now display summary details of all your fixed assets.

♦ If you wish to delete a fixed asset record select the asset in the **Fixed Assets** window and click the **Delete** button in either the **Fixed Assets** window or the **Fixed Asset Record** window.

♦ **Close** the **Fixed Assets** window.

At this stage no depreciation has been posted to the ledger accounts. You have simply set up your asset records which contain, amongst other things, the necessary posting details.

Posting depreciation

Before proceeding:

♦ Set the program date to 29/02/96.

Then carry on as follows:

♦ Open the **Period End** menu and select **Month End**.

♦ The following **Month End** dialogue box should now appear:

```
┌─────────────────────────────────────────┐
│ ▬           Month End                     │
│ ┌─Period────────────────────────────────┐│
│ │  Current Month :    February 1996      ││
│ │  Last Ran :         January 1996       ││
│ └───────────────────────────────────────┘│
│ ┌─Options───────────────────────────────┐│
│ │  Post Prepayments              ☐       ││
│ │  Post Accruals                 ☐       ││
│ │  Post Depreciation             ☐       ││
│ │  Clear Turnover Figures        ☐       ││
│ └───────────────────────────────────────┘│
│    WARNING: You should backup your data    │
│         prior to running this routine.     │
│        ┌────────┐     ┌────────┐          │
│        │   OK   │     │ Cancel │          │
│        └────────┘     └────────┘          │
└─────────────────────────────────────────┘
```

♦ Select the **Post Depreciation** check box (a cross will appear when selected) and click the **OK** button. A small **Confirm** dialogue box should now appear asking you to confirm that you wish to process a Month End for February 1996. Click the **Yes** button and the depreciation for February will now be posted to the ledger accounts.

The program uses a date check to prevent assets being depreciated more than once in a month.

Accounting entries

The entries made to the ledger accounts to record the depreciation will be as follows:

CREDIT Furniture and Fixtures Depreciation A/c (0041) in the
Nominal Ledger   104.66 (in total)
CREDIT Motor Vehicles Depreciation A/c (0051) in the
Nominal Ledger   592.21 (in total)
DEBIT   Furniture and Fittings Depreciation A/c (8002) in the
Nominal Ledger   104.66 (in total)
DEBIT   Vehicles Depreciation A/c (8003) in the Nominal Ledger   592.21 (in total)

Check that these entries have been made by examining the transaction details of each of the accounts affected.

The first two depreciation accounts (0041 and 0051) hold the accumulated depreciation of the asset category concerned. At the end of the financial period when the Final Accounts are being prepared these two accounts will be entered in the Balance Sheet as deductions from the appropriate fixed asset category. The other two accounts (8002 and 8003) will be entered in the Profit and Loss Account as expenses for the period.

Fixed Asset reports

To view an asset valuation report on all or selected fixed assets showing cost price, accumulated depreciation and net book value select the **Asset Valuation** button in the **Fixed Assets** window.

If you wish to print this report select the asset(s) in the **Fixed Assets** window and click the **Reports** button. When the **Fixed Assets Reports** window opens select the **Fixed Assets Valuation** report in the **Layout** panel and **Printer** in the **Output** panel then click the **Run** button.

Note: You can also print a **Fixed Assets List** report from the **Fixed Assets Reports** window.

Depreciation postings by Journal

An alternative to the automated depreciation posting routine is to make the entries to the ledger accounts on a monthly or yearly basis using the **Journals** routine in the **Nominal Ledger**.

PREPAYMENTS AND ACCRUALS

Prepayments are payments in advance. The payment for the expense is made during one accounting period but the expense really belongs to a future accounting period, e.g. rent paid in advance. Accruals are arrears of payments. The benefit of the expense has been received during one accounting period but at the end of that period the expense has not yet been paid, e.g. rent in arrears. If you wish to calculate an accurate profit figure then expenses must be allocated to the period in which they 'belong' no matter whether they have been paid during that period or not.

An example of a prepayment

Let's say we pay a year's rent in advance on 1 January and this amounts to £3600. If we did not take the prepayment into account then the Profit and Loss Account at the end of the first month might look like the following:

		£	£
	Sales		20000
less	Purchases		15000
	Gross profit		5000
less	Rent	3600	
	Other expenses	2400	6000
	NET LOSS		1000

However, if we take the prepayment into consideration the Profit and Loss Account would appear as follows:

		£	£
	Sales		20000
less	Purchases		15000
	Gross profit		5000
less	Rent	300	
	Other expenses	2400	2700
	NET PROFIT		2300

The Balance Sheet at the end of month 1 would show a prepayment of £3300 as an asset.

An example of an accrual

Let's say we pay our telephone bill at the end of each quarter in arrears. We estimate the charge to be £150 per month. At the end of the first month we have paid nothing but we have incurred telephone charges of £150. If we did not take this accrual into consideration then the Profit and Loss Account might appear as follows:

		£	£
	Sales		2000
less	Purchases		1200
	Gross profit		800
less	Telephone charges	–	
	Other expenses	700	700
	NET PROFIT		100

However if we take the accrual into consideration the Profit and Loss Account would appear as follows:

		£	£
	Sales		2000
less	Purchases		1200
	Gross profit		800
less	Telephone charges	150	
	Other expenses	700	850
	NET LOSS		50

The Balance Sheet at the end of month 1 would show an accrual of £150 as a liability.

Setting up a prepayment

On 25 February 1996 we make a cheque payment (cheque No. 249191) of £2200 to Phoenix Insurance, being our vehicles insurance for the period January–December 1996. Record this payment in the following way:

♦ Select the **Bank** option in the **Desktop** window.

♦ When the **Bank Accounts** window opens ensure that the **Bank Current Account**, nominal code 1200, is selected then click the **Payment** button.

♦ Record the details of the payment in the **Bank Payment** window (nominal code for vehicle insurance is 7303, tax code should be T2 and department No. should be 1).

♦ When you have entered and checked the details select the **Save** button to post to the ledger accounts then **Close** the **Bank Payment** window.

♦ **Close** the **Bank Accounts** window.

We'll now record this payment in a Prepayments file so that we can spread the expense over the year on a monthly basis.

♦ Select the **Nominal Ledger** option in the **Desktop** window.

♦ Click the **Prepayments** button in the **Nominal Ledger** window and the following **Prepayments** window should open:

	Prepayments						
Prepayments							
N/C				Current Item	1		
PRP				No Of Items	0		

N/C	Details	PRP N/C	Value	Mth	Monthly	Post	
			0.00	0	0.00	0	

Save	Wizard					Close

♦ Enter the following details:

N/C	:	7303	Nominal code for Vehicle Insurance.
Details	:	Vehicle insurance	
PRP N/C	:	1103	Nominal code for Prepayments. This code should already appear in the field.
Value	:	2200	
Mth	:	11	This prepayment would normally be spread over 12 months but since February is the second month of our financial year we will spread it over 11.
Monthly	:	200	This field will show the monthly expense and will be calculated automatically by the program.
Post	:		This field will show the number of monthly postings made to date.

♦ Check that your entries are accurate then select the **Save** button to store the details. Click **OK** in the **Information** dialogue box. If a small **Confirm** dialogue box appears asking if you are sure you wish to exit click the **Yes** button.

Note that no entries in the accounts are made as a result of saving these details. You have merely set up a Prepayments file. Postings to the accounts are only made when the **Month End** routine is run.

Prepayments Wizard

The **Wizard** button in the **Prepayments** window activates the **Prepayments Wizard** tool. This is a series of dialogue boxes which lead you, in a step-by-step manner, through the process of setting up a prepayment.

Setting up an accrual

Let's say we decide to do some advertising and we enter into an agreement with a local agency to advertise on our behalf. The contract is to run for three months, it is expected to cost £600 per month and the total is to be settled at the end of the three-month period.

To set this up proceed as follows:

♦ From the **Nominal Ledger** window select **Accruals** and the **Accruals** window, similar to that for Prepayments should open.

♦ Click the **Wizard** button at the bottom of the window and the first **Accruals Wizard** dialogue box should appear inviting you to select a nominal code.

♦ Select the nominal code for Advertising, 6201 (you will have to scroll the list) and click the **Next** button.

♦ When the Step 2 dialogue box opens enter the description as Advertising and select **Next**.

♦ In the Step 3 dialogue box enter the total amount of the accrual as 1800 and click **Next**.

♦ In the Step 4 box enter the number of months as 3 and click **Next**.

The final dialogue box will display the details you have just entered.

♦ Check the entries; if there are any changes to be made you can move back to the appropriate dialogue box using the **Back** button.

♦ If the entries are accurate click the **Finish** button and you will be returned to the **Accruals** window where the details of the accrual should be shown on the first line.

♦ Select the **Save** button and click **OK** in the **Information** dialogue box. Again, no entries have been made to the accounts, an Accruals file has simply been set up.

♦ **Close** the **Nominal Ledger** window.

Deleting prepayments and accruals

Entries on the Prepayments or Accruals files can be removed by highlighting any field on the line to be removed and pressing the **[F8]** function key or selecting the **Delete Row** option from the **Edit** menu. Then select the **Save** button at the bottom of the **Prepayments** or **Accruals** window.

Posting prepayments and accruals

Before proceeding:

♦ Set the program date to 29/02/96.

Then carry on as follows:

♦ **Open** the **Period End** menu and select **Month End**.

♦ When the **Month End** dialogue box appears select the **Post Prepayments** and **Post Accruals** check boxes (a cross will appear when selected) and click the **OK** button.

♦ A small **Confirm** dialogue box should now appear asking you to confirm that you wish to process a Month End for February 1996. Click the **Yes** button and the accruals and prepayments for February will now be posted to the ledger accounts.

Accounting entries

The following tables show the accounting entries which have been made and those which will be made over the next few months to record the prepayment and accrual.

(a) *Prepayment*:

Date	Transaction	A/c debited		A/c credited		Notes
25/02/96	Paid insurance by cheque	Insurance	£2200	Bank	£2200	1 year's insurance paid in advance
END-FEB	Month-end routine	Prepayments	£2200	Insurance	£2200	
		Insurance	£200	Prepayment	£200	£2200/11
END-MARCH	Month-end routine	Insurance	£200	Prepayment	£200	

and so on in like manner.

After 11 months (end December) the Insurance A/c will have a debit balance of £2200 and the Prepayments A/c will have a *nil* balance.

(b) *Accrual*:

Date	Transaction	A/c debited		A/c credited		Notes
END-FEB	Month-end routine	Advertising	£600	Accruals	£600	£1800/3
END-MAR	Month-end routine	Advertising	£600	Accruals	£600	
END-APR	Month-end routine	Advertising	£600	Accruals	£600	
		Accruals	£1800	Advertising	£1800	
END-APR	Paid advertising by cheque	Advertising	£1800	Bank	£1800	

Check that these entries have been made for the month of February by examining the transaction details of each of the accounts affected:

Vehicle Insurance A/c   (7303)
Prepayments A/c   (1103)
Advertising A/c   (6201)
Accruals A/c   (2109)
Bank A/c   (1200)

Prepayments and accruals postings by Journal

An alternative to the automated prepayments and accruals posting routines is to make the entries to the ledger accounts using the **Journals** routine in the Nominal Ledger.

VAT RETURN ANALYSIS

♦ Select the **Financials** option in the **Desktop** window.

♦ Click the **VAT Return** button in the **Financials** window.

♦ When the **Value Added Tax Return** window opens enter the dates as follows:

For the period : 010196
to   : 290296

♦ Select the **Calculate** button.

♦ When the small **VAT Return** dialogue box opens indicating the number of transactions found click the **OK** button.

♦ When the figures have been calculated for the period note the tax due to Customs and Excise (box 5 on the VAT Return) and **Close** the **Value Added Tax Return** window.

♦ **Close** the **Financials** window.

♦ Check this figure with the *net* balance of the Sales and Purchase Tax Control Accounts (2200 and 2201) in the Nominal Ledger. They should agree.

FINAL ACCOUNTS

We will now produce a Profit and Loss Account and Balance Sheet at the end of February. Before doing this we must update our Cost of Goods Sold Account (5300).

Cost of Goods Sold

This account will have to be updated with February's net purchases. In addition, last month's closing stock will have to be removed and replaced with the stock figure at the end of February.

From the **Nominal Ledger** window note the balances on the three Purchases Accounts (5000–5002) and the Closing Stock (Balance Sheet) Account (1001). These balances should be as follows:

Nominal Code	A/c Name	Balance	
		Dr	Cr
1001	Closing Stock (Balance sheet)	46200	
5000	Purchases – Kitchen equipment	3740	
5001	Purchases – TV/Hi-Fi	3220	
5002	Purchases – Personal care	440	

Assume that after a stock check the Closing Stock at the end of February is valued at £49000.

♦ From the **Nominal Ledger** window select the **Journals** option and enter the following details to the **Journal Entry** window:

Ref : COGS
Date : 290296

N/C	Dept	Details	Tc	Debit	Credit
5300	0	Remove January closing stock	T9	46200	0
1001	0	Zeroing	T9	0	46200
5000	0	Transfer to COGS	T9	0	3740
5001	0	Transfer to COGS	T9	0	3220
5002	0	Transfer to COGS	T9	0	440
5300	0	Purchases for February	T9	7400	0
1001	0	Stock at 29 February	T9	49000	0
5300	0	Stock at 29 February	T9	0	49,000

♦ Check your entries carefully (the **Balance** at the top should be 0.00) then select the **Save** button.

♦ **Close** the **Journal Entry** window then **Close** the **Nominal Ledger** window.

The balance on the Cost of Goods Sold Account (5300) now represents the Cost of Sales for the period 1 January–29 February and this will be used in the Profit and Loss Account. The three Purchases Accounts have been zeroed – balances transferred to Cost of Goods Sold Account. The balance on the Closing Stock Account (1001), which represents the value of stock held at the end of February, will be used in the Balance Sheet.

Print Trial Balance

We now require a printout of the current Trial Balance to enable us to update the design of our Final Accounts. Before proceeding:

♦ Set the program date to 29/02/96.

Then carry on as follows:

♦ Open the **Financials** window and click the **Trial Balance** button.

♦ When the **Trial Balance Report** dialogue box appears ensure that the **Current** option button is selected in the **Accounting Range** panel. **February 1996 Mth 2** should already be displayed in the **Period Range** panel.

♦ Select the **Printer** option in the **Output** panel then click the **Run** button.

♦ When the **Print** dialogue box appears click the **OK** button and the Trial Balance at the end of February 1996 should be printed. It should be similar to the following:

ASCOT ENTERPRISES
Current Trial Balance

N/C	Name	Debit	Credit
0040	Furniture and fixtures	6280.00	
0041	Furniture/fixtures depreciation		104.66
0050	Motor vehicles	25000.00	
0051	Motor vehicles depreciation		592.21
1001	Closing stock (balance sheet)	49000.00	
1100	Debtors control account	16934.15	
1103	Prepayments	2000.00	
1200	Bank current account	3018.25	
1230	Cash	96.30	
2100	Creditors control account		12077.05
2109	Accruals		600.00
2200	Sales tax control account		4252.15
2201	Purchase tax control account	2858.00	
2300	Bank loan		4000.00
3000	Capital		80000.00
4000	Sales – kitchen equipment		11740.00
4001	Sales – TV/Hi-Fi		12080.00
4002	Sales – personal care		1018.00
4009	Discounts allowed	240.00	
4500	Returns in – kitchen equipment	300.00	
5009	Discounts taken		100.00
5300	Cost of goods sold	10890.00	
6201	Advertising	600.00	
7003	Salaries	5350.00	
7100	Rent	2000.00	
7103	Rates	150.00	
7200	Electricity	165.00	
7303	Vehicle insurance	200.00	

7305	Vehicle repairs	102.00	
7504	Office stationery	84.00	
7801	Cleaning	77.00	
7850	Gardening expenses	75.00	
8002	Furniture/fittings depreciation	104.66	
8003	Vehicles depreciation	592.21	
8100	Bad debt write-off	399.50	
8204	Insurance	48.00	
		126564.07	126564.07

♦ When you have obtained the printout **Close** the **Financials** window.

Update Chart of Accounts

Since we designed the Final Accounts 'last month' it will now simply be a case of modifying them slightly to accommodate some new entries.

♦ Select the **Nominal Ledger** option in the **Desktop** window.

♦ Click the **Chart of Accounts** button in the **Nominal Ledger** window.

♦ When the **Chart of Accounts** window opens select (highlight) **Layout2** – the layout you designed 'last month' – and click the **Edit** button.

The **Chart of Accounts** dialogue box should now display the design for Layout2.

The **Sales** and **Purchases** categories do not need to be altered.

♦ Select the **Overheads** category in the **Category Type** column and complete the **Category Account** panel on the right with the following details:

Overheads	Low	High
Discount allowed	4009	4009
Salaries	7003	7003
Rent	7100	7100
Electricity	7200	7200
Vehicle repairs	7305	7305
Office stationery	7504	7504
Cleaning	7801	7801
Advertising	6201	6201
Rates	7103	7103
Vehicle insurance	7303	7303
Gardening expenses	7850	7850
Depreciation – Furn./Fixts.	8002	8002
Depreciation – Vehicles	8003	8003
Bad Debt write-off	8100	8100
Buildings insurance	8204	8204
less Discount received	5009	5009

♦ Once you have completed and checked these entries (especially the ranges) select the **Fixed Assets** category and enter the following details to the **Category Account** panel:

Fixed Assets	Low	High
Furniture and fixtures	0040	0040
less depreciation	0041	0041
Motor vehicles	0050	0050
less depreciation	0051	0051

◆ Select the **Current Assets** category and complete the **Category Account** panel with the following details:

Current Assets	Low	High
Stock	1001	1001
Debtors	1100	1100
Cash	1230	1230
Prepayments	1103	1103

◆ Check that the following details appear on *lines 46 and 47* of the **Category Account** panel (the panel has 50 lines, you'll have to scroll to the end):

Current Assets	Low	High
Bank	1200	1200
VAT reclaimable	2200	2201

◆ Select the **Current Liabilities** category and complete the **Category Account** panel with the following details:

Current Liabilities	Low	High
Creditors	2100	2100
Bank loan	2300	2300
Accruals	2109	2109

◆ Check that the following details appear on *lines 46 and 47* of the **Category Account** panel:

Current Liabilities	Low	High
Bank overdraft	1200	1200
VAT liability	2200	2201

◆ No alterations are needed to the **Capital and Reserves** category, so select the **Save** button and your updated layout will be saved.

◆ **Close** the **Chart of Accounts** dialogue box and if a small **Confirm** dialogue box appears asking if you are sure you wish to exit click the **Yes** button.

◆ **Close** the **Chart of Accounts** window then **Close** the **Nominal Ledger** window.

Print Profit and Loss Account for the period to end February

◆ Set the program date to 290296.

◆ Select the **Financials** option in the **Desktop** window and click the **Profit & Loss** button in the **Financials** window.

◆ When the **Profit & Loss** dialogue box opens ensure that the **Current** option button is selected in the **Accounting Range** panel. **February 1996 Mth 2** should already be displayed in the **Period Range** boxes. Ensure that **Layout 2** is displayed in the

Layout panel, if not select from the drop-down list.

♦ Select **Printer** in the **Output** panel and click the **Run** button.

♦ When the **Print** dialogue box opens click the **OK** button.

♦ The Profit and Loss Account for the first two months of the financial year should now be printed showing figures for This Month (February) and the Year-To-Date (January and February).

Print Balance Sheet at end of February

♦ Ensure that the program date is set to 290296.

♦ Select the **Financials** option in the **Desktop** window and click the **Balance Sheet** button in the **Financials** window.

♦ When the **Balance Sheet** dialogue box opens check the following settings:

Accounting Range panel	:	**Current** should be selected.
Period Range panel	:	**February 1996 Mth2** should be displayed in each box.
Output panel	:	**Printer** should be selected.
Layout panel	:	**Layout2** should be displayed.

♦ Click the **Run** button and when the **Print** dialogue box opens click the **OK** button.

The Balance Sheet as at 29 February 1996 should now be printed.

The figures in the Year-To-Date column are the values of the assets and liabilities at 29/02/96. The figures in the This Month column are the changes in these values during the month, i.e. from 31/01/96 to 29/02/96.

♦ **Close** the **Financials** window.

YEAR-END PROCEDURE

This routine should obviously be run at the end of the financial year only. The Year-End procedure will carry out the following tasks:

1 The balances on all expense and revenue accounts are transferred to the Retained Profit Control Account (No. 3200). The balances on the expense and revenue accounts are thereby zeroed and the accounts are then ready to accept the transactions for the new financial year.

2 The balances on the asset and liability accounts are carried forward to the beginning of the new financial year.

3 The Actual monthly balances are transferred to Prior Year for each nominal account record. This enables you to print comparison reports in the new financial year.

4 The Year-To-Date turnover figure on all customer and supplier records is transferred to the Prior YTD field.

5   The financial year start date is incremented.

As an option in the Year-End procedure you can transfer Actuals to Budgets if you wish to transfer this period's actual nominal account balances into the budget fields to be used for next year. You can also specify a percentage by which the budget figures are to be increased.

You should always ensure that you have taken a backup copy of your data files before carrying out the Year-End procedure.

The **Year-End** routine is accessed from the **Period End** pull-down menu in the **Desktop** window. *However, you should not carry out this procedure right now* since all the expense and revenue accounts would be zeroed and the financial year date would be automatically incremented (from 1996 to 1997).

The following is an example of what your current Trial Balance would look like after the **Year-End** routine had been run:

ASCOT ENTERPRISES
Current Trial Balance

N/C	Name	Debit	Credit
0040	Furniture and fixtures	6280.00	
0041	Furniture/fixtures depreciation		104.66
0050	Motor vehicles	25000.00	
0051	Motor vehicles depreciation		592.21
1001	Closing stock (balance sheet)	49000.00	
1100	Debtors control account	16934.15	
1103	Prepayments	2000.00	
1200	Bank current account	3018.25	
1230	Cash	96.30	
2100	Creditors control account		12077.05
2109	Accruals		600.00
2200	Sales tax control account		4252.15
2201	Purchase tax control account	2858.00	
2300	Bank loan		4000.00
3000	Capital		80000.00
3200	Profit and Loss account		3560.63
		105186.70	105186.70

Note that the Profit and Loss Account items (expense and revenue accounts) have been zeroed and the Balance Sheet items (asset and liability accounts) have been carried forward to the beginning of next year. 'Last year's' net profit has been credited to the Retained Profit Control Account (3200).

The first job which would be necessary at the beginning of the new year would be to transfer the balance on the Closing Stock Account (1001) to the Opening Stock Account (5200) by means of a Journal Entry, i.e.

DEBIT   Opening Stock (5200)   49000
CREDIT Closing Stock (1001)   49000

CHAPTER 6

Report Generator

Creating a New Report · Layout Wizard · Layout Editor – Report Presentation · Layout Editor – Report Variables

CREATING A NEW REPORT

The Report Generator routine allows you to design your own reports and run them using the details stored in the data files.

Creating a new report essentially involves designing a layout file and there are four stages to this:

1   *Layout Wizard.* The Layout Wizard tool allows you to select the type of report (Sales Purchase, Nominal, etc.), give the report a title, select the variables to include and assign a sort order.

    The report layout file can actually be saved at this stage and run using your data from the Report Generator window. Alternatively you can move on to stages (2) and (3) and enhance your report layout using the features in the Layout Editor.

2   *Layout Editor – Report Presentation.* The Layout Editor can be used to set margins, alter font characteristics, add graphics, organise the position of the variables and so on.

3   *Layout Editor – Report Variables.* The Layout Editor has a Report Variable List which can be used to specify the data to be included in the report. A sort order can be set and adjusted, breaks and subtotals included and new calculated variables created. Selection criteria can also be applied to the variables so that only data which meets specified criteria is included in the report.

4   *Saving the Report Layout.* Once the report layout has been designed it should be saved. The layout file will then be listed in the Report Generator window from where it can be run using your data.

LAYOUT WIZARD

We'll now design a simple report which will allow you to familiarise yourself with some of the facilities available in Report Generator and Layout Editor. The report will have the following layout:

AREA	CUSTOMER	NET SALES
MIDLANDS	Ashraf Hi-Fi Ltd	xxx
	Deacon Showrooms Ltd	xxx
		xxx
NORTH	Budget Electric	xxx
	James Buyandsell	xxx
	Sandar Brothers Ltd	xxx
		xxx

etc.

♦ Select the **Report Generator** option in the **Desktop** window and when the **Report Generator** window opens click the **New** button.

♦ The **Layout Wizard** tool should now be activated. This is a series of four dialogue boxes which lead you through the first stage in the design of your report in easy-to-follow steps. The following Step 1 dialogue box should be displayed at the moment:

Step 1

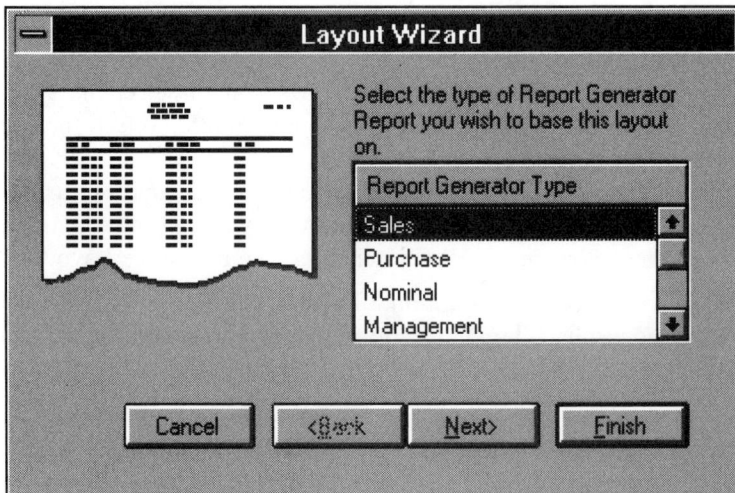

The Step 1 dialogue box allows you to select the report type. This indicates which area of the program the data for your report will be drawn from and you can choose from the following list:

Sales (Customers)
Purchase (Suppliers)
Nominal
Management
Products
Invoicing
Sales Order Processing
Purchase Order Processing

♦ We wish to produce a report on our customers so select **Sales** from the **Report Generator Type** list and click the **Next** button. The following Step 2 dialogue box should now appear:

Step 2

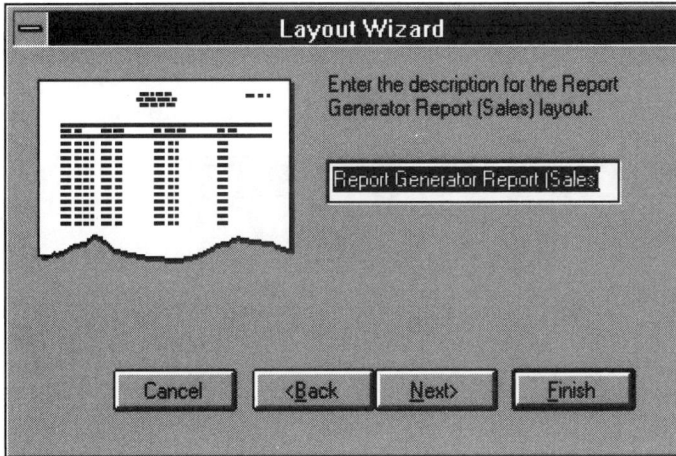

The Step 2 dialogue box allows you to give the report a title.

♦ Enter the title, Sales by Area, in the text box and click the **Next** button. (You can move backwards and forwards through the dialogue boxes using the **Back** and **Next** buttons.) The Step 3 dialogue box, similar to the following, should now be displayed:

Step 3

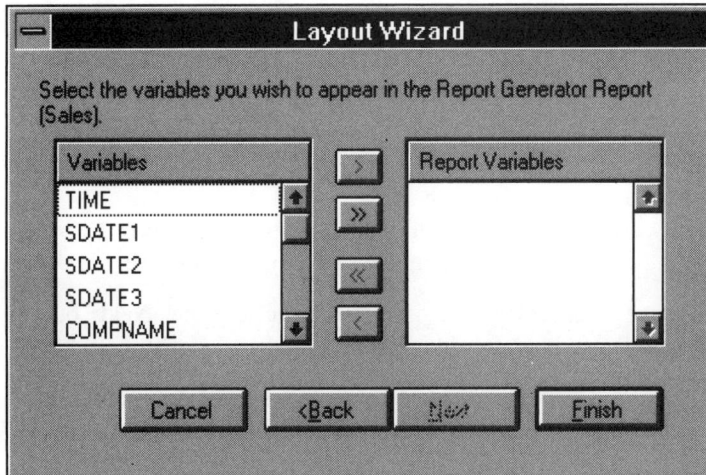

The Step 3 dialogue box enables you to specify the type of data you wish to include in the report. The **Variables** list box shows the data items which are available for inclusion in the report type previously specified.

To select data items for inclusion in the report the name of the variable must be moved from the **Variables** list box to the **Report Variables** list box.

♦ Select (highlight) **ANALYSIS 1** in the **Variables** list box (you'll have to scroll the box to bring it into view) and click the [>] button.

ANALYSIS 1 should now appear as the first item in the **Report Variables** list box.

♦ Select **A/C NAME** in the **Variables** list box and click the [>] button.

♦ Select **TOVRYTD** (Turnover Year-to-Date) in the **Variables** list box and click the ⊳ button.

The **Report Variables** list box should now be similar to the following:

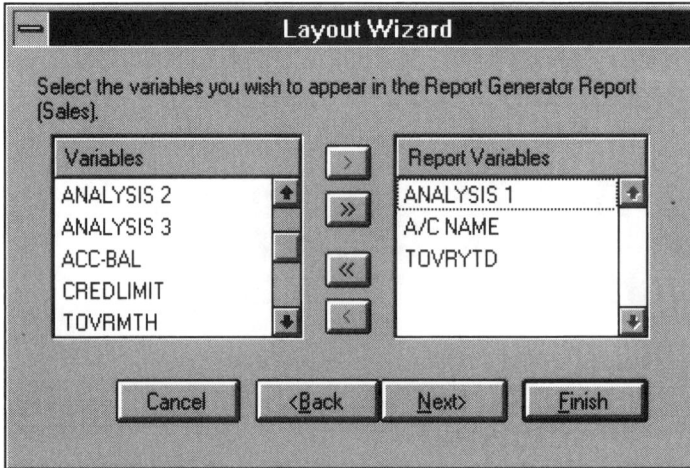

The order in which the variables appear in the **Report Variables** list box determines their position on the final report; the first variable in the list box becomes the first column in the report, etc. Your report should therefore have the following format:

ANALYSIS 1	A/C NAME	TOVRYTD
MIDLANDS	Ashraf Hi-Fi Ltd	xxx

The column headings can be altered later from the Layout Editor and variables can be added, removed or reordered at this stage also.

You can remove variables from the **Report Variables** list box by selecting them and then clicking the ◁ button. The ◀◀ button will remove them all.

♦ When your **Report Variables** list is accurate click the **Next** button and the following Step 4 dialogue box should appear:

Step 4

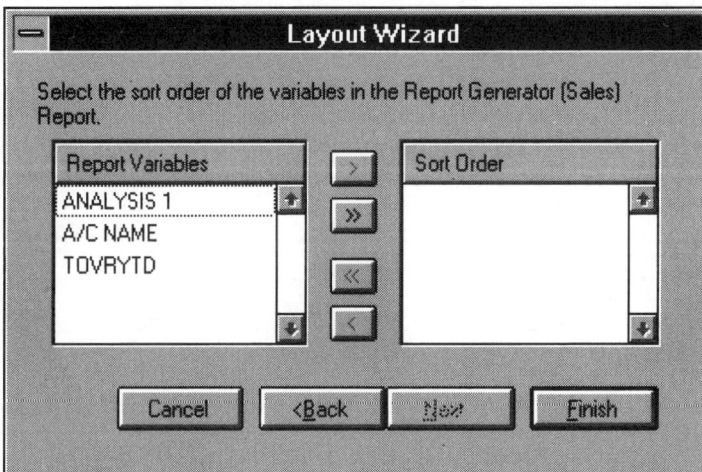

This box enables you to specify how you want the report sorted. A sorting priority can be defined using up to nine variables. Let's say that we want the entries in the first column of our report (**ANALYSIS 1** codes) to be listed alphabetically, i.e. in the order: MIDLANDS, NORTH, SCOTLAND, SOUTH. In addition, within each area group, we would like our customers (**A/C NAME**) in the second column of our report to be shown in alphabetical order.

To specify a sort order the appropriate variable name(s) should be moved from the **Report Variables** list box to the **Sort Order** list box.

♦ Select **ANALYSIS 1** in the **Report Variables** list box and click the ⊳ button.

ANALYSIS 1 should now appear as the first item in the **Sort Order** list box.

♦ Select **A/C NAME** in the **Report Variables** list box and click the ⊳ button.

Your dialogue box should now be similar to the following:

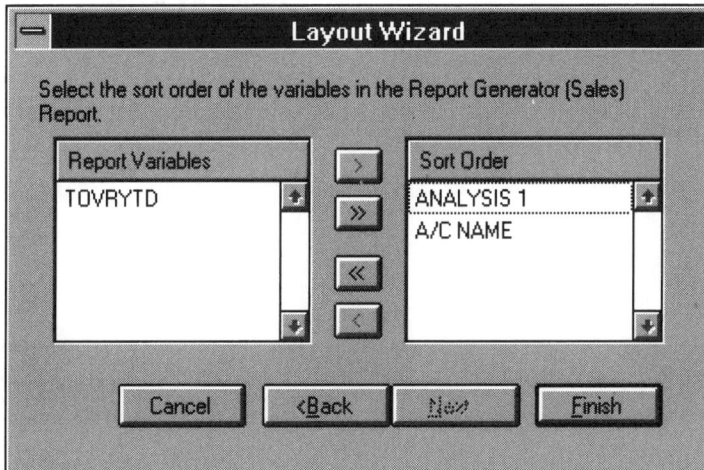

♦ The first stage in the creation of your new report is now complete so click the **Finish** button and the **Layout Editor** window should open displaying the report layout.

LAYOUT EDITOR – REPORT PRESENTATION

The **Layout Editor** window should be similar to the following:

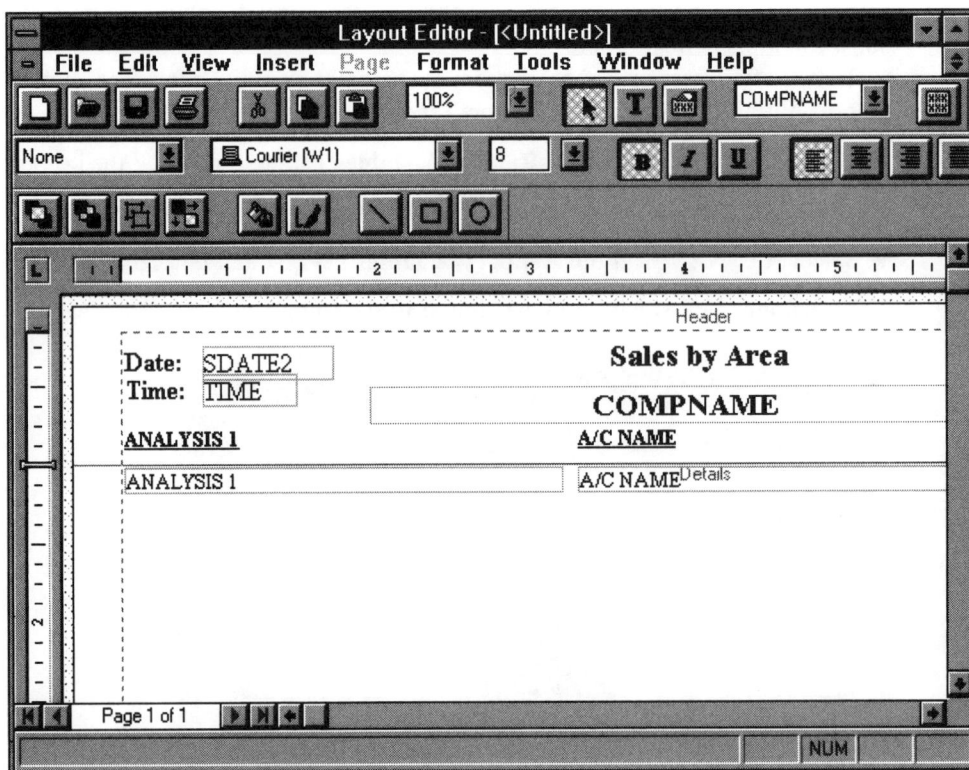

The facilities in the **Layout Editor** enable you to enhance the presentation of your report.

Save the report layout

At the moment we have a report layout file which, once saved, can be used on our data. It would be wise to save this file before proceeding.

♦ Open the **File** menu in the **Layout Editor** window and select **Save**.

♦ When the **Save As** dialogue box opens enter the **File Name** as AREA and click the **OK** button. The file will be saved and **AREA.SRP** should now appear in the **Layout Editor's** title bar.

Print the report

We'll now print the report to see what it looks like using the existing layout. That will help us decide what changes, if any, to make to the layout.

♦ Open the **File** menu in the **Layout Editor** window and select **Exit**. You will be returned to the **Report Generator** window where your report, **Sales by Area**, should be listed in the **Layout** panel (you may have to scroll the list to see it).

♦ Ensure that the report, **Sales by Area**, is selected (highlighted), select **Printer** in the **Output** panel then click the **Run** button.

♦ When the **Print** dialogue box opens click the **OK** button and the report should be printed. It should be similar to the following:

Date: Time:	**Sales by Area** **ASCOT ENTERPRISES**	
ANALYSIS 1	**A/C NAME**	**TOVRYTD**
MIDLANDS	Ashraf Hi-Fi Ltd	2840.00
MIDLANDS	Deacon Showrooms Ltd	1270.00
NORTH	Budget Electric	340.00
NORTH	James BuyandSell	1600.00
NORTH	Sandar Brothers Ltd	1626.00
SCOTLAND	Boyd Brothers	2180.00
SCOTLAND	Imran & Sons	1660.00
SCOTLAND	Mackay Electrical	1410.00
SOUTH	Abbey Brothers Ltd	3424.00
SOUTH	Acorn Electrics Ltd	3232.00
SOUTH	Canon & Sons Ltd	1226.00
SOUTH	Napier Stores PLC	1610.00
SOUTH	Seddon Enterprises	2080.00

Edit the report layout

We'll now edit the report layout to improve its presentation.

♦ In the **Report Generator** window ensure that the report, **Sales by Area**, is selected then click the **Edit** button.

The **Layout Editor** window should now open displaying your report layout.

The **Layout Editor** window has three Toolbars (Main, Options and Advanced Options) which are located immediately below the Menu bar. These Toolbars can be 'switched' on or off (displayed or hidden). We shall be using the facilities on the Main and Options Toolbars to modify the layout and presentation of the report.

♦ If these Toolbars are not displayed at the moment open the **View** menu, choose the **Toolbars** command and select the appropriate check boxes when the **Toolbars** dialogue box opens. Ensure also that the **Variable Names, Margins** and **Rulers** commands on the **View** menu are all selected (a tick will appear in front of the command name when it is selected).

The **Layout Editor** window should now be similar to the following:

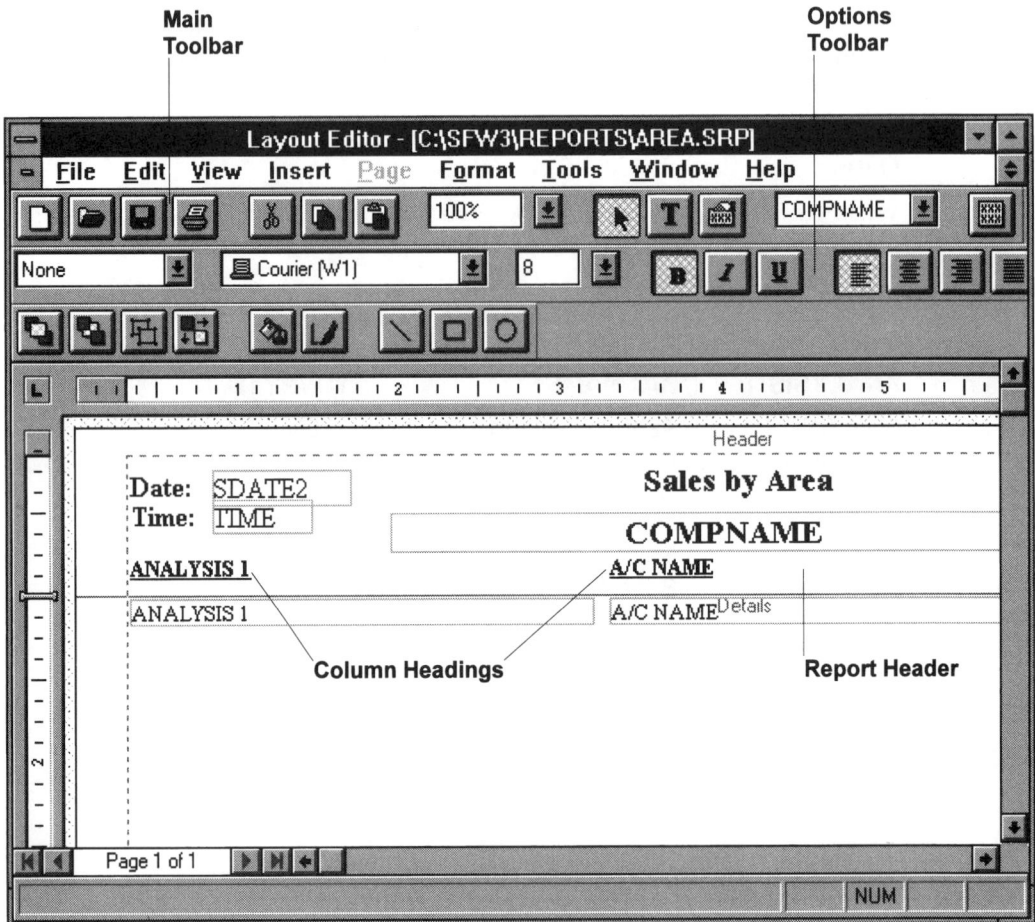

First of all we'll give the column headings in the Report Header section – ANALYSIS 1, A/C NAME AND TOVRYTD – more meaningful names.

♦ Click on **ANALYSIS 1** in the Header section (above the Header line) and the name will be surrounded by small square 'handles' to indicate that it has been selected.

♦ When you have selected **ANALYSIS 1** open the **Edit** menu and select **Clear**. ANALYSIS 1 will be removed from the Header.

♦ Now click on the **Text** button, T, on the Main Toolbar. Locate the mouse pointer in the Header section immediately above ANALYSIS 1 (the pointer will be in the shape of a cross). When you have located the cross at the position you want the new column heading to begin, click the mouse button and an insertion cursor (vertical bar) will begin flashing.

♦ If you do not locate the insertion cursor correctly first time, click anywhere in the report layout area to remove it. You can then click on the **Text** button again and repeat the procedure.

♦ When the insertion cursor is correctly located type AREA then click anywhere in the report layout area.

♦ Now select the new column heading, **AREA**, by pointing and clicking. When **AREA** is surrounded by the small 'handles', indicating that it is selected, click the **Bold** button, B, then the **Underlined** button, U, on the Options Toolbar. Click anywhere in the report layout area to deselect **AREA** and view the result. The new column heading, **AREA**, should now be in bold text and underlined.

You can alter the font type and size of a text item by selecting the item and then choosing from the Font Type and Font Size boxes on the Options Toolbar. Text items can also be moved once they have been selected by 'clicking and dragging', i.e. point to the selected item, click and hold down the left mouse button then drag the pointer to a new location.

So, the procedure for carrying out an operation on an item of text is as follows:

(a) Click on the item to select it – square 'handles' appear round the item.

(b) Carry out the operation – e.g. delete, embolden, move, alter font size.

(c) Click anywhere in the report area to deselect the item – square 'handles' disappear.

You should now change the other two column headings – **A/C NAME** and **TOVRYTD** – to CUSTOMER and NET SALES respectively. Embolden and underline the new headings. You may have to scroll the window to bring the third column heading (**TOVRYTD**) in to view.

Undoing mistakes

The Layout Editor keeps a record of everything that you do and allows you to 'undo' any mistakes that you make. If you make a mistake open the **Edit** menu and select the **Undo** command. The last action which you carried out will be undone. The **Undo** command then reverts to the action you carried out before the one you have just undone, so you can step back and undo a whole sequence of actions one at a time.

You can also undo an undo. This is known as **Redo** and this command is also accessed from the **Edit** menu.

In addition you can always abandon the report layout completely, revert back to the previously saved layout and start from scratch again. If you wish to do this:

♦ Open the **File** menu and select **Exit**.

♦ When the small **Save** dialogue box opens asking if you wish to save the file click the **No** button and you will be returned to the **Report Generator** window.

♦ You can then select your previously saved file in the **Report Generator** window, click the **Edit** button and start again.

Saving the edited report layout

Once you have entered the new column headings and formatted them correctly, your report layout should be similar to the following:

Date: Time:	Sales by Area COMPNAME	Page:
AREA	CUSTOMER	NET SALES
ANALYSIS 1	A/C NAME	TOVRYTD

◆ When your report layout is accurate open the **File** menu and select **Save**.

Your report layout will be saved and this will replace the previously saved version. The **Save As** dialogue box will not open this time – the program knows the name and location of your file.

LAYOUT EDITOR – REPORT VARIABLES

You can now specify any special conditions you wish to be applied to the variables themselves and thereby control the content and structure of the final report.

◆ Ensure that the **Layout Editor** window is open with your report layout file displayed.

◆ Open the **Tools** menu and select **Report Variable List** (**Report Settings** if you are using Version 3.10 of the program).

The following **Report Variables** dialogue box should now appear displaying each of the variables you have included in the report, one variable per line.

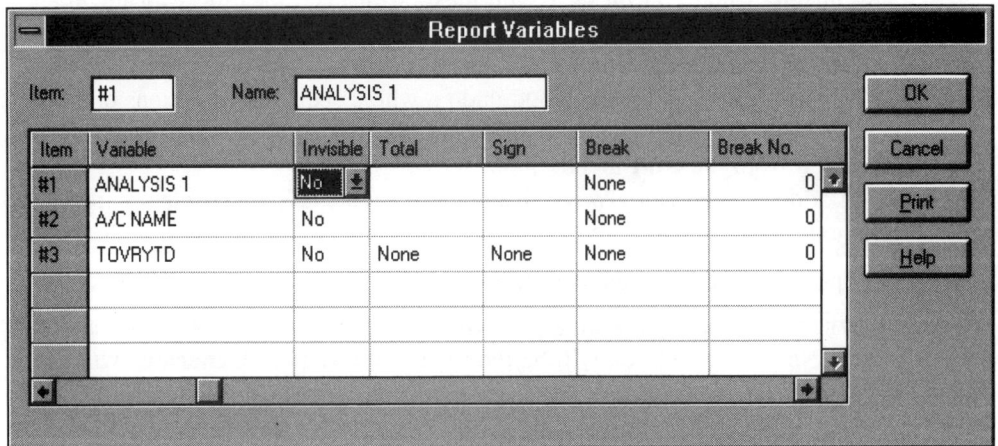

Note: There will also be a **Calculated** column in the dialogue box if you are using Version 3.10 of the program.

The columns following the variable names (**Invisible, Total, Sign**, etc.) allow you to specify conditions for each variable. The purpose of each column will now be explained and we'll apply some of these conditions to the variables in our report.

Invisible

If you select **Yes** from the drop-down list box the variable concerned will not be printed on the report. Note, however, that although a variable may be omitted from a report in this way it can still be used in calculations and have selection criteria applied to it.

We want all the variables to be printed on the report so ensure that **No** is displayed against each variable name in this column.

Total

This column can be used to specify whether totals and subtotals are required for numeric variables. The following options are available from the drop-down list boxes in this column:

(a) **None**   – If this is selected no subtotals are printed for this variable.

(b) **Print Totals** – This option will print a subtotal for the variable every time there is a break in the report (see later). A grand total is also printed at the end of the report.

(c) **Totals Only** – This will print a totals only report for this variable. The subtotals for the variable will be printed every time there is a break but the individual transaction lines will be omitted. A grand total will also be printed.

♦ Click in or **[Tab]** to the **Total** field for the **TOVRYTD** variable.

♦ Click the 🔽 button and select **Print Totals** from the drop-down list.

Sign

This column applies to numeric variables and the options are:

(a) **None**   – Don't print any sign before numeric values.

(b) **All**   – Print all numeric values preceded by a minus (–) sign if appropriate. Credit postings are regarded as negative numbers so they would be preceded with a minus sign.

(c) **Debits** – Prints only debit values.

(d) **Credits** – Prints only credit values.

We will not use this facility in our report so ensure that **None** is displayed in the **Sign** field for the **TOVRYTD** variable.

Break

This column can be used to specify a line or a page break at certain points in the report. The options are as follows:

(a) **None** – No breaks in the report.

(b) **Line** – This option will break the list and leave a blank line whenever this variable changes. For example, the following report:

Department number	Employee surname
1	CLARK
1	DAVIES
1	GRANGER
2	BLAND
2	MEADOWS
2	WALLACE
3	ABRAHAM
3	KINNING
3	YOUNGER

could be re-structured using the line break facility to produce the following:

Department number	Employee surname
1	CLARK
	DAVIES
	GRANGER
2	BLAND
	MEADOWS
	WALLACE
3	ABRAHAM
	KINNING
	YOUNGER

(c) **Page** – This option will break the list and start a new page whenever this variable changes.

(d) **On Characters** – This option will cause the report to break only when it sees a change in this variable within the first *n* characters of the data, where *n* is the number you enter in the **Break No.** field in the next column.

The **Break** facility can be used in conjunction with the **Total** option to produce subtotals for numeric variables where breaks occur in the report.

♦ In our report we want a line break after each area's listing so click in or **[Tab]** to the **Break** field for the **ANALYSIS 1** variable.

♦ Click the ⬇ button and select **Line** from the drop-down list.

♦ Ensure that **None** is displayed in the **Break** fields for the other two variables.

Break No.

This is used in conjunction with the **On Characters** option in the **Break** column to specify a value for *n*.

We are not using this facility so 0 should appear in each of the three fields.

Sort Level

You'll have to scroll the variables list box horizontally to bring this column into view. The report can be sorted on up to nine variables. The **Sort Level** column allows you to allocate a sort sequence to the variables which are being sorted.

♦ Click in or **[Tab]** to the **Sort Level** field for the **ANALYSIS 1** variable. **Level One** should already be displayed since we set this in **Layout Wizard**, if not click the ▣ button and select **Level One** from the drop-down list.

♦ Similarly, ensure the **Sort Level** for the **A/C NAME** variable is set to **Level Two**. The **Sort Level** for the **TOVRYTD** variable should be **Level None**.

These settings will result in a primary sort being carried out on the Area names (ANALYSIS 1 variable) then within each Area group a secondary sort will be carried out on the Customer names (A/C NAME variable).

Sort Order

A sort can be carried out in ascending (A–Z or 1–9) or descending (Z–A or 9–1) order.

♦ Ensure that **Ascending** is displayed in each of the three fields.

The settings in your **Report Variables** dialogue box should now be as follows:

Item	Variable	Invisible	Total	Sign	Break	Break No.	Sort Order	Sort Order
#1	ANALYSIS 1	No			Line	0	Level One	Ascending
#2	A/C NAME	No			None	0	Level Two	Ascending
#3	TOVRYTD	No	Print Totals	None	None	0	Level None	Ascending

Note: If there is a **Calculated** column in your dialogue box **No** should be displayed in each of the three fields.

♦ The last two columns in the dialogue box (**Criteria** and **Calculation**) should be blank.

♦ When your settings are accurate click the **OK** button in the dialogue box and you will be returned to the **Layout Editor** window.

♦ Open the **File** menu and select **Save**.

♦ Open the **File** menu again and select **Exit** and you will be returned to the **Report Generator** window.

Print the report

♦ Ensure that your report file, **Sales by Area**, is selected in the **Report Generator** window.

♦ Select **Printer** as the **Output** medium then click the **Run** button.

♦ When the **Print** dialogue box opens click the **OK** button and the report should be printed. It should be similar to the following:

Date:	Sales by Area	
Time:		
	ASCOT ENTERPRISES	
AREA	**CUSTOMER**	**NET SALES**
MIDLANDS	Ashraf Hi-Fi Ltd	2840.00
	Deacon Showrooms Ltd	1270.00
		4110.00
NORTH	Budget Electric	340.00
	James BuyandSell	1600.00
	Sandar Brothers Ltd	1626.00
		3566.00
SCOTLAND	Boyd Brothers	2180.00
	Imran & Sons	1660.00
	Mackay Electrical	1410.00
		5250.00
SOUTH	Abbey Brothers Ltd	3424.00
	Acorn Electrics Ltd	3232.00
	Canon & Sons Ltd	1226.00
	Napier Stores PLC	1610.00
	Seddon Enterprises	2080.00
		11572.00
		24498.00

Adding selection criteria

We will now edit the report to limit the printout to customers whose turnover exceeds £2000.

♦ In the **Report Generator** window select the report, **Sales by Area**, and click the **Edit** button.

♦ When the **Layout Editor** window appears, open the **Tools** menu and select **Report Variables List** (**Report Settings** if you are using Version 3.10 of the program).

♦ When the **Report Variables** dialogue box appears scroll the list horizontally until the **Criteria** column is brought into view. The **Criteria** column is used to apply selection criteria to the variables so that only those records which meet the specified criteria will be printed in the report.

♦ Enter >2000 in the **Criteria** field for the **TOVRYTD** variable (third line) then click the **OK** button.

♦ In the **Layout Editor** window open the **File** menu and select **Save**.

♦ Open the **File** menu again and select **Exit**.

♦ In the **Report Generator** window ensure that your report, **Sales by Area**, is selected. Select **Printer** as thc **Output** medium then click the **Run** button.

♦ When the **Print** dialogue box opens click the **OK** button and your report should be printed.

This time the report should be restricted to those customers whose turnover is greater than £2000.

CHAPTER 7

Stock Control and Invoicing

Stock Control · Invoicing · Product-based Invoices · Credit Notes · Service Invoices · Invoice Deletion · Product Reports

The Sage Stock Control routine operates on the FIFO (first in, first out) basis and is integrated with the Invoicing and Order Processing routines. When an invoice is created and posted using the Invoicing routine it updates the Sales and Nominal Ledgers and also the stock records.

STOCK CONTROL

Sage allows you to classify your items of stock in two ways. First of all, they can be allocated to a broad category then each item within the category can be given a meaningful code. In our case, for example, we could have categories for washing machines, refrigerators, televisions, hi-fi, etc. All televisions would fall into the same category but different makes of TV would have a different stock code.

Example

```
Category 1   TV
Category 2   Hi-fi
Category 3   Washing machine
etc.
```

The system allows 999 categories to be established. The following coding system could be used for TVs to identify the manufacturer and size:

```
TV-PAN-51
TV-PAN-55   (i.e. manufacturer: Panvision; screen size: 55 cm)
TV-PAN-59

TV-SON-51
TV-SON-55
TV-SON-59   (i.e. manufacturer: Sonvision; screen size: 59 cm)
```

The stock code can consist of up to 16 characters. Thoughtful design of stock codes can greatly facilitate reporting. The type of information required from reports should be given careful consideration and codes should be designed in such a way as to make the production of meaningful reports easy.

Product categories

Let's say that our company has started to sell wooden hi-fi cabinets in two sizes, each size having either a mahogany, yew or ash finish.

First of all we will set up a category for cabinets.

◆ Open the **Defaults** menu and select **Product Categories**.

A **Product Categories** dialogue box similar to the following should now open:

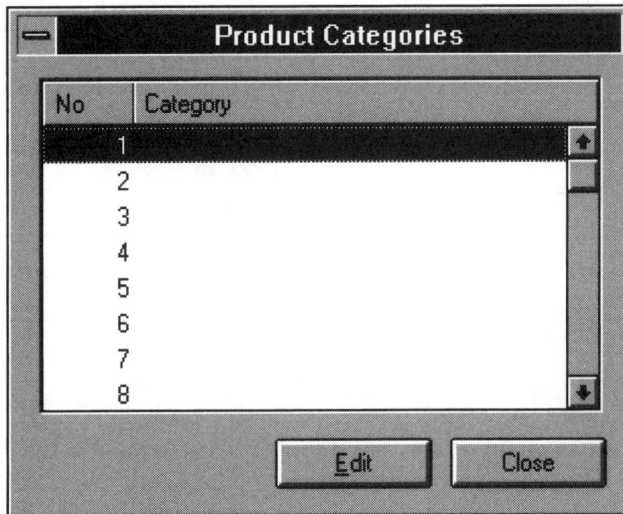

◆ Select (highlight) **Category No 1** and click the **Edit** button.

◆ The **Edit Product Category** dialogue box should now open allowing you to enter a name for the first category. Enter the **Name** as CABINETS and click the **OK** button.

◆ You should be returned to the **Product Categories** dialogue box and CABINETS should appear as **Category No 1**. Click the **Close** button to return to the **Desktop** window.

Product records

Before we set up the stock records for our cabinets we will establish two new nominal accounts to record the sales of these cabinets.

◆ Select the **Nominal Ledger** option in the **Desktop** window.

◆ Click the **Record** button in the **Nominal Ledger** window.

◆ Set up the following accounts, remembering to **Save** each one:

N/C	Name	Total Budget (last field in the **Budgets** column)
4003	Sales – Small Cabinets	27000
4004	Sales – Large Cabinets	50000

♦ Once you have created these accounts **Close** the **Nominal Record** window then **Close** the **Nominal Ledger** window.

Now set up the stock records:

♦ Select the **Products** option in the **Desktop** window.

♦ Click the **Product Record** button in the **Products** window.

A **Product Record** data entry window, similar to the following, should now open:

♦ Ensure that the **Details** 'page' is displayed. This will allow you to enter the relevant details for the first stock item – equivalent to the stock record card in a manual system.

It is not necessary to make entries to all the fields in the record and some of the fields are updated automatically by the program. The following are the details which you should enter for your first item of stock:

Product Code	: C-YEW-S	
Description	: Small Yew Cabinet	
Department	: 3 TV/Hi-Fi	Select from the drop-down list.
Category	: 1 CABINETS	
Nominal Code	: 4003	Nominal Sales A/c used when an invoice including this item is posted to the ledgers.
Tax Code	: T1 17.50	
Sales Price	: 80	Net of VAT.
Unit of Sale	: each	
Ignore Stock Levels	: Check box should be blank	
Re-order Level	: 5	

♦ Once these details have been entered check them then select the **Save** button.

The following are the details for another five product records. Set them up in similar manner and remember to **Save** each one.

	2	3	4	5	6
Product Code	C-ASH-S	C-MAH-S	C-YEW-L	C-ASH-L	C-MAH-L
Description	Small Ash Cabinet	Small Mahogany Cabinet	Large Yew Cabinet	Large Ash Cabinet	Large Mahogany Cabinet
Department	3 TV/Hi-Fi	3 TV/Hi-Fi	3 TV/Hi-Fi	3 TV/Hi-Fi	3 TV/Hi-Fi
Category	1 CABINETS	1 CABINETS	1 CABINETS	1 CABINETS	1 CABINETS
Nominal Code	4003	4003	4004	4004	4004
Tax Code	T1 17.50	T1 17.50	T1 17.50	T1 17.50	T1 17.50
Sales Price	70	75	120	110	115
Unit of Sale	each	each	each	each	each
Ignore Stock	Check box	Check box	Check box	Check box	Check box
Levels	should be blank	should be blank	should be blank	should be blank	should be blank
Re-order Level	5	5	8	8	8

♦ Once the details for the last product record have been entered and **Saved** select the **Close** button and you will be returned to the **Products** window where the code, description and price for each stock item will be listed. Remember, the column headings (**Product Code, Description, Qty** and **Sales Price**) are also sort buttons which allow you to order the list.

Editing a product record

If you wish to edit a product record select the record in the **Products** window and click the **Product Record** button. When the **Product Record** window opens make the necessary amendment(s) and click the **Save** button.

Deleting a product record

If you wish to delete a product record select the record in the **Products** window and click the **Delete** button. The **Delete** button in the **Product Record** window can also be used for this purpose. You can only delete a product record when all of the following conditions are met:

1 there are no outstanding orders;

2 the product has both an 'In Stock' and an 'Allocated' balance of zero;

3 any history on the product's activity has been removed using the **Clear Stock** option from the **Period End** menu.

Setting up budget report details

♦ Select the **Product Record** option in the **Products** window.

♦ In the **Product Record** window enter the **Product Code** as C-YEW-S (you can use 'Finder' here) and the product details for small yew cabinets should appear.

♦ Click the **Sales** tab button at the top of the window and a sales analysis 'page', similar to the following, should appear:

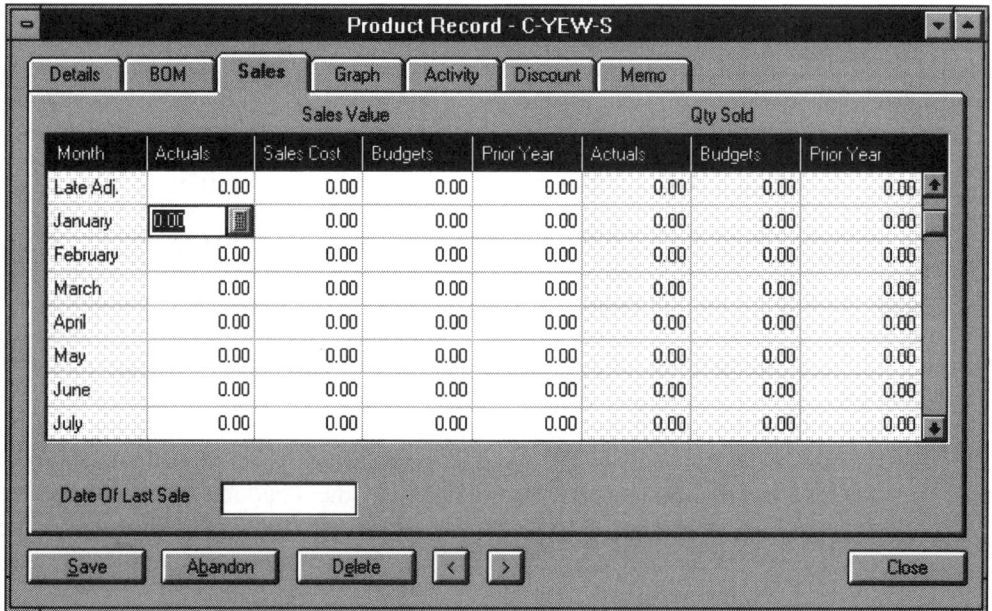

Product Record - C-YEW-S						

	Sales Value				Qty Sold		
Month	Actuals	Sales Cost	Budgets	Prior Year	Actuals	Budgets	Prior Year
Late Adj.	0.00	0.00	0.00	0.00	0.00	0.00	0.00
January	0.00	0.00	0.00	0.00	0.00	0.00	0.00
February	0.00	0.00	0.00	0.00	0.00	0.00	0.00
March	0.00	0.00	0.00	0.00	0.00	0.00	0.00
April	0.00	0.00	0.00	0.00	0.00	0.00	0.00
May	0.00	0.00	0.00	0.00	0.00	0.00	0.00
June	0.00	0.00	0.00	0.00	0.00	0.00	0.00
July	0.00	0.00	0.00	0.00	0.00	0.00	0.00

Date Of Last Sale

Save · Abandon · Delete · [<] [>] · Close

♦ In the **Budgets** column for **Sales Value** enter 800 for each month from March to December. The **[Tab]** key (or **[Shift]** + **[Tab]**) will move the insertion cursor from field to field. The [↑] and [↓] keys will move the cursor up or down a particular column. Fields can also be selected by pointing and clicking with the mouse.

♦ In the **Budgets** column for **Qty Sold** enter 10 for each month from March to December.

♦ Once these figures have been entered select the **Save** button and you will be returned to the **Details** 'page'.

♦ In a similar way enter the budget figures for the following cabinets and remember to **Save** each record.

Product Code	C-ASH-S	C-MAH-S	C-YEW-L	C-ASH-L	C-MAH-L
Monthly budget for **Sales Value** (March–December)	700	750	1440	1320	1380
Monthly budget for **Qty Sold** (March–December)	10	10	12	12	12

The program will insert the Actual figures automatically when transactions take place.

♦ Once the figures for the last stock item have been entered and saved **Close** the **Product Record** window.

Initial stock balances

To enter opening stock balances proceed as follows:

♦ Select the **Product Record** option in the **Products** window.

♦ In the **Product Record** window enter the **Product Code** as C-YEW-S and the product details for small yew cabinets should appear.

♦ Now select the opening balance button, %, in the **In Stock** field and an **Opening Product Setup** dialogue box, similar to the following, should open:

```
┌──────────────────────────────────────────────────────────┐
│ ▬              Opening Product Setup                       │
├──────────────────────────────────────────────────────────┤
│   Ref        Date        Quantity        Cost Price        │
│  ┌──────┐  ┌──────────┐  ┌──────────┐  ┌──────────────┐   │
│  │O/BAL │  │01/03/96 🖩│  │0.00      🖩│  │     0.00   🖩│   │
│  └──────┘  └──────────┘  └──────────┘  └──────────────┘   │
│        ┌─────────────┐        ┌─────────────┐             │
│        │    Save     │        │   Cancel    │             │
│        └─────────────┘        └─────────────┘             │
└──────────────────────────────────────────────────────────┘
```

♦ Enter the **Date** as 010396.

♦ Enter the **Quantity** as 15.

♦ Enter the **Cost Price** as 50.

♦ Select the **Save** button in the dialogue box and you will be returned to the **Product Record** window where the **In Stock**, **Free Stock** and **Cost Price** fields will have been updated.

♦ In similar fashion enter the following opening balances:

Code	Date	Quantity	Cost Price
C-ASH-S	010396	15	40
C-MAH-S	010396	15	45
C-YEW-L	010396	20	70
C-ASH-L	010396	20	60
C-MAH-L	010396	20	65

♦ When you have finished entering the opening balances **Close** the **Product Record** window.

♦ The **Products** window should now display the opening balances for each stock item in the **Qty** column.

Stock movements

Stock movements can be entered 'manually' using the **Adjustment In** and **Adjustment Out** routines. These routines should be used when the stock movement is not being recorded using the program's **Invoicing** or **Order Processing** options. However, it should be noted that these routines are not linked to the ledgers – the Purchases, Sales and Personal accounts are not updated automatically.

Stock receipts

Receipts of stock can be entered using the **Adjustment In** routine but remember there will be no automatic updating of Supplier A/c and Purchases A/c. These entries would have to be made separately.

♦ Select the **Adjustment In** option in the **Products** window.

A **Stock Adjustments In** data entry window, similar to the following, should now open:

♦ Enter the following details for the first stock receipt:

Product Code	:	C-YEW-S
Details	:	Small Yew Cabinet
Date	:	020396
Ref	:	GRN123
Qty	:	5
Cost Price	:	55

♦ Ensure that the insertion cursor is in the **Product Code** field on the second line of the window and enter the details for the following five stock receipts:

Product Code	Details	Date	Ref	Qty	Cost Price
C-ASH-S	Small Ash Cabinet	020396	GRN124	5	45
C-MAH-S	Small Mahogany Cabinet	020396	GRN125	5	50
C-YEW-L	Large Yew Cabinet	040396	GRN126	10	75
C-ASH-L	Large Ash Cabinet	040396	GRN127	10	65
C-MAH-L	Large Mahogany Cabinet	040396	GRN128	10	70

♦ When you have entered the details for the six receipts check the entries and click the **Save** button.

♦ **Close** the **Stock Adjustments In** window.

The **Products** window should now display the updated balances for each stock item in the **Qty** column.

Posting Adjustments In causes the following entries to be made:

(a) the **In Stock** quantity on the **Product Record** is increased;

(b) the **Cost Price** on the **Product Record** is updated;

(c) the **Product Activity** file is updated with details of the transaction.

Posting Adjustments Out causes the following entries to be made:

(a) the **In Stock** quantity on the **Product Record** is decreased on a FIFO basis;

(b) the **Product Activity** file is updated with details of the transaction.

To view details relating to stock movements for each product:

♦ Select the **Clear** button at the bottom of the **Products** window to ensure that all products are deselected, then click the **Activity** button.

♦ When the small **Date Range** dialogue box opens click the **OK** button and the following **Product Activity** window should open showing details of your first stock item (Large Ash Cabinet):

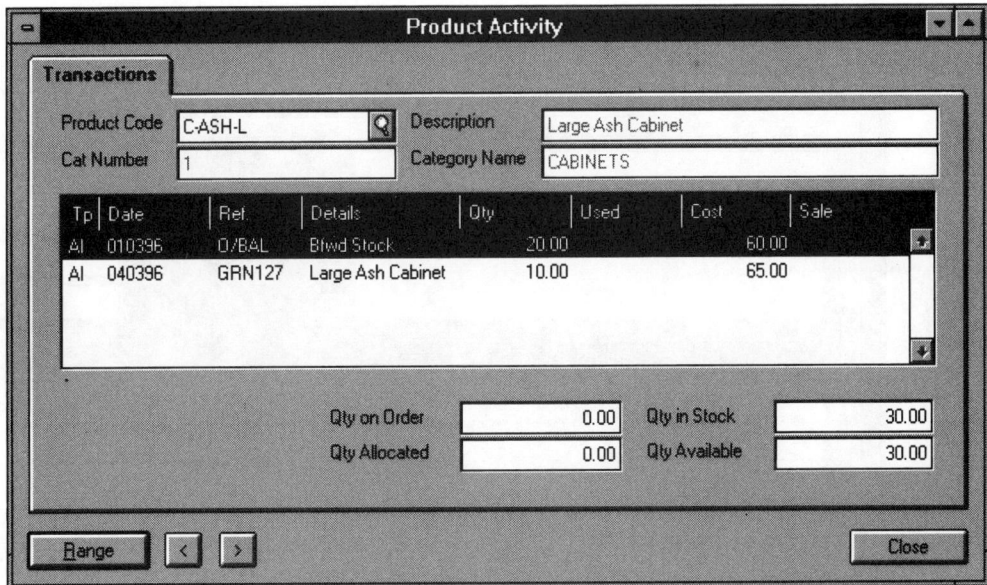

♦ The ▷ and ◁ buttons will move you forwards and backwards through the **Product Activity** windows to allow you to view details for the other items of stock.

♦ When you have finished examining the activity details **Close** the **Product Activity** window then **Close** the **Products** window.

INVOICING

Invoices and credit notes have so far been posted to the ledger accounts using the **Batch Invoices** and **Batch Credits** options in the **Customers** window. The program also has an **Invoicing** routine which interacts with the stock files. This function can be used to create invoices and credit notes, print them and update the Sales and Nominal Ledger accounts and product records.

The Invoicing routine allows you to produce either product (stock) based invoices and credit notes or those which are text-based. The latter are suitable for companies which provide a service, e.g. repairs and maintenance.

The invoices and credit notes can include items which are recorded in the stock files or not. The layout of the documents can be amended to suit user requirements.

PRODUCT-BASED INVOICES

Enter invoice details

♦ Select the **Invoicing** option in the **Desktop** window.

♦ Click the **Product Invoice** button in the **Invoicing** window and the following **Product Invoice** data entry window should now open:

Invoices and credit notes are produced in three sections: **Invoice/Credit Details,**
Order Details and **Footer Details**. The **Invoice Details** 'page' should be displayed at
the moment.

♦ Enter the following details for your first invoice:

Invoice No.	: 1225	
Invoice Date	: 060396	
Order No.	: 6655	
A/C Ref	: ACORN	Customer reference. This field allows 'live account creation' for a new customer.
Product Code	: C-YEW-S	Again, in this field you can set up a new product record if necessary.

Note at this point that the **Description** and the **Net** and **VAT** figures have all been
retrieved from the stock files and inserted in the appropriate fields. These details can
be edited and additional information inserted to the invoice using the **Product Item**
Line dialogue box.

Activate this in the following way:

♦ Ensure that the insertion cursor is in the **Description** field for Small Yew Cabinet and
click the edit button at the end of the field. The following **Product Item Line** dialogue
box should now appear allowing you to enter one-off details for this item if you wish:

Note that many of the details relating to the product have already been inserted using information taken from the product records. These details can be edited in this dialogue box for this invoice only with no effect on the product record.

♦ Check the following details and alter where necessary:

Product Code	: C-YEW-S	
Description	: Small Yew Cabinet	
Comment 1	: –	
Comment 2	: –	
Quantity	: 5	This value will appear in the **Qty** field on the **Invoice Details** 'page'.
Unit Price	: 80.00	The price can be altered for this invoice only with no effect on the product record.
Discount %	: 0.00	This field can be used to enter discount (e.g. trade discount) relating to a particular item on the invoice and the **Net** and **VAT** fields on the **Invoice Details** 'page' would be recalculated automatically. Settlement discount relating to the full invoice total is entered on the **Footer Details** 'page'.
Discount	: 0.00	
Nominal Code	: 4003	This is the nominal code for Small Cabinet Sales. Enter code here to analyse each line item to Nominal Ledger separately. If whole invoice is to be analysed to one code (account) this can be entered on the **Footer Details** 'page'.
Tax Code	: T1 17.50	Enter code here to apply VAT to each line item on invoice separately. If whole invoice is to be analysed to one VAT code then this code can be entered on the **Footer Details** 'page'.
Department	: 3 TV/Hi-Fi	This can be entered by line item or for the invoice as a whole.

♦ Select **OK** at the bottom of the **Product Item Line** dialogue box and you will be returned to the **Invoice Details** 'page'.

The **Product Item Line** dialogue box can be recalled for amendment by selecting the **Description** field on the **Invoice Details** 'page' and clicking the **Edit** button at the end of the field.

We will enter the details of one more item on this invoice – this time a non-stock item (i.e. an item which is not yet recorded on the product record files).

♦ Click in the **Product Code** field on the second line of the **Invoice Details** 'page'.

♦ If you wish to process a non-stock item you must enter one of the following codes:

M   to add a message text (simply a line of text without quantity, price or VAT).
S1   to add a non-stock item which is taxable.
S2   to add a non-stock item which is zero rated for VAT.

♦ Enter S1 to the **Product Code** field and press the **[Tab]** key.

The **Product Item Line** dialogue box will open and show the **Product Code** as S1.

♦ Enter the following details:

Description	:	Food processors	
Comment 1	:	as per telephone call	
Comment 2	:	–	
Quantity	:	6	
Unit Price	:	40	
Discount %	:	0.00	
Discount	:	0.00	
Nominal Code	:	4000	Kitchen Equipment Sales A/c.
Tax Code	:	T1 17.50	Select from drop-down list.
Department	:	2 KITCHEN EQUIPMENT	Select from drop-down list.

♦ Click the **OK** button at the bottom of the **Product Item Line** dialogue box and you will be returned to the **Invoice Details** 'page' again where the details of the food processors will be shown on the second line.

♦ To enter the Footer details for the invoice select the **Footer Details** tab button at the top of the **Product Invoice** window.

The **Footer Details** 'page', similar to the following, should now be displayed:

The **Footer Details** 'page' is divided into three sections allowing you to input details relating to **Carriage, Settlement Terms** and **Global** values.

In the **Carriage** section you can enter details of any charge on the invoice total such as delivery charges, postage and packing, insurance, etc.

♦ Leave this section blank.

The **Settlement Terms** section allows you to enter details of any settlement terms which apply to the invoice total. Any discount entered here will affect the value of VAT for the invoice. VAT will be calculated on the discounted amount.

♦ Enter the following details:

Days   : 30
Discount % : 10

If there are several items on the invoice they can each be analysed to separate tax codes, nominal codes and departments. To do this the appropriate codes for each item would be entered in the **Product Item Line** dialogue box. Alternatively the whole invoice can be analysed to one tax code, nominal code and department if all items are similar. To do this the appropriate codes should be entered in the **Global** section of the **Footer Details** 'page' and these codes override any which have already been entered in the **Product Item Line** dialogue boxes.

You don't need to enter anything in this section.

◆ Select the **Invoice Details** tab button at the top of the window and the **Invoice Details** 'page' will be redisplayed. Note that the VAT figures have been adjusted to allow for the settlement discount.

Once the invoice has been completed you can choose either to print a copy or save it for batch printing later. You can also use the **Abandon** button to clear the entries you have made and start again. We will save this one and print it later so:

◆ Click the **Save** button at the bottom of the **Product Invoice** window. The window will refresh ready to receive details of the next invoice.

Note: If you wish to edit an existing invoice after it has been saved enter the invoice No. in the **Invoice No.** field in the **Product Invoice** window and press the [**Tab**] key. The invoice details should appear and you can amend where necessary.

◆ Enter the following details for the second invoice:

Invoice No.	: 1226	This should appear automatically (previous invoice No. incremented by one).
Invoice Date	: 060396	
Order No.	: 7766	
A/C Ref	: OCHIL	Since this is a new customer and we have not yet created an account for them the small Customer Accounts selection box should open.

◆ Click the **New** button in the selection box and a **Customer Record** window should open.

◆ Enter the following details for your new customer:

A/C	: OCHIL
Name	: Ochil Valley Electrics
Street 1	: 51–56 High Street
Street 2	: –
Town	: Dollar
County	: –
Post Code	: FK22 4DL
Credit Limit	
(**Defaults** 'page')	: 2000
Analysis1	
(**Defaults** 'page')	: SCOTLAND

◆ **Save** these details and you will be returned to the Customer Accounts selection box. Ensure that your new customer, OCHIL, is selected (highlighted) and click the **OK** button to return to the **Invoice Details** 'page'. Again, you have experienced the 'live' account creation facility of the program.

◆ Continue and enter the remainder of the invoice details:

Product Code   :   C-MAH-S

◆ There is no need to change anything in the **Product Item Line** dialogue box so [**Tab**] to or click in the **Qty** field and enter the quantity as 10.

♦ Click in the **Product Code** field on the second line of the **Invoice Details** 'page' and enter the following:

Product Code : C-ASH-S
Qty : 6

♦ There is nothing to be entered on the **Order** or **Footer Details** 'pages' so select the **Save** button at the bottom of the **Product Invoice** window. This will store the details for printing and updating of ledgers later.

♦ Enter the following details for the third invoice:

Invoice No. : 1227
Invoice Date : 060396
Order No. : 8855
A/C Ref : ASHRAF

ITEM 1
Product Code : C-ASH-L
Qty : 6

ITEM 2
Product Code : C-MAH-L
Qty : 8

ITEM 3
Product Code : C-YEW-S
Qty : 25

♦ When you press the **[Tab]** key after the last entry an 'Insufficient Stock' **Warning** dialogue box should appear. Click the **OK** button and move back to the **Qty** field for Small Yew Cabinets. Re-enter the quantity as 5.

♦ Again, nothing to enter on the **Footer Details** 'page', so select the **Save** button. If a 'credit limit exceeded' dialogue box appears click the **Yes** button to continue.

♦ Enter the following details for the last invoice:

Invoice No. : 1228
Invoice Date : 060396
Order No. : 9977
A/C Ref : BOYD

ITEM 1
Product Code : C-YEW-S

Product Item Line details:
Comment 1 : 5 per cent trade discount
Quantity : 12
Unit Price : 80.00
Discount % : 5
Discount : 48.00
Nominal Code : 4003
Tax Code : T1 17.50
Department : 3 TV/Hi-Fi

♦ When you have entered these details to the **Product Item Line** dialogue box click the **OK** button.

ITEM 2
Product Code : C-MAH-S

Product Item Line details:

Comment 1	:	10 per cent trade discount
Quantity	:	6
Unit Price	:	75.00
Discount %	:	10
Discount	:	45.00
Nominal Code	:	4003
Tax Code	:	T1 17.50
Department	:	3 TV/Hi-Fi

♦ Click the **OK** button in the **Product Item Line** dialogue box and you will be returned to the **Invoice Details** 'page'. Note that trade discount has been deducted from the **Net** figure for each item and **VAT** calculated on the discounted amount.

♦ Select the **Footer Details** tab button at the top of the **Customer Invoice** window.

Since both items on this invoice are small cabinets we can analyse the whole invoice amount to one VAT code, nominal account and department and these will override any already specified for the item lines of the invoice.

♦ Enter the following details in the **Global** section of the **Footer Details** 'page':

N/C	:	4003
Details	:	Yew & Mahogany Cabinets
Tax Code	:	T1 17.50
Dept	:	3 TV/Hi-Fi

This means that when the invoice is posted only one line representing the total amount will be added to the Audit Trail.

♦ Click the **Save** button at the bottom of the **Product Invoice** window and you will be returned to a clear **Invoice Details** 'page'.

♦ **Close** the **Product Invoice** window.

The **Invoicing** window should display the four invoices showing the invoice No., type, date, customer name and amount for each.

Editing an invoice

If you wish to edit an invoice before it has been used to update the product records and ledger accounts select the invoice in the **Invoicing** window and click the **Product Invoice** button. When the **Product Invoice** window opens the invoice details will be displayed. You can then make the necessary amendments and re-save.

Update product records and ledgers

♦ In the **Invoicing** window select all four invoices (1225–1228) and click the **Update Ledgers** button.

♦ When the **Update Ledgers** dialogue box opens select the **Output** medium as **Preview** and click the **OK** button.

A report of the update should now be produced and displayed in a Preview window.

♦ Maximise the Preview window if necessary and then use the scroll buttons to view all the report details. Notice from the report that invoice 1228 has not been posted due to insufficient stock for item 1 (Small Yew Cabinet).

♦ **Close** the Preview window.

When you return to the **Invoicing** window you should note that the **Posted** status for invoices 1225, 1226 and 1227 is **Yes** but invoice 1228 has not been posted.

♦ Click the **Clear** button at the bottom of the **Invoicing** window to deselect all invoices then select the **Product Invoice** button.

♦ In the **Product Invoice** window enter the **Invoice No.** as 1228 and press the **[Tab]** key. The details of invoice 1228 should now be displayed.

♦ Select the **Qty** field for the first line item (C-YEW-S) and re-enter the quantity as 8.

♦ Select the **Save** button.

♦ **Close** the **Product Invoice** window.

♦ In the **Invoicing** window select invoice 1228 and click the **Update Ledgers** button.

♦ In the **Update Ledgers** dialogue box select the **Output** medium as **Preview** and click the **OK** button.

The update report this time should confirm that invoice 1228 has been posted to the ledgers.

♦ **Close** the Preview window and when you return to the **Invoicing** window the **Posted** status for invoice 1228 should be **Yes**.

♦ **Close** the **Invoicing** window.

We'll now check the entries which have been made in the product records and the ledger accounts to record the posting of the invoices.

♦ Select the **Products** option in the **Desktop** window.

♦ When the **Products** window opens select the five products included in your invoices: Small Mahogany, Yew and Ash Cabinets and Large Ash and Mahogany Cabinets.

♦ Click the **Activity** button. Click **OK** in the **Date Range** dialogue box and the **Product Activity** window should display the transaction details for the first product, Large Ash Cabinet.

There should be a Goods Out entry of 6. Notice that the cost price of the cabinets sold was 60 indicating that the sale was made from opening stock rather than the stock receipt (which has a cost price of 65). This is correct according to the FIFO system –

first in, first out. The stock value for Large Ash Cabinet should now be $(14 \times 60) + (10 \times 65) = 1490$. You can check this by running the **Product Valuation** report later.

You can display the activity details for the selected products using the ▷ button and check that the sales invoices have been recorded.

♦ **Close** the **Product Activity** window when you are finished viewing.

♦ Click the **Clear** button at the bottom of the **Products** window to deselect all records.

♦ Select Large Ash Cabinet in the **Products** window and click the **Reports** button. When the **Product Reports** window opens run the **Product Valuation** report and check that the stock value for Large ash cabinets is 1490.

♦ When you have done this **Close** the **Product Reports** window then **Close** the **Products** window.

The following entries should have been made to the ledger accounts when the invoices were posted. Check the transaction details of the accounts concerned.

Invoice No. 1225

Acorn Electrics Ltd A/c (ACORN) in the Sales Ledger (**Customers**)	Dr	740.80
Small Cabinet Sales A/c (4003) in the **Nominal Ledger**	Cr	400.00
Kitchen Equipment Sales A/c (4000) in the **Nominal Ledger**	Cr	240.00
Sales Tax Control A/c (2200) in the **Nominal Ledger**	Cr	100.80
Debtors Control A/c (1100) in the **Nominal Ledger**	Dr	740.80

Note: In the **Activity** window there is a 'drill down' facility which allows you to view the individual line items which make up the invoice total. Double click on the invoice concerned to display these details.

Invoice No. 1226

Ochil Valley Electrics A/c (OCHIL) in the Sales Ledger (**Customers**)	Dr	1374.75
Small Cabinet Sales A/c (4003) in the **Nominal Ledger**	Cr	750.00
Small Cabinet Sales A/c (4003) in the **Nominal Ledger**	Cr	420.00
Sales Tax Control A/c (2200) in the **Nominal Ledger**	Cr	204.75
Debtors Control A/c (1100) in the **Nominal Ledger**	Dr	1374.75

Invoice No. 1227

Ashraf Hi-Fi Ltd A/c (ASHRAF) in the Sales Ledger (**Customers**)	Dr	2326.50
Small Cabinet Sales A/c (4003) in the **Nominal Ledger**	Cr	400.00
Large Cabinet Sales A/c (4004) in the **Nominal Ledger**	Cr	660.00
Large Cabinet Sales A/c (4004) in the **Nominal Ledger**	Cr	920.00
Sales Tax Control A/c (2200) in the **Nominal Ledger**	Cr	346.50
Debtors Control A/c (1100) in the **Nominal Ledger**	Dr	2326.50

Invoice No. 1228

Boyd Brothers A/c (BOYD) in the Sales Ledger (**Customers**)	Dr	1190.28
Small Cabinet Sales A/c (4003) in the **Nominal Ledger**	Cr	1013.00
Sales Tax Control A/c (2200) in the **Nominal Ledger**	Cr	177.28
Debtors Control A/c (1100) in the **Nominal Ledger**	Dr	1190.28

Notice that invoices 1225, 1226 and 1227 have been analysed to the Sales Accounts in the Nominal Ledger by item line whereas invoice 1228 has been entered in the Sales A/c as one total. The reason for this is that the nominal code, tax code and department number were entered in the **Global** section of the **Footer Details** 'page' for invoice 1228.

♦ When you have finished viewing the accounts return to the **Desktop** window.

You should now be convinced that the **Invoicing** routine is fully integrated with the product files and the ledgers.

Print invoices

♦ Select the **Invoicing** option in the **Desktop** window.

♦ One or more invoices can be printed by first of all selecting the invoice(s) in the **Invoicing** window and then selecting the **Print Invoices** button.

♦ We'll print invoice 1225 so select (highlight) this in the **Invoicing** window and click the **Print Invoices** button.

♦ When the **Print Invoice** window opens select the file **New Product Invoice/Credit Note (A4)** in the **Layout** panel; this is one of the standard product invoice layout files supplied by Sage and is designed for A4 paper. Select **Printer** in the **Output** panel and click the **Run** button. Click the **Yes** button in the **Confirm** dialogue box to confirm that it is a product invoice layout that you wish.

♦ Click the **OK** button in the **Print** dialogue box and the invoice should be printed.

♦ **Close** the **Print Invoice** window.

When you return to the **Invoicing** window the **Printed** status for invoice 1225 should now be Yes. You can only post invoices once but you can print them as many times as you wish.

Note: The invoice which you have just produced is using one of the standard layouts supplied with the program. However, invoice layout and content can be amended to suit your requirements or you can design a new layout.

CREDIT NOTES

Credit notes can be produced in exactly the same way by selecting the **Product Credit Note** option from the **Invoicing** window. The credit note data entry windows are identical to the invoice entry windows with '**Credit No.**' replacing '**Invoice No.**'.

SERVICE INVOICES

These invoices are not based on items held in stock. They are invoices which require textual description of a service carried out. This type of invoice would be used by a company which sells a service rather than physical items of stock, e.g. landscape gardening, painting and decorating, etc. Let's say that our company operates a repair service for items which have been damaged in transit and on the customer's premises.

First of all we will need a nominal account to record 'sales' of this service.

♦ Set up a new account in the nominal ledger for Stock Repairs with a code of 4005. Don't enter anything for Yearly Budget.

♦ When you have **Saved** this account return to the **Desktop** window and select the **Invoicing** option.

♦ When the **Invoicing** window opens ensure that none of the existing invoices are selected then click the **Service Invoice** button. A **Service Invoice** data entry window, similar to the following, should now open:

♦ Enter the following details:

Invoice No.	:	1229
Invoice Date	:	100396
A/C Ref	:	OCHIL
Details	:	Repair of small mahogany cabinet.

♦ Now press the [**Tab**] key and when the insertion cursor is in the **Price** field click the Edit button in the Item No box or press the [**F3**] function key and the **Service Item Line** dialogue box, similar to the following, should appear:

```
┌────────────────────────────────────────────────────────┐
│  ─            Service Item Line                          │
│ ┌─Details──────────────────────────────────────────────┐│
│ │ Repair of small mahogany cabinet.                  ▲ ││
│ │                                                      ││
│ │                                                    ▼ ││
│ └──────────────────────────────────────────────────────┘│
│ ┌─Item Details─────────────────────────────────────────┐│
│ │ Invoice Value   [    0.00 🖩] Tax Code [T1 17.50  ±] ││
│ │ Discount %      [    0.00 🖩] Net      [      0.00] ││
│ │ Discount        [    0.00 🖩] VAT      [      0.00] ││
│ └──────────────────────────────────────────────────────┘│
│ ┌─Posting Details──────────────────────────────────────┐│
│ │ Details      [Goods\Services                    ]   ││
│ │ Nominal Code [4000      🔍]                          ││
│ │ Department   [0                                  ±] ││
│ └──────────────────────────────────────────────────────┘│
│ [Calc. Net] [Discounts]        [  Ok  ]  [ Cancel ]     │
└────────────────────────────────────────────────────────┘
```

♦ The dialogue box allows you to complete text input if you wish and to enter item and posting details. Enter the following text to lines 2 and 3 in the **Details** panel:

Replacement of broken glass door.
Cabinet re-polished to remove scratches.

♦ Now enter the following **Item** and **Posting Details**:

Invoice Value	: 25	
Discount %	: 0.00	
Discount	: 0.00	
Tax Code	: T1 17.50	
Details	: Cabinet repairs	
Nominal Code	: 4005	Stock Repairs A/c.
Department	: 3 TV/Hi-Fi	

♦ Click the **OK** button at the bottom of the **Service Item Line** dialogue box and you will be returned to the **Invoice Details** 'page' where the completed text and the price, net and VAT figures should now be shown.

You can continue to add further text items in a similar way.

♦ Select the **Save** button at the bottom of the **Service Invoice** window and these details will be stored for future printing and updating of ledgers.

♦ **Close** the **Service Invoice** window and you will be returned to the **Invoicing** window where your new invoice (1229) should be listed with the others.

Update ledgers

♦ Select (highlight) invoice No. 1229 in the **Invoicing** window and click the **Update Ledgers** button.

♦ When the **Update Ledgers** dialogue box opens select the **Output** medium as **Preview** and click the **OK** button.

A report of the update should now be produced and displayed in the Preview window.

♦ **Close** the Preview window.

When you return to the **Invoicing** window the **Posted** status for invoice 1229 should be Yes.

♦ The following entries should have been made to the ledger accounts to record the posting. Check the transaction details of the accounts concerned.

Ochil Valley Electrics' A/c (OCHIL) in the Sales Ledger (**Customers**)	Dr	29.38
Stock Repairs A/c (4005) in the **Nominal Ledger**	Cr	25.00
Sales Tax Control A/c (2200) in the **Nominal Ledger**	Cr	4.38
Debtors Control A/c (1100) in the **Nominal Ledger**	Dr	29.38

Print invoice

♦ Ensure that the service invoice (1229) only is selected in the **Invoicing** window and click the **Print Invoices** button.

♦ When the **Print Invoice** window opens this time select the file **New Service Invoice/Credit Note (A4)** in the **Layout** panel (the file description is **A4 Service Inv\Cnd** in Version 3.10 of the program); this is one of the standard service invoice layout files supplied by Sage and is designed for A4 paper. Select **Printer** in the **Output** panel and click the **Run** button. Click the **Yes** button in the **Confirm** dialogue box to confirm that it is a service invoice layout that you wish.

♦ When the **Print** dialogue box opens click the **OK** button and the service invoice should be printed.

♦ **Close** the **Print Invoice** window.

When you return to the **Invoicing** window the **Printed** and **Posted** status for invoice 1229 should now be Yes.

♦ **Close** the **Invoicing** window.

INVOICE DELETION

When your invoices have been successfully printed and posted you will no longer require to store them on disc. They can be removed to create additional disc space by selecting the invoices for deletion in the **Invoicing** window and then selecting the **Delete** button. It is a good idea to take a backup copy of your data files before doing this.

Before deletion the program will check that the invoices have been printed and posted and if either of these two conditions is not met an appropriate warning message will be printed.

Once deleted the invoices will be removed from the list but you will need to use the **Compress** files option in the **Disk Doctor** routine (accessed from the **Data** pull-down menu) in order to remove the deleted records from the data files and free disc space.

PRODUCT REPORTS

Record enquiries

1 The **Product Record** option in the **Products** window can be used to call up the details relating to a particular item of stock. In addition to the information entered when the stock record 'card' was set up the program will maintain and display the 'In Stock', 'Allocated', 'Free Stock' and 'On Order' figures for the product. The latest 'Cost Price' will also be shown. For example:

♦ In the **Products** window select the item Small Yew Cabinet and click the **Product Record** button. The **Product Record** window for Small Yew Cabinet should now open and the quantity **In Stock** and the latest **Cost Price** will be displayed on the **Details** 'page'.

♦ Select the **Sales** tab button at the top of the **Product Record** window and a Sales Analysis 'page' will be displayed giving a comparison of actual with budgeted sales figures on a monthly basis.

♦ Select the **Graph** tab button at the top of the **Record** window and the **Graph** 'page' will enable you to produce various forms of graphs/charts showing actual and/or budgeted figures for Sales Value or Quantity Sold on a monthly basis.

♦ Select the **Activity** tab button at the top of the **Record** window and the **Activity** 'page' will allow you to view details relating to stock movements. Quantities 'On Order', 'In Stock', 'Allocated' and 'Available' should also be displayed for the product concerned.

♦ **Close** the **Product Record** window.

2 The **Activity** option in the **Products** window can also be used to display details relating to stock movements for the product selected. This is similar to the **Activity** 'page' in the **Product Record** window.

Pre-designed reports

Several standard reports can be previewed, printed or saved to file using the **Reports** button in the **Products** window.

(a) *Product List.* This shows the product code, description, selling price and nominal account.

(b) *Product Price List.* This produces a list of products showing code, description and selling price.

(c) *Product Profit – Month and Year.* These reports show, for the period chosen, a profit figure and a profit margin for the selected product(s).

(d) *Product Re-Order Levels.* Lists all products whose 'In Stock' quantity is below the 'Re-Order' level.

(e) *Product Valuation.* Produces a stock valuation based on a FIFO calculation for the selected product(s).

(f) *Product History (or Product Activity).* Shows a transaction history for the selected product(s).

(g) *Product Details.* Lists all the details shown on the Product Record card.

When you have finished examining these reports return to the **Desktop** window.

User-designed reports

The Report Generator can be used to design reports based on the data held in the product files. Let's say we hope to start selling our products in Germany and we want to produce a report showing their prices in Deutschmarks. Assume that the £ Sterling/Deutschmark exchange rate is £1 Sterling = 2.27 Deutschmarks.

We will design a report with the following format:

Price List (Germany)

Code	Product	Sterling	Marks
XXX	XXX	XXX	XXX
XXX	XXX	XXX	XXX
XXX	XXX	XXX	XXX

♦ Select the **Report Generator** option in the **Desktop** window.

♦ When the **Report Generator** window opens click the **New** button and the **Layout Wizard** tool will be activated.

♦ In the **Layout Wizard** Step 1 dialogue box select **Products** from the **Report Generator Type** list and click the **Next** button.

♦ In the Step 2 dialogue box enter the Report Description as Price List (Germany) and click the **Next** button.

♦ When the Step 3 dialogue box opens select the variable **CODE** in the **Variables** list box then click the > button to move it into the **Report Variables** list box. In a similar manner move the variables **PRODDESC**, **PRICE** and **<CALC>** into the **Report Variables** list box. The last variable, **<CALC>**, allows you to insert a calculated field into the report layout.

The **Report Variables** list box should now be similar to the following:

```
┌─────────────────────────────┐
│ Report Variables            │
├─────────────────────────────┤
│ CODE                        │
│ PRODDESC                    │
│ PRICE                       │
│ <CALC>                      │
└─────────────────────────────┘
```

♦ Click the **Next** button to move on to the **Layout Wizard** Step 4 dialogue box.

♦ In the Step 4 dialogue box select **CODE** in the **Report Variables** list box and click the ☒ button to move it into the **Sort Order** list box.

♦ Click the **Finish** button and the **Layout Editor** window should open displaying the report layout. The layout should be similar to the following:

```
┌───────────────────────────────────────────────────────────────┐
│ Date:              Price List (Germany)            Page:        │
│ Time:                  COMPNAME                                  │
│                                                                 │
│ CODE          PRODDESC              PRICE        <CALC>          │
│─────────────────────────────────────────────────────────────   │
│ CODE          PRODDESC              PRICE        <CALC>          │
└───────────────────────────────────────────────────────────────┘
```

♦ In the Header section of the layout delete the column headings PRODDESC, PRICE and <CALC> and replace them with PRODUCT, STERLING and MARKS respectively. Embolden and underline these new headings. The procedure for doing this is described in Chapter 6 on the Report Generator.

♦ Once you have inserted and formatted the new headings open the **Tools** menu and select **Report Variable List** (**Report Settings** if you are using Version 3.10 of the program).

♦ When the **Report Variables** dialogue box opens scroll the box horizontally to bring the **Sort Level** column into view. Ensure that **Level One** appears in the **Sort Level** field for the variable, **CODE**, if not, select from the drop-down list.

♦ Scroll the box again to bring the **Calculation** column into view.

♦ Click in the **Calculation** field for the variable <CALC> (fourth line) and enter #3*2.27. #3 is the Item No. of the variable **PRICE** in the report layout. The calculation we have inserted will multiply the sterling price by 2.27 and this will give the price in marks.

♦ When you have completed the **Report Variables** list box accurately click the **OK** button.

♦ In the **Layout Editor** window open the **File** menu and select **Save**.

♦ When the **Save As** dialogue box opens enter the **File Name** as PRICLIST and click the **OK** button.

♦ Open the **File** menu again and select **Exit**. You should be returned to the **Report Generator** window where your new file should be listed (you may have to scroll the list to see it).

♦ Select the new report file, **Price List (Germany)**, in the **Layout** panel, select **Printer** as the **Output** medium then click the **Run** button.

♦ When the **Print** dialogue box opens click the **OK** button and the report should be printed. It should be similar to the following:

Date:	Price List (Germany)		Page:
Time:	ASCOT ENTERPRISES		

CODE	PRODUCT	STERLING	MARKS
C-ASH-L	Large Ash Cabinet	110.00	249.70
C-ASH-S	Small Ash Cabinet	70.00	158.90
C-MAH-L	Large Mahogany Cabinet	115.00	261.05
C-MAH-S	Small Mahogany Cabinet	75.00	170.25
C-YEW-L	Large Yew Cabinet	120.00	272.40
C-YEW-S	Small Yew Cabinet	80.00	181.60

♦ **Close** the **Report Generator** window.

CHAPTER 8

Order Processing

Sales and Purchase Order Processing · **Sales Order Processing** · **Purchase
Order Processing** · **Processing Back Order for Sales** · **Processing
Outstanding Purchase Order** · **Delete Orders**

SALES AND PURCHASE ORDER PROCESSING

The order processing routines allow you to enter and progress orders from customers
and to suppliers and to record the despatch and delivery of goods. The routines are
integrated with the stock files and the product records are updated automatically when
goods are despatched or delivered.

SALES ORDER PROCESSING

This routine enables you to record the details of orders received from customers and to
print them. You can allocate stock to these orders and record the despatch of goods and
these entries will be reflected in the product records. When the goods are despatched a
delivery note can be printed and an invoice is automatically generated from the order.
The invoice can then be used to update the relevant accounts in the Sales and Nominal
ledgers.

Enter order details

♦ Select the **Sales Orders** option in the **Desktop** window.

♦ Click the **Sales Order Entry** button in the **Sales Orders** window and the following
Sales Order Entry window will open:

```
┌──────────────────────────────────────────────────────────────────┐
│ ▭                           Sales Order                      ▼ ▲  │
├──────────────────────────────────────────────────────────────────┤
│  ┌Main─┐┌ Order Details ┐┌ Footer Details ┐                      │
│                                                                    │
│   ┌───────────────────────────────────┐   Order No.  │ 1    │     │
│   │                                   │   Order Date │10/03/96│📅  │
│   │                                   │   A/C Ref    │      │🔍    │
│   │                                   │                            │
│   └───────────────────────────────────┘                          │
│   ┌──────────────┬──────────────┬──────┬────────┬────────┐        │
│   │ Product Code │ Description   │ Qty  │ Net    │ V.A.T. │▲       │
│   ├──────────────┼──────────────┼──────┼────────┼────────┤        │
│   │              │              │      │        │        │        │
│   │              │              │      │        │        │        │
│   │              │              │      │        │        │        │
│   │              │              │      │        │        │▼       │
│   └──────────────┴──────────────┼──────┼────────┼────────┤        │
│                          │ Totals │      │  0.00  │  0.00  │       │
│                          │ Carriage│     │  0.00  │  0.00  │       │
│   ┌──────────────────┐   ├────────┤              ┌────────┤       │
│   │   Item 1 of 0    │   │ Gross  │              │  0.00  │       │
│   └──────────────────┘   └────────┘              └────────┘       │
│                                                                    │
│   ┌──Save──┐ ┌─Abandon─┐ ┌─Print─┐ ┌─Complete─┐      ┌─Close─┐    │
└──────────────────────────────────────────────────────────────────┘
```

Orders are recorded in sections, similar to Invoices and Credit Notes, using **Main**, **Order Details** and **Footer Details** 'pages'. The **Main** 'page' for the first order should now be displayed.

♦ Enter the following details:

Order No.	: 1	
Order Date	: 100396	
A/C Ref	: BUDGET	Customer reference. This field allows 'live' account creation for a new customer.
Product Code	: C-YEW-S	Again, in this field you can set up a new product record if necessary. You can also enter a non-stock item here using the code S1 or S2.

♦ Ensure that the insertion cursor is in the **Description** field showing Small Yew Cabinet and click the Edit button at the end of the field. The following **Product Item Line** dialogue box should appear allowing you to apply one-off product details for this item if you wish.

```
┌─────────────────────────────────────────────────────────────────┐
│ ▭                        Product Item Line                        │
├─────────────────────────────────────────────────────────────────┤
│ ┌─Product Details──────────────────────────────────────────────┐ │
│ │   Product Code    │C-YEW-S                              │     │ │
│ │   Description     │Small Yew Cabinet                    │     │ │
│ │   Comment 1       │                                     │     │ │
│ │   Comment 2       │                                     │     │ │
│ └──────────────────────────────────────────────────────────────┘ │
│ ┌─Product Line Details─────────────────────────────────────────┐ │
│ │  Quantity    │1.00      │▣│  Discount %  │    0.00 │▣│        │ │
│ │  Unit Price  │   80.00  │▣│  Discount    │    0.00 │▣│        │ │
│ │  Net         │   80.00  │    VAT         │   14.00 │           │ │
│ │  Allocated   │    0.00  │    Despatched  │    0.00 │           │ │
│ └──────────────────────────────────────────────────────────────┘ │
│ ┌─Posting Details──────────────────────────────────────────────┐ │
│ │  Nominal Code │4003   │🔍│  Tax Code  │T1  17.50 │▼│          │ │
│ │  Department   │3 TV/Hi-Fi                        │▼│          │ │
│ └──────────────────────────────────────────────────────────────┘ │
│ │ Calc. Net │  │ Discounts │            │   Ok   │  │ Cancel │    │
└─────────────────────────────────────────────────────────────────┘
```

Note that some of the details relating to the product have already been inserted using information taken from the product records. However, these details can be edited in this dialogue box for this order only with no effect on the product record.

♦ Check the following details and alter where necessary:

Product Code	:	C-YEW-S	
Description	:	Small Yew Cabinet	
Comment 1	:	–	
Comment 2	:	–	
Quantity	:	2	This value will appear in the **Qty** field on the **Main** 'page'.
Unit Price	:	80.00	You can alter the price for this order but any amendment made here will have no effect on the product record.
Discount %	:	0.00	
Discount	:	0.00	

Nominal Code	: 4003	Enter code here to analyse each line item on order to Nominal Ledger separately. If whole order is to be analysed to one code (account) this can be entered on the **Footer Details** 'page'.
Tax Code	: T1 17.50	Enter code here to apply VAT to each line item on order separately. If whole order is to be analysed to one VAT code then this code can be entered on the **Footer Details** 'page'.
Department	: 3 TV/Hi-Fi	This can be entered by line item or for the order as a whole.

♦ Click **OK** at the bottom of the **Product Item Line** dialogue box and you will be returned to the **Main** 'page' where the details on line 1 should now be complete.

The **Product Item Line** dialogue box can be recalled for amendment by selecting the **Description** field on the **Main** 'page' and clicking the Edit button at the end of the field.

We will enter one more item on this order.

♦ Select the **Product Code** field on the second line of the **Main** 'page' and enter the **Product Code** as C-MAH-S.

♦ There is no need to change anything in the **Product Item Line** dialogue box so [**Tab**] to or click in the **Qty** field and enter the quantity as 5. When you press the [**Tab**] key after the last entry an 'Insufficient Stock' warning should appear. Ignore this and click the **OK** button to remove the warning from the screen. A back order for the outstanding amount will be generated automatically when this order is processed further.

♦ Select the **Order Details** tab button at the top of the **Sales Order** Entry window.

The following **Order Details** 'page' should now be displayed allowing you to enter additional details relating to the order:

♦ Enter the following details:

Customer Order No.	654765
Due Despatch	150396

♦ To enter the Footer details for the order select the **Footer Details** tab button at the top of the **Sales Order** Entry window. The **Footer Details** 'page', similar to the following, should now be displayed:

```
 ─                          Sales Order                        ▼  ▲
┌──────────────────────────────────────────────────────────────┐
│  │  Main  │  Order Details  │ Footer Details                  │
│  ┌─Carriage────────────────────────────────────────────────┐ │
│  │  Net      [0.00        🔳]  T/c   [T1  17.50   ±]         │ │
│  │  V.A.T.        [0.00   🔳]  Gross [          0.00]        │ │
│  │  N/C      [          🔍]  Dept.  [0                    ±] │ │
│  └─────────────────────────────────────────────────────────┘ │
│  ┌─Settlement Terms────────────────────────────────────────┐ │
│  │  Days     [0      ]       Amount [          0.00]        │ │
│  │  Discount %    [     0.00] Total [        628.63]        │ │
│  └─────────────────────────────────────────────────────────┘ │
│  ┌─Global──────────────────────────────────────────────────┐ │
│  │  N/C      [          🔍]  Details [                    ] │ │
│  │  Tax Code [T1  17.50  ±]  Dept.  [0                    ±]│ │
│  └─────────────────────────────────────────────────────────┘ │
│  [ Save ] [ Abandon ] [ Print ] [ Complete ]      [ Close ]   │
└──────────────────────────────────────────────────────────────┘
```

♦ Again, similar to Invoice entry, the **Footer Details** 'page' for the order is divided into three sections allowing you to input details relating to **Carriage**, **Settlement Terms** and **Global** values. Enter the following details in the **Settlement Terms** section:

Days   : 30
Discount %   : 10

♦ Since both items on the order are Small Cabinets the whole order can be analysed to one tax code, nominal code and department. Make the following entries in the **Global** section and these will override the corresponding entries made in the **Product Item Line** dialogue box.

N/C   : 4003
Details   : Mahogany and Yew Cabinets
Tax Code   : T1 17.50
Dept   : 3 TV/Hi-Fi

This means that when the invoice produced from this order is posted only one line representing the total amount will be added to the Audit Trail.

♦ Select the **Main** tab button at the top of the **Sales Order** Entry window and the **Main** 'page' will be redisplayed. Note that the VAT figures have been adjusted to reflect settlement discount.

The entries for order No. 1 are complete and you now have the following options:

1 **Print**   This button enables you to print the order straight away.

2 **Save**   This button will save the order for batch printing and further processing later.

3 **Complete**   This button allows you to save and despatch the order, print the delivery note, update the product records and create an invoice for the order.

4 **Abandon**   Use this button to clear the entries you have made and start again.

♦ We will save our order for batch printing later so click the **Save** button. The **Sales Order** Entry window will refresh, ready to receive details of the next order.

Note: If you wish to edit an existing sales order after it has been saved enter the order No. in the **Order No.** field in the **Sales Order** Entry window and press the **[Tab]** key. An **Information** dialogue box may appear displaying the current status of the order. If so, click the **OK** button in this dialogue box and the order should appear allowing you to amend where necessary.

If you have already despatched all or part of a sales order you cannot decrease the quantity of any product ordered to less than the quantity which has already been despatched.

We will now record the details of another two orders.

♦ Enter the following details for order No. 2:

Order No.	: 2
Order Date	: 110396
A/C Ref	: BOYD
Product Code	: C-ASH-S
Qty	: 4

♦ Select the **Save** button at the bottom of the **Sales Order** Entry window and the window will clear, ready to receive the details of the next order.

♦ Enter the following details for order No. 3:

Order No.	: 3
Order Date	: 110396
A/C Ref	: ABBEY
Product Code	: C-ASH-L
Qty	: 3

♦ Select the **Save** button at the bottom of the **Sales Order** Entry window then **Close** the **Sales Order** Entry window.

♦ The **Sales Orders** window should display the three orders showing the order No., date, customer name and amount for each. If you wish to edit an order at this point you should select it in this window and click the **Sales Order Entry** button.

At this point the orders have simply been recorded, no processing has been done and no entries have been made to the product records.

Print sales order

One or more sales orders can be printed by first of all selecting the order(s) in the **Sales Orders** window and then selecting the **Print Sales Orders** button.

♦ We'll print order No. 1 so select (highlight) this in the **Sales Orders** window and click the **Print Sales Orders** button.

♦ When the **Print Sales Order** window opens select the file **New Sales Order (A4)** in the **Layout** panel (the file description is **A4 Sales Order** in Version 3.10 of the program); this is one of the standard sales order layout files supplied by Sage and is designed for A4 paper. Select **Printer** in the **Output** panel and click the **Run** button.

♦ Click the **OK** button in the **Print** dialogue box and order No. 1 should be printed.

♦ **Close** the **Print Sales Order** window.

Note: The sales order which you have just produced is using one of the standard layouts supplied with the program. However, sales order layout and content can be amended to suit your requirements or you can design a new layout.

Allocate stock to order

There are two option buttons in the **Sales Orders** window which allow you to allocate stock to selected sales orders. Stock must be allocated to an order before you can record its despatch.

(a) The **Amend Despatches** option enables you to manually allocate (and despatch) all or part of the stock required for an order. This option can also be used to alter an allocation which has already been made, cancel an order, put an order on hold and to keep track of orders.

(b) The **Allocate** option allows you to automatically allocate stock to selected orders. A full allocation will be made if possible and if there is insufficient stock to satisfy any of the orders you will be advised of this and as much stock as possible will be allocated. If you wish to make a part-allocation only you should use the **Amend Despatches** option.

To allow us to examine both options we'll allocate stock to order No. 1 using the **Amend Despatches** button and to order Nos. 2 and 3 using the **Allocate** button.

♦ Select (highlight) sales order No. 1 in the **Sales Orders** window and click the **Amend Despatches** button. The **Amend Allocations** and **Despatches** window, similar to the following, should now open:

Amend Allocations & Despatches							

Budget Electric
12 Old School Walk

Newcastle

NC5 6DF

Order No. 1
Date 10/03/96
Order Value 619.26
A/C Ref BUDGET

Product Code	Description	Ordered	Despatched	Outstanding	Allocated	This Despatch
C-YEW-S	Small Yew Cabinet	2.00	0.00	2.00	0.00	0.00
C-MAH-S	Small Mahogany Cabinet	5.00	0.00	5.00	0.00	0.00

Off Order   Allocate All   Despatch   <   >   Close

The **Amend Allocations** and **Despatches** window lists each product from the sales order and manual stock allocations and despatches for each product can be made by entering the appropriate amounts in the **Allocated** and **This Despatch** fields. If there is not enough stock to cover the amount entered in the **Allocated** field you will be given a warning and the maximum amount possible will be allocated to the order.

The **Allocate All** button at the bottom of the window can be used to allocate the full amount of stock to each product item on the order and once again a warning will be given if there is insufficient stock to satisfy the order for any item.

♦ Since we wish to make a full allocation of stock, if possible, to each product item on order No. 1 click the **Allocate All** button now.

♦ When the small **Amend Despatch** dialogue box opens asking if you wish to fully allocate all items with available stock click the **Yes** button.

♦ A **Warning** dialogue box should now appear advising you that there is insufficient stock to allocate all items. Click the **OK** button to remove the warning from the screen. The **Allocated** field for each product item should now show the amount of stock which has been allocated to the order. Note that there has been a full allocation of 2 for Small Yew Cabinets and a part-allocation of 4 for Small Mahogany Cabinets. The **Allocated** quantity for each product also appears in the **This Despatch** field. These entries have simply been made in preparation for recording a despatch and can be amended if necessary when the details of the actual despatch are entered.

♦ If you wish to alter an allocation which has already been made simply change the entry in the **Allocated** field. If you wish to unallocate all allocated stock for the entire order or cancel the order select the **Off Order** button at the bottom of the **Amend Allocations** and **Despatches** window. When the **Order Status** dialogue box opens you can then select to unallocate stock, cancel the order or put the order on hold.

◆ **Close** the **Amend Allocations & Despatches** window and you will be returned to the **Sales Orders** window where the **Allocated** status for order No. 1 should be PART.

We'll now automatically allocate stock to order Nos. 2 and 3.

◆ Click the **Clear** button at the bottom of the **Sales Orders** window to deselect order No. 1.

◆ Select (highlight) order Nos. 2 and 3 and click the **Allocate** button.

◆ A small dialogue box should now appear asking you to confirm that you wish to allocate all stock to selected orders. Click the **Yes** button.

The **Sales Orders** window should now show the **Allocated** status for order Nos. 2 and 3 to be FULL indicating that there is sufficient stock to fully satisfy both orders.

◆ Ensure that order Nos. 2 and 3 are still selected in the **Sales Orders** window and click the **Amend Despatches** button. The **Amend Allocations & Despatches** window should now open displaying the details for order No. 2. As you have already seen the facilities in this window can be used to manually allocate and record the despatch of stock. However, it can also be used as an 'enquiries' window to check on the 'allocated' and 'despatched' status of individual items on an order.

The **Allocated** field for order No. 2 should show a full allocation of 4 Small Ash Cabinets.

◆ Click the ⊟ button at the bottom of the **Amend Allocations & Despatches** window and the details for order No. 3 should be displayed showing a full allocation of 3 Large Ash Cabinets.

◆ **Close** the **Amend Allocations & Despatches** window then **Close** the **Sales Orders** window.

Product records and sales order reports

When stock is allocated to an order the **Allocated** and **Free Stock** fields in the appropriate product record are updated. We'll now check that this has taken place.

◆ Select the **Products** option in the **Desktop** window and when the **Products** window opens select (highlight) the four products included in your sales orders: Large Ash, Small Yew, Small Ash and Small Mahogany Cabinets.

◆ Click the **Product Record** button and the first record should be displayed showing an entry in the **Allocated** field. The **Free Stock** field should have been reduced to reflect the allocation. You can 'move' through your records using the ⊟ button and check that the stock allocations have been made.

◆ **Close** the **Product Record** window when you are finished viewing.

The **Activity** button in the **Products** window gives you access to transaction details for the selected products. The **Qty Allocated** and **Qty Available** fields in the **Product Activity** windows should have also been updated to reflect the stock allocations.

◆ **Close** the **Products** window.

The following three reports can be accessed using the **Reports** button in the **Sales Orders** window:

(a) *Despatched Sales Orders* – This report shows orders that have been partly or wholly despatched.

(b) *Outstanding Sales Orders* – This report shows orders that have been partly or fully allocated and are awaiting despatch.

(c) *Back Orders* – This report shows orders that are not yet fully allocated, i.e. they may be totally unallocated or only part allocated.

♦ Select all three orders in the **Sales Orders** window and click the **Reports** button.

♦ When the **Sales Order Processing Reports** window opens select **Outstanding Sales Orders** in the **Layout** panel, select the **Output** medium as **Preview** and click the **Run** button.

The Preview window should now open and display the Outstanding Sales Orders report. All three orders should be shown on the report.

♦ **Close** the Preview window.

♦ When you return to the **Sales Order Processing Reports** window select **Back Orders** in the **Layout** panel, select the **Output** medium as **Preview** and click the **Run** button.

The Back Orders report should show order No. 1.

Note: Version 3.10 of the program has an additional report called **Sales Orders Shortfalls**. If you are using this version the report will show the shortfall of one Small Mahogany Cabinet for order No. 1.

♦ **Close** the Preview window then **Close** the **Sales Order Processing Reports** window.

Record despatch of stock

There are two option buttons in the **Sales Orders** window which enable you to record the despatch of stock for selected sales orders.

(a) The **Amend Despatches** option enables you to manually record the despatch of all or part of the stock required for an order.

(b) The **Despatch** option allows you to automatically record the despatch of stock for selected orders. This option assumes that you are despatching all the stock which has been previously allocated to the selected orders. If you wish to despatch only a part of an order you should use the **Amend Despatches** option.

In both cases you can only record the despatch of stock which has already been allocated to the order.

When you record the despatch of stock you can also print a delivery note, update the product records and create a product invoice for the amount of stock being despatched.

We'll record the despatch of stock for order No. 1 using the **Amend Despatches** option and for order Nos. 2 and 3 we'll use the **Despatch** option.

These routines involve an automatic posting where the date on the computer's clock will be used as the transaction date. So, before proceeding:

♦ Set the program date to 15/03/96.

When you have set the date proceed as follows:

♦ Ensure that the **Sales Orders** window is open.

♦ Click the **Clear** button at the bottom of the **Sales Orders** window to deselect any orders which may still be selected.

♦ Select (highlight) order No. 1 and click the **Amend Despatches** button.

The details for order No. 1 should now be displayed in the **Amend Allocations & Despatches window**.

When stock was allocated to this order the amounts allocated were automatically entered in the **This Despatch** fields. However, these figures can be amended if you wish to record a part despatch.

♦ Since we wish to record a full despatch of the amounts allocated click the **Despatch** button at the bottom of the window.

♦ The **Despatch Order** dialogue box should now open giving you the option to print a delivery note and/or update the product records and create an invoice. Ensure that the **Update Stock and Invoicing** option button is selected and that the others are deselected. Click the **OK** button and you will be asked to confirm that you wish to update stock and invoicing. Click the **Yes** button and you will be returned to the **Amend Allocations &· Despatches** window where the **Despatched** fields should now show the quantities despatched for each product and the **Allocated** and **This Despatch** fields should be clear. The **Outstanding** field for Small Mahogany Cabinets should show an amount outstanding of 1.

♦ **Close** the **Amend Allocations & Despatches** window and you will be returned to the **Sales Orders** window where the **Despatched** status for order No. 1 should be PART.

We'll now automatically record the despatch of stock for order Nos. 2 and 3.

♦ Click the **Clear** button at the bottom of the **Sales Orders** window to deselect order No. 1.

♦ Select (highlight) order Nos. 2 and 3 and click the **Despatch** button.

♦ A small dialogue box should appear asking if you wish to print a delivery note for the orders. Click the **No** button. A small **Confirm** dialogue box should now open asking you to confirm that you wish to create invoices and update stock for the selected orders. Click the **Yes** button.

When you return to the **Sales Orders** window the **Despatched** status for order Nos. 2 and 3 should be COMPLETE.

♦ **Close** the **Sales Orders** window.

Note that at this point the product records have been updated to record the despatches and invoices have been generated. *No entries have been made yet to the ledger accounts.*

Product records and sales order reports

We'll now check the product records to note the effect of the despatch.

♦ Select the **Products** option in the **Desktop** window and when the **Products** window opens select (highlight) the four products concerned: Large Ash, Small Yew, Small Ash and Small Mahogany Cabinets.

♦ Click the **Product Record** button and the first record should be displayed.

♦ The **Allocated** field should be blank and the **In Stock** field should have been reduced to reflect the despatch. You can 'move' through your records using the ⯈ button and check that the product despatches have been recorded appropriately.

♦ **Close** the **Product Record** window when you have finished viewing.

♦ From the **Products** window click the **Activity** button. Click **OK** in the **Date Range** dialogue box and the **Product Activity** window should display the transaction details for the first product. There should be a Goods Out entry (with a transaction date of 15/03/96) to record the despatch and the **Qty Allocated** field should now be blank. Again you can use the ⯈ button to display the activity details for the selected products.

♦ **Close** the **Product Activity** window then **Close** the **Products** window.

♦ Select the **Sales Orders** option in the **Desktop** window.

♦ When the **Sales Orders** window opens select all three orders and click the **Reports** button.

♦ When the **Sales Order Processing Reports** window opens select the **Output** medium as **Preview** and **Run** each of the sales order report files.

Order No. 1 should be listed as a back order for one Small Mahogany Cabinet. Order Nos. 1, 2 and 3 should be listed as despatched with a complete delivery for 2 and 3 and a part delivery for order No. 1.

♦ Close the **Sales Order Processing Reports** window then **Close** the **Sales Orders** window.

Cancel sales orders

A sales order can be cancelled provided its **Despatched** status in the **Sales Orders** window is not COMPLETE. When you cancel an order its details will be retained and it will remain in the **Sales Orders** window with a status of CANCEL until it is deleted using the **Delete** option.

The procedure is as follows:

♦ Select the sales order(s) you wish to cancel in the **Sales Orders** window and click the **Amend Despatches** button.

♦ When the **Amend Allocations & Despatches** window opens click the **Off Order** button.

♦ When the **Order Status** dialogue box appears select the **Cancel Order** option button and then click **OK**.

When an order is cancelled the **Off Order** button in the **Amend Allocations** and **Despatches** window changes to **Order**. The **Allocated** and **Free Stock** fields on the appropriate product record(s) will be updated to reflect the cancellation.

Note: The **Cancel Order** button cancels the entire order. If you only wish to cancel one item on the order, select the **Sales Order Entry** option in the **Sales Orders** window and when the **Sales Order** Entry window opens select any field on the required row then delete the row using the **Delete Row** option on the **Edit** menu.

If you wish to put a cancelled order back on order select the **Order** button in the **Amend Allocations** and **Despatches** window.

Print invoice and update ledgers

You have seen that recording the despatch of an order through Sales Order Processing updates the product records automatically since the Order Processing and Product routines are integrated. However, the ledger accounts (customer, sales and tax) have not yet been affected. The transaction details will be entered in these accounts when the invoices generated from the orders are used to update the ledgers. We'll do that now.

♦ Select the **Invoicing** option in the **Desktop** window.

When the **Invoicing** window opens, invoices 1230, 1231 and 1232 should appear at the bottom of the list.

These invoices can be printed using the **Print Invoices** button and the ledger accounts can be updated with the invoice details using the **Update Ledgers** button.

♦ Select Invoices 1230, 1231 and 1232 and click the **Update Ledgers** button.

♦ When the **Update Ledgers** dialogue box appears select the **Output** medium as **Preview** and click the **OK** button.

A report of the update should now appear on screen in the Preview window.

♦ **Close** the Preview window and when you return to the **Invoicing** window the **Posted** status of all three invoices should be **Yes**.

♦ **Close** the **Invoicing** window.

Accounting entries

The following entries should have been made to the ledger accounts. Check the transaction details of the accounts concerned.

Order No. 1 (Invoice No. 1230)
Budget Electric's A/c (BUDGET) in the Sales Ledger (**Customers**)	Dr	532.45
Small Cabinet Sales A/c (4003) in the **Nominal Ledger**	Cr	460.00
Sales Tax Control A/c (2200) in the **Nominal Ledger**	Cr	72.45
Debtors Control A/c (1100) in the **Nominal Ledger**	Dr	532.45

Order No. 2 (Invoice No. 1231)

Boyd Brothers A/c (BOYD) in the Sales Ledger (**Customers**)	Dr	329.00
Small Cabinet Sales A/c (4003) in the **Nominal Ledger**	Cr	280.00
Sales Tax Control A/c (2200) in the **Nominal Ledger**	Cr	49.00
Debtors Control A/c (1100) in the **Nominal Ledger**	Dr	329.00

Order No. 3 (Invoice No. 1232)

Abbey Brothers Ltd A/c (ABBEY) in the Sales Ledger (**Customers**)	Dr	387.75
Large Cabinet Sales A/c (4004) in the **Nominal Ledger**	Cr	330.00
Sales Tax Control A/c (2200) in the **Nominal Ledger**	Cr	57.75
Debtors Control A/c (1100) in the **Nominal Ledger**	Dr	387.75

PURCHASE ORDER PROCESSING

This routine enables you to create and print purchase orders for the products you buy and update the product records with the order details. You can keep track of the purchase orders you've raised and record any deliveries you've had for them.

Enter order details

The procedure for entering Purchase Order details is very similar to that for Sales Orders.

♦ Select the **Purchase Orders** option in the **Desktop** window.

♦ Click the **Purchase Order Entry** button in the **Purchase Orders** window.

The **Purchase Order Entry** window should now open with the **Main** 'page' displayed.

♦ Enter the following details:

Order No.	:	1
Order Date	:	120396
A/C Ref	:	CHEUNG
Product Code	:	C-MAH-S You can enter a non-stock item here using the code S1 or S2.

♦ Ensure that the insertion cursor is in the **Description** field showing Small Mahogany Cabinet and click the Edit button at the end of the field.

♦ Enter the following details to the **Product Item Line** dialogue box:

Quantity	:	10
Unit Price	:	55.00 The change to the cost price here will be saved back to the Product Record.
Discount %	:	0.00
Discount	:	0.00

♦ Click **OK** at the bottom of the **Product Item Line** dialogue box and you will be returned to the **Main** 'page' where the details on line 1 should now be complete.

◆ Select the **Product Code** field on the second line and enter the following details:

Product Code : C-YEW-S

Product Item Line details

Quantity	: 10
Unit Price	: 60.00
Discount %	: 0.00
Discount	: 0.00

◆ Click the **OK** button to return to the **Main** 'page'.

There is nothing to be entered on the **Order** or **Footer Details** 'pages'.

The entries for order No. 1 are complete and you now have the following options:

(a) **Print**   This button allows you to print the order straight away.

(b) **Save**   This button will save the order for batch printing and further processing later.

(c) **Complete** This button enables you to save the order, put it 'on order', record the full delivery of it now and update the product records.

(d) **Abandon** Use this button to clear the entries you have made and start again.

◆ We will save our order for batch printing and further processing later so click the **Save** button.

The **Purchase Order Entry** window will refresh, ready to receive details of the next order.

Note: If you wish to edit an existing purchase order after it has been saved enter the order No. in the **Order No.** field in the **Purchase Order Entry** window and press the **[Tab]** key. An **Information** dialogue box may appear displaying the current status of the order. If so, click the **OK** button in this dialogue box and the order should appear allowing you to amend where necessary.

◆ We have another two purchase orders to enter now. Enter the following details for order No. 2:

Order No.	: 2
Order Date	: 120396
A/C Ref	: BEAVER
Product Code	: C-ASH-S

Product Item Line details

Quantity	: 10
Unit Price	: 50
Discount %	: 0.00
Discount	: 0.00

◆ Click **OK** at the bottom of the **Product Item Line** dialogue box and you will be returned to the **Main** 'page'.

♦ Select the **Save** button at the bottom of the **Purchase Order Entry** window and order No. 2 will be saved for further processing later.

♦ Enter the following details for order No. 3:

Order No.	:	3
Order Date	:	120396
A/C Ref	:	KEENAN
Product Code	:	C-ASH-L

Product Item Line details

Quantity	:	10
Unit Price	:	70
Discount %	:	0.00
Discount	:	0.00

♦ Click **OK** at the bottom of the **Product Item Line** dialogue box.

♦ Select the **Save** button at the bottom of the **Purchase Order Entry** window then **Close** the **Purchase Order Entry** window.

♦ The **Purchase Orders** window should display the three orders showing the order No., date, supplier name and amount for each. If you wish to edit an order at this point you should select it in this window and click the **Purchase Order Entry** button.

At this point the orders have simply been recorded, no processing has been done and no entries have been made to the product records.

Print purchase order

♦ One or more purchase orders can be printed by first of all selecting the order(s) in the **Purchase Orders** window and then selecting the **Print Purchase Orders** button.

♦ We'll print order No. 1 so select (highlight) this in the **Purchase Orders** window and click the **Print Purchase Orders** button.

♦ When the **Print Purchase Order** window opens select the file **New Purchase Order (A4)** in the **Layout** panel (the file description is **A4 Purchase Order** in Version 3.10 of the program); this is one of the standard purchase order layout files supplied by Sage and is designed for A4 paper. Select **Printer** in the **Output** panel and click the **Run** button. Click the **OK** button in the **Print** dialogue box and purchase order No. 1 should be printed. **Close** the **Print Purchase Order** window.

Note: The purchase order which you have just produced is using one of the standard layouts supplied with the program. However, purchase order layout and content can be amended to suit your requirements or you can design a new layout.

Record order as 'On Order'

There are two option buttons in the **Purchase Orders** window which allow you to record your purchase orders as being 'on order'. An order must be put 'on order' before you can record any deliveries for it.

(a) The **Amend Deliveries** option allows you to manually record a purchase order as being 'on order'. This updates the 'On Order' level for the appropriate product record. You can also use this option to keep track of purchase orders and to cancel them if necessary.

(b) The **Order** option allows you to automatically record a batch of selected purchase orders as being 'on order'. This will update the 'On Order' level for each of the appropriate product records.

To allow us to examine both options we'll place order No. 1 'on order' using the **Amend Deliveries** option and we'll use the **Order** option for order Nos. 2 and 3.
Before proceeding:

♦ Set the program date to 12/03/96.

When you have set the date proceed as follows:

♦ Select (highlight) order No. 1 in the **Purchase Orders** window and click the **Amend Deliveries** button. The **Amend Deliveries** window, similar to the following, should now open:

The **Amend Deliveries** window lists each product from the purchase order and displays the **Ordered, Delivered, Outstanding** and **This Delivery** amounts for each item. These fields cannot be edited.

♦ To put purchase order No. 1 'on order' click the **Order** button at the bottom of the window. The **Order** button should now change to **Off Order** and if this is selected the products would be taken off order.

♦ **Close** the **Amend Deliveries** window and you will be returned to the **Purchase Orders** window where the **On Order** status for order No. 1 should be ON ORDER.

We'll now place order Nos. 2 and 3 'on order' automatically.

♦ Click the **Clear** button at the bottom of the **Purchase Orders** window to deselect order No. 1.

♦ Select (highlight) orders 2 and 3 and click the **Order** button.

♦ A small dialogue box should now appear asking you to confirm that you wish to place all selected items On Order. Click the **Yes** button.

♦ Another **Confirm** dialogue box should now appear asking if you wish to print the Purchase Orders. Click the **No** button.

When you return to the **Purchase Orders** window the **On Order** status for order Nos. 2 and 3 should be **ON ORDER**.

♦ **Close** the **Purchase Orders** window.

Product records and purchase order reports

When an order is put 'on order' the 'On Order' field in the appropriate product record is updated. We'll now check that this has taken place.

♦ Select the **Products** option in the **Desktop** window and when the **Products** window opens select (highlight) the four products included in your purchase orders: large ash, small yew, small ash and small mahogany cabinets.

♦ Click the **Product Record** button and the first record should be displayed showing an entry in the **On Order** field. Note that the **Last Ord Date** field has an entry which should be the program date when the product was placed 'on order'.

The **Cost Price** field should also have been updated with the latest cost price entered on the order.

♦ You can 'move' through your records using the ▷ button and check that the entries have been made.

♦ **Close** the **Product Record** window when you are finished viewing.

♦ The **Activity** button in the **Products** window gives you access to transaction details for the selected products. The **Qty On Order** field in the **Product Activity** window should also have been updated for the products on order.

♦ **Close** the **Products** window.

The following two reports can be accessed using the **Reports** button in the **Purchase Orders** window:

(a) **Outstanding Purchase Orders**;
(b) **Delivered Purchase Orders**.

♦ **Run** the **Outstanding Purchase Orders** file in the Preview window and all three orders should be displayed.

Record delivery of stock

There are two option buttons in the **Purchase Orders** window which enable you to record the delivery of stock for selected purchase orders.

(a) The **Amend Deliveries** option allows you to manually record a part or complete delivery of stock for an order.

(b) The **Deliver** option enables you to automatically record complete deliveries of stock for selected orders. This option assumes that you are recording a full delivery of stock for all selected orders. If you wish to record a part-delivery you should use the **Amend Deliveries** option.

In both cases you can only record deliveries for orders which have already been placed 'On Order'.

We'll record the delivery of stock for order No. 1 using the **Amend Deliveries** button and for order Nos. 2 and 3 we'll use the **Deliver** button.

These routines involve an automatic posting where the date on the computer's clock will be used as the transaction date so before continuing:

♦ Set the program date to 17/03/96.

When you have set the date proceed as follows:

♦ Click the **Clear** button at the bottom of the **Purchase Orders** window to deselect any orders which may still be selected.

♦ Select (highlight) order No. 1 and click the **Amend Deliveries** button.

The details for order No. 1 should now be displayed in the **Amend Deliveries** window.

Let's say that when the goods arrive there are only 8 cabinets of each type instead of 10.

♦ Click in the **This Delivery** field for the first product, delete the existing amount and enter 8. [Tab] to the **This Delivery** field for the second product, delete the existing amount and enter 8.

♦ Select the **Deliver** button at the bottom of the **Amend Deliveries** window.

♦ A small dialogue box should now appear asking you to confirm that you want to update your stock levels. Click the **Yes** button.

The **Delivered** fields for each product should both show an entry of 8 and the **Outstanding** fields should show an entry of 2.

♦ **Close** the **Amend Deliveries** window and you will be returned to the **Purchase Orders** window where the **Delivered** status for order No. 1 should be **PART**.

We'll now automatically record a complete delivery of stock for order Nos. 2 and 3.

♦ Click the **Clear** button at the bottom of the **Purchase Orders** window to deselect order No. 1.

♦ Select (highlight) order Nos. 2 and 3 and click the **Deliver** button.

♦ A small dialogue box should appear asking you to confirm that you wish to complete deliveries and update stock for the selected orders. Click the **Yes** button.

When you return to the **Purchase Orders** window the **Delivered** status for order Nos. 2 and 3 should be **COMPLETE**.

♦ **Close** the **Purchase Orders** window.

Product records and purchase order reports

We'll now check the product records to note the effect of the delivery.

♦ Select the **Products** option in the **Desktop** window and when the **Products** window opens select (highlight) the four products concerned: large ash, small yew, small ash and small mahogany cabinets.

♦ Click the **Product Record** button and the first record should be displayed.

♦ The **In Stock** and **Free Stock** fields should have increased by the amount of the delivery and the **On Order** field should have reduced by the delivery amount. You can 'move' through your records using the ⊳ button and check that the product deliveries have been recorded appropriately.

♦ **Close** the **Product Record** window when you are finished viewing.

♦ From the **Products** window click the **Activity** button. Click **OK** in the **Date Range** dialogue box and the **Product Activity** window should display the details for the first product. There should be a Goods In entry (with a transaction date of 17/03/96) to record the delivery and the **Qty on Order** field should have been reduced by the amount of the delivery. Again you can use the ⊳ button to display the activity details for the selected products.

♦ **Close** the **Product Activity** window then **Close** the **Products** window.

♦ Select the **Purchase Orders** option in the **Desktop** window.

♦ When the **Purchase Orders** window opens select all three orders and click the **Reports** button.

♦ When the **Purchase Order Processing Reports** window opens select the **Output** medium as **Preview** and **Run** the two purchase order report files. Order No. 1 should be listed as outstanding for 2 small mahogany and 2 small yew cabinets. Order Nos. 1, 2 and 3 should be listed as delivered with a complete delivery for 2 and 3 and a part delivery for order No. 1.

♦ **Close** the **Purchase Order Processing Reports** window then **Close** the **Purchase Orders** window.

Cancel purchase orders

A purchase order can be cancelled provided its **Delivered** status in the **Purchase Orders** window is not COMPLETE. When you cancel an order its details will be retained and it will remain in the **Purchase Orders** window with a status of CANCEL until it is deleted using the **Delete** option.

The procedure is as follows:

♦ Select the purchase order(s) you wish to cancel in the **Purchase Orders** window and click the **Amend Deliveries** button.

♦ When the **Amend Deliveries** window opens click the **Off Order** button.

When an order is cancelled the **Off Order** button in the **Amend Deliveries** window changes to **Order**. The **On Order** fields on the appropriate product record(s) will be updated to reflect the cancellation.

Note: The **Off Order** button cancels the entire order. If you only wish to cancel one item on the order, select the **Purchase Order Entry** option in the **Purchase Orders** window and when the **Purchase Order** Entry window opens select any field on the required row then delete the row using the **Delete Row** option on the **Edit** menu.

If you wish to put a cancelled order back on order, select the **Order** button in the **Amend Deliveries** window.

Update ledgers

You have seen that recording the delivery of an order through Purchase Order Processing updates the product records automatically since the Order Processing and Product routines are integrated. However, the ledger accounts (supplier, purchases and tax) are not affected. The transaction details would be entered to these accounts in the usual way using the **Batch Invoices** routine in the **Suppliers** window when the invoice arrives from the supplier.

PROCESSING BACK ORDER FOR SALES

We now have enough small mahogany cabinets in stock to satisfy the back order for Budget (sales order No. 1). To process this proceed as follows:

♦ Set the program date to 18/03/96.

♦ In the **Sales Orders** window select order No. 1 and click on the **Amend Despatches** button.

The **Amend Allocations** and **Despatches** window should now open and the **Outstanding** field for small mahogany cabinets should show that there is one outstanding.

♦ Click in the **Allocated** field for small mahogany cabinets, enter 1 and press the **[Tab]** key. The **Allocated** and **This Despatch** fields should now show an entry of 1 for this product.

♦ Now click the **Despatch** button.

♦ When the **Despatch Order** dialogue box appears ensure that the **Update Stock and Invoicing** option button is selected and that the others are deselected.

♦ Click the **OK** button and you will be asked to confirm that you wish to update stock and invoicing. Click the **Yes** button and you will be returned to the **Amend Allocations** and **Despatches** window where the **Despatched** field for small mahogany

cabinets should show a quantity despatched of 5 and the **Outstanding** field should
be clear.

♦ **Close** the **Amend Allocations** and **Despatches** window and you will be returned to
the **Sales Orders** window where the **Despatched** status for order No. 1 should now
be COMPLETE.

Product records and sales order reports

♦ From the **Products** window check the **Activity** report for small mahogany cabinets.
This should show a Goods Out entry of 1 with a transaction date of 18/03/96.

♦ **Close** the **Product Activity** and **Products** windows and return to the **Sales Orders**
window.

♦ Select all three orders in the **Sales Orders** window and click the **Reports** button. If
you now **Run** the **Despatched Sales Orders** file in the Preview window all three
orders should be listed as being despatched complete. The **Outstanding Sales
Orders** and **Back Orders** files should both be blank.

♦ **Close** the **Sales Order Processing Reports** window then **Close** the **Sales Orders**
window.

Print invoice and update ledgers

♦ Select the **Invoicing** option from the **Desktop** window.

When the **Invoicing** window opens the new invoice (1233) to Budget Electric should
be listed with the others. Select this invoice and click the **Update Ledgers** button.

♦ When the **Update Ledgers** dialogue box appears select the **Output** medium as
Preview and click the **OK** button. A report of the update should now appear on
screen in the Preview window.

♦ **Close** the Preview window.

When you return to the **Invoicing** window the **Posted** status for invoice 1233 should
now be **Yes**.

♦ **Close** the **Invoicing** window.

Accounting entries

The following entries should have been made to the ledger accounts to record the
posting of invoice 1233. Check the transaction details of the accounts concerned.

Budget Electric A/c (BUDGET) in the Sales Ledger (**Customers**)	Dr	86.81
Small Cabinet Sales A/c (4003) in the **Nominal Ledger**	Cr	75.00
Sales Tax Control A/c (2200) in the **Nominal Ledger**	Cr	11.81
Debtors Control A/c (1100) in the **Nominal Ledger**	Dr	86.81

Note: A settlement discount of 10 per cent was offered on sales order No. 1 so the tax
is calculated on a net figure of £67.50 rather than £75.00.

PROCESSING OUTSTANDING PURCHASE ORDER

We will now record the delivery of two small yew and two small mahogany cabinets from our supplier Cheung-Li Production PLC. This delivery will complete purchase order No. 1.

♦ Set the program date to 20/03/96.

♦ In the **Purchase Orders** window select order No. 1 and click on the **Amend Deliveries** button.

The **Amend Deliveries** window should now open and the **Outstanding** fields for Small Mahogany and Small Yew Cabinets should each have an entry of 2. Enter 2 in the **This Delivery** fields for Small Mahogany and Small Yew Cabinets.

♦ Click the **Deliver** button at the bottom of the window. When the **Confirm** dialogue box opens asking you to confirm that you wish to update stock levels with all items allocated click the **Yes** button.

The **Delivered** fields for each product should both show an entry of 10 and the **Outstanding** fields should be clear.

♦ **Close** the **Amend Deliveries** window and you will be returned to the **Purchase Orders** window where the **Delivered** status for order No. 1 should now be shown as **COMPLETE**.

Product records and purchase order reports

The **Activity** report for Small Yew and Small Mahogany Cabinets should now show a Goods In (GI) entry of 2 and the **Qty on Order** should be 0.

Update ledgers

Remember the ledger accounts would still have to be updated when the invoice arrives from the supplier.

DELETE ORDERS

When orders are complete they can be deleted using the **Delete** button on the **Order Processing** windows. Before doing this you should take a backup copy of your data files.

To remove the deleted records from the data files the **Compress** files option within the **Disk Doctor** routine would have to be used.

CHAPTER 9

Exercise and Suggested Solution

COMPUTERISED ACCOUNTING: ASSESSMENT EXERCISE FOR USE WITH SAGE STERLING FOR WINDOWS

A small computer dealer Crinan Systems who buys and sells hardware and software has decided to computerise his accounting system from 1 January 1996 using Sage software. As the accounts clerk for the dealer you are required to set up the necessary accounts, enter opening balances thereto, record the transactions for the month of January and produce a Profit and Loss A/c and Balance Sheet at the end of January.

Carry out the following tasks:

1   Zero the data files using the **New Data** (or **Rebuild**) option in **Disk Doctor**. During this routine you should indicate that you wish to use the default nominal structure and set the financial year start date to January 1996.

2   Set up a tax code (T3) for VAT on fuel and power at 8 per cent.

3   Set up the following accounts:

Sales Ledger (Customer) Accounts		*Purchase Ledger (Supplier) Accounts*	
Account reference	*Name, Town and Credit Limit*	*Account reference*	*Name, Town and Credit Limit*
(a) LEX	Lexicon Enterprises GLASGOW CL 8000	(a) HARD	Hardware Supplies BOURNEMOUTH CL 4000
(b) SUN	Sun Valley Electronics CARDIFF CL 5000	(b) SOFT	Software Supplies NEWCASTLE CL 5000
(c) MILLER	Miller Promotions OXFORD CL 4000	(c) POWER	Central Electric BIRMINGHAM CL 0
(d) IRIS	Iris Fashion Supplies HASTINGS CL 3000	(d) FROST	Frost & Fraser COVENTRY CL 0

4   You will need the following nominal ledger accounts. Set them up or modify the default nominal ledger accounts as necessary.

Account code	Account name	Account code	Account name
0040	Office Furniture	5000	Purchases
0050	Motor Vehicles	5200	Opening Stock
0051	M/V Depreciation	5300	Cost of Goods Sold
1001	Closing Stock (BS)	5500	Purchases Returns
1100	Debtors Control	6201	Advertising
1103	Prepayments	7003	Salaries
1200	Bank Current Account	7100	Rent
1230	Cash Account	7200	Electricity
2100	Creditors Control	7301	Motor Repairs
2109	Accruals	7801	Cleaning
2200	Sales Tax Control	8003	Vehicle Depreciation
2201	Purchase Tax Control	9998	Suspense
3000	Capital		
4000	Sales		
4500	Sales Returns		

5 Enter the following balances to your customer and supplier accounts at 1 January:

Customers Ref.	Opening balance (£)	Suppliers Ref.	Opening balance (£)
LEX	1500 (Dr)	HARD	1300 (Cr)
IRIS	1200 (Dr)	SOFT	900 (Cr)

6 Zero the balances in the Nominal Ledger accounts (Debtors Control, Creditors Control and Suspense), which have been created automatically as a result of entering opening balances to the customer and supplier accounts.

7 The opening nominal Ledger Balances at 1 January 1996 were as follows:

	£
Office Furniture	2000
Motor Vehicles	13000
Opening Stock	15500
Cash	800
Bank Current Account	2200
Debtors	2700
Creditors	2200
Capital	34000

Enter these balances to the accounts at 1 January using the Journal Entry routine.

8 The following transactions took place during January. Make the necessary entries to the ledger accounts.

(a) Sales invoices sent out:

Date	Customer	Details	Net amount (£)	Tax code	Invoice number
Jan 3	Lexicon Enterprises	Computers (4), Printers (3)	5500	T1	1250
Jan 6	Sun Valley Electronics	Portable computers (3)	4000	T1	1251
Jan 11	Miller Promotions	Wordprocessing software	280	T1	1252

(b) Purchase invoices received:

Date	Supplier	Details	Net amount (£)	Tax code	Invoice number
Jan 12	Hardware Supplies	Computer and Printer	1900	T1	9343
Jan 15	Software Supplies	Games Software and discs	387	T1	5634
Jan 29	Central Electric	Electricity	81.60	T3	001249
Jan 29	Frost & Fraser	Rent (1 Jan – 31 Mar)	720	T2	004315

(c) Credit notes sent out:

Date	Customer	Details	Net amount (£)	Tax code	CN number
Jan 12	Lexicon Enterprises	Computer (damaged in transit)	1000	T1	1350

(d) Credit notes received:

Date	Supplier	Details	Net amount (£)	Tax code	CN number
Jan 26	Software Supplies	Floppy discs damaged	47	T1	00431

(e) Cheques received from customers:

Date	Customer	Cheque number	Amount (£)
Jan 19	Miller Promotions	667588	200
Jan 19	Sun Valley Electronics	946454	4700

(f) Cheques paid to suppliers:

Date	Supplier	Cheque number	Amount (£)	
Jan 21	Hardware Supplies	421412	3000	– use to pay off opening balance and part-pay invoice 9343
Jan 31	Frost & Fraser	421414	720	

(g) Nominal ledger transactions:

(i)   £100 transferred from Bank Current A/c to Cash A/c on 18 January.

(ii) Paid £18.80 (inc. VAT) cash for motor repairs on 22 January (petty cash voucher number PC30).

(iii) Paid £15 cash for office cleaning on 26 January (petty cash voucher number PC31). This is a non-VAT transaction.

(iv) £3000 withdrawn from Bank Current A/c on 28 January to pay the salaries bill for the month of January (cheque number 421413).

(v) Sold four boxes of blank discs for cash on 28 January. The price was £35.25 including VAT.

Record these transactions using the routines in the **Bank Accounts** window.

9 Transfer the balances on the Opening Stock, Purchases and Purchases Returns Accounts to the Cost of Goods Sold Account. Enter a closing stock figure of £14500 to the Cost of Goods Sold Account and the Closing Stock (BS) Account.

10 The following adjustments should be made to the accounts at the end of January:

(a) Depreciate the motor vehicles by £300.

(b) Rent paid in advance at 31 January is £480.

(c) An advertising bill for £500 is due but unpaid.

These adjustments should be made by journal entry.

11 Produce a printout of the VAT Return Analysis and the Trial Balance at 31 January.

12 Using the Trial Balance as a guide design a Chart of Accounts layout for the Final Accounts – Profit and Loss A/c and Balance Sheet.

13 Produce a printout of the Final Accounts.

14 Take a backup copy of your data files.

SUGGESTED SOLUTION

Trial Balance

Date: 31/01/96   **CRINAN SYSTEMS**
Current Trial Balance

N/C	Name	Debit	Credit
0040	Office Furniture	2000.00	
0050	Motor Vehicles	13000.00	
0051	Motor Vehicles Depreciation		300.00
1001	Closing Stock (BS)	14500.00	
1100	Debtors Control Account	8116.50	
1103	Prepayments	480.00	
1200	Bank Current Account	280.00	
1230	Cash	901.45	
2100	Creditors Control Account		1920.13
2109	Accruals		500.00
2200	Sales Tax Control Account		1541.75
2201	Purchase Tax Control Account	401.33	
3000	Capital		34000.00
4000	Sales		9810.00
4500	Sales Returns	1000.00	
5300	Cost of Goods Sold	3240.00	
6201	Advertising	500.00	
7003	Salaries	3000.00	
7100	Rent	240.00	
7200	Electricity	81.60	
7301	Motor Repairs	16.00	
7801	Cleaning	15.00	
8003	Vehicle Depreciation	300.00	
	Totals:	48071.88	48071.88

Profit and Loss Account

Date: 31/01/96

CRINAN SYSTEMS
Current Profit & Loss Financial Report

		This Month	**Year-To-Date**
Turnover			
Sales		9810.00	9810.00
less Returns In		−1000.00	−1000.00
	Totals:	8810.00	8810.00
Cost of Sales			
Cost of Goods Sold		3240.00	3240.00
	Totals:	3240.00	3240.00
	Gross Profit:	5570.00	5570.00
Overheads			
Advertising		500.00	500.00
Salaries		3000.00	3000.00
Rent		240.00	240.00
Electricity		81.60	81.60
Motor Repairs		16.00	16.00
Cleaning		15.00	15.00
Depreciation − Vehicles		300.00	300.00
	Totals:	4152.60	4152.60
	Net Profit:	1417.40	1417.40

Balance Sheet

Date: 31/01/96

CRINAN SYSTEMS
Current Balance Sheet

		This Month		Year-To-Date	
Fixed Assets					
Office Furniture		2000.00		2000.00	
Motor Vehicles		13000.00		13000.00	
less depreciation		−300.00		−300.00	
	Totals:		14700.00		14700.00
Current Assets					
Stock		14500.00		14500.00	
Debtors		8116.50		8116.50	
Bank		280.00		280.00	
Cash		901.45		901.45	
Prepayments		480.00		480.00	
	Totals:		24277.95		24277.95
Current Liabilities					
Creditors		1920.13		1920.13	
Accruals		500.00		500.00	
VAT Liability		1140.42		1140.42	
	Totals:	3560.55		3560.55	
	Current Assets less Liabilities:	20717.40		20717.40	
	Net Assets:	35417.40		35417.40	
Capital & Reserves					
Capital		34000.00		34000.00	
P&L Account		1417.40		1417.40	
	Totals:	35417.40		35417.40	

PART 2

An Introduction to the Use and Application of Spreadsheets using Microsoft® Excel: Version 5

CHAPTER 10

Introduction

What is a Spreadsheet? · **Loading Microsoft® Excel** · **The Spreadsheet Screen** · **Maximise the Worksheet Window** · **The Keyboard – Useful Keys** · **Moving Around the Worksheet** · **Help** · **Exiting Microsoft® Excel**

WHAT IS A SPREADSHEET?

A spreadsheet is essentially the electronic equivalent of a pencil, an eraser, a calculator and a large paper worksheet ruled with lines to give rows and columns. The computer's screen can only display a small portion of the worksheet at any one time – the full worksheet is much too big to be displayed all at once.

The worksheet consists of a large number of cells, each cell being the intersection of a row and a column. You can enter text or numbers to these cells and where you want to perform a calculation you would enter a formula. The software will carry out calculations very quickly and perform update calculations equally quickly when the initial data is changed. Spreadsheets are ideal for answering 'what if' questions. Given a set of assumptions (e.g. prices, costs, rate of inflation, etc.) the spreadsheet can be used as a tool to show what would happen if the parameters were to change. This kind of sensitivity analysis can be carried out accurately with ease and speed if care has been taken when building the initial model. A well-designed model would provide the new results in seconds, whereas the paper model would need to be recalculated from scratch. Most spreadsheets also have a graphics facility which allows results shown in a table to be displayed in the form of a graph or chart.

Spreadsheets are principally used for dealing with numeric data – sales, costs, profit projections, financial forecasting, budgeting, statistical modelling, etc. Consequently, they are an excellent tool for anyone working in the field of accounting and finance.

LOADING MICROSOFT® EXCEL

Microsoft® Excel is a spreadsheet program with graphics and database facilities which runs in the Windows® operating system.

Load the program and in a few seconds the spreadsheet screen should appear.

THE SPREADSHEET SCREEN

The spreadsheet screen showing the worksheet and the 'tools' should be similar to the following:

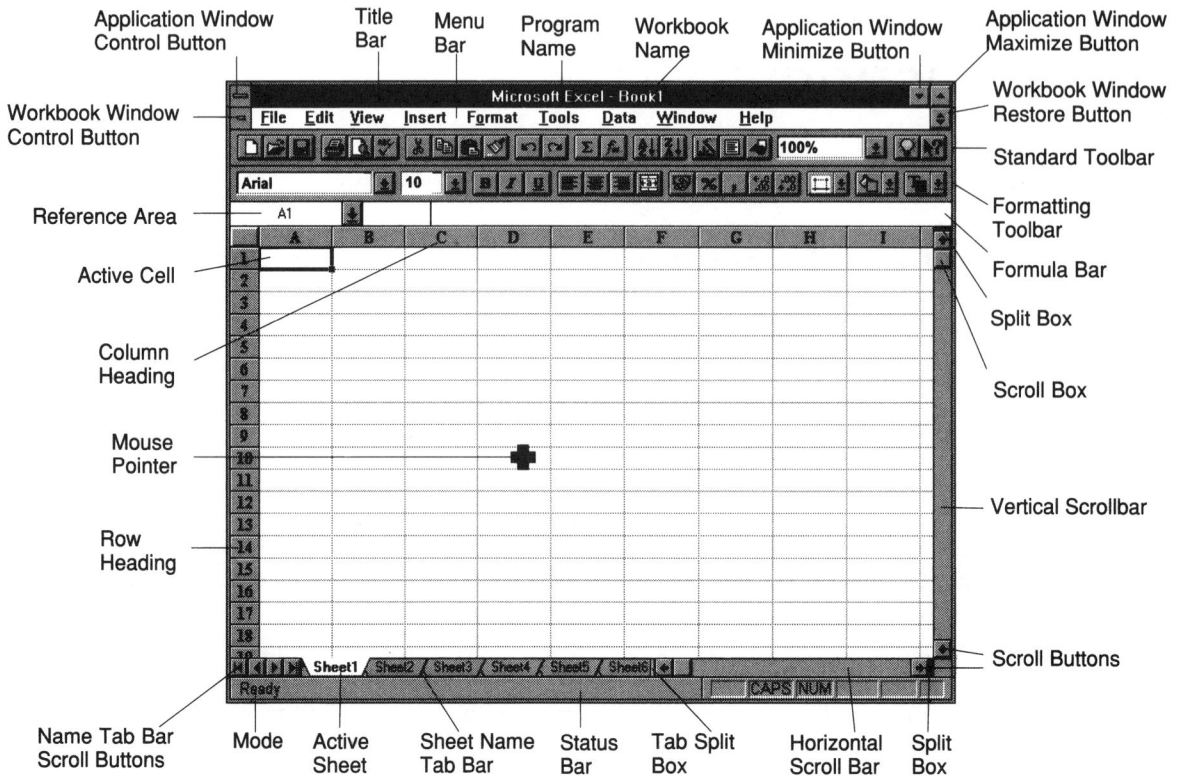

Your screen may not be exactly the same as this but you'll be shown how to modify it later in the chapter (see Maximise the Worksheet Window).

Worksheet, cell and active cell

Most of the work done in a spreadsheet package is carried out on a *worksheet*. The worksheet is like a grid of rows and columns. A *cell* occurs at the intersection of a row and column and each one has a unique address or reference, e.g. A1 (the home cell), B2 (column B, row 2), H5 (column H, row 5), etc. You can enter text, numbers or formulae into cells but before you can do this you must first make the cell ACTIVE. To make a cell active move the mouse pointer over it and click. The cell should now be surrounded by a heavy border. A cell can also be activated using the arrow keys on the keyboard. The four arrow keys can be used to move the active cell designator (the heavy border) around the worksheet.

At any one time you can only see a small portion of the full worksheet which consists of 256 columns and 16384 rows (4194304 cells).

Mouse pointer

Application programs for the Windows® operating system such as Microsoft® Excel and Microsoft® Word are designed to be used with a mouse. Moving the mouse causes the mouse pointer on the screen to move also. This can be used instead of the keyboard to carry out certain functions such as opening a menu, selecting a command from a menu, activating a Toolbar button or selecting a text box for data entry. The mouse pointer will change its shape depending on what it is 'pointing' at, e.g. it will be a cross shape (⊕) when located over a worksheet cell and an arrow shape (↖) when located over a menu option or a Toolbar button. If the pointer is not visible on the screen, move the mouse a little.

Title bar

The Title bar displays the name of the active file, i.e. the file currently being used. Microsoft® Excel gives each new file a name – Book1, Book2, Book3, etc. – until one is allocated by the user. Book1 is probably displayed in the Title bar at the moment.

Menu bar

This displays a list of the menu options – **File**, **Edit**, **View**, etc. These are 'pull-down' menus which contain the commands for carrying out specific tasks. Move the mouse pointer over the word **File** and click the left mouse button (this is called 'point and click'). The **File** menu containing the list of associated commands – **Open**, **Close**, **Save**, **Print**, **Exit**, etc. – should drop down. A command itself can be selected by pointing and clicking. Point and click anywhere outside the menu to close it.

Menu options and commands can also be selected using the keyboard. Notice that each menu option on the Menu bar has one of its letters underlined: **F**ile, **E**dit, **F**ormat, etc. To open a menu using the keyboard, hold down the [**Alt**] key and press the appropriate underlined letter. The corresponding menu should now drop down. Notice that each command on the menu also has one of its letters underlined. To activate one of the menu commands simply press the appropriate underlined letter or move the highlight bar over the command using the arrow key and press [**Enter**]. Press the [**Alt**] or [**F10**] key to close the menu.

Many commands can be activated directly from the keyboard without using the Menu. The key combinations for these commands are given alongside the command name on the menu.

Toolbar

This consists of a row of buttons which allow you to perform some of the most common spreadsheet activities at speed – sometimes called the 'speedbar' for this reason. The Toolbar acts as a shortcut to the menu commands for the more common tasks such as opening files, saving files, summing a column of figures, emboldening text, etc. Each button is activated by clicking on it.

If you allow the mouse pointer to hover over a button for a few seconds its name will appear next to the pointer and a short description of its function will be shown in the Status bar at the bottom of the screen. This is a very helpful feature and if it is not active you should 'switch it on' now in the following way:

♦ Open the **View** menu and select **Toolbars** from the list of commands.

The **Toolbars** dialogue box should now appear on screen listing the Toolbars which are available and identifying those which are currently displayed.

♦ Click the **Show ToolTips** check box at the bottom of the dialogue box and a cross should appear in it to show that it has been selected.

♦ Click the **OK** button in the dialogue box and you will be returned to the worksheet.

The Toolbar button names should now appear when you hover the pointer over the button.

Microsoft® Excel initially displays two Toolbars – *Standard* and *Formatting* – in the positions shown. However, Toolbars can be moved to different positions on the screen or removed altogether to give you more workspace. They can also be customised. You can choose the Toolbars you wish displayed by selecting the appropriate check boxes in the **Toolbars** dialogue box.

Formula bar

This bar shows the address of the active cell, e.g. A1, B2, C3, etc., in the reference area at the extreme left of the bar. Further along the bar the data or formula in the active cell is displayed.

Status bar

This bar displays information relating to a menu command when it is activated. Click on some of the menu options on the Menu bar and watch the information in the Status bar change. It performs a similar function for Toolbar buttons.

Row headings

These are the row references, e.g. 1, 2, 3, 4, etc.

Column headings

These are the column references, e.g. A, B, C, D, etc.

Scroll bars

These allow you to scroll the worksheet vertically and horizontally to bring other parts of it into view.

Active sheet and Sheet name tab bar

The main Microsoft® Excel document is called a workbook. A workbook is like a folder which contains several sheets, e.g. worksheets, chart sheets. The default number of sheets is 16 but you can have more. If you look at the bottom of the screen just above the Status bar you should see a series of tab buttons marked Sheet1, Sheet2, Sheet3 and so on. These are the default names for the sheets in the workbook and the tab buttons enable you to activate different sheets, i.e. bring them into the foreground so that you can work on them.

♦ If the tab buttons are not visible open the **Tools** menu and select **Options**. When the **Options** dialogue box opens click the **View** tab button at the top and select the **Sheet Tabs** check box (a cross will appear when selected). Click the **OK** button in the dialogue box and you will be returned to the worksheet where the sheet tab buttons should now be visible. If you still don't see them double click the tab split box at the extreme left of the horizontal scroll bar.

To activate a sheet click on its name tab button. This will bring the sheet into the foreground and the name on its tab button will become bold.

MAXIMISE THE WORKSHEET WINDOW

If your worksheet does not fill the screen completely as in the following example, point and click on the maximise button, ▲, at the extreme right of the Book1 Title bar. This will expand the worksheet area to display more rows.

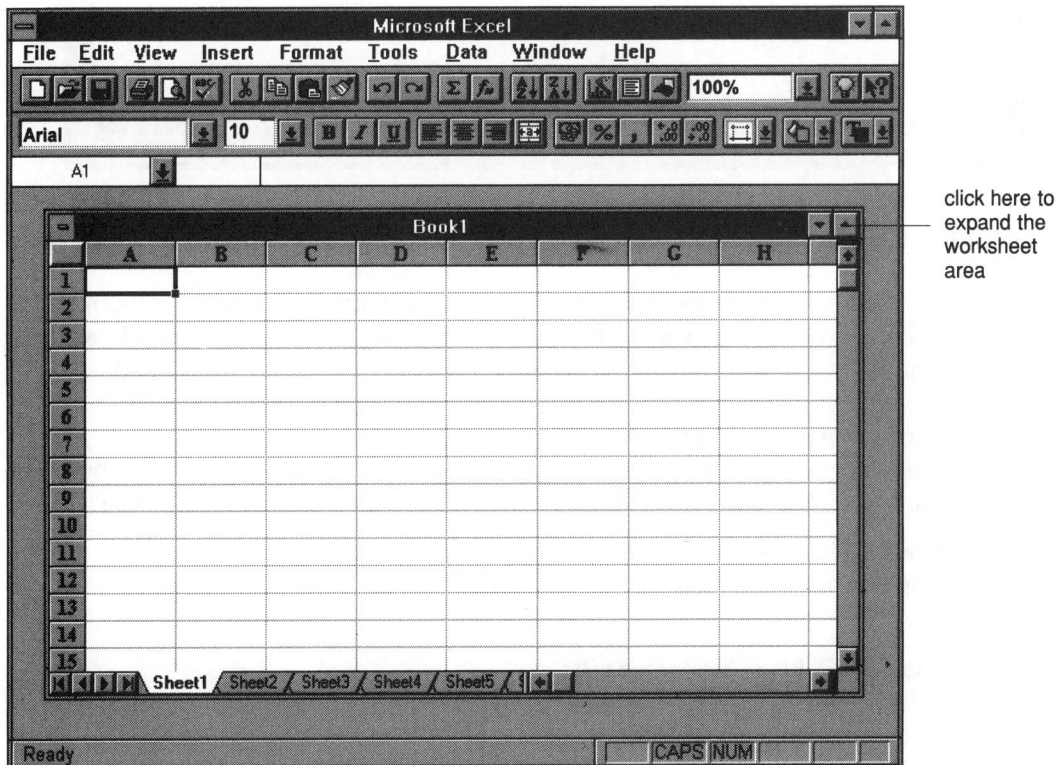

click here to expand the worksheet area

To allow you maximum visible work area, your screen should be similar to the following:

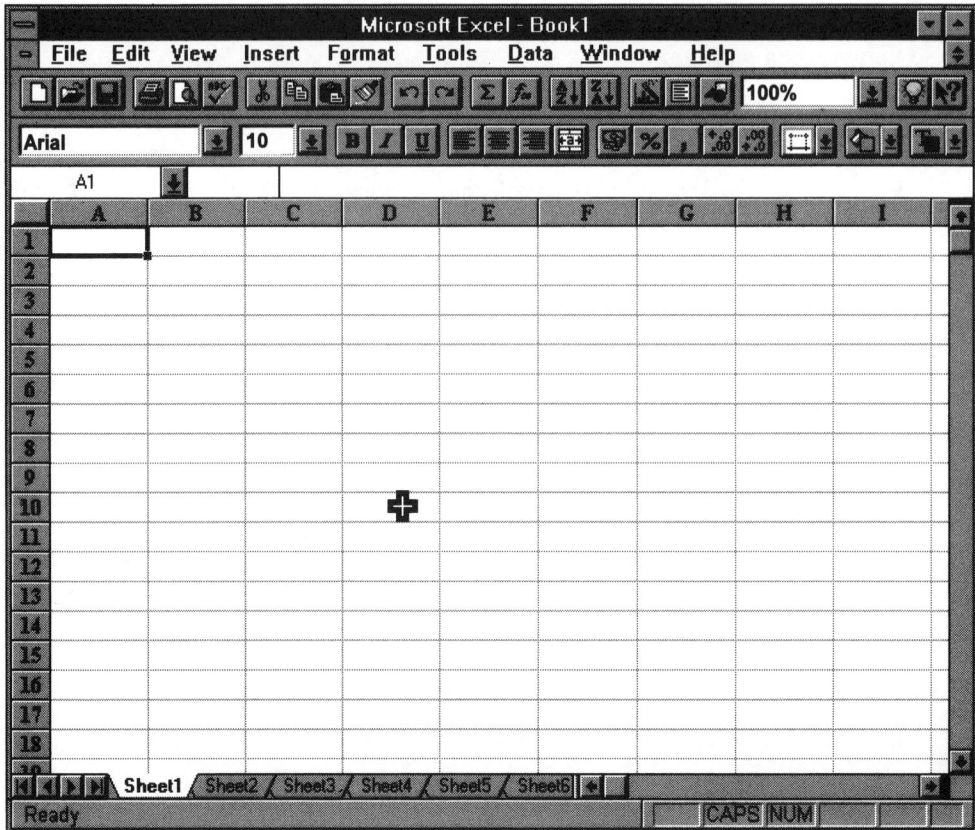

THE KEYBOARD – USEFUL KEYS

Before starting to learn about spreadsheets, it is important to know the location and function of several keys which you will use regularly. Familiarise yourself with the position of the following on your keyboard:

1   **The four ARROW keys: [↑] [↓] [←] [→]**
These keys will move the active cell designator (the heavy border) around the worksheet. They can also be used to make selections from pull-down menus.

2   **The ENTER key: [Enter], or [↵], or [Enter ↵]**
This key 'tells' the program you have selected a command or finished keying in an entry.

3   **The SHIFT key: [⇑], or [⇑ Shift]**
As on a normal typewriter, this key produces capital letters and the upper symbols on the non-letter keys. There is one located on each side of the letter keys on the keyboard.

4   **The ESCAPE key: [Esc]**
If pressed during a command sequence, it usually cancels the command and returns you step-by-step to the 'Ready' mode (Ready is displayed in the Status bar).

5   **The CONTROL key: [Ctrl]**
    Used when moving around the worksheet and selecting ranges of cells.

6   **The ALT key: [Alt]**
    Used to activate the pull-down menus and command sequences if you are using the keyboard instead of the mouse.

7   **The BACKSPACE key: [←]**
    Usually positioned above the **[Enter]** key. The backspace key is used to delete individual characters to the left of the insertion cursor when correcting or amending cell contents.

8   **The DELETE keys: [Del] and [Delete]**
    Used to delete individual characters to the right of the insertion cursor when correcting or amending cell contents. These keys can also be used to delete highlighted text.

9   **FUNCTION KEYS: [F1] . . . [F12]**
    These are located along the top of the keyboard and they are programmed to perform specific functions when Microsoft Excel is loaded, e.g. **[F1]** is the help key and **[F2]** is the edit key.

MOVING AROUND THE WORKSHEET

You can move around the worksheet using the mouse or the keyboard keys.

Mouse

1   *Vertical Scroll Bar*. This bar allows you to scroll the worksheet vertically. Click on the arrow button at the top or bottom of the bar to move up or down one row at a time. There is a third button on the bar; the scroll box. If you click and drag this button you can move several rows at a time. Click and drag means point to the box, click and hold down the mouse button and drag the pointer along the scroll bar (the box will follow). If you click the scroll bar area below or above the scroll box the worksheet will scroll down or up a screenful at a time.

2   *Horizontal Scroll Bar*. This operates in a similar way to the vertical bar and allows you to scroll the worksheet horizontally.

Keyboard keys

Key(s)	Movement
[↑] [↓] [←] [→]	One cell at a time (in direction of arrow).
[PageUp] and [PageDown]	Up or down one screen.
[Alt] + [PageUp]	Left one screen.
[Alt] + [PageDown]	Right one screen.

Note: [**Alt**] + [**PageUp**]	Means press and hold down the [**Alt**] key while pressing the [**PageUp**] key.
[**Home**]	To the beginning of the row.
[**Ctrl**] + [**Home**]	To the beginning of the sheet (cell A1).
[**Ctrl**] + [**End**]	To the last cell containing data in the sheet.
[**F5**] function key	This activates the **Go To** dialogue box where you can specify the exact cell reference you wish to move to.

The **Go To** dialogue box and the Name box on the Formula bar can also be used to move from one position in the worksheet to another.

The Go To Dialogue box

♦ Select the **Edit** pull down menu.

♦ Select the **Go To** option from the **Edit** menu.

♦ The **Go To** dialogue box should now open allowing you to enter a cell reference. If you enter a cell reference here and click the **OK** button, you will be returned to the worksheet which will have moved to the area of the new cell (now the active cell).

The Formula bar

In the reference area at the extreme left of the Formula bar the address of the active cell is displayed. If you click in this area, type a new address and press the [**Enter**] key, the worksheet will move to the area of the new cell address (now the active cell).

HELP

When first learning how to use spreadsheets, some of the detailed information is difficult to remember. Even users who have become familiar with spreadsheet techniques require help from time to time in performing certain tasks. However, assistance is constantly available from the comprehensive **Help** facility. This can be accessed by pressing the [**F1**] function key or by selecting the **Help** option from the Menu bar.

Click on the word **Help** on the Menu bar and the **Help** pull-down menu will appear. Click on the **Contents** option on this menu and the **Help** window will open displaying a list of contents. If you move the mouse pointer slowly over the list of contents, the pointer will change from an arrow to a hand shape as it passes over a topic. So for help on a particular topic, move the mouse pointer to that topic and when it changes to a hand, click the mouse button. A further **Help** window displaying contents on the selected topic should open and the selection procedure is similar (point and click).

To close the **Help** window, open the **File** menu on the **Help** menu bar and select **Exit**. This should return you to the worksheet.

Microsoft® Excel can also search for **Help** on a particular topic entered by the user. This facility can be accessed using the **Search for Help On ...** option on the **Help** menu.

The help system is context-sensitive. You will find that most of the dialogue boxes have a **Help** button and selecting this will give you assistance in the particular task you are carrying out.

There is also a **Help** button on the standard Toolbar marked thus ⬚.

◆ Click on this button and a question mark sign will attach itself to the mouse pointer.

◆ Place this on top of another Toolbar button and click. A **Help** window should now open up explaining the use and purpose of this button.

Help may be obtained for any command, key combination or screen area using the same procedure.

◆ If the **Help** button just described is not available on the Toolbar, press the **[Shift]** + **[F1]** keys together and this will produce the context-sensitive pointer.

◆ The help pointer can be removed from the screen by pressing the **[Esc]** key.

There is also an on-line tutorial facility covering the essential features of the software. This can be accessed from the **Help** menu.

EXITING MICROSOFT® EXCEL

The following is the exit procedure, although you are not required to do this at the moment.

◆ Select the **Exit** command from the **File** menu.

If you have forgotten to save your work you will be prompted to do so now.

CHAPTER 11

Creating a Worksheet and Working with Files

Selecting Cells and Cell Ranges · Entering Text and Numbers to Worksheet Cells · Editing and Clearing Cell Contents · Altering Column Width and Row Height · Entering Formulae to Worksheet Cells · Saving a File · Backup Copies of Files · Closing a File · Opening a File

Ensure that Microsoft® Excel is 'loaded' and Sheet1 displayed on screen.

SELECTING CELLS AND CELL RANGES

Before you can perform an operation on the contents of a cell or range of cells such as entering data, copying, formatting or printing, you must first select that cell or range.

Selecting a single cell

Make sure you are in Ready mode – bottom left corner of screen (in Status bar) should display 'Ready'. A cell can be selected using the arrow keys or by pointing and clicking with the mouse.

When a cell is selected it becomes active – it is surrounded by a heavy dark border and the address and contents of the cell are displayed in the Formula bar.

Selecting a range of cells

Range of adjacent cells

♦ Using the mouse, point to cell D1.

♦ Press and hold down the left mouse button while you drag the pointer down to cell D10. Release the mouse button. This operation is referred to as 'click and drag'.

Cells D1 to D10 should be surrounded by a heavy dark border and D2 to D10 should be dark. You have just selected the range of cells D1 to D10, referred to as D1:D10, and your worksheet should be similar to the following:

	A	B	C	D	E	F	G	H	I
1									
2									
3									
4									
5									
6									
7									
8									
9									
10									
11									
12									
13									
14									
15									
16									
17									
18									

♦ To deselect, click anywhere on the worksheet.

Range containing several rows and columns

♦ Point to cell D1.

♦ Click and hold down the left mouse button while you drag the pointer down to cell D10 then, without releasing the button, pull the pointer to the right over columns E and F. When the three columns are dark release the mouse button and the range of cells D1:F10 should now be selected, similar to the following:

	A	B	C	D	E	F	G	H	I
1									
2									
3									
4									
5									
6									
7									
8									
9									
10									
11									
12									
13									
14									
15									
16									
17									
18									

♦ Click anywhere on the worksheet to deselect the range.

Range of non-adjacent cells

♦ Select the cell range D1:D10.

♦ Now, *while holding down the [Ctrl] key on the keyboard*, point to cell F1, click and drag down to F10 and release the mouse button then the **[Ctrl]** key.

♦ Hold down the **[Ctrl]** key again and select the range H1:H10.

When you have finished, you should have selected three separate ranges of non-adjacent cells, similar to the following:

	A	B	C	D	E	F	G	H	I
1									
2									
3									
4									
5									
6									
7									
8									
9									
10									
11									
12									
13									
14									
15									
16									
17									
18									

♦ Click anywhere on the worksheet to deselect these ranges.

Selecting all cells in the worksheet

All cells in the worksheet can be selected by clicking the Select All button. This is located in the top left corner of the worksheet immediately above the row 1 heading and to the left of the column A heading. This can be used for global formatting, e.g. if you want to change the font of all cells in the worksheet.

Click anywhere on the worksheet to deselect all cells.

If you have experienced any difficulty with the cell selection procedure, you should practise since it is a skill you will be using quite often.

ENTERING TEXT AND NUMBERS TO WORKSHEET CELLS

We will now build a small, fairly simple worksheet and use this task to describe some of the main spreadsheet features. Using forecasts for sales and costs for a new product, we will produce a profit projection for a 12 month period for Consumer Gadgets, a company which has recently been set up to manufacture food processors. It is anticipated that the costs for each processor will be as follows:

Material   : £15
Labour   : £10
Variable overhead   : £2.50

In addition, fixed costs of £50000 per month will be incurred.

The marketing manager has produced the following sales forecast based on a price of £50 per processor:

	JAN	FEB	MAR	APR	MAY	JUN
Sales (units)	4000	4000	4000	4300	4300	4500

In the first instance we'll produce a worksheet which is similar to the following and extend it to cover 12 months later:

MONTH	JAN	FEB	MAR	APR	MAY	JUN
Sales (units)	4000	4000	4000	4300	4300	4500
Selling price	50	50	50	50	50	50
Sales revenue	200000	200000	200000	215000	215000	225000
COSTS:						
Material per unit	15	15	15	15	15	15
Total material	60000	60000	60000	64500	64500	67500
Labour per unit	10	10	10	10	10	10
Total labour	40000	40000	40000	43000	43000	45000
Variable overheads per unit	2.50	2.50	2.50	2.50	2.50	2.50
Total variable overheads	10000	10000	10000	10750	10750	11250
Fixed overheads	50000	50000	50000	50000	50000	50000
Total costs	160000	160000	160000	168250	168250	173750
Profit/Loss	40000	40000	40000	46750	46750	51250

We will build the worksheet in stages. Don't worry if we deviate from this layout initially – we'll modify it later. Carry out the following tasks:

♦ Click on cell A1 to activate it. When selected, the cell should be surrounded by a heavy border and A1 should appear in the reference area of the Formula bar.

♦ Type MONTH and press the [**Enter**] key (or click the 'tick' button, ☑, in the Formula bar). You must press [**Enter**] or click the 'tick' button to complete an entry to a cell.

The label, MONTH, should now appear in cell A1.

♦ Click on cell B1 (or 'move' to cell B1 using the arrow keys).

♦ Type JAN and press [**Enter**] or click the 'tick' button.

JAN should now appear in cell B1.

♦ Click on cell A3.

♦ Type Sales revenue and press [**Enter**].

The label, Sales revenue, should now appear in cell A3. The text is actually too wide and will overflow into column B but don't worry about this – we'll adjust the column width later.

♦ Click on cell B3.

♦ Type 4000 and press [**Enter**].

The value 4000 should now appear in cell B3.

By making an entry to cell B3 the overflow from cell A3 has been removed. Don't worry, it's still there, you just can't see it.

Notice also at this point that text is automatically aligned to the left of the cell and numbers are right-aligned. You will learn later how to alter alignment to suit your requirements.

EDITING AND CLEARING CELL CONTENTS

If you notice a mistake before clicking the 'tick' button or pressing the **[Enter]** key you can cancel the entry completely using the **[Esc]** key or the cancel button, **X**, on the Formula bar or you can correct the mistake using the **[Backspace]** key to delete the characters in the usual way. If the entry has been made to the cell and you wish to cancel it select the **Undo Entry** command from the **Edit** menu or click the **Undo** button on the standard Toolbar. If an entry has been made to a cell and you wish to change it, you can simply activate the cell again and retype the entry. The new entry will overwrite existing cell contents. If you wish to edit a cell's contents, you must first activate the cell and this will display the cell entry in the Formula bar. You then have two choices; you can make the alteration in the Formula bar or in the cell itself.

We will change the contents of cell A3 from Sales revenue to Sales (units).

♦ Activate cell A3 and watch the text, Sales revenue, appear in the Formula bar.

♦ Move the mouse pointer on to the Formula bar. The shape of the pointer will change from a cross to an I shape. Position the pointer at the end of the word revenue and click. An insertion cursor (vertical bar) will now flash allowing you to edit the contents. Using the **[Backspace]** key delete the word revenue, replace it with (units) and press the **[Enter]** key. The contents of cell A3 should have changed to Sales (units), although it will not all be visible yet.

♦ You can do the editing in the cell itself rather than in the Formula bar. To do this, simply *double click* on the cell (or activate the cell and press the **[F2]** function key) and the insertion cursor will appear allowing you to edit the contents. When editing is complete, click outside the cell or press the **[Enter]** key.

When you edit a cell containing a formula, the formula is displayed and the value is temporarily hidden.

♦ Try editing cell B3 directly; change the value from 4000 to 5000 then change it back again.

It is an easy matter to clear the contents of a cell or range of cells completely. To describe the procedure, enter the following values to the cells shown:

Cell	Value	Cell	Value
D1	1	E1	4
D2	2	E2	5
D3	3	E3	6

♦ Select cell D1 and open the **Edit** menu.

♦ From the **Edit** menu select **Clear** and from the **Clear** sub-menu select **All**.

You will be returned to the worksheet and the contents of cell D1 should have been cleared.

♦ Select the range D2:D3 and repeat the **Clear** procedure.

♦ Select the range E1:E3. Position the mouse pointer somewhere in the selected range and click the *right* mouse button. A shortcut menu should appear displaying the most useful commands for the selected cells. Select **Clear Contents** from the menu and you will be returned to the worksheet where cells E1:E3 should have been cleared.

Microsoft® Excel has a useful feature which allows you to '**Undo**' your last command in case you make a mistake.

♦ To illustrate, select **Edit** from the Menu bar and **Undo Clear** from the **Edit** menu.

The figures should reappear in cells E1:E3.

♦ Clear the range once again, by pressing the [**Del**] or [**Delete**] key.

Note: The **Clear Contents** command on the shortcut menu does not remove any formatting from the cell(s), nor does the [**Del**] or [**Delete**] key.

Now, to get back to building the worksheet. Carry on and complete the cell entries for column A as follows. Some of the entries will run over into the next column(s). Don't worry about this.

	A
1	MONTH
2	
3	Sales (units)
4	Selling price
5	Sales revenue
6	COSTS:
7	Material per unit
8	Total material
9	Labour per unit
10	Total labour
11	Var.o/heads per unit
12	Total var.o/heads
13	Fixed overheads
14	Total costs
15	Profit/Loss

ALTERING COLUMN WIDTH AND ROW HEIGHT

Column A is not wide enough to accommodate the labels we have inserted. However, it is a simple matter to alter the column width. There are several ways to do it.

1 ♦ Using the mouse, position the pointer on the border between column heading A and column heading B.

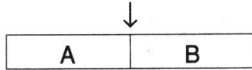

A	B

♦ When correctly located the pointer will change to a double headed arrow: ↔. Now click and hold down the mouse button and drag the pointer to the right until the column is wide enough to accommodate the labels fully. Note that the column width will be displayed in the reference area of the Formula bar while you are doing this.

2 ♦ Point to the column heading (A) and click. This will select the whole column (it will become dark).
♦ From the Menu bar select the **Format** option.
♦ From the **Format** menu select **Column** and from the **Column** menu select **Width**. The **Column Width** dialogue box should now open prompting you to enter a width.
♦ Enter the width as 8.43 and click the **OK** button.

The column width should have returned to its original size.

♦ You can deselect the column (remove the dark shading) by clicking on any cell.

3 ♦ Again point to the column heading (A) and click to select the whole column.
♦ From the Menu bar select **Format**.
♦ From the **Format** menu select **Column** and from the **Column** menu select **AutoFit Selection**. This will adjust the width to fit the longest entry.

4 ♦ Reset the width of column A to 8.43 (default width).
♦ If column A is still darkened deselect it.
♦ Position the mouse pointer on the border between column heading A and column heading B and double click the mouse button.

The width will be adjusted automatically to fit the longest entry.

You can adjust the widths of several columns at once. If several columns are selected and the width of one is adjusted using any of the methods described the other columns will be adjusted to the same width automatically.

Note: The heights of the rows can be altered in similar manner. However, the row height will adjust automatically to suit the largest font in the row.

Column A should now be wide enough to accommodate the longest entry.

ENTERING FORMULAE TO WORKSHEET CELLS

♦ Activate cell B4 and enter the value 50.
♦ Activate cell B5.

The contents of this cell should be the product of cells B3 and B4 (unit sales × selling price). The program will do the calculation for us if we enter the correct formula.

♦ Enter the formula =B3*B4 to cell B5 (* is used for multiply). The = sign at the beginning 'tells' the program that this is a formula to be solved rather than a piece of text.

The contents of cells B3 and B4 should have been multiplied together and the result entered in cell B5.

♦ Select cell B5 once again and enter B3*B4.

The contents of cell B5 should now be B3*B4 because the program interpreted the entry as text since it begins with a letter, rather than a formula.

♦ Now correct the entry in B5 to =B3*B4.

The worksheet should now show the number 200000 in cell B5 and if you select this cell the formula, =B3*B4, will be displayed in the Formula bar.

It is important to remember that when you enter a formula to a worksheet cell, you must precede it with the = sign.

Cell B5 is now linked to cells B3 and B4. If the contents of either of the latter two cells is changed, then B5 will change automatically.

♦ Select cell B3 and enter 6000.

Note that the contents of cell B5 have also changed, to 300000.

♦ Re-enter the correct value, 4000, to cell B3.

♦ Continue and enter the following values and formulae to the appropriate cells:

Cell	Value/Formula
B7	15
B8	=B3*B7
B9	10
B10	=B3*B9
B11	2.5
B12	=B3*B11
B13	50000
B14	=B8+B10+B12+B13
B15	=B5-B14

We can now show the advantage of entering formulae instead of actual values:

♦ Select cell B3 and change the value to 5000.

Changing the value in cell B3 will affect the values in cells B5, B8, B10, B12, B14 and B15 since they are all linked by formulae, directly or indirectly, to cell B3.

By linking cells using formulae in this way, a change to one cell will have a ripple effect throughout the worksheet. The spreadsheet is so powerful that these changes take place almost instantaneously. We have demonstrated the rapid recalculation facility in our worksheet which has only a few entries at the moment. Imagine the savings in time and effort with a very large worksheet. It may take some time at the beginning to build the model, but once designed, the template (model) can be used over and over again with different parameters.

♦ Re-enter the correct sales figure, 4000, to cell B3.

Your worksheet should now appear as follows:

	A	B	
1	MONTH	JAN	
2			
3	Sales (units)	4000	
4	Selling price	50	
5	Sales revenue	200000	← =B3*B4
6	COSTS:		
7	Material per unit	15	
8	Total material	60000	← =B3*B7
9	Labour per unit	10	
10	Total labour	40000	← =B3*B9
11	Var o/heads per unit	2.5	
12	Total var o/heads	10000	← =B3*B11
13	Fixed overheads	50000	
14	Total costs	160000	← =B8+B10+B12+B13
15	Profit/Loss	40000	← =B5–B14

The underlying formula will be displayed on the Formula bar when the relevant cell is selected.

♦ Select cell A17 in the worksheet and enter the label, MARGIN.

♦ Select cell B17 and enter a formula which will show the Profit as a percentage of Sales revenue (note the sign used for division is the forward slash, /).

The formula =(B15*100)/B5 will give you the correct margin, i.e. 20. We'll modify this later when dealing with percentage formats.

SAVING A FILE

You should get into the habit of saving your work regularly otherwise if the power goes down, you will lose everything you've done.

To save the worksheet you will need a formatted 'floppy' disc in drive a: or b:.

♦ Open the **File** menu (click on **File** in the Menu bar) and select the **Save** command.

Since this is the first time you have saved your file the following **Save As** dialogue box should open:

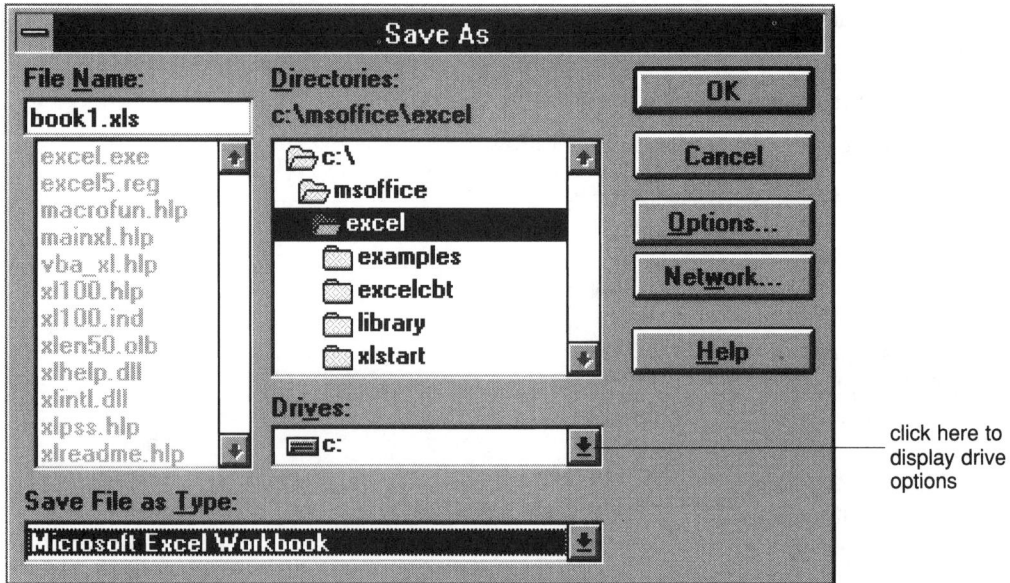

click here to display drive options

If you have not used the **Save As** dialogue box before it may appear confusing. However, in common with all dialogue boxes, there is a **Cancel** button which will return you to the worksheet if you make a mistake. The dialogue box allows you to give your file a name, specify the drive and directory it will be saved to (c:, a:, b:, etc.) and select the type of file it will be saved as. Be careful not to press the [**Enter**] key or click the **OK** button until the correct entries and selections have been made.

♦ Make the following entries:

1   *File name.* You must give your workbook file a name and this should be meaningful (for future recognition). Filenames can consist of up to 8 alphanumeric characters (including the _ sign) but there must be no spaces between characters. For example EXAMPLE1 is an acceptable filename; EX 1 is not, but EX_1 is. The **File Name** field at the top of the dialogue box should display a default name at the moment (e.g. book1.xls). Type the new name, LearnXL, and this will replace the default name – *do not press the* [**Enter**] *key after typing* in case your file is saved to the wrong drive.

2   *Drives.* The **Drives** field near the bottom of the dialogue box will display the name of the drive to which your file will be saved. The common options are c: for hard disc and a: or b: for floppy disc. You should save your file to floppy disc, so ensure that the correct letter is displayed in the **Drives** field; a: or b: depending on which drive your floppy is in. If the correct drive letter is not displayed, click on the [↓] button at the corner of the field and select (click on) the letter from the 'drop-down' list. Your selection (a: or b:) should now appear in the **Drives** field.

3   *File type.* Ensure that Microsoft® Excel Workbook is displayed in the **Save File as Type** field.

Note: You can 'move' from one field to the next in a dialogue box by clicking on the field, by pressing [**Alt**] and the underlined letter or by pressing the [**Tab**] key.

♦ Now select the **OK** button in the dialogue box. A **Summary Information** dialogue box may now open allowing you to enter details of the file's title, subject, author, key words and comments. Microsoft® Excel can use this information when searching for files (the analogy is searching for a book in a library). Do not enter anything to this dialogue box if it opens, simply click on the **OK** button and you will be returned to the worksheet. Either way, at this point your file should have been saved to floppy disc.

Note: If the **Summary Information** dialogue box does appear and you do not wish to use this facility, you can 'switch it off' in the following way:

♦ Select **Tools** from the Menu bar and **Options** from the **Tools** menu.

♦ Select the **General** index tab button from the **Options** dialogue box and click the **Prompt for Summary Info** check box (to remove the cross).

♦ Select the **OK** button in the **Options** dialogue box and you will be returned to the worksheet.

When you return to the worksheet after saving your file, note that the filename LearnXL.XLS is displayed in the Title bar at the top of the screen. Microsoft® Excel adds the file extension .XLS automatically.

You should develop the habit of saving your data regularly – it only takes a few seconds. If a 'disaster' happens, you can always revert to a previously saved file.

There is a **Save** button on the standard Toolbar to make saving even quicker.

BACKUP COPIES

You can elect to have a backup copy of your file made every time you save it. If you use this facility Microsoft® Excel will save the previous version of your file as a backup every time you save the updated version. To activate this facility select the **Options** button in the **Save As** dialogue box and when the **Save Options** dialogue box opens click the **Always Create Backup** check box (a cross will appear in it when selected). The backup copy will be created in the same directory as the original file. It will be given the same name as the original file but with the filename extension of .BAK.

CLOSING A FILE

To confirm that your file has been saved properly, you may wish to close down the workbook and open it up again from disc.

♦ Open the **File** menu and select the **Close** option.

The workbook will be closed and the worksheet part of the screen should be blank since there is no workbook in use.

OPENING A FILE

♦ Open the **File** menu.

Your file name should be listed near the bottom of the **File** menu. It can be opened by simply clicking on the name, but don't do that this time.

♦ Select the **Open** option from the **File** menu and the **Open** dialogue box should appear (similar to the **Save** box).

♦ Make sure that the correct floppy drive letter, a: or b:, appears in the **Drives** field. If not, change it.

♦ Select the file you wish to open (LearnXL.XLS) from the list displayed on the left side of the dialogue box and the name should appear in the **File Name** field.

♦ Click the **OK** button and your workbook file should be retrieved from disc and displayed on the screen.

There is an **Open** file button on the standard Toolbar.

If, when you tried to open your file, the name was not displayed in the dialogue box, it means that it has not been saved properly or it may have been saved to the hard disc instead of the floppy. If it has not been saved you will have to build the worksheet again. This time, save after every few entries and make sure you're doing it correctly.

CHAPTER 12

Extending the Worksheet

Entering a Data Series using Autofill · Entering Values to a Range of Cells · Copying a Value to a Range of Cells · Copying a Formula to a Range of Cells · Copying a Range of Cells · Copying using Fill Right · Copying a Formula using Autofill · Moving Data · Copying and Moving using 'Drag and Drop' · Inserting Rows, Columns and Blank Cells · Deleting Rows, Columns and Cells · Relative and Absolute Addressing

♦ Ensure that your workbook file, LearnXL, is open and Sheet1 displayed on screen.

ENTERING A DATA SERIES USING AUTOFILL

We'll now complete the entries to the worksheet for the six-month period and we'll try to make the process as easy and quick as possible by using the program's copying and automated data filling procedures.

First, we will complete row 1 with the months of the year. We could do this mechanically, entering each cell individually. However, the program has an automated procedure for completing data series such as months of the year, days of the week, number series, etc.

♦ Select cell B1.

Notice at the bottom right corner of the cell there is a small dark square. This is called the *fill handle*.

Active Cell → | JAN ■ | ← fill handle

♦ Position the mouse pointer over the fill handle, the pointer will change from a light cross to a dark cross when located correctly. Click and drag the pointer to the right through the range of cells C1:G1. Release the mouse button when you reach cell G1 and the first six months of the year will be entered automatically.

♦ If cells B1:G1 are still selected (darkened) click anywhere on the worksheet to deselect.

This procedure can be used to increment any value(s), which Microsoft® Excel recognises as a series, through a range. The following are some examples of values which the program would automatically increment:

This/these value(s):	*Would be extended to:*
1, 2 (selected in two adjacent cells)	3, 4, 5, etc.
10, 20 (selected in two adjacent cells)	30, 40, 50, etc.
January (Jan)	February (Feb), March (Mar), etc.
1st Quarter	2nd Quarter, 3rd Quarter, etc.
Period 1	Period 2, Period 3, etc.
1/3/96	2/3/96, 3/3/96, etc.

The values will only be incremented if Microsoft® Excel recognises them as a series.

Note: A value can also be incremented by choosing the **Fill** command from the **Edit** menu then **Series** from the sub-menu.

ENTERING VALUES TO A RANGE OF CELLS

The unit sales for each month can now be entered. These values can be inserted by selecting each cell individually and making the appropriate entry. However, there is a quicker method.

♦ Select the range of cells C3:G3.

♦ While this range is selected type the following values pressing the **[Enter]** key after each entry: 4000, 4000, 4300, 4300, 4500. These values should now appear in the cells as follows:

Cell no:	C3	D3	E3	F3	G3
Value:	4000	4000	4300	4300	4500

♦ Deselect the range C3:G3 by clicking anywhere on the worksheet.

COPYING A VALUE TO A RANGE OF CELLS

The following values are not expected to change over the six-month period: selling price, material cost per unit, labour cost per unit and variable overheads per unit. We therefore want to copy these values over the next five columns (C:G). There are several different ways of copying cell contents. We'll use a different method for each value and you can decide which you prefer.

Copying using the Main menu

♦ Select cell B4.

♦ Select **Edit** from the Menu bar then **Copy** from the **Edit** menu.

The selected area (cell B4) should now be surrounded by a flowing border. What the program has done so far is to copy the contents of the selected cell to an area in memory called the Clipboard.

♦ You must now 'tell' the program where you want the data copied to. Select the cell range C4:G4.

♦ Select **Edit** from the Menu bar then **Paste** from the **Edit** menu.

The price, 50, should now be copied (pasted) from the Clipboard into the cells C4:G4.

Notice that the flowing border remains around cell B4 allowing you to paste again if you require.

♦ Press the [**Esc**] key to remove the flowing border.

The procedure you have just completed is called **Copy** and **Paste** – copy from the worksheet to the clipboard and paste from the clipboard to another area in the worksheet. The information in one cell can be copied to another cell or to several cells as you have just seen.

Copying using the shortcut menu

♦ Select cell B7.

♦ Make sure the pointer is over cell B7 and click the right mouse button.

♦ When the shortcut menu opens select **Copy** and cell B7 will be surrounded by a flowing border.

♦ Select the cell range C7:G7.

♦ Make sure the pointer is located somewhere in the selected range and click the right mouse button.

♦ This time select **Paste** from the shortcut menu and the value 15 should be pasted into the cells C7:G7.

♦ Press [**Esc**] to remove the flowing border.

Copying using the Toolbar

♦ Select cell B9.

♦ Select (click) the **Copy** button on the standard Toolbar and cell B9 will be surrounded by the flowing border.

♦ Select the cell range C9:G9.

♦ Select (click) the **Paste** button on the standard Toolbar and the value 10 should be pasted into the cells C9:G9.

♦ Press [**Esc**] to remove the flowing border.

Copying using Autofill

♦ Select cell B11.

♦ Position the mouse pointer directly over the fill handle at the bottom right corner of the cell. When the pointer changes to a dark cross, click and drag the pointer to the right through cells C11:G11.

When you release the mouse button, the value 2.5 should be inserted to the cells C11:G11.

Notice that this time Autofill did not increment the value since Microsoft® Excel did not recognise it as a series.

Copying and pasting can also be carried out using the keyboard keys shown on the **Edit** menu.

The copy procedures you have just learned can be used on numbers, text and formulae.

COPYING A FORMULA TO A RANGE OF CELLS

The Sales revenue formula in cell B5 is =B3*B4 (sales*price). This formula will be the same (relatively) for the next five months so we can copy it across the range C5:G5.

♦ Select cell B5.

♦ Select **Edit** from the Menu bar then **Copy** from the **Edit** menu.

Cell B5 should be surrounded by a flowing border.

♦ Select the cell range C5:G5.

♦ Select **Edit** from the Menu bar then **Paste** from the **Edit** menu.

The sales revenue figures for the six-month period should now appear in the appropriate cells.

♦ Press **[Esc]** to remove the flowing border from cell B5.

Select cell B5 and examine the formula which appears in the Formula bar. It should be =B3*B4. We copied this formula across the next five columns. However, when the spreadsheet program copies a formula into one or more cells *it is not an absolute copy*, otherwise the same figure for sales revenue (200000) would appear in all six cells. The program copies formulae *relative to position*. To illustrate this, select cell B5 and then C5 and then D5 and so on. Stop each time and examine the formula in the Formula bar. You should see the following:

Selected cell:	B5	C5	D5	E5
Corresponding formula:	=B3*B4	=C3*C4	=D3*D4	=E3*E4

So remember, *when formulae are copied the program adjusts them automatically, relative to position.*

♦ Using one of the copying methods available to you, copy the formulae in cells B8 (total material costs) and B10 (total labour costs) over the next five months.

COPYING A RANGE OF CELLS

The copy command can be used to even greater effect to copy several cells at once. The cells to be copied become a range and they can contain text, numbers, formulae or any combination of these.

♦ Select the cell range B12:B15.

♦ Select **Edit** from the Menu bar then **Copy** from the **Edit** menu.

The flowing border should surround the cell range B12:B15.

♦ Select the cell range C12:G15 and press [**Enter**] (or select **Edit** and **Paste**).

Again the figures for each of the next five months will be calculated and entered in the worksheet almost instantaneously. Values (fixed overheads) are copied over unchanged and formulae are copied relative to position.

♦ If the flowing border around the range B12:B15 is still there, remove it by pressing the [**Esc**] key.

Note: A range of cells can also be copied by dragging the fill handle at the bottom of the selected range or by using the Toolbar buttons or the shortcut menu.

COPYING USING FILL RIGHT

There is an alternative and quicker way to perform the previous operation using the **Fill Right** facility. To illustrate this, clear the range of cells you have just filled, C12:G15, by selecting the range then **Edit/Clear/All**.

♦ Select the range B12:G15.

♦ Select **Edit** from the Menu bar.

♦ Select **Fill** from the **Edit** menu and **Right** from the **Fill** sub-menu.

Once again values and formulae will be copied across to the next five months.

COPYING A FORMULA USING AUTOFILL

♦ Select cell B17.

♦ Position the pointer over the fill handle and drag to the right through cells C17:G17.

♦ The profit margin figures for the next five months should be inserted to the appropriate cells.

MOVING DATA

Data can be moved from one location in the worksheet to another using one of a variety of techniques. To demonstrate the procedure we'll move the cell range, A17:G17, from row 17 to row 16.

♦ Select the cell range A17:G17.

♦ Open the **Edit** menu and choose **Cut**.

♦ Select cell A16:G16.

♦ Open the **Edit** menu and choose **Paste**.

The MARGIN label and figures should now be located in row 16.

The procedure you have just completed is called **Cut** and **Paste** and is used for moving data to a new location. This should not be confused with **Copy** and **Paste** which copies data to another location but also leaves the data in its original position.

As with **Copy**, the **Move** procedure can be carried out using the Toolbar (**Cut** and **Paste** buttons), shortcut menu and the keyboard keys.

COPYING AND MOVING USING 'DRAG AND DROP'

Copying and moving data over short distances on a worksheet can be carried out quickly with the mouse using the 'drag and drop' procedure.

To demonstrate, we'll move the cell range A16:G16 back to row 17.

♦ Select the range A16:G16.

♦ Position the mouse pointer anywhere along the lower or upper border of the selected range. When the pointer changes to an arrow shape (↖) click and hold down the left mouse button, drag the pointer down to row 17 and release the button. The MARGIN label and figures should now be relocated in row 17.

This procedure can be used to move selected cells in any direction across the worksheet. If you are moving the selection to a part of the worksheet which is not visible, the window will scroll when the pointer reaches the edge.

Drag and drop can also be used to copy selected cells to another location. In this case hold down the **[Ctrl]** key while you drag and drop.

Your worksheet should now appear as follows:

	A	B	C	D	E	F	G
1	MONTH	JAN	FEB	MAR	APR	MAY	JUN
2							
3	Sales (units)	4000	4000	4000	4300	4300	4500
4	Selling price	50	50	50	50	50	50
5	Sales revenue	200000	200000	200000	215000	215000	225000
6	COSTS:						
7	Material per unit	15	15	15	15	15	15
8	Total material	60000	60000	60000	64500	64500	67500
9	Labour per unit	10	10	10	10	10	10
10	Total labour	40000	40000	40000	43000	43000	45000
11	Var. o/heads per unit	2.5	2.5	2.5	2.5	2.5	2.5
12	Total var. o/heads	10000	10000	10000	10750	10750	11250
13	Fixed overheads	50000	50000	50000	50000	50000	50000
14	Total costs	160000	160000	160000	168250	168250	173750
15	Profit/Loss	40000	40000	40000	46750	46750	51250
16							
17	MARGIN	20	20	20	21.74419	21.74419	22.77778

INSERTING ROWS, COLUMNS AND BLANK CELLS

Our worksheet does not have a heading at the moment. We will first insert two blank rows at the top of the worksheet and then insert a heading.

♦ Select the first two rows in the worksheet by clicking on row heading 1 (located to the left of cell A1) and dragging the pointer down to row heading 2.

When you have successfully selected rows 1 and 2 they will both be darkened.

♦ Select **Insert** from the Menu bar then **Rows** from the **Insert** menu.

The worksheet should have moved down creating two blank rows at the top. When the worksheet is moved in this way the program automatically adjusts formulae references to reflect the new locations of data.

Note: Columns can be inserted to the worksheet in similar manner by selecting the column heading(s) and choosing **Columns** from the **Insert** menu. New blank column(s) are inserted to the left of the selected column(s).

If you wish to insert blank cells within a range of data first select the range of cells which are located at the position of insertion. Open the **Insert** menu and select the **Cells** command. When the **Insert** dialogue box opens choose the direction in which you want the selected cells to move in order to create space for the blank cells.

♦ Select cell A1 and enter the heading: CONSUMER GADGETS – PROFIT FORECAST 199X. Don't worry that the heading extends over several cells in row 1, we are not going to use these cells for anything else.

♦ Now **Save** your updated file.

♦ The **Save** dialogue box will not open this time since the program knows the name and drive location of your file. Should you wish a duplicate copy of your file for any reason, you would choose the **Save As** command from the **File** menu and when the dialogue box opens, give it a different name.

DELETING ROWS, COLUMNS AND CELLS

Rows, columns and cells can be deleted by first selecting then choosing **Delete** from the **Edit** menu. Once deleted, the following rows, columns or cells move to fill the space created and any formulae references are adjusted automatically.

Note: When you **Delete** cells they are removed from the worksheet and the surrounding cells move to fill the space created. When you **Clear** cells you simply clear the contents or formats and the cells themselves are left on the worksheet.

RELATIVE AND ABSOLUTE ADDRESSING

It is important that a spreadsheet model is designed in such a way as to be able to 'answer' easily 'what if' questions, e.g. *what* would the profit figures be *if* the price were dropped to £40? Or *what* would total costs be *if* the variable costs changed to

£2.75 per unit? The effect of these changes can be shown using the existing design but it would mean changing formulae in the main body of the worksheet and this could become quite time-consuming if the spreadsheet was large and complex. Ideally, these key variables – crucial values which are liable to change and which affect most of the other figures in the model – should be listed in a separate area of the worksheet so that they are easily identifiable and easy to alter.

We will list selling price, material cost per unit, labour cost per unit, variable overheads per unit and fixed overheads per month in a separate section of the worksheet similar to the following:

```
KEY VARIABLES
Selling price              50
Material cost per unit     15
Labour cost per unit       10
Var. o/heads per unit      2.5
Fixed o/heads per month    50000
```

To create space in the worksheet for the Key Variables section, we'll insert seven rows near the top:

♦ Select the row headings 3–9 (located to the left of cells A3:A9).

The seven rows, 3–9, should now be selected and darkened.

♦ Select **Insert** from the Menu bar and **Rows** from the **Insert** menu.

The worksheet should have moved down creating seven blank rows for the insertion of our new section.

In case any prior formatting remains in the space we have created, we'll clear the cell contents before proceeding:

♦ Select the cell range A3:G9.

♦ Select **Edit** from the Menu bar and **Clear** from the **Edit** menu then **Formats** from the **Clear** sub-menu.

♦ Select cell A3 and enter the section heading, KEY VARIABLES.

♦ Select cell range A13:B13 (Selling price label and value).

♦ Select **Edit** from the Menu bar and **Copy** from the **Edit** menu.

Cells A13:B13 should now be surrounded by a flowing border.

♦ Select the cell range A4:B4.

♦ Select **Edit** from the Menu bar and **Paste** from the **Edit** menu.

♦ Press the [Esc] key to remove the flowing border.

The selling price (label and value) should have been copied to its new location.

We'll copy the next four items (material, labour, variable and fixed overheads) in one operation:

♦ Select the cell range A16:B16.

♦ Hold down the **[Ctrl]** key and *keep it depressed while making the next three selections.*

♦ Select the cell range A18:B18, then A20:B20 (you may have to scroll the window to bring these cells into view), then A22:B22. Release the **[Ctrl]** key.

Four cell ranges should now be selected; A16:B16, A18:B18, A20:B20 and A22:B22.

♦ Select **Edit** from the Menu bar and **Copy** from the **Edit** menu.

♦ Select cell A5 (one cell is enough).

♦ Select **Edit** from the Menu bar and then **Paste**.

♦ Press **[Esc]** to remove the flowing borders.

The four labels and values should have been copied to their new locations.

♦ Edit cell A5 to read: Material cost per unit.

♦ Edit cell A6 to read: Labour cost per unit.

♦ Edit cell A8 to read: Fixed o/heads per month.

♦ You may now have to widen column A slightly.

Your worksheet should now be similar to the following:

	A	B	C	D	E	F	G
1	CONSUMER GADGETS – PROFIT FORECAST 199X						
2							
3	KEY VARIABLES						
4	Selling price	50					
5	Material cost per unit	15					
6	Labour cost per unit	10					
7	Var. o/heads per unit	2.5					
8	Fixed o/heads per month	50000					
9							
10	MONTH	JAN	FEB	MAR	APR	MAY	JUN
11							
12	Sales (units)	4000	4000	4000	4300	4300	4500
13	Selling price	50	50	50	50	50	50
14	Sales revenue	200000	200000	200000	215000	215000	225000
15	COSTS:						
16	Material per unit	15	15	15	15	15	15
17	Total material	60000	60000	60000	64500	64500	67500
18	Labour per unit	10	10	10	10	10	10
19	Total labour	40000	40000	40000	43000	43000	45000
20	Var. o/heads per unit	2.5	2.5	2.5	2.5	2.5	2.5
21	Total var. o/heads	10000	10000	10000	10750	10750	11250
22	Fixed overheads	50000	50000	50000	50000	50000	50000
23	Total costs	160000	160000	160000	168250	168250	173750
24	Profit/Loss	40000	40000	40000	46750	46750	51250
25							
26	MARGIN	20	20	20	21.74419	21.74419	22.77778

We now no longer need rows 13, 15, 16, 18, 20 and 22 so we can delete them, but before doing so **Save** *your file.*

♦ Select row heading 13 (the complete row should be darkened).

♦ Select **Edit** from the Menu bar and **Delete** from the **Edit** menu.

Several things should have happened to your worksheet now.

● The whole worksheet from row 14 downwards should have moved up a row.

● The sign #REF! should appear in several of the worksheet cells. This indicates an error and it has been caused by removing the price figures from the main body of the worksheet. The values which were linked by formula to the price (Sales revenue directly and Profit/Loss and Margin indirectly) cannot now be solved and the error message #REF! is displayed. We will rebuild the worksheet in a moment but before we do so, we still have another five rows to remove.

When a worksheet row is deleted, the succeeding rows move up to fill the gap and consequently the row numbers will change. So be careful to make the correct deletions. The following rows should be deleted one at a time:

COSTS:	(row 14 at the moment)
Material per unit	(row 15 at the moment)
Labour per unit	(row 17 at the moment)
Var. o/heads per unit	(row 19 at the moment)
Fixed overheads	(row 21 at the moment)

Your worksheet should now appear as follows:

	A	B	C	D	E	F	G
1	CONSUMER GADGETS – PROFIT FORECAST 199X						
2							
3	KEY VARIABLES						
4	Selling price	50					
5	Material cost per unit	15					
6	Labour cost per unit	10					
7	Var. o/heads per unit	2.5					
8	Fixed o/heads per month	50000					
9							
10	MONTH	JAN	FEB	MAR	APR	MAY	JUN
11							
12	Sales (units)	4000	4000	4000	4300	4300	4500
13	Sales revenue	#REF!	#REF!	#REF!	#REF!	#REF!	#REF!
14	Total material	#REF!	#REF!	#REF!	#REF!	#REF!	#REF!
15	Total labour	#REF!	#REF!	#REF!	#REF!	#REF!	#REF!
16	Total var. o/heads	#REF!	#REF!	#REF!	#REF!	#REF!	#REF!
17	Total costs	#REF!	#REF!	#REF!	#REF!	#REF!	#REF!
18	Profit/Loss	#REF!	#REF!	#REF!	#REF!	#REF!	#REF!
19							
20	MARGIN	#REF!	#REF!	#REF!	#REF!	#REF!	#REF!

We will now rebuild the worksheet so that the formulae take account of the new locations for the key variables:

♦ Edit cell A14 to read: Total material cost.

♦ Edit cell A15 to read: Total labour cost.

♦ Select cell B13 and we'll enter a new formula for Sales revenue.

What do you think it should be?

You are probably thinking that the formula is =B4*B12. That formula would give you the correct result for January, but remember we are going to copy this formula across the next five columns (February–June). This formula would produce the following results after copying:

	A	B	C	D	E	F	G
10	MONTH	JAN	FEB	MAR	APR	MAY	JUN
11							
12	Sales (units)	4000	4000	4000	4300	4300	4500
13	Sales revenue	=B4*B12	=C4*C12	=D4*D12	=E4*E12	=F4*F12	=G4*G12

Can you see the problem? When the spreadsheet program copies formulae, it copies *relative to position*. So the formula, =B4*B12, in cell B13 would become =C4*C12 when copied into cell C13 and =D4*D12 when copied into cell D13 and so on. The problem is that the price is now located in one cell only – B4. There is nothing in cell C4 or D4, etc.

We have to find some way of anchoring the first part of the formula (the price) so that it does not change when copied. We can do this using the $ sign.

♦ Enter the following formula to cell B13: =$B$4*B12 (*Note:* You can type the dollar sign directly into the formula or press the [**F4**] function key to change a relative address to an absolute address.)

When this formula is copied, the first part (the price, in B4) will remain fixed but the second part (the sales figure, in B12) will change relative to position. This is how the program interprets the dollar sign in this context.

♦ Now copy the formula in cell B13 to the range C13:G13.

♦ Activate the cells C13, D13, E13 and so on in turn and examine the formula each time in the Formula bar. You'll notice that the first part of the formula (price) remains fixed at $B$4 while the second part (sales) changes relative to position.

You have now learned the difference between relative and absolute addressing.

♦ Enter the formula for Total material cost, =$B$5*B12, to cell B14 and copy it across the next five months. Do the same for Total labour cost and Total var. o/heads.

The formula for Total costs in cell B17 should be =$B$8+B14+B15+B16.

♦ Enter this formula and copy to the next five months.

The Profit/Loss formula in cells B18:G18 and the MARGIN formula in cells B20:G20 should both still be accurate and the values will be entered automatically. When cell contents are moved to new positions the program automatically adjusts formulae which refer to these cells to reflect their new location.

It has now become very easy to show the effect of a change to any of the influencing parameters – selling price, material cost, labour cost, variable and fixed overheads. An alteration to one cell will have a ripple effect throughout the entire worksheet.

Practise this, but make sure you return the key variables to their original values:

KEY VARIABLES

Selling price	50
Material cost per unit	15
Labour cost per unit	10
Var. o/heads per unit	2.5
Fixed o/heads per month	50000

Your worksheet should now be similar to the following:

	A	B	C	D	E	F	G
1	CONSUMER GADGETS – PROFIT FORECAST 199X						
2							
3	KEY VARIABLES						
4	Selling price	50					
5	Material cost per unit	15					
6	Labour cost per unit	10					
7	Var. o/heads per unit	2.5					
8	Fixed o/heads per month	50000					
9							
10	MONTH	JAN	FEB	MAR	APR	MAY	JUN
11							
12	Sales (units)	4000	4000	4000	4300	4300	4500
13	Sales revenue	200000	200000	200000	215000	215000	225000
14	Total material cost	60000	60000	60000	64500	64500	67500
15	Total labour cost	40000	40000	40000	43000	43000	45000
16	Total var. o/heads	10000	10000	10000	10750	10750	11250
17	Total costs	160000	160000	160000	168250	168250	173750
18	Profit/Loss	40000	40000	40000	46750	46750	51250
19							
20	MARGIN	20	20	20	21.74419	21.74419	22.77778

♦ **Save** your file.

CHAPTER 13

Formatting and Printing the Worksheet

The Formatting Toolbar · Font Style and Size · Underlining · Alignment · Formatting Numbers · Expressing Values in Percentage Format · Naming Cells · Clearing Cell Formats · Cell Borders · Worksheet Gridlines · Autoformat · Moving through the Workbook and Naming a Worksheet · Printing · Printing the Underlying Formulae

THE FORMATTING TOOLBAR

In this chapter we will refer to and use the facilities on the formatting Toolbar quite often. If this does not appear on the screen you should display it now by choosing **Toolbars** from the **View** menu and selecting the **Formatting** check box in the **Toolbars** dialogue box. As with the standard Toolbar each button on the formatting Toolbar has a name. If you allow the mouse pointer to hover over a button for a few seconds its name will appear and a short description of its function will be shown in the Status bar at the bottom of the screen.

♦ Ensure that your workbook file, LearnXL, is open and Sheet1 displayed on screen.

FONT STYLE AND SIZE

We will first embolden the heading and the row labels.

♦ Select the cell range A1:A20.

♦ Select **Format** from the Menu bar and **Cells** from the **Format** menu (or **Format Cells** from the shortcut menu).

The **Format Cells** dialogue box will open. It should be similar to the following but may not be identical depending on which option 'page' is displayed:

Format Cells

| Number | Alignment | Font | Border | Patterns | Protection |

Category:

All
Custom
Number
Accounting
Date
Time
Percentage
Fraction
Scientific
Text
Currency

Format Codes:

General
0
0.00
#,##0
#,##0.00
#,##0;-#,##0
#,##0;[Red]-#,##0
#,##0.00;-#,##0.00
#,##0.00;[Red]-#,##0.00
£#,##0;-£#,##0
£#,##0;[Red]-£#,##0

OK
Cancel
Help
Delete

Code: General

Sample:

To create a custom format,
type in the Code box.

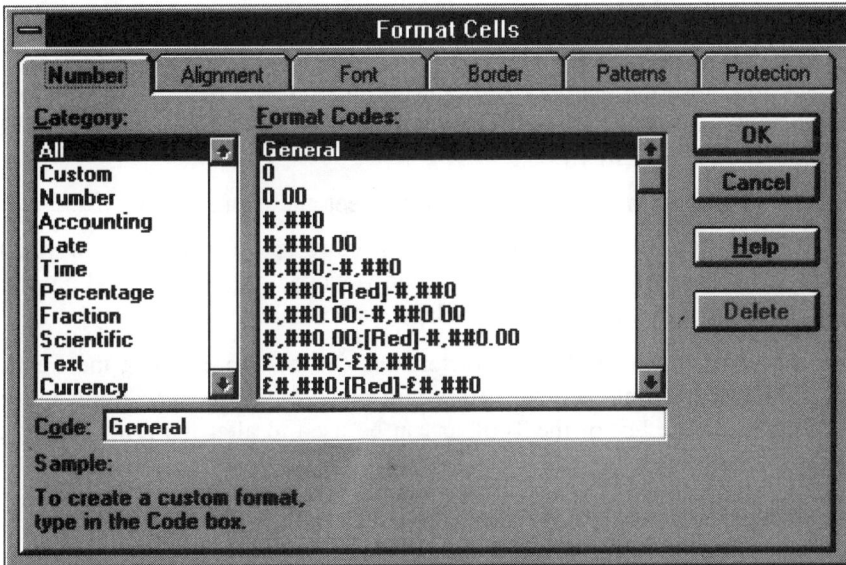

Notice that the dialogue box has index tab buttons arranged along the top – **Number, Alignment, Font, Border, Patterns, Protection**. This means that the one dialogue box has several 'pages' which can be used to carry out a number of related tasks such as altering the alignment, font characteristics, border highlighting, etc. of a selected cell or range of cells.

♦ Click on the **Font** tab button and the following 'page' should be displayed:

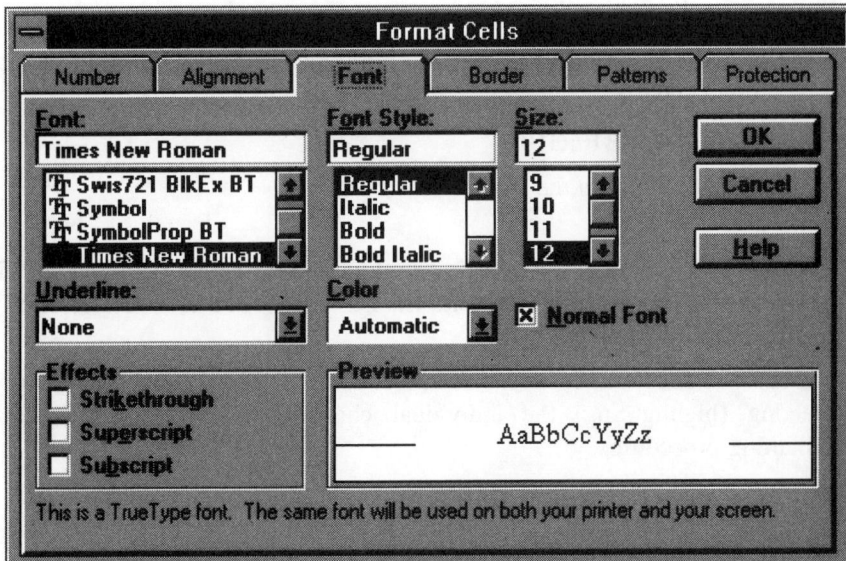

Format Cells

| Number | Alignment | Font | Border | Patterns | Protection |

Font:

Times New Roman

Swis721 BlkEx BT
Symbol
SymbolProp BT
Times New Roman

Font Style:

Regular

Regular
Italic
Bold
Bold Italic

Size:

12

9
10
11
12

OK
Cancel
Help

Underline:

None

Color

Automatic

[X] **Normal Font**

Effects

☐ Strikethrough
☐ Superscript
☐ Subscript

Preview

AaBbCcYyZz

This is a TrueType font. The same font will be used on both your printer and your screen.

The **Font** options will allow you to change the font type, style, size and colour. You can also choose to have your entry underlined. Experiment with the different types, styles and sizes and examine the result in the **Preview** panel.

♦ Before you close the dialogue box, set the **Font** to MS Sans Serif (you may have to scroll the **Font** list using the arrow buttons to bring this into view), the **Font Style** to Bold and the **Size** to 10.

♦ Click the **OK** button to return to the worksheet and examine the effect.

♦ Emboldening the text causes it to take up more space in the cell so you may now have to widen column A slightly (don't worry about the heading overrunning column A but make sure all the row labels are displayed completely).

As you have just seen, the font characteristics can be altered using the **Format** menu. However, the formatting Toolbar offers quicker alternatives. The **Font** and **Font Size** boxes located on the left of the Toolbar can be used to alter the font and character size of selected text.

♦ If you select any cell in column A, MS Sans Serif should be displayed in the **Font** box and 10 in the **Font Size** box.

We will enlarge our heading. Although the heading spreads over several cells, it is actually located in cell A1.

♦ Select cell A1 and click the ⬇ button in the **Font Size** box on the formatting Toolbar.

♦ Select 12 from the drop-down list.

The heading should be enlarged and row 1 will have widened automatically to accommodate the larger character size.

♦ Now select the cell range B10:G10, click the ⬇ button in the **Font** box on the formatting Toolbar and select MS Sans Serif from the drop-down list.

Emboldening can also be carried out much more quickly using the **Bold** button, **B** , on the formatting Toolbar.

♦ Select the cell range B10:G10.

♦ Click the **Bold** button on the Toolbar.

Notes:

1   There are also **Italic** and **Underline** buttons on the formatting Toolbar. These are toggle buttons (as is the **Bold** button), i.e. click once to activate, click again to deactivate.

2   Individual characters in a cell can be formatted by double clicking the cell, selecting (highlighting) the individual character(s) and then carrying out the formatting procedure.

UNDERLINING

If you wish to underline the heading proceed as follows:

♦ Select cell A1.

♦ Select **Format** from the Menu bar and **Cells** from the **Format** menu.

♦ When the **Format Cells** dialogue box opens, select the **Font** tab button at the top.

♦ When the **Font** options are displayed, click the ▾ button in the **Underline** box. Select single or double underlining and then select the **OK** button in the dialogue box.

When you return to the worksheet the heading should be underlined.

♦ Click the **Underline** button on the formatting Toolbar to remove the underlining (you may have to do this twice if you double underlined).

♦ Click on the button again to replace the underlining.

ALIGNMENT

At the moment, all text is aligned to the left and all numbers to the right of their cells. These are the default settings but they can be altered. You can left, centre or right align text and numbers.

♦ Select the cells containing the month names – cell range B10:G10.

♦ Select **Format** from the Menu bar and **Cells** from the **Format** menu.

♦ When the **Format Cells** dialogue box opens, select the **Alignment** tab button.

♦ When the alignment options are displayed, select **Center** from the **Horizontal** section and click the **OK** button.

The month names should now appear in the centre of their cells.

We will now centre the worksheet heading.

♦ Select cells A1:G1 (we will align the heading in the centre of this range).

♦ Select **Format** from the Menu bar and **Cells** from the **Format** menu.

♦ Select the **Alignment** tab button in the **Format Cells** dialogue box.

♦ Select **Center across selection** from the **Horizontal** section and click the **OK** button. The worksheet heading should now be centred within the selected cells.

Note: There are four alignment buttons on the formatting Toolbar which allow you to **Align Left**, **Center**, **Align Right** and **Center Across Columns**.

FORMATTING NUMBERS

♦ Select the cell range B13:G20.

♦ Select **Format** from the Menu bar and **Cells** from the **Format** menu.

♦ Select the **Number** tab button at the top of the **Format Cells** dialogue box.

The **Number** format 'page' offers a considerable list of options of how to display numeric values. Changing the selection in the **Category** section will change the options displayed in the **Format Codes** section.

♦ Select **Number** from the **Category** section and the codes displayed should be similar to the following:

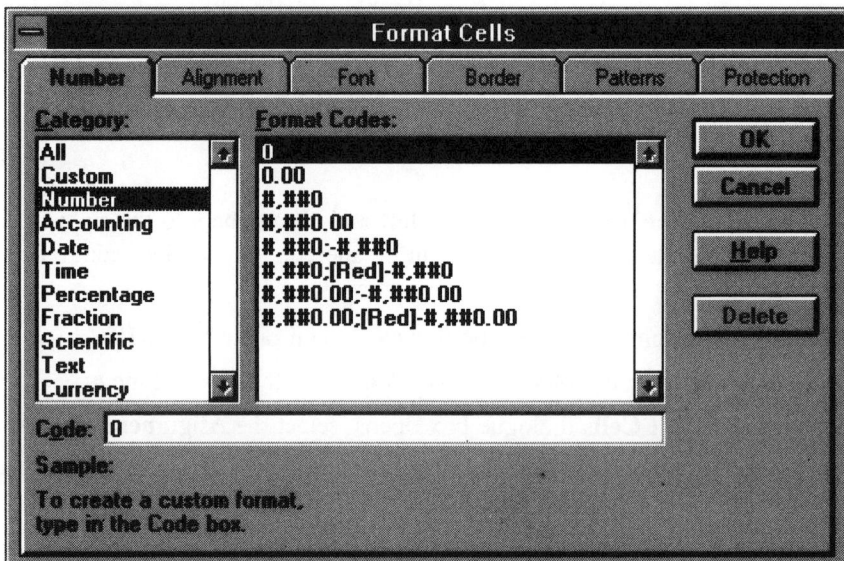

♦ Select the style **0.00** from the **Format Codes** section and click the **OK** button.

♦ The worksheet values will now be redisplayed in decimal format with two digits after the point. However, hash signs (####) may now appear in some of the cells. This indicates that the number entered is too wide for the cell or the format chosen is too wide to be displayed. The solution is to widen the column so do that where necessary.

Numeric values can be displayed preceded by the £ sign. This is achieved by selecting the **Currency** option from the **Category** section in the **Format Cells** dialogue box and then choosing an appropriate code. However, the formatting Toolbar offers a quicker method of doing this.

♦ Select the cell range B13:G13.

- Click the **Currency Style** button on the formatting Toolbar and the Sales revenue figures will be preceded by the £ sign. If you get hash signs in the cells widen the columns again.

- Having one line only in the worksheet formatted in the currency style looks odd so change it back to conform with the rest of the worksheet using the shortcut menu.

- Using the Main menu format cell range B4:B8 to display in currency style with two decimals. The code for this style in the **Format Codes** dialogue box is £#,##0.00.

- Reformat cell B8 to display in currency style with no decimals.

EXPRESSING VALUES IN PERCENTAGE FORMAT

We'll now display the MARGIN figures in cells B20:G20 in percentage format.

- Select cell B20 and click the **Percent Style** button on the formatting Toolbar.

The value displayed will be 2000 per cent and this is obviously wrong. However, it is not the program's mistake. When Microsoft® Excel displays a number in percentage format, it multiplies the number by 100 and adds the percent sign (%). You must bear this in mind when inserting formulae to the worksheet. The formula in cell B20 is =(B18*100)/B13, i.e. we have already multiplied by 100. So when we wish one figure to be expressed as a percentage of another, we should allow the program to do that part of the calculation when it is formatting in percentage style.

- Change the formula in B20 to =B18/B13. The percentage value should now be correct, i.e. 20 per cent.

- When B20 is selected, point to the fill handle and drag the pointer to the right through the range C20:G20.

- Release the mouse button and the correct percentage figures should now be displayed for each month. When you copy the contents of a cell, any formatting which has been applied to that cell is also copied.

At the moment some of the percentage figures have been rounded so we'll format the range to two decimal places.

- Select the range B20:G20.

- Select **Format** from the Menu bar and **Cells** from the **Format** menu.

- Select the **Number** tab button from the top of the **Format Cells** dialogue box to display the options for number formatting.

- Select **Percentage** from the **Category** section and **0.00%** from the **Format Codes** section.

- Click the **OK** button in the dialogue box.

The worksheet should now display the margin figures correctly formatted in percentage style to two decimal places.

It is important that you understand how to express percentage values when working with a spreadsheet since many calculations in the field of accounting and finance involve percentages. A simple exercise should make it clear. We'll set this up in a blank area of the worksheet then erase it when we've finished.

♦ Enter the following labels, values and formulae to the cells as shown:

Cell	Label	Cell	Value/formula
A25	Cost price	B25	160
A26	Selling price	B26	200
A27	Profit	B27	=B26–B25
A28	Mark-up	B28	=B27/B25

♦ Format cells B25, B26 and B27 to currency style with two decimal places.

♦ Note that the mark-up in cell B28 is shown as 0.25. Format this cell to percentage style with no decimal places.

The result should be as follows:

	Column A	Column B
Row 25	Cost price	£160.00
Row 26	Selling price	£200.00
Row 27	Profit	£40.00
Row 28	Mark-up	25%

So percentages should be calculated in the worksheet as decimals and then formatted to display in percentage style.

However, if you wish to insert a percentage figure directly to a cell there is no need to enter it as a decimal. If you type the number and add the per cent sign (%) Microsoft® Excel will recognise this and format the cell to percentage style automatically. To illustrate this we'll clear the contents of cells B27 and B28 and re-enter the data in a different way.

♦ Select the cell range B27:B28, open the **Edit** menu and choose **Clear**, then select **All** from the sub-menu.

♦ Select cell B28, type 25% and press [**Enter**].

♦ Select cell B28 again and note that 0.25 appears in the Formula bar. Excel has recognised the % sign and formatted the cell in percentage style although the contents will be stored as a decimal.

♦ Select cell B27 and enter the formula =B25*B28. 40 should now appear in cell B27. Format the cell to currency style with two decimal places.

NAMING CELLS

A cell or a range of cells can be given a name which can then be used to replace a cell reference in a formula to make the formula more meaningful. For example, the formula =Gross_Profit – Expenses is easier to read and understand than =C10-C20.

To demonstrate this feature we'll give the cells B25 and B26 a name and use these names in the formula in cell B27.

♦ Select cell B25.

♦ Select **Insert** from the Menu bar, **Name** from the **Insert** menu then **Define** from the **Name** sub-menu.

The following **Define Name** dialogue box should appear with Cost_price displayed in the **Names in Workbook** box:

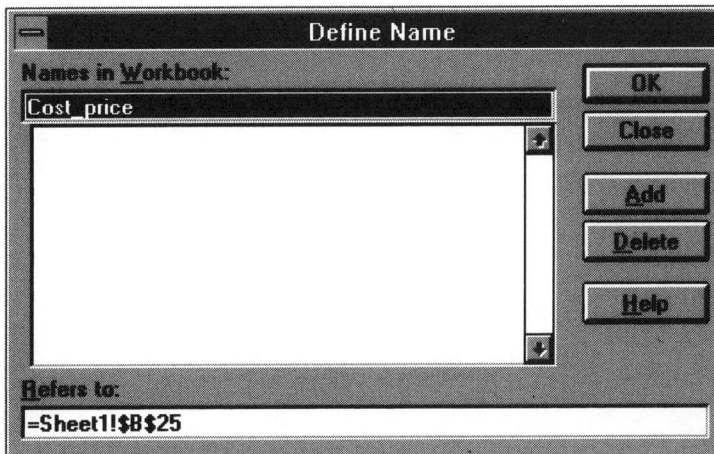

```
┌─────────────────────────────────────────────────────┐
│ ─              Define Name                            │
├─────────────────────────────────────────────────────┤
│ Names in Workbook:                    ┌──────────┐    │
│ ┌─────────────────────────────────┐   │   OK     │    │
│ │Cost_price                       │   └──────────┘    │
│ └─────────────────────────────────┘   ┌──────────┐    │
│ ┌───────────────────────────────┬─┐   │  Close   │    │
│ │                               │▲│   └──────────┘    │
│ │                               │ │   ┌──────────┐    │
│ │                               │ │   │   Add    │    │
│ │                               │ │   └──────────┘    │
│ │                               │ │   ┌──────────┐    │
│ │                               │ │   │  Delete  │    │
│ │                               │ │   └──────────┘    │
│ │                               │ │   ┌──────────┐    │
│ │                               │▼│   │   Help   │    │
│ └───────────────────────────────┴─┘   └──────────┘    │
│ Refers to:                                            │
│ ┌─────────────────────────────────────────────────┐  │
│ │=Sheet1!$B$25                                     │  │
│ └─────────────────────────────────────────────────┘  │
└─────────────────────────────────────────────────────┘
```

♦ Cost_price is being offered as a suggested name for cell B25 although you can type in a different name if you wish. Accept the name Cost_price by clicking the **OK** button.

You will be returned to the worksheet and the cell name, Cost_price, should be displayed in the Name box at the extreme left of the Formula bar.

♦ Select cell B26. Click in the Name box on the Formula bar, type in the name, Selling_price, and press the **[Enter]** key. This is an alternative and quicker method of allocating a name to a cell or range of cells.

♦ Select cell B27 and open the **Edit** menu.

♦ Select **Clear** from the **Edit** menu and **Contents** from the **Clear** sub-menu.

We'll now enter the formula to cell B27 using names instead of references. You can type the formula in as normal but it is quicker and more accurate to use the Name box. Carry out the following tasks:

♦ Ensure that cell B27 is selected.

♦ Type = .

♦ Click the ⬇ button at the side of the Name box and select Selling_price from the drop-down list. Selling_price should now be inserted to the formula.

♦ Type – .

♦ Click the ⬇ button in the Name box and select Cost_price.

♦ Click the ☑ button in the Formula bar.

The Profit of £40.00 should now appear in cell B27.

Since this exercise was for demonstration purposes only we'll now delete the names.

♦ Open the **Define Name** dialogue box. Delete each name in turn by selecting the name from the panel below the **Names in Workbook** box and clicking the **Delete** button.

♦ When all names have been deleted click the **OK** button to return to the worksheet.

The error message #NAME? will now appear in cell B27 because the formula cannot now be solved since the cell names no longer exist. Don't worry about this because we'll shortly be deleting this cell.

CLEARING CELL FORMATS

Now clear the cell range A25:B28 in the following way:

♦ Select the range A25:B28 and while 'pointing' to the selected area click the right mouse button.

♦ Select **Clear Contents** from the shortcut menu.

The cell contents will have been cleared but the cell formatting will be retained. Enter the value 8 to cell B25 and it will be displayed in currency style: £8.00. Enter the value 30 to cell B28 and it will be displayed in percentage style: 3000%.

To clear contents and formatting from cells you should use the **Edit** menu from the Menu bar:

♦ Select the cell range B25:B28.

♦ Select **Edit** from the Menu bar.

♦ Select **Clear** from the **Edit** menu and **All** from the **Clear** sub-menu.

Formatting is applied to a cell rather than cell contents. Any data entered to the cell will adopt the cell format style. You can format a blank cell and any data entered thereto will adopt this format. You can also copy cell formats to another cell or range of cells using the normal 'copy' commands.

If a cell contains formatted data and you wish to copy only the format(s) you should use the **Format Painter** button on the standard Toolbar or the **Paste Special** command on the **Edit** menu.

CELL BORDERS

To emphasise the Profit/Loss figures we will embolden them and put a border round the cell range.

♦ Select the range B18:G18 and click the **Bold** button on the formatting Toolbar. Widen the columns if necessary.

♦ With the cells still selected open the **Format** menu and choose the **Cells** option.

♦ When the **Format Cells** dialogue box opens, select the **Border** tab button at the top and the list of **Border** options and **Styles** should be displayed as follows:

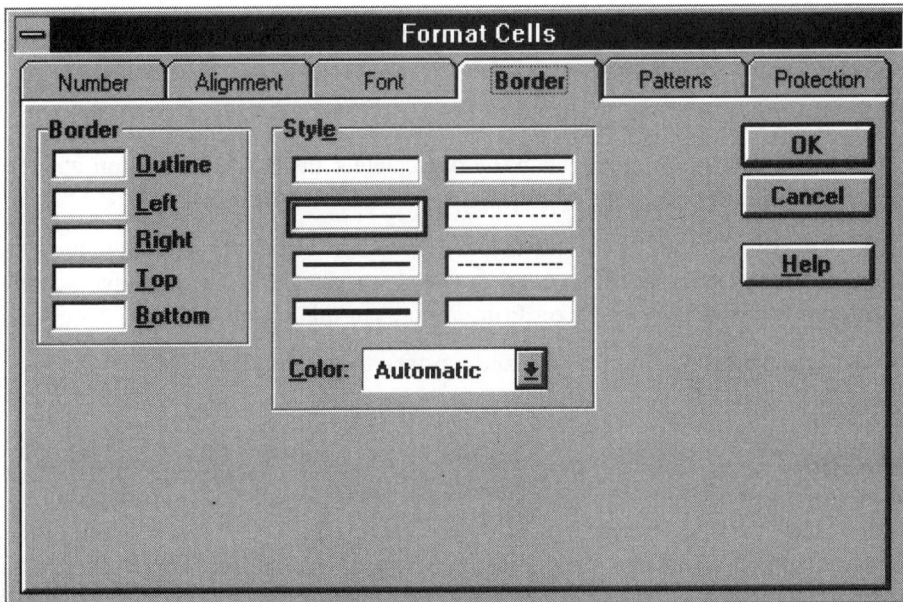

```
┌────────────────────────────────────────────────────────┐
│ ▬              Format Cells                             │
├────────────────────────────────────────────────────────┤
│ ╱Number ╲╱Alignment╲╱ Font ╲╱ Border ╲╱Patterns╲╱Protection╲ │
│ ┌─Border──────┐ ┌─Style───────────────────┐  ┌────────┐ │
│ │ ┌──┐ Outline │ │ ┌──────┐   ┌──────┐     │  │   OK   │ │
│ │ └──┘         │ │ └──────┘   └──────┘     │  └────────┘ │
│ │ ┌──┐ Left    │ │ ┌══════┐   ┌──────┐     │  ┌────────┐ │
│ │ └──┘         │ │ └══════┘   └──────┘     │  │ Cancel │ │
│ │ ┌──┐ Right   │ │ ┌──────┐   ┌──────┐     │  └────────┘ │
│ │ └──┘         │ │ └──────┘   └──────┘     │  ┌────────┐ │
│ │ ┌──┐ Top     │ │ ┌──────┐   ┌──────┐     │  │  Help  │ │
│ │ └──┘         │ │ └──────┘   └──────┘     │  └────────┘ │
│ │ ┌──┐ Bottom  │ │                         │             │
│ │ └──┘         │ │ Color:│ Automatic  ▼│   │             │
│ └─────────────┘ └─────────────────────────┘             │
└────────────────────────────────────────────────────────┘
```

You can put a border at the top, bottom, left or right of a cell or range of cells or surround the cell(s) completely. You can also choose the thickness and pattern of the border.

♦ Select a style by clicking on one of the **Style** boxes and then select the **Top** and **Bottom** boxes in the **Border** section.

♦ Click the **OK** button in the dialogue box and you will be returned to the worksheet showing a border along the top and bottom of the selected cells.

♦ To remove borders use the same commands, i.e. select cells, then **Format/Cells/ Border** and deselect the **Border** box(es) in the **Format Cells** dialogue box.

To emphasise the Key Variables section we will surround it with a border:

♦ Select the cell range A3:B8.

♦ Select **Format** from the Menu bar and **Cells** from the **Format** menu.

♦ Select the **Border** tab button at the top of the **Format Cells** dialogue box.

♦ Select a style, click on the **Border Outline** box and select **OK**.

Note: There is a **Borders** box on the formatting Toolbar which allows you to select a border style from a drop-down display.

WORKSHEET GRIDLINES

To obtain a clearer view of the border we have just added, we can turn off the gridline display for a moment.

♦ Select **Tools** from the Menu bar and **Options** from the **Tools** menu.

♦ When the **Options** dialogue box opens, select the **View** tab button at the top, click the **Gridlines** check box to remove the x and then select **OK**.

The worksheet should now be displayed without gridlines although they would still appear on any printout. If you do not wish to print gridlines, a separate procedure is required (refer to the section on Printing later in this chapter).

♦ Repeat the last series of commands to turn the gridlines back on again.

AUTOFORMAT

Microsoft® Excel can offer you a choice from a list of pre-defined format combinations to apply to a range of cells in your worksheet. The facility allows you to format a range of cells or a complete worksheet to a pre-designed style which suits your needs very quickly. *Before experimenting with **AutoFormat** you should Save your updated file.*

♦ To demonstrate, select all the worksheet cells containing data (A1:G20).

♦ Select **Format** from the Menu bar and **AutoFormat** from the **Format** menu.

The **AutoFormat** dialogue box should now appear as follows:

```
┌─────────────────────────────────────────────────────────────────────┐
│ ═                              AutoFormat                             │
├─────────────────────────────────────────────────────────────────────┤
│ Table Format:          ┌─Sample──────────────────────┐   ┌────────┐  │
│ ┌──────────────┬─┐     │                             │   │   OK   │  │
│ │ Simple       │▲│     │        Jan  Feb  Mar  Total │   └────────┘  │
│ │ Classic 1    │ │     │                             │   ┌────────┐  │
│ │ Classic 2    │ │     │  East    7    7    5    19  │   │ Cancel │  │
│ │ Classic 3    │ │     │  West    6    4    7    17  │   └────────┘  │
│ │ Accounting 1 │ │     │  South   8    7    9    24  │   ┌──────────┐│
│ │ Accounting 2 │ │     │  Total  21   18   21    60  │   │Options >>││
│ │ Accounting 3 │ │     │                             │   └──────────┘│
│ │ Accounting 4 │ │     │                             │   ┌────────┐  │
│ │ Colorful 1   │ │     │                             │   │  Help  │  │
│ │ Colorful 2   │ │     │                             │   └────────┘  │
│ │ Colorful 3   │▼│     └─────────────────────────────┘              │
│ └──────────────┴─┘                                                   │
└─────────────────────────────────────────────────────────────────────┘
```

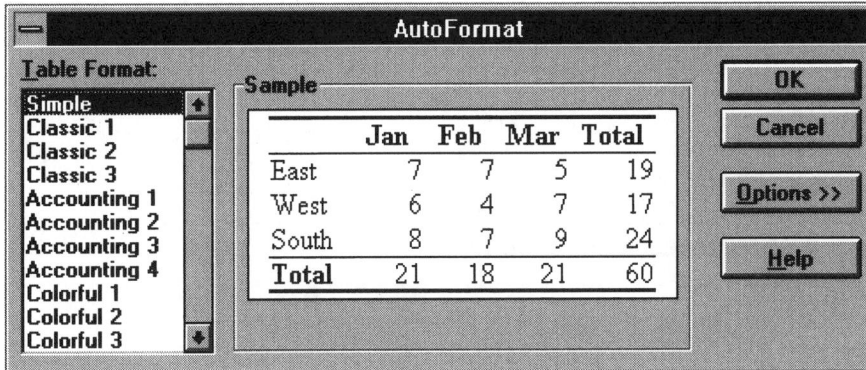

◆ As you select a format from the **Table Format** section, the **Sample** will change to correspond with the format selected.

◆ You can use the **Options** button if you wish to adopt a particular autoformat but at the same time preserve some of the formats you have already applied.

◆ When you see a format style which suits you, click on the **OK** button and you will be returned to the worksheet which will be formatted in the chosen style.

◆ Select **Undo AutoFormat** from the **Edit** menu to revert back to your original style.

◆ If for some reason you cannot recover your original style, select **Close** from the **File** menu and when 'asked' if you want to save changes to the file click the **No** button. You can then re-open the file which you had the good sense to save before experimenting with **AutoFormat**.

Your worksheet should now appear as follows:

	A	B	C	D	E	F	G
1	CONSUMER GADGETS – PROFIT FORECAST 199X						
2							
3	KEY VARIABLES						
4	Selling price	£50.00					
5	Material cost per unit	£15.00					
6	Labour cost per unit	£10.00					
7	Var. o/heads per unit	£2.50					
8	Fixed o/heads per month	£50,000					
9							
10	MONTH	JAN	FEB	MAR	APR	MAY	JUN
11							
12	Sales (units)	4000	4000	4000	4300	4300	4500
13	Sales revenue	200000.00	200000.00	200000.00	215000.00	215000.00	225000.00
14	Total material cost	60000.00	60000.00	60000.00	64500.00	64500.00	67500.00
15	Total labour cost	40000.00	40000.00	40000.00	43000.00	43000.00	45000.00
16	Total var. o/heads	10000.00	10000.00	10000.00	10750.00	10750.00	11250.00
17	Total costs	160000.00	160000.00	160000.00	168250.00	168250.00	173750.00
18	Profit/Loss	40000.00	40000.00	40000.00	46750.00	46750.00	51250.00
19							
20	MARGIN	20.00%	20.00%	20.00%	21.74%	21.74%	22.78%

MOVING THROUGH THE WORKBOOK AND NAMING A WORKSHEET

If you look at the bottom of the screen just above the Status bar, you'll see several tab buttons marked Sheet1, Sheet2, Sheet3, etc. These are the default names of the sheets (pages) in your workbook file. If they are not visible refer to the section on the spreadsheet screen in Chapter 10. There are 16 sheets in the workbook at the moment and you can add more. Dragging the tab split box to the right or left along the horizontal scroll bar will display more or fewer respectively of the name tabs. Immediately to the left of these tab buttons there are four arrow buttons:

⏮	Clicking this one will move you to the beginning of the name tab bar (the first few sheet names will be visible).
⏭	Clicking this one will move you to the end of the name tab bar (the last few sheet names will be visible).
◀ and ▶	These will move you along the bar one sheet at a time. To scroll by several tabs at a time hold down the [Shift] key and click.

◆ Click the button to take you to the end of the bar, ⏭.

◆ Sheet16 name tab should now be in view, select it by pointing and clicking. A blank worksheet should now appear; you've 'turned' to the last 'page' in your workbook.

◆ Click the button to take you to the beginning of the name tab bar, ⏮.

◆ Sheet1 name tab should now be in view, select it by pointing and clicking and your worksheet should be displayed again. You've moved back to the first 'page' in the workbook.

♦ Select **Format** from the Menu bar and **Sheet** from the **Format** menu.

♦ Select **Rename** from the **Sheet** sub-menu and when the **Rename Sheet** dialogue box opens, enter the name as Forecast and click the **OK** button.

Forecast will now replace Sheet1 in the sheet name tab bar at the bottom of the screen.

Giving the workbook sheets meaningful names in this way makes it easier for you to identify them.

Note:

(a) The **Rename Sheet** dialogue box can be opened by double-clicking the sheet name tab button.

(b) The **Rename** sheet command is also available on the shortcut menu.

♦ **Save** your file.

PRINTING

Printing is usually carried out in three steps:

(a) Design the page layout.

(b) Preview the layout to display the page as it will look when printed.

(c) Print.

Page setup

♦ Select **File** from the Menu bar and **Page Setup** from the **File** menu.

The **Page Setup** dialogue box should now open similar to the following:

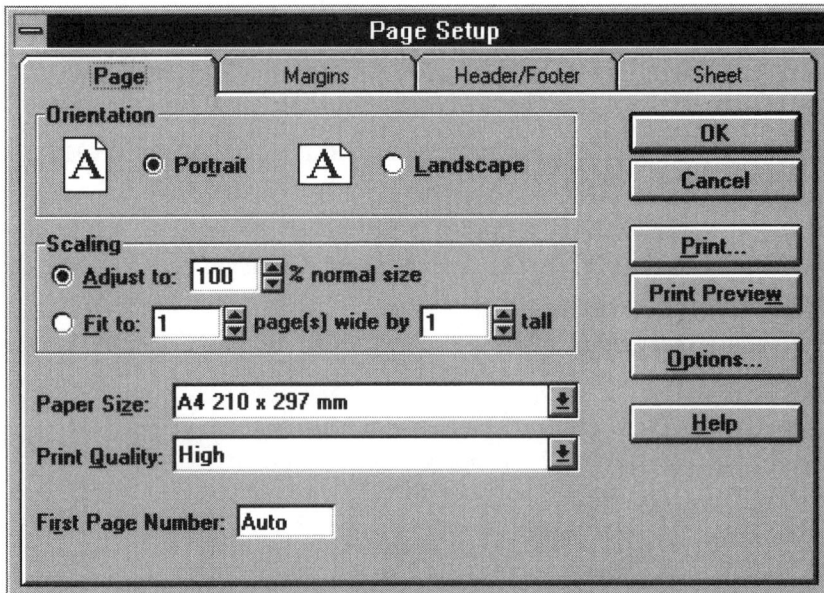

As with the **Format Cells** dialogue box, **Page Setup** has several 'pages' accessed by clicking the tab buttons at the top (**Page**, **Margins**, **Header/Footer**, **Sheet**). This allows you to design different aspects of your layout from the one dialogue box.

♦ Select the **Page** tab button. This 'page' can be used to specify the orientation (portrait or landscape) and scaling of your printout. Microsoft® Excel can fit a wide worksheet to the specified paper size by automatically adjusting the print size to suit, i.e. print the worksheet to fit the page.

Your worksheet is quite small so there is no need to alter anything on this 'page' of the dialogue box.

♦ Select the **Margins** tab button. This 'page' allows you to adjust the widths of the margins at the left, right, top and bottom and to centre the worksheet horizontally and/or vertically.

♦ Click the **Center on Page Horizontally** check box and note the effect in the **Preview** panel.

♦ Select the **Header/Footer** tab button. This 'page' allows you to insert custom header and footer labels on your printout or select from a list of standard labels (page no., filename, date, etc.).

♦ Click the ⊞ button at the end of the **Header** box and select **(none)** from the drop-down list. You may have to scroll the list to bring this into view. **(None)** should now appear in the **Header** box.

♦ Click the ⊞ button at the end of the **Footer** box and select **(none)** from the drop-down list. We have just elected to have no header or footer labels on our print page.

♦ Select the **Sheet** tab button. This 'page' allows you to specify a print area, i.e. a cell range for printing, if you only want part of the worksheet printed. In addition, you can specify titles for printing on multiple pages and elect to have gridlines and row and column headings on or off.

♦ Change nothing on this 'page'.

Print preview

♦ Select the **Print Preview** button from the dialogue box. A preview of the printed page should now be displayed.

♦ If you can't read it, you can enlarge it by clicking the **Zoom** button. Clicking the **Zoom** button again will return the worksheet to normal size. If you want to zoom in on a particular section of the worksheet, position the mouse pointer (which should be a magnifying glass when it is on the print page) over the area for enlarging and click the mouse button. Click again to return to normal size.

♦ If you are not happy with any part of the layout you can return to the **Page Setup** dialogue box (by clicking the **Setup** button) and make the necessary adjustments.

Print

♦ Select the **Print** button at the top of the **Preview** window and the **Print** dialogue box, similar to the following should open:

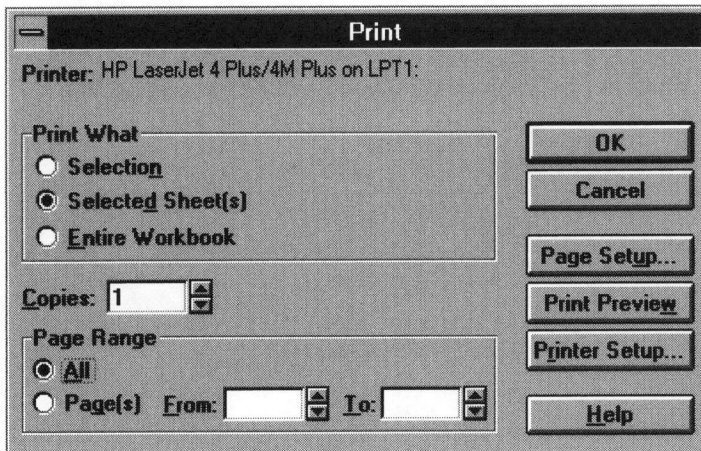

```
┌───────────────────────────────────────────────────────┐
│ ▬                          Print                        │
├───────────────────────────────────────────────────────┤
│ Printer: HP LaserJet 4 Plus/4M Plus on LPT1:            │
│                                                         │
│ ┌─Print What────────────────┐  ┌──────────────────┐    │
│ │ ○ Selection               │  │       OK         │    │
│ │ ● Selected Sheet(s)       │  └──────────────────┘    │
│ │ ○ Entire Workbook         │  ┌──────────────────┐    │
│ │                           │  │     Cancel       │    │
│ └───────────────────────────┘  └──────────────────┘    │
│                                 ┌──────────────────┐    │
│ Copies: [1]  ▲▼                 │   Page Setup...  │    │
│ ┌─Page Range────────────────┐  └──────────────────┘    │
│ │ ● All                     │  ┌──────────────────┐    │
│ │ ○ Page(s) From: [  ]▲▼    │  │   Print Preview  │    │
│ │           To: [  ]▲▼      │  └──────────────────┘    │
│ └───────────────────────────┘  ┌──────────────────┐    │
│                                 │  Printer Setup...│    │
│                                 └──────────────────┘    │
│                                 ┌──────────────────┐    │
│                                 │      Help        │    │
│                                 └──────────────────┘    │
└───────────────────────────────────────────────────────┘
```

This dialogue box allows you to specify exactly what you want printed and you can select from the following:

1 **Selection**. This option will print previously selected worksheet cells and will override any print area specified in **Page Setup**.

2   **Selected Sheet(s)**. This option will print the area specified in **Page Setup** or the active sheet if no area has been specified.

3   **Entire Workbook**. This option will print all sheets in the workbook which have printing on them.

You can also select a page range for printing and the number of copies.

♦ Click on **Selected Sheet(s)** in the **Print What** section of the dialogue box and select **OK**.

The worksheet should now be printed.

♦ You should now **Save** your workbook and these worksheet print settings will be saved with it.

Once the page layout has been designed, files can be previewed and printed directly using the appropriate commands on the **File** menu.

There are also **Print** and **Print Preview** buttons on the standard Toolbar. However, the **Print** button will not display the **Print** dialogue box before printing.

PRINTING THE UNDERLYING FORMULAE

♦ Select **Tools** from the Menu bar and **Options** from the **Tools** menu.

♦ When the **Options** dialogue box opens, select the **View** tab button at the top, click the **Formulas** check box in the **Window Options** section and select **OK**.

Your worksheet should now be redisplayed showing the underlying formula for each cell. Notice that the column widths have been expanded to accommodate the formulae.

♦ You will have to scroll the window horizontally to view the complete worksheet.

♦ If you wish to print the worksheet showing the formulae, you would now carry on and print in the manner described.

♦ Reset the worksheet to normal display by deselecting the **Formulas** check box in the **Options** dialogue box.

CHAPTER 14

Functions

Introduction to Functions · Useful Financial Functions · Help with Functions · Function Wizard · Alphabetical List of Financial and Statistical Functions

INTRODUCTION TO FUNCTIONS

In addition to the commands which you have been using, the spreadsheet **program** contains an extensive library of functions which you can call on. You can think of them as built-in calculation routines. Each function has a name, followed by brackets which usually contain 'arguments' and with Microsoft® Excel it should be preceded with the = sign.

For example, the formula A1+A2+A3+A4 could be replaced with the function =SUM(A1:A4). The formula A1+A3+A5 could be replaced with the function =SUM(A1,A3,A5).

Microsoft® Excel has several hundred functions which fall into categories such as finance, statistics, engineering, etc. A complete list with descriptions can be accessed through the **Help** system. In this section, a few simple functions will be described as a means of introduction and to this end we will build a new but small worksheet showing the accounting marks for a group of first-year undergraduates.

We'll continue to use your file, LearnXL, so make sure it's open. We'll take a new 'page' in the workbook for this exercise. In fact, we'll use the 'back page' which you can keep for reference.

♦ Click the ▶ button to move to the end of the name tab bar.

♦ When the Sheet16 name tab is visible, select it by pointing and clicking and a blank worksheet should appear.

♦ Double-click on the Sheet16 name tab and when the **Rename Sheet** dialogue box opens, enter the new name as Reference and click the **OK** button.

♦ Set up the following worksheet:

	A	B	C
1	ABC UNIVERSITY		
2	Accounting Results – General Degree, Year 1		
3			
4	NAME	MARK	PASS/FAIL
5	Alice	55	
6	Dave	38	
7	Fred		
8	Jean	76	
9	Jim	78	
10	John	56	
11	Liz	47	
12	Mary	39	
13	Peggy		
14	Tom	45	
15	Willie	62	
16	Wilma	69	
17	TOTAL		
18	AVERAGE		
19	NUMBER SAT		
20	HIGHEST MARK		
21	LOWEST MARK		
22	NUMBER PASSED		

Fred and Peggy missed the examination so there are no marks for them. You will have to widen columns A and C.

We will now use functions to make the following calculations:

1 *Class total:*

♦ Select cell B17 and insert the function =SUM(B5:B16).

This function will add the values in the stated range and enter the total to the selected cell. Blank cells will be interpreted as 0.

♦ There is an **Autosum** button on the standard Toolbar which makes an 'educated guess' at the range of figures you want to add up. To demonstrate this, clear the contents of cell B17.

♦ Select cell B17 and click the **Autosum** button, Σ, on the Toolbar.

♦ The SUM function with the suggested range will be inserted to the cell and displayed in the Formula bar. You can accept it by clicking the tick button, ✓, (or pressing [**Enter**]), reject it by clicking the cross button, ✗, (or pressing [**Esc**]) or edit the range if this is not accurate. In our case, the range is **not accurate** because there are gaps in our column of figures. If there had been no gaps, **Autosum** would have suggested the range B5:B16 for totalling.

♦ Change the range to B5:B16 (the editing can be done in the cell itself or in the Formula bar) and click the tick button or press [**Enter**].

♦ If you select the range for totalling before you click the **Autosum** button this will ensure that the correct range is inserted to the function. The program will enter the function in the first empty cell below the selected range if the values are located in a column or the first empty cell to the right of the range if the values are located in a row.

2 *Class average:*

♦ Select cell B18 and insert the function =AVERAGE(B5:B16).

♦ The cell range can be inserted between the brackets by clicking and dragging the mouse pointer over the range.

This function will produce the average based on the number of students sitting the exam.

3 *Number sat:*

♦ Insert the function =COUNT(B5:B16) in cell B19.

This function will count number entries only in the cell range and ignore text such as 'ABSENT'.

4 *Highest and lowest marks:*

♦ Insert the functions =MAX(B5:B16) and =MIN(B5:B16) in cells B20 and B21 respectively.

Suppose you have forgotten to enter the marks for two students – George whose mark was 36 and Grace whose mark was 65. We'll insert these two students to the list but we'll keep the list in alphabetical order as it is at the moment.

♦ Select the row headings 8 and 9.

Rows 8 and 9 should now be completely darkened.

♦ Select **Insert** from the Menu bar and **Rows** from the **Insert** menu.

Two blank rows should have been inserted between Fred and Jean.

♦ Enter the names and marks for George and Grace.

♦ Now check the formula in each of the cells B19:B23 and notice that in each case the range has been altered automatically to accommodate the two insertions.

5 *Pass/fail:*

♦ To test for pass or fail we'll use one of the program's logical functions. Insert the following function to cell C5: =IF(B5>=50,"P","F"). This means, if the value in B5 is greater than or equal to 50 insert the letter P to cell C5, else insert the letter F. If you wish text to be inserted to a cell using this function, it must be surrounded by double quotes, but there is no need to do this for numbers.

♦ Copy this function to the range C6:C18.

6 *Number passed:*

♦ Select cell B24 and insert the following function, =COUNTIF(C5:C18,"P"). This function will count the number of entries in a specified range (C5:C18) which meet a certain criterion (=P).

A related function, **Sumif**, will add the entries in a specified range which conform to a particular criterion.

♦ **Save** your file.

USEFUL FINANCIAL FUNCTIONS

In addition to the functions you have already used in this chapter, the following are useful for making calculations in the field of finance and accounting.

PMT

=PMT (rate, nper, pv, [fv,type])

This function calculates an annuity. An annuity is a number of periodic payments or receipts (nper) of equal amounts needed to repay a principal (pv) at a certain rate of interest (rate). It can be used to calculate the repayments on a loan. Optional arguments in the function are fv and type. Fv is the future value, or a cash balance you want to attain after the last payment is made. If fv is omitted it is assumed to be 0 (the future value of a loan, for example, is 0). Type can be either 0 or 1 and indicates whether payments or receipts are due at the end of the period (0) or the beginning (1). If type is omitted it is assumed to be 0.

For example, the following function would produce the yearly payment on a £30000 loan which had to be repaid over 25 years at an annual interest rate of 10 per cent:

=PMT (10%,25,–30000)

Notes:

(a) The units used to express 'rate' and 'nper' must be consistent. In the example, 10 per cent represents a *yearly* interest rate and 25 relates to *years*. The function is often used to calculate monthly repayments on a loan by dividing the rate by 12 and multiplying the nper by 12.

(b) The negative sign in front of pv avoids the result being negative.

PPMT

=PPMT (rate, per, nper, pv, [fv,type])

This function calculates the payment on the principal for a given period for an investment based on periodic, constant payments and a constant interest rate. It can be used to calculate the principal portion of a loan repayment for a given period.

IPMT

=IPMT (rate, per, nper, pv, [fv,type])

This function calculates the interest payment for a given period for an investment based on periodic, constant payments and a constant interest rate. It can be used to calculate the interest portion of a loan repayment for a given period.

FV

=FV (rate, nper, pmt, [pv,type])

This function calculates the future value of an investment based on periodic, constant payments, the number of payments and a constant interest rate.

PV

=PV (rate, nper, pmt, [fv,type])

This function calculates the present value of an investment. The present value is the amount that a series of future payments is worth now.

NPV

=NPV (rate, value1, value2, . . .)
or   =NPV (rate, range)

This function calculates the net present value of an investment based on a discount rate and a given series of periodic cash flows or a series of cash flows within a given range.

IRR

=IRR (values, guess)

This function calculates the internal rate of return for a series of periodic cash flows represented by the numbers in values. Guess is optional.

SLN

=SLN (cost, salvage, life)

This function returns the straight line depreciation of an asset for one period given the initial cost, salvage value when depreciation is complete and the number of periods over which it is being depreciated.

Lookup

Strictly speaking, lookup functions are not categorised as financial but they can be very useful in this area for looking up values in tables. They are dealt with separately in Chapter 23.

A complete list of financial and statistical functions is given at the end of this chapter.

HELP WITH FUNCTIONS

A detailed description of all Microsoft® Excel functions including syntax and examples of use should be available through the **Help** system. To gain access to this information the procedure is as follows:

♦ Select **Help** from the Menu bar and **Search for Help on** . . . from the **Help** menu.

♦ When the **Search** dialogue box opens type functions, select the item **functions, worksheet** from the list then click the **Show Topics** button.

A list of topics on worksheet functions should now be displayed in the topics section at the bottom of the **Search** dialogue box.

♦ Select the item **Alphabetical List of Worksheet Functions** and click the **Go To** button.

♦ The **Help** window should now display an alphabetical list of worksheet functions with brief descriptions. You will have to scroll the window to see all the functions in the list since there are several hundred.

♦ If you move the mouse pointer slowly over the function names the pointer will change from an arrow to a hand shape as it passes over a name. So for help on a particular function, locate the pointer over the function name and when it changes to a hand shape click the mouse button. This should display a **Help** window giving a detailed description of the function chosen.

♦ To return to the worksheet open the **File** menu in the **Help** window and select **Exit**.

FUNCTION WIZARD

The program's Function Wizard can be used to assist you when inserting functions to cells or cell formulae. It enables you to choose the required function, assemble the arguments and insert the function to the cell or formula. Function Wizard can be activated using the **Function** command on the **Insert** menu or by selecting the **Function Wizard** button, [fx], on the standard Toolbar.

The **Function Wizard** consists of two dialogue boxes. The first box allows you to view all functions or to view by category. You can select a function name and the arguments and a short description for that function will be displayed. The second dialogue box allows you to enter the values for each argument in the function and displays the calculated value when the function is complete.

ALPHABETICAL LIST OF FINANCIAL AND STATISTICAL FUNCTIONS

Financial functions

ACCRINT	Returns the accrued interest for a security that pays periodic interest.
ACCRINTM	Returns the accrued interest for a security that pays interest at maturity.

AMORDEGRC	Returns the depreciation for each accounting period.
AMORLINC	Returns the depreciation for each accounting period.
COUPDAYBS	Returns the number of days from the beginning of the coupon period to the settlement date.
COUPDAYS	Returns the number of days in the coupon period that contains the settlement date.
COUPDAYSNC	Returns the number of days from the settlement date to the next coupon date.
COUPNCD	Returns the next coupon date after the settlement date.
COUPNUM	Returns the number of coupons payable between the settlement date and maturity date.
COUPPCD	Returns the previous coupon date before the settlement date.
CUMIPMT	Returns the cumulative interest paid between two periods.
CUMPRINC	Returns the cumulative principal paid on a loan between two periods.
DB	Returns the depreciation of an asset for a specified period using the fixed-declining balance method.
DDB	Returns the depreciation of an asset for a specified period using the double-declining balance method or some other method you specify.
DISC	Returns the discount rate for a security.
DOLLARDE	Converts a dollar price, expressed as a fraction, into a dollar price, expressed as a decimal number.
DOLLARFR	Converts a dollar price, expressed as a decimal number, into a dollar price, expressed as a fraction.
DURATION	Returns the annual duration of a security with periodic interest payments.
EFFECT	Returns the effective annual interest rate.
FV	Returns the future value of an investment.
FVSCHEDULE	Returns the future value of an initial principal after applying a series of compound interest rates.
INTRATE	Returns the interest rate for a fully invested security.
IPMT	Returns the interest payment for an investment for a given period.
IRR	Returns the internal rate of return for a series of cash flows.
MDURATION	Returns the Macauley modified duration for a security with an assumed par value of $100.
MIRR	Returns the internal rate of return where positive and negative cash flows are financed at different rates.
NOMINAL	Returns the annual nominal interest rate.

NPER	Returns the number of periods for an investment.
NPV	Returns the net present value of an investment based on a series of periodic cash flows and a discount rate.
ODDFPRICE	Returns the price per $100 face value of a security with an odd first period.
ODDFYIELD	Returns the yield of a security with an odd first period.
ODDLPRICE	Returns the price per $100 face value of a security with an odd last period.
ODDLYIELD	Returns the yield of a security with an odd last period.
PMT	Returns the periodic payment for an annuity.
PPMT	Returns the payment on the principal for an investment for a given period.
PRICE	Returns the price per $100 face value of a security that pays periodic interest.
PRICEDISC	Returns the price per $100 face value of a discounted security.
PRICEMAT	Returns the price per $100 face value of a security that pays interest at maturity.
PV	Returns the present value of an investment.
RATE	Returns the interest rate per period of an annuity.
RECEIVED	Returns the amount received at maturity for a fully invested security.
SLN	Returns the straight-line depreciation of an asset for one period.
SYD	Returns the sum-of-years' digits depreciation of an asset for a specified period.
TBILLEQ	Returns the bond-equivalent yield for a Treasury bill.
TBILLPRICE	Returns the price per $100 face value for a Treasury bill.
TBILLYIELD	Returns the yield for a Treasury bill.
VDB	Returns the depreciation of an asset for a specified or partial period using a declining balance method.
XIRR	Returns the internal rate of return for a schedule of cash flows that is not necessarily periodic.
XNPV	Returns the net present value for a schedule of cash flows that is not necessarily periodic.
YIELD	Returns the yield on a security that pays periodic interest.
YIELDDISC	Returns the annual yield for a discounted security, for example a Treasury bill.
YIELDMAT	Returns the annual yield of a security that pays interest at maturity.

Statistical functions

AVEDEV	Returns the average of the absolute deviations of data points from their mean.
AVERAGE	Returns the average of its arguments.
BETADIST	Returns the cumulative beta probability density function.
BETAINV	Returns the inverse of the cumulative beta probability density function.
BINOMDIST	Returns the individual term binomial distribution probability.
CHIDIST	Returns the one-tailed probability of the chi-squared distribution.
CHIINV	Returns the inverse of the one-tailed probability of the chi-squared distribution.
CHITEST	Returns the test for independence.
CONFIDENCE	Returns the confidence interval for a population mean.
CORREL	Returns the correlation coefficient between two data sets.
COUNT	Counts how many numbers are in the list of arguments.
COUNTA	Counts how many values are in the list of arguments.
COVAR	Returns covariance, the average of the products of paired deviations.
CRITBINOM	Returns the smallest value for which the cumulative binomial distribution is less than or equal to a criterion value.
DEVSQ	Returns the sum of squares of deviations.
EXPONDIST	Returns the exponential distribution.
FDIST	Returns the F probability distribution.
FINV	Returns the inverse of the F probability distribution.
FISHER	Returns the Fisher transformation.
FISHERINV	Returns the inverse of the Fisher transformation.
FORECAST	Returns a value along a linear trend.
FREQUENCY	Returns a frequency distribution as a vertical array.
FTEST	Returns the result of an F-test.
GAMMADIST	Returns the gamma distribution.
GAMMAINV	Returns the inverse of the gamma cumulative distribution.
GAMMALN	Returns the natural logarithm of the gamma function, $\Gamma(x)$.
GEOMEAN	Returns the geometric mean.
GROWTH	Returns values along an exponential trend.
HARMEAN	Returns the harmonic mean.
HYPGEOMDIST	Returns the hypergeometric distribution.
INTERCEPT	Returns the intercept of the linear regression line.

KURT	Returns the kurtosis of a data set.
LARGE	Returns the kth largest value in a data set.
LINEST	Returns the parameters of a linear trend.
LOGEST	Returns the parameters of an exponential trend.
LOGINV	Returns the inverse of the lognormal distribution.
LOGNORMDIST	Returns the cumulative lognormal distribution.
MAX	Returns the maximum value in a list of arguments.
MEDIAN	Returns the median of the given numbers.
MIN	Returns the minimum value in a list of arguments.
MODE	Returns the most common value in a data set.
NEGBINOMDIST	Returns the negative binomial distribution.
NORMDIST	Returns the normal cumulative distribution.
NORMINV	Returns the inverse of the normal cumulative distribution.
NORMSDIST	Returns the standard normal cumulative distribution.
NORMSINV	Returns the inverse of the standard normal cumulative distribution.
PEARSON	Returns the Pearson product moment correlation coefficient.
PERCENTILE	Returns the kth percentile of values in a range.
PERCENTRANK	Returns the percentage rank of a value in a data set.
PERMUT	Returns the number of permutations for a given number of objects.
POISSON	Returns the Poisson distribution.
PROB	Returns the probability that values in a range are between two limits.
QUARTILE	Returns the quartile of a data set.
RANDBETWEEN	Returns a random number between the numbers you specify.
RANK	Returns the rank of a number in a list of numbers.
RSQ	Returns the square of the Pearson product moment correlation coefficient.
SKEW	Returns the skewness of a distribution.
SLOPE	Returns the slope of the linear regression line.
SMALL	Returns the kth smallest value in a data set.
STANDARDIZE	Returns a normalised value.
STDEV	Estimates standard deviation based on a sample.
STDEVP	Calculates standard deviation based on the entire population.
STEYX	Returns the standard error of the predicted y-value for each x in the regression.
TDIST	Returns the student's t-distribution.

TINV	Returns the inverse of the student's t-distribution.
TREND	Returns values along a linear trend.
TRIMMEAN	Returns the mean of the interior of a data set.
TTEST	Returns the probability associated with a student's t-test.
VAR	Estimates variance based on a sample.
VARP	Calculates variance based on the entire population.
WEIBULL	Returns the Weibull distribution.
ZTEST	Returns the two-tailed P-value of a z-test.

CHAPTER 15

Consolidation and Additional Worksheet Features

PRACTICE EXERCISE 1: Freezing labels and headings · Extending the forecast · Full screen view and display magnification · Printing the updated file
PRACTICE EXERCISE 2: Moving columns · Sorting data · Adding shading and patterns to cells

PRACTICE EXERCISE 1

This exercise is designed to consolidate your knowledge of the material you have learned so far and also to introduce a few new features.

Open the workbook LearnXL and display the worksheet Forecast on screen. We are going to extend the worksheet for a further six months to produce a forecast until the end of the year. However, inserting another six columns to the worksheet will involve scrolling the window to the right and thereby losing sight of the labels in column A. Keeping row labels and column headings fixed on the screen can give us guidance when we are scrolling to the right or downwards in a large worksheet.

Freezing labels and headings

When extending our worksheet it would help greatly if we could keep the row labels in column A in sight at all times. We can do this by splitting the worksheet into panes and freezing the pane containing the labels to prevent scrolling. The rest of the worksheet can scroll normally. You can freeze the left pane, the top pane or both. The window is split at the active cell, i.e. the rows above and columns to the left of the cell are frozen when the **Freeze Panes** command is activated. If an entire row or column is selected, the window is split above the row or to the left of the column.

♦ Select the column heading B. The whole of column B will be darkened indicating that it has been selected.

♦ Select **Window** from the Menu bar and **Freeze Panes** from the **Window** menu.

♦ Deselect column B by clicking anywhere on the worksheet.

♦ If you now scroll the worksheet to the right, the labels in column A will remain fixed on the screen.

Extending the forecast

Extend the worksheet for another six months (Jul.–Dec.) based on the following figures for unit Sales:

JUL	AUG	SEP	OCT	NOV	DEC
4500	4600	4600	4500	4400	4200

◆ These are the only figures you should have to enter. Complete the other cells by copying the formulae from the June column. Cell formatting will be copied automatically. After copying you may have to widen some of the columns to display the results.

◆ When you have completed this, add a further column at the end to display totals for the year for the following:

Sales (units)
Sales revenue
Total material costs
Total labour costs
Total var. o/heads
Total costs
Profit/Loss

◆ The heading for column N should be TOTAL and the **Sum** function should be inserted once (**Autosum** could be used) and copied.

◆ Insert or copy a formula for the MARGIN for the year in cell N20.

◆ Format column N to correspond with the other columns and surround cell N18 completely with a border to highlight the Profit/Loss for the year.

◆ When you have completed the worksheet, select **Window** from the Menu bar and **Unfreeze Panes** from the **Window** menu.

Since the worksheet is now much wider, we will have to recentre the heading.

◆ Select cells A1:N1.

◆ Select **Format** from the Menu bar and **Cells** from the **Format** menu.

◆ When the **Format Cells** dialogue box opens, click on the **Alignment** tab button and select **Center Across Selection**.

◆ Click **OK** in the dialogue box to return to the worksheet and the heading should be re-centred.

Note: The re-centring task could have been carried out using the **Center Across Columns** button on the formatting Toolbar.

◆ Now **Save** your updated workbook.

Full screen view and display magnification

The worksheet has now become too large to view completely on the screen. You can see a bit more of it by 'switching off' the Title and Status bars and the Toolbars.

♦ Select **View** from the Menu bar and **Full Screen** from the **View** menu. This allows you to see more rows in the worksheet.

♦ Select **View** again and **Zoom** from the **View** menu.

♦ When the **Zoom** dialogue box opens select the **75% Magnification** option button and click **OK**. This will allow you to see more columns.

♦ Now return to the original screen: select **View** and **Full Screen**, then select **View**, **Zoom**, **100% Magnification**, and click **OK**.

Note: There is a **Zoom Control** box on the standard Toolbar which you can use to change the magnification of the worksheet.

Printing the updated file

The page layout has already been designed but since the worksheet is now quite a bit wider it might be better to have it printed in landscape rather than portrait orientation.

♦ Select **File** from the Menu bar and **Print** from the **File** menu.

♦ When the **Print** dialogue box opens, ensure that the **Selected Sheet(s)** check box is selected in the **Print What** section and click the **Page Setup** button.

♦ In the **Page Setup** dialogue box click the **Page** tab button and select **Landscape Orientation**.

♦ In the **Scaling** section click the button marked, **Fit to 1 page wide by 1 tall**.

♦ Select **OK**.

♦ You will be returned to the **Print** dialogue box where you should select the **Print Preview** button. If you are satisfied with the presentation, select the **Print** button from the top of the **Preview** window and your worksheet should be printed.

♦ **Save** your worksheet again with the updated print settings.

The printed worksheet should be similar to the following:

	A	B	C	D	E	F	G	H	I	J	K	L	M	N
1				CONSUMER GADGETS – PROFIT FORECAST 199X										
2														
3	KEY VARIABLES													
4	Selling price	£50.00												
5	Material cost per unit	£15.00												
6	Labour cost per unit	£10.00												
7	Var. o/heads per unit	£2.50												
8	Fixed o/heads per month	£50000												
9														
10	MONTH	JAN	FEB	MAR	APR	MAY	JUN	JUL	AUG	SEP	OCT	NOV	DEC	TOTAL
11														
12	Sales (units)	4000	4000	4000	4300	4300	4500	4500	4600	4600	4500	4400	4200	51900
13	Sales revenue	200000.00	200000.00	200000.00	215000.00	215000.00	225000.00	225000.00	230000.00	230000.00	225000.00	220000.00	210000.00	2595000.00
14	Total material cost	60000.00	60000.00	60000.00	64500.00	64500.00	67500.00	67500.00	69000.00	69000.00	67500.00	66000.00	63000.00	778500.00
15	Total labour cost	40000.00	40000.00	40000.00	43000.00	43000.00	45000.00	45000.00	46000.00	46000.00	45000.00	44000.00	42000.00	519000.00
16	Total var. o/heads	10000.00	10000.00	10000.00	10750.00	10750.00	11250.00	11250.00	11500.00	11500.00	11250.00	11000.00	10500.00	129750.00
17	Total costs	160000.00	160000.00	160000.00	168250.00	168250.00	173750.00	173750.00	176500.00	176500.00	173750.00	171000.00	165500.00	2027250.00
18	Profit/Loss	40000.00	40000.00	40000.00	46750.00	46750.00	51250.00	51250.00	53500.00	53500.00	51250.00	49000.00	44500.00	567750.00
19														
20	MARGIN	20.00%	20.00%	20.00%	21.74%	21.74%	22.78%	22.78%	23.26%	23.26%	22.78%	22.27%	21.19%	21.88%

PRACTICE EXERCISE 2

Once again this exercise is designed to consolidate learning so far and to introduce a few additional spreadsheet facilities.

♦ Select Sheet2 in your workbook, LearnXL.

♦ Set up the following worksheet which is designed to hold the examination results for students on a one-year diploma course in Business Administration.

♦ All students study four subjects: Economics, Accounting, Law and either Marketing or French.

	A	B	C	D	E	F	G	H	I	J
1	SURNAME	INITS	ECONS	ACCTS	MKTING	LAW	FRENCH	STUDENT	STUDENT	PASS/
2								TOTAL	AVERAGE	FAIL
3	Thomas	R	47	65		42	38			
4	Turner	R	50	62	50	62				
5	Hawkins	M	65	57		55	65			
6	Philips	B	49	68	47	45				
7	Davies	N	51	65	41	50				
8	Jones	K	64	77		58	72			
9	Jones	B	36	51	36	42				
10	Smith	L	59	56		51	67			
11	Wilson	J	57	65	55	69				
12	Short	A	48	56	51	51				
13	Rowan	P	45	55	41	50				
14	Dale	M	60	66		59	68			
15	Watson	I	62	60	62	54				
16	Dunn	S	62	61	70	49				
17	Meadows	G	48	54	52	54				
18										
19	SUBJECT TOT									
20	SUBJECT AVG									
21	NUMBER SAT									

Carry out the following tasks:

1 Rename Sheet2 in your workbook to Sturecs.

2 **Save** the workbook, LearnXL.

3 Embolden headings and names and centre column headings. Adjust column widths where necessary.

4 Use appropriate functions to calculate totals and averages for each student and subject. Each of these functions should be entered to the appropriate cell and copied to the others. Format all average figures to two decimal places (0.00).

5 Insert a function to calculate the number of students who sat each examination. Again, insert once and copy.

♦ Complete the PASS/FAIL column using an appropriate function. Student average must be 50 or above to pass.

♦ Centre all values in their cells.

♦ We forgot to put a heading in. Insert three blank rows at the top of the worksheet and enter the following:

BUSINESS ADMINISTRATION DIPLOMA
EXAMINATION RESULTS JUNE 199X

The heading should be located in cells A1 and A2 (although it will stretch over several columns). It should be in bold print, underlined and the font size should be 12.

Moving columns

It is decided to put the option subjects (Marketing and French) in adjacent columns. This will involve moving the Marketing column. First we'll insert a blank column between Law and French.

♦ Select the column heading G.

♦ When column G is completely darkened, select **Insert** from the Menu bar and **Columns** from the **Insert** menu.

There should now be a blank column (G) between Law and French.

♦ Now select the column heading E. When column E is completely darkened select **Edit** from the Menu bar and **Cut** from the **Edit** menu.

Column E should now be surrounded by a flowing border and the contents will have been transferred to the clipboard.

♦ Select column heading G, then **Edit** from the Menu bar, then **Paste** from the **Edit** menu.

The column containing the Marketing results should now appear between Law and French and column E will be blank.

♦ We'll now delete column E so select the column heading.

♦ When column E is darkened, select **Edit** from the Menu bar and **Delete** from the **Edit** menu. The worksheet data should have moved along to fill the gap.

Data can be moved and relocated between existing data much more quickly by selecting and dragging to the new location. To demonstrate this feature we'll now move the Accounts column (D) and relocate it between Law and Marketing. However, before you try this save the workbook and if you experience any difficulty with the move you can always revert back to this version of your worksheet.

♦ Select column heading D and the column will be darkened.

♦ Locate the mouse pointer over the right border of the selected column. When correctly located the pointer will be in the shape of an arrow.

♦ Hold down the **[Shift]** key then click and drag the pointer to the right into column C. When you see the column border relocate itself release the mouse button and then the **[Shift]** key. The Accounts column should now be located between Law and Marketing.

♦ If the move has been unsuccessful for some reason you can cancel a mistake using **Edit/Undo**. Alternatively you can revert back to the previously saved version of your file by **Closing** the workbook and *not* saving changes when prompted.

Sorting data

We'll now sort the data into alphabetical order by student surname.

♦ Select that part of the worksheet containing the names *and results* (cell range A6:J20). If you sort the names only, the results will remain in their existing positions and end up against the wrong names.

♦ Select **Data** from the Menu bar and **Sort** from the **Data** menu.

The following **Sort** dialogue box should now open allowing you to specify sort fields:

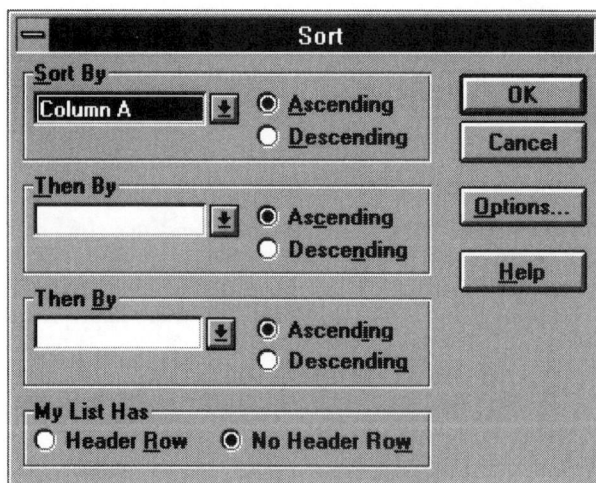

♦ We want the primary sort to be carried out using the data in column A (surname) so make sure that Column A is displayed in the small **Sort By** box. If not, clicking on the ▣ button at the end of the box will allow you to make the selection from a drop-down list. Now select the **Ascending** button in the **Sort By** section.

♦ Ascending means A–Z or 1, 2, 3, . . ., etc.; descending means Z–A or 3, 2, 1.

♦ In case there are several students with the same surname, we will specify a secondary sort field. In the first **Then By** section, click the ▣ button and select Column B (initials) from the drop-down list. Also select the **Ascending** button in the **Then By** section.

♦ Click the **OK** button and you'll be returned to the worksheet where the students' names should now be arranged in alphabetical order. Notice that a secondary sort has been carried out on the two students with the surname Jones and they are listed alphabetically by initials.

Shading and patterns

When producing reports, presentation is an important factor. When a report consists of columns of data it is often easier to read the figures when alternate columns are shaded. We'll try this on the Sturecs worksheet to see the effect.

♦ Select the cell range C4:C24 (Economics results).

♦ Hold down the **[Ctrl]** key and select the ranges E4:E24, G4:G24 and I4:I24.

♦ When the four ranges have been darkened, select **Format** from the Menu bar and **Cells** from the **Format** menu.

♦ When the **Format Cells** dialogue box opens, select the **Patterns** tab button at the top and you will be allowed to select a pattern and colour for the selected cell ranges.

♦ The **Pattern** choices can be displayed by clicking the ⬇ button. Selections are made by pointing to the appropriate square and clicking. Experiment with the different colours and patterns and observe the different effects in the **Sample** window. Remember, the objective is to make the figures easier to locate and read and not to print pretty patterns on the worksheet. When you find a shading you think might be suitable, click the **OK** button and check out the result on the worksheet.

♦ If you would like to see how it will look when printed select **File** from the Menu bar then **Print Preview**. If the full worksheet is not displayed on one page in Print Preview mode this means that it is too wide to fit on one page. You would then have to adjust the scaling or the orientation in the **Page Setup** dialogue box before printing.

Your worksheet should be similar to the following:

	A	B	C	D	E	F	G	H	I	J
1	BUSINESS ADMINISTRATION DIPLOMA									
2	EXAMINATION RESULTS		JUNE 199X							
3										
4	SURNAME	INITS	ECONS	LAW	ACCTS	MKTING	FRENCH	STUDENT	STUDENT	PASS/
5								TOTAL	AVERAGE	FAIL
6	Dale	M	60	59	66		68	253	63.25	Pass
7	Davies	N	51	50	65	41		207	51.75	Pass
8	Dunn	S	62	49	61	70		242	60.50	Pass
9	Hawkins	M	65	55	57		65	242	60.50	Pass
10	Jones	B	36	42	51	36		165	41.25	Fail
11	Jones	K	64	58	77		72	271	67.75	Pass
12	Meadows	G	48	54	54	52		208	52.00	Pass
13	Philips	B	49	45	68	47		209	52.25	Pass
14	Rowan	P	45	50	55	41		191	47.75	Fail
15	Short	A	48	51	56	51		206	51.50	Pass
16	Smith	L	59	51	56		67	233	58.25	Pass
17	Thomas	R	47	42	65		38	192	48.00	Fail
18	Turner	R	50	62	62	50		224	56.00	Pass
19	Watson	I	62	54	60	62		238	59.50	Pass
20	Wilson	J	57	69	65	55		246	61.50	Pass
21										
22	SUBJECT TOT		803	791	918	505	310			
23	SUBJECT AVG		53.53	52.73	61.20	50.50	62.00			
24	NUMBER SAT		15	15	15	10	5			

♦ **Save** the workbook.

CHAPTER 16

Managing Workbooks

**Copying and Moving Worksheets · Inserting and Deleting Worksheets ·
Protection · Opening a New Workbook · Protecting the Worksheet · Protecting
Individual Cells · Protecting the Workbook · Deleting a Workbook**

COPYING AND MOVING WORKSHEETS

If you wish to produce a duplicate copy of your worksheet or move it to a different
position in the workbook, the procedure is as follows:

♦ Activate (display) the worksheet.

♦ Select **Edit** from the Menu bar then **Move or Copy Sheet** from the **Edit** menu.

The following **Move or Copy** dialogue box should now open:

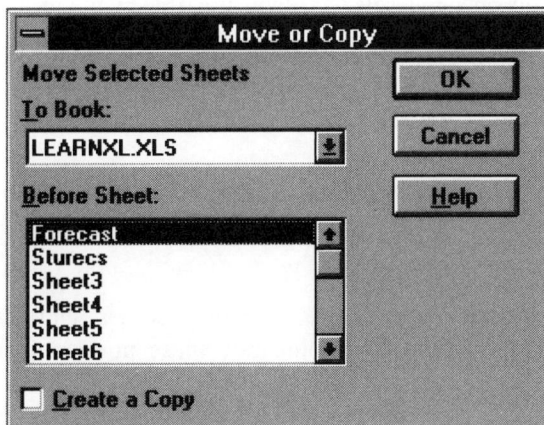

♦ The **To Book** section in the dialogue box allows you to specify the workbook to
which the sheet is to be moved or copied – the existing workbook, another
workbook which has already been created or a new workbook. Simply choose from
the drop-down list.

♦ The **Before Sheet** section allows you to select the location in the workbook the
sheet is to be moved or copied to, e.g. before Sheet4. Again, simply choose from the
list displayed.

◆ If you select the **Create a Copy** check box, a copy of the sheet will be placed in the selected location and the original sheet will remain in its existing location.

◆ If you do not select the **Create a Copy** check box, the original sheet will be moved to the new location.

The move or copy operation can be carried out within the same workbook by clicking the sheet's name tab and dragging to a new position on the name tab bar. The procedure is as follows:

◆ Activate (display) the sheet you wish to move or copy.

◆ Point to the sheet's name tab.

◆ Press and hold down the mouse button; a small sheet will attach itself to the pointer and an arrow, ▼, will appear above the sheet's name. If you want to move the sheet, drag the pointer along the name tab bar and release when the arrow indicates the new position. If you want to copy the sheet, hold down the [**Ctrl**] key while you drag and release the button.

INSERTING AND DELETING WORKSHEETS

When a new workbook is opened it contains 16 sheets but it is a simple matter to insert more if required. It is also easy to remove unwanted sheets from the workbook.

1   *To insert a sheet:*

◆ Select any existing sheet by clicking on its name tab button (the new sheet will be inserted in front of the one you select). Open the **Insert** menu and choose **Worksheet**.

2   *To delete a sheet:*

◆ Select the sheet for deletion by clicking on its name tab button. Open the **Edit** menu and choose **Delete Sheet**.

PROTECTION

Microsoft® Excel offers protection options for restricting access and preventing alterations to workbooks and worksheets. To demonstrate these protection measures, we'll open a new workbook.

Once you have become familiar with the operation and effects of the protection facilities available you can then use them, if you wish, on the workbook LearnXL.

OPENING A NEW WORKBOOK

◆ **Close** any workbook which is open at the moment using **File/Close**.

The worksheet part of the screen should now be blank.

◆ Select **File** from the Menu bar and **New** from the **File** menu (or click the **New Workbook** button on the standard Toolbar).

A new workbook should now open and Sheet1 should be displayed on the screen.

♦ Enter the following details to the worksheet:

	A	B
1	EMPLOYEES' SALARIES	
2		
3	Karen	19000
4	Bob	21000
5	Stewart	15000
6	Ali	18000
7	Mary	16000

Protecting the worksheet

A worksheet or chartsheet (see later) can be protected so that other people cannot change its contents.

♦ To demonstrate this select **Tools** from the Menu bar. Choose **Protection** from the **Tools** menu, then **Protect Sheet** from the sub-menu.

The following **Protect Sheet** dialogue box should now appear:

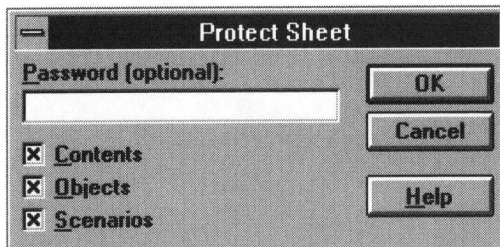

By selecting the **Contents** check box, you will prevent changes being made to cells or embedded charts on a worksheet or items on a chartsheet. Password protection is also available here to prevent anyone unprotecting the sheet without knowledge of the password.

♦ Enter the password as OPENUP and note that asterisks only appear in the entry field. Passwords are case sensitive so if you use capital letters here you must also use capital letters when asked for the password in the future.

♦ Ensure that the **Contents** check box has been selected and click the **OK** button.

A **Confirm Password** dialogue box will now open.

♦ Re-enter the password in exactly the same style and click the **OK** button.

♦ Now try to make a change to any cell in the worksheet. A dialogue box will warn you that the cells have been locked and cannot be changed. Remove the dialogue box from the screen by clicking **OK**.

♦ To unprotect the worksheet, open the **Tools** menu, select **Protection** then **Unprotect Sheet**. You should now be prompted for the password. Enter the password openup in lower case and click **OK**. You will be advised that the password is incorrect. Click the **OK** button and you will be returned to the worksheet.

♦ Select **Tools/Protection/Unprotect Sheet** again and this time enter the password correctly in upper case and click the **OK** button.

You should now be able to make alterations to the sheet.

PROTECTING INDIVIDUAL CELLS ON THE WORKSHEET

Depending on what the worksheet is used for, it is sometimes advisable to protect some of the cells whilst leaving others unprotected to allow data entry.

Let's say we wish to prevent alteration to the heading and names in our worksheet but we want to be able to amend the salary figures.

♦ Select the cell range B3:B7.

♦ Open the **Format** menu and select the **Cells** command.

♦ When the **Format Cells** dialogue box opens, select the **Protection** tab button at the top and when the Protection 'page' appears, clear the **Locked** check box (the cross should disappear).

♦ Select **OK**.

Note: This operation has to be carried out before you protect the sheet: you cannot unlock cells on a protected sheet.

♦ Now select **Tools** from the menu bar then **Protection** then **Protect Sheet**.

♦ When the **Protect Sheet** dialogue box opens, ensure that the **Contents** check box is selected and click **OK**.

You should now be able to make changes to the data in the worksheet but not the heading or the names.

♦ Remove the protection from Sheet1 in the normal way – **Tools/Protection/Unprotect Sheet**.

PROTECTING THE WORKBOOK

Password Protection

This level of protection denies access to the workbook file unless the correct password is entered.

♦ Select **File** from the Menu bar and **Save As** from the **File** menu.

♦ When the **Save As** dialogue box opens, enter the **File Name** as Trial, ensure that the **Drives** box displays the floppy drive (a: or b:) and then select the **Options** button.

♦ When the **Save Options** dialogue box opens, enter the password LETMEIN to the **Protection Password** field and six asterisks will appear.

♦ Click the **OK** button and a **Confirm Password** dialogue box will open.

♦ Re-enter the password in exactly the same style and click the **OK** button.

♦ When returned to the **Save As** dialogue box, select **OK**.

♦ **Close** the workbook using **File/Close**.

♦ Select **File** from the Menu bar.

♦ If the file TRIAL.XLS is listed near the bottom of the **File** menu, select it, otherwise **Open** it in the normal way.

The **Password** dialogue box should now appear.

♦ Enter the password LETMEIN, making sure that you use the correct case, and click the **OK** button.

The workbook should now open and display Sheet1.

Read-only and Write Protection

Two other levels of protection are available:

(a) The first allows other people to open the workbook and make changes to it but prevents them from replacing the original copy.

(b) The second allows other people to open the workbook but not change its contents.

DELETING A WORKBOOK

Since the workbook, TRIAL, was only used to demonstrate the protection facilities and it's almost empty, we'll delete it from our disc.

♦ **Close** the workbook TRIAL using **File/Close**.

♦ Open the **File** menu and select the **Find File** command.

The following **Find File** dialogue box should now open unless this is the first time **Find File** has been used, in which case the **Search** dialogue box should appear (covered next).

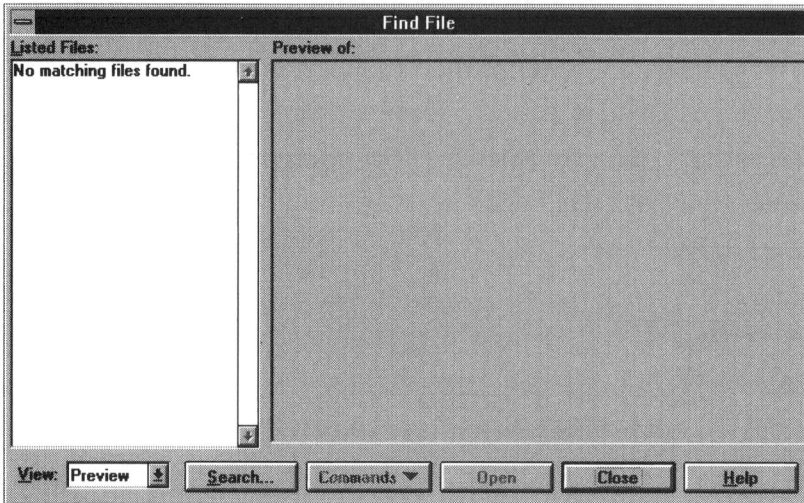

♦ If the file, TRIAL.XLS, is not listed in the **Listed Files** section of the dialogue box click on the **Search** button and the following **Search** dialogue box should appear:

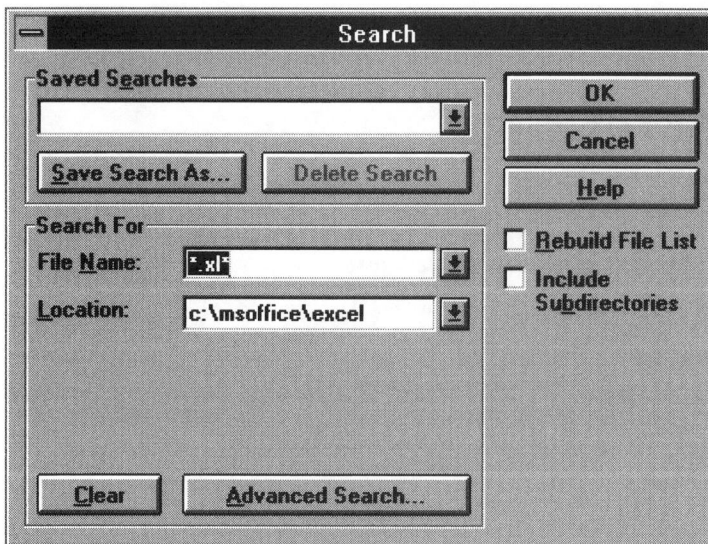

♦ Type TRIAL.XLS in the **File Name** box.

♦ Click the ⬇ button at the end of the **Location** box and select the floppy drive letter (a: or b: depending on where your file is located) from the drop-down list.

♦ When the correct drive letter appears in the **Location** box click the **OK** button and you will be returned to the **Find File** dialogue box where TRIAL.XLS should now be displayed in the **Listed Files** section.

♦ Ensure that TRIAL.XLS is selected (highlighted).

♦ Select the **Commands** button at the bottom of the dialogue box and choose **Delete** from the pop-up list.

♦ You will be asked to confirm that you want to delete TRIAL.XLS. Select **Yes**.

♦ Select the **Close** button to close the **Find File** dialogue box.

Note: You cannot delete a workbook file which is open.

CHAPTER 17

Charts and Graphs

Charts and Graphs · Creating a Pie Chart Sheet · Deleting a Chart Sheet · Creating a Multiple Column Chart Sheet · Creating a Line Chart from Non-Adjacent Selections

CHARTS AND GRAPHS

Worksheet data can often be shown to greater effect and produce greater impact by displaying it in the form of a chart. Excel offers a number of two- and three-dimensional chart types to choose from including column, pie, bar and line.

A chart can be created directly on the worksheet and in this case it is referred to as an *embedded* chart. This is useful when you want the chart printed alongside the data to which it relates. Alternatively, the chart can be produced on a separate chart sheet in the workbook. Either way, the chart is linked to the worksheet and is automatically updated when changes are made to the worksheet data.

We will use the following worksheet as a basis to demonstrate the construction of some of the chart types which are available.

♦ Open the workbook LearnXL and select Sheet3. Rename the sheet PROFITS and set up the worksheet as shown below:

	A	B	C	D	E	F
1	**COUNTRYWIDE ELECTRONICS PLC**					
2	**AREA PROFIT STATEMENT – 1st QUARTER 199X**					
3						
4	**AREA INCOME**					
5		JAN	FEB	MAR	TOTAL	%TOTAL
6	NORTH	6000	5000	7000		
7	EAST	7000	8000	8500		
8	SOUTH	500	4500	6500		
9	WEST	4500	7000	8000		
10	TOTAL INCOME					
11						
12	**AREA COSTS**					
13	NORTH	4500	3000	4500		
14	EAST	3500	6000	6000		
15	SOUTH	1000	3500	5000		
16	WEST	5000	4500	4500		
17	TOTAL COSTS					
18						
19	**AREA PROFIT**					
20	NORTH					
21	EAST					
22	SOUTH					
23	WEST					
24	TOTAL PROFIT					

◆ Carry out the following tasks:

1 Widen column A to accommodate the entries.

2 Calculate total quarterly income for each area (cells E6:E9).

3 Calculate total income for all areas for each month and a grand total (cells B10:E10).

4 Calculate each area's total quarterly income as a percentage of the total quarterly income for all areas (cells F6:F9). Use absolute cell referencing here. Format the figures to percentage style with no decimal places.

5 Calculate total quarterly costs for each area (cells E13:E16).

6 Calculate total costs for all areas for each month and a grand total (cells B17:E17).

7 Calculate each area's total quarterly costs as a percentage of the total quarterly cost for all areas (cells F13:F16). Format the figures to percentage style with no decimal places.

8 Calculate profit for each month for each area (Income – Costs).

9 Calculate total quarterly profit for each area (cells E20:E23).

10 Calculate total profit for all areas for each month and a grand total (cells B24:E24).

11 Calculate each area's total quarterly profit as a percentage of the total quarterly profit for all areas (cells F20:F23). Format the figures to percentage style with no decimal places.

12 Format all the figures (except percentages) to display in currency style (£) with no decimal places and centre all values in their cells.

When complete the worksheet should be similar to the following:

	A	B	C	D	E	F
1	**COUNTRYWIDE ELECTRONICS PLC**					
2	**AREA PROFIT STATEMENT – 1st QUARTER 199X**					
3						
4	**AREA INCOME**					
5		JAN	FEB	MAR	TOTAL	%TOTAL
6	NORTH	£6000	£5000	£7000	£18000	25%
7	EAST	£7000	£8000	£8500	£23500	32%
8	SOUTH	£500	£4500	£6500	£11500	16%
9	WEST	£4500	£7000	£8000	£19500	27%
10	TOTAL INCOME	£18000	£24500	£30000	£72500	
11						
12	**AREA COSTS**					
13	NORTH	£4500	£3000	£4500	£12000	24%
14	EAST	£3500	£6000	£6000	£15500	30%
15	SOUTH	£1000	£3500	£5000	£9500	19%
16	WEST	£5000	£4500	£4500	£14000	27%
17	TOTAL COSTS	£14000	£17000	£20000	£51000	
18						
19	**AREA PROFIT**					
20	NORTH	£1500	£2000	£2500	£6000	28%
21	EAST	£3500	£2000	£2500	£8000	37%
22	SOUTH	(£500)	£1000	£1500	£2000	9%
23	WEST	(£500)	£2500	£3500	£5500	26%
24	TOTAL PROFIT	£4000	£7500	£10000	£21500	

♦ **Save** your workbook.

CREATING A PIE CHART SHEET

Creating a chart sheet is like producing the chart on a separate 'page' to the related worksheet data. As with all other sheets in the workbook, the chart sheet can be printed independently and it is automatically saved when the workbook is saved.

We will first produce a simple pie chart of January's income for each area.

♦ Select the data you wish to plot: cell range A5:B9 (it is necessary to include the blank cell A5 in the selection).

♦ Select **Insert** from the Menu bar then **Chart** from the **Insert** menu then **As New Sheet** from the **Chart** sub-menu.

The **ChartWizard** tool will now be activated. This is a series of dialogue boxes which lead you through the design of your chart in five easy-to-follow steps.

Step 1

The Step 1 dialogue box, which should be displayed at the moment, allows you to enter the data range you wish to chart. Normally row and column labels should be included in this range and these will be used to identify the figures in the chart.

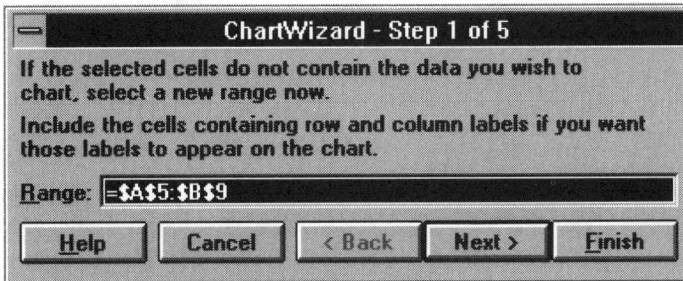

♦ The range displayed should be the range you selected: A5:B9 (shown as $A$5:$B$9), so click the **Next** button.

Step 2

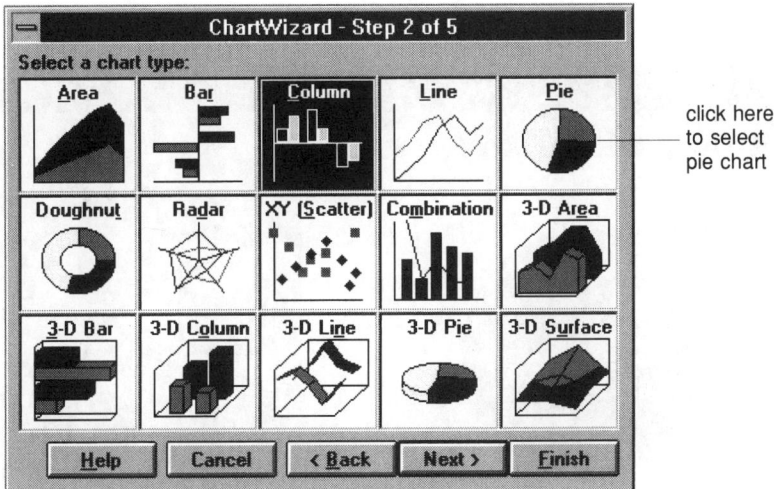

click here
to select
pie chart

♦ The Step 2 dialogue box should now appear allowing you to select a chart type. Select **Pie** (point and click on the **Pie** box) and click the **Next** button. You can move backwards and forwards through the dialogue boxes using the **Back** and **Next** buttons.

Step 3

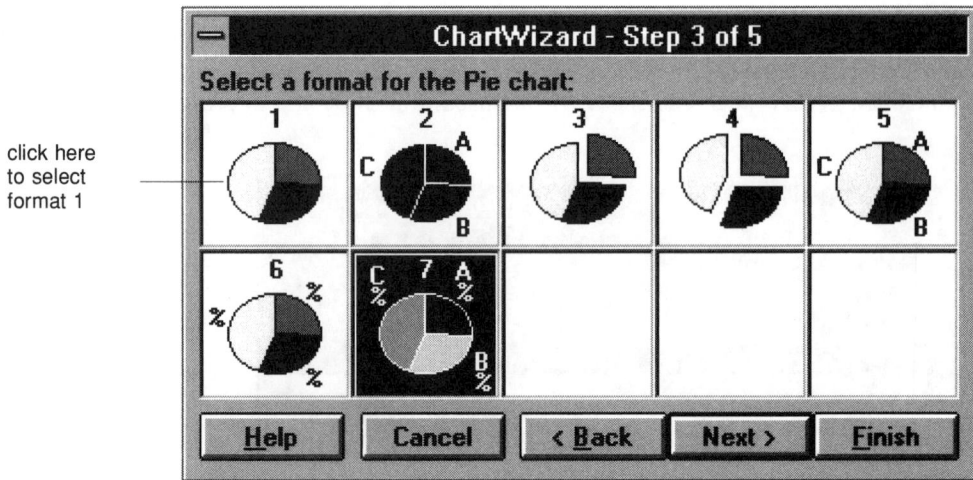

click here
to select
format 1

♦ The Step 3 dialogue box allows you to choose a format for the pie chart. We'll keep it very simple at the moment so select the basic pie chart with no labels (No.**1**) and click the **Next** button.

Step 4

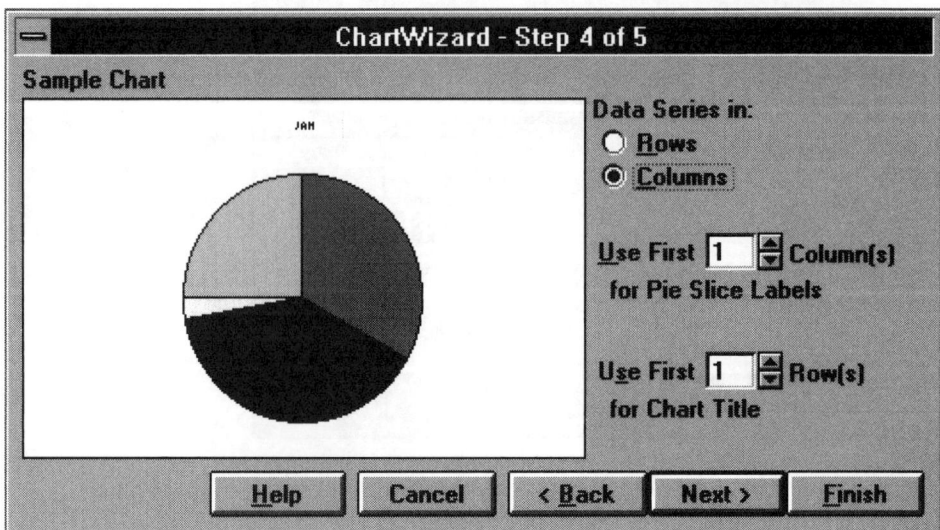

♦ The Step 4 dialogue box allows you to specify how you wish the data to be plotted and displays a sample chart – more on this later. Ensure that the following selections are made:

(a) **Data Series in Columns**;

(b) **Use First 1 Column for Pie Slice Labels**;

(c) **Use First 1 Row for Chart Title** (we'll modify the title later).

♦ Click the **Next** button.

Step 5

The Step 5 dialogue box allows you to add a legend, a chart title and axis titles where appropriate (e.g. bar charts and line graphs).

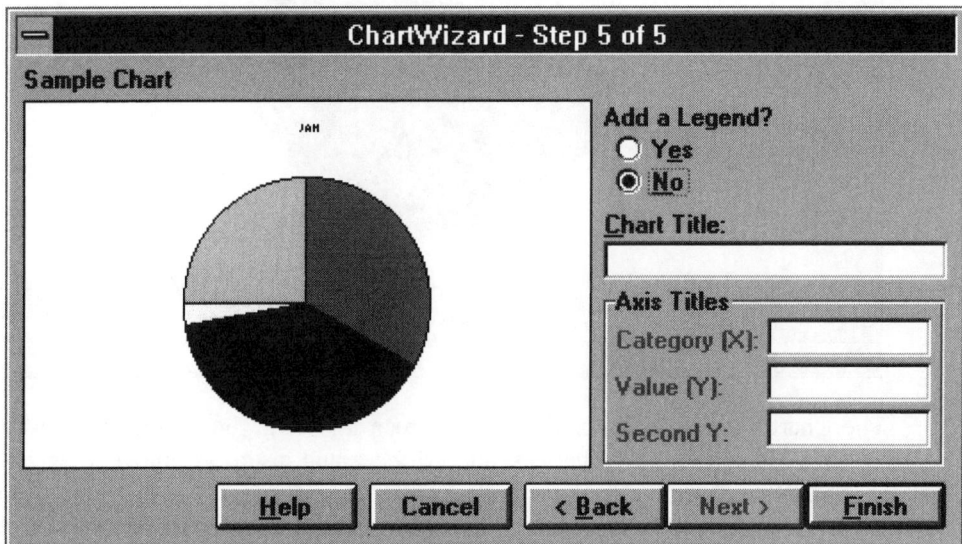

♦ Click the **Yes** button for **Add a Legend**.

♦ Click in the **Chart Title** box and enter the title as Area Income (Jan). *Do not press the* **[Enter]** *key* after typing the title – this will close the dialogue box.

♦ Examine the result in the **Sample Chart** panel and if you are satisfied select **Finish**.

The Chart Sheet should now be displayed similar to the following:

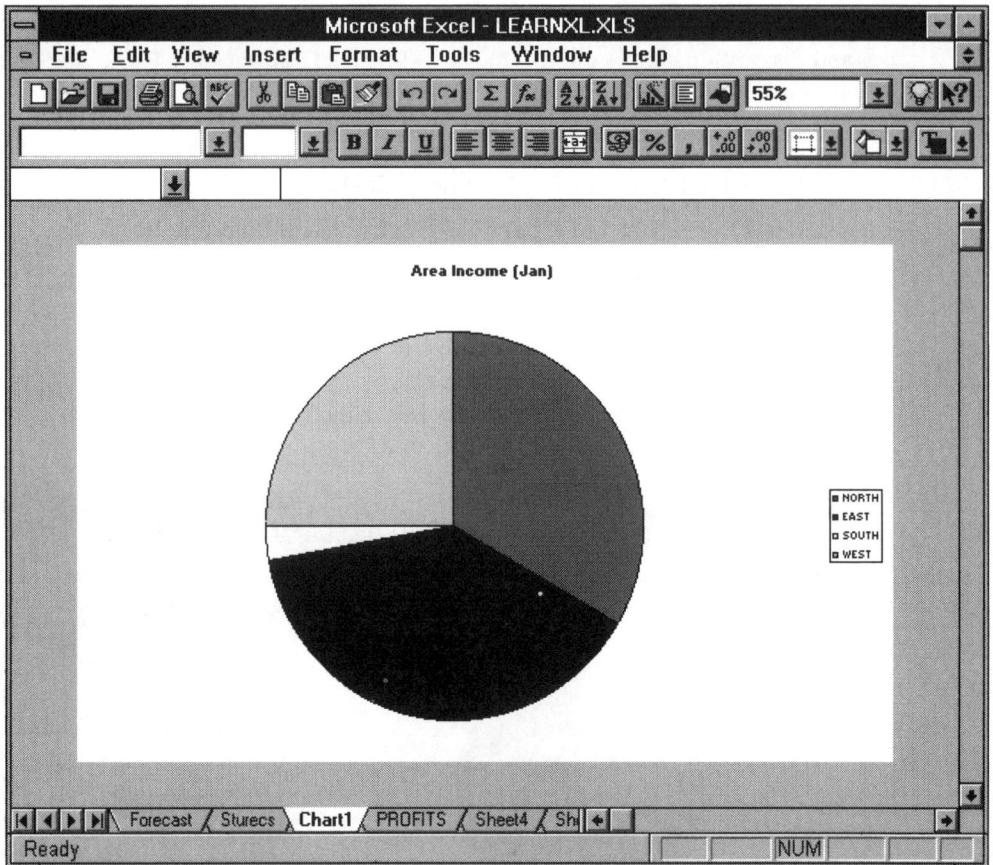

The Chart Toolbar may appear on the screen allowing you to alter the chart type, call up ChartWizard to make changes, add gridlines and insert or remove a legend.

ChartWizard can also be recalled from the standard Toolbar and some of the dialogue boxes will be redisplayed allowing you to make certain changes.

The chart sheet can be modified and formatted using the commands from the **Insert** and **Format** menus. We'll cover this later.

Note that the chart sheet has been inserted in the workbook in front of the related worksheet and given the name Chart1. We'll give it a more meaningful name.

♦ Select **Format** from the Menu bar then **Sheet** from the **Format** menu and **Rename** from the **Sheet** sub-menu.

♦ When the **Rename Sheet** dialogue box opens, enter the name as Piechart and click **OK**.

♦ **Save** the workbook.

DELETING A CHART SHEET

If you wish to remove a chart sheet from the workbook, simply activate (i.e. display) the sheet concerned and select the **Delete Sheet** option from the **Edit** menu.

CREATING A MULTIPLE COLUMN CHART SHEET

This time we'll create a multiple column chart to display each area's income for each of the three months.

♦ Activate (display) the worksheet PROFITS.

♦ Select the data which will be used for the chart – A5:D9 (the blank cell A5 must be included in the selection).

♦ Select **Insert** from the Menu bar then **Chart** from the **Insert** menu then **As New Sheet** from the **Chart** sub-menu.

The first **ChartWizard** dialogue box should now be displayed.

♦ *Step 1*. The Step 1 dialogue box should display the range which you have just selected – A5:D9 (it will be displayed as $A$5:$D$9). Click the **Next** button.

♦ *Step 2*. Select the chart type, **Column**, from the Step 2 dialogue box and click the **Next** button.

♦ *Step 3*. Select format **1** from the Step 3 dialogue box and click the **Next** button.

♦ *Step 4*. The Step 4 dialogue box will display a sample chart based on the information supplied so far. The columns in the chart can either represent months or areas depending on the selection made in this box. If the **Data Series in Columns** button is selected, the columns will represent months. If the **Data Series in Rows** button is selected, the columns will represent areas. Experiment by selecting each of these buttons in turn and watch the sample chart change. The legend and the *x*-axis data labels will obviously change to suit the selection. Select the **Data Series in Rows** button and click on **Next**.

♦ *Step 5*. The Step 5 dialogue box allows you to add a legend, a chart title and axis titles. The legend has already been added.

♦ Click in the **Chart Title** box and enter the title as Area Income (Jan–Mar). *Do not press the* [**Enter**] *key* after typing the title.

♦ Click in the **Axis Titles Category [X]** box and enter the title as Month. Again, *do not press the* [**Enter**] *key* after typing the axis title.

These results should appear on the **Sample Chart**.

♦ If you are satisfied with the result, click on the **Finish** button.

The multiple column chart sheet should now be displayed similar to the following:

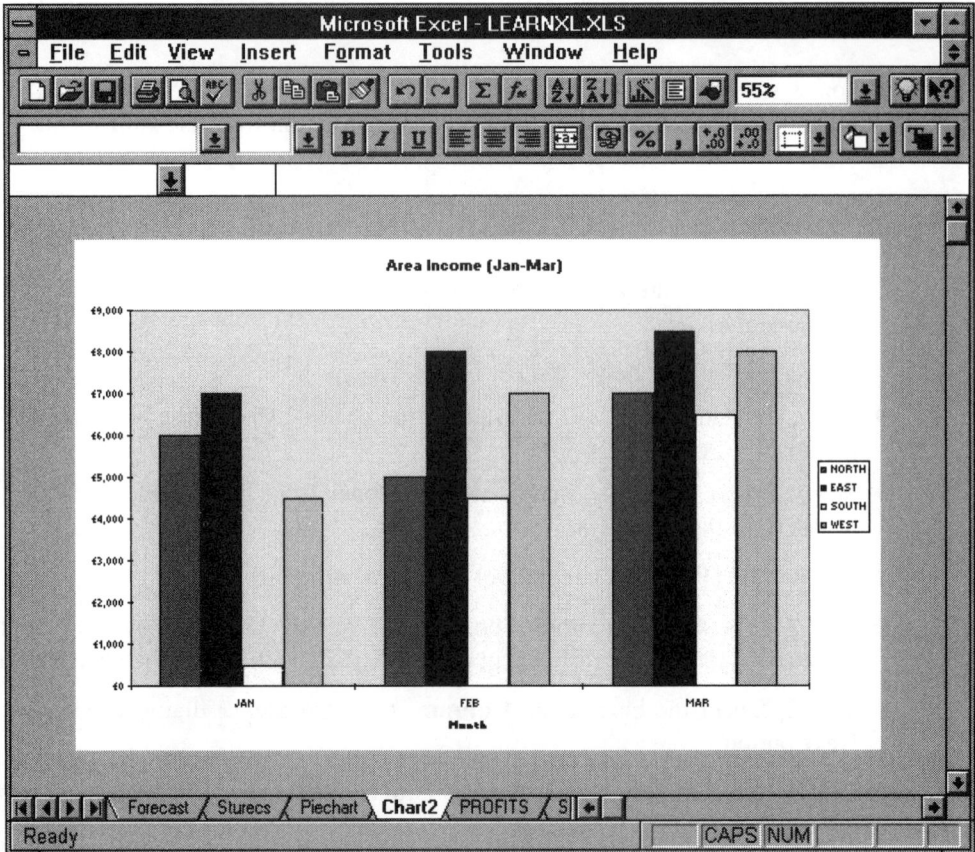

♦ Your new chart sheet will have been given the default name, Chart2. Rename this to Colchart.

♦ **Save** the workbook.

CREATING A LINE CHART FROM NON-ADJACENT SELECTIONS

We'll produce a line chart this time to compare the costs of the North and South areas for each of the three months. This will involve making *non-adjacent selections* from the worksheet.

♦ Activate (display) the worksheet PROFITS.

♦ Select the range A5:D5 (the complete selection must be a rectangular shape therefore the blank cell A5 must be included).

♦ Hold down the **[Ctrl]** key and select the two ranges A13:D13 and A15:D15. Release the **[Ctrl]** key.

The three ranges A5:D5, A13:D13 and A15:D15 should now be selected and darkened.

♦ Select **Insert** from the Menu bar then **Chart** from the **Insert** menu then **As New Sheet** from the **Chart** sub-menu.

The first **ChartWizard** dialogue box should now be displayed showing the selected ranges.

♦ Click the **Next** button in the Step 1 dialogue box.

♦ Select **Line** from the Step 2 dialogue box and click the **Next** button.

♦ Select format **2** from the Step 3 dialogue box and click **Next**.

♦ The Step 4 box will display a sample of the chart. Let's modify the format slightly. Click on the **Back** button and you will be returned to the Step 3 box. Select format **1** and click the **Next** button.

♦ The Step 4 box will now display the new format. Click the **Next** button.

♦ In the Step 5 dialogue box enter the **Chart Title** as Area Costs (Jan–Mar) and the **Category [X] Axis Title** as Month, remember not to press the **[Enter]** key after making these entries.

♦ If you are satisfied with the **Sample Chart**, click the **Finish** button.

The line chart should now be displayed similar to the following:

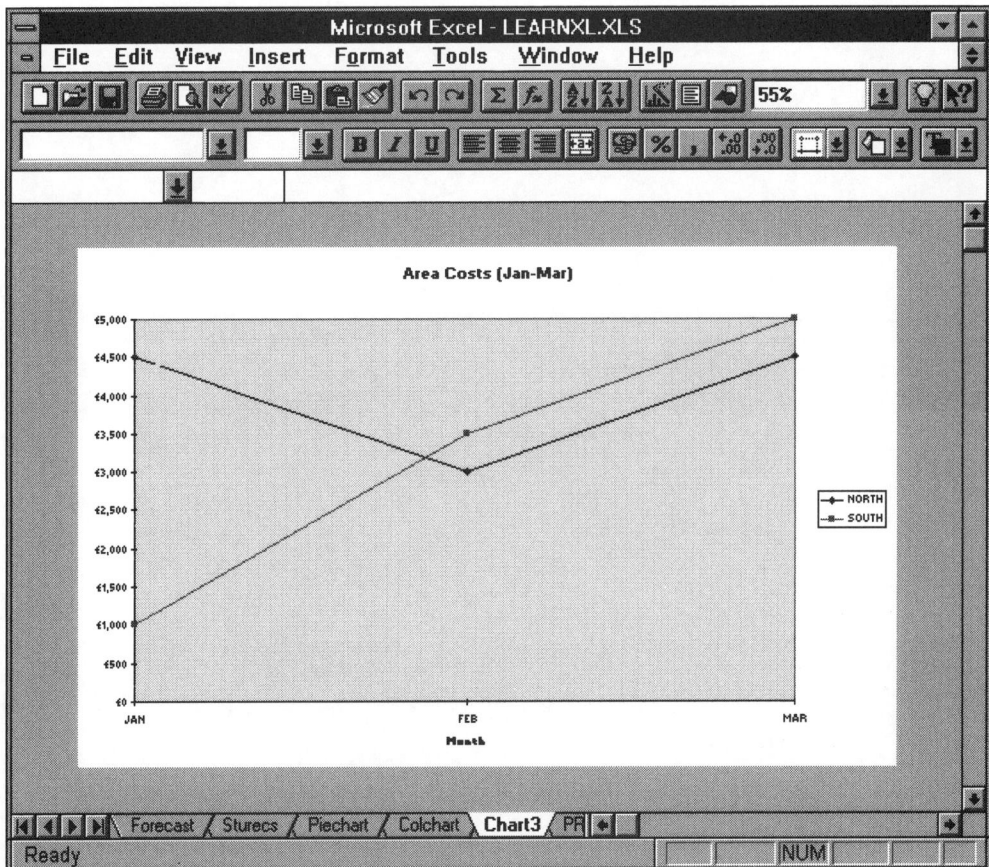

♦ Rename the chart sheet to Linechart.

♦ **Save** the workbook.

CHAPTER 18

Modifying and Formatting a Chart Sheet

Chart Commands · Adding Data Labels · Changing Chart Type · Selecting and Modifying Items on the Chart Sheet · Copying a Chart Sheet · Printing a Chart Sheet · Link between Worksheet and Chart · Displaying Worksheet and Chart Sheet Simultaneously

CHART COMMANDS

When a chart sheet is active (i.e. displayed on screen) the Chart commands are available from the Menu bar options and these can be used to perform operations on the chart itself or selected items within the chart area, e.g. the legend or the title. For example, the **Insert** menu can be used to add chart and axis titles, data labels or a legend and the **Format** menu can be used to carry out formatting operations on selected items and to change the chart type.

♦ Open the workbook, LearnXL, and activate the chart sheet, PieChart.

ADDING DATA LABELS

♦ Select **Insert** from the Menu bar and **Data Labels** from the **Insert** menu. When the **Data Labels** dialogue box opens, select the **Show Value** option button and click **OK**.

The chart should now display values against each pie slice.

CHANGING CHART TYPE

♦ Select **Format** from the Menu bar and **Chart Type** from the **Format** menu. When the **Chart Type** dialogue box opens, select **Column** and click the **OK** button.

The chart should now display the data in columnar format.

♦ Repeat the last operation and change the chart type back to **Pie**.

SELECTING AND MODIFYING ITEMS ON THE CHART SHEET

The existing chart sheet consists of a chart area, a plot area, the pie chart itself, a title, a legend and data labels. Each of these items can have operations such as formatting, moving, sizing, deleting carried out on them separately *once the item concerned has been selected.*

Selecting the chart area

This is basically the entire chart sheet consisting of the pie diagram, legend, title and data labels. To select this item, click anywhere within the chart area, making sure the pointer is clear of any other item. When the chart area is selected, small square 'handles' will appear round the rectangular perimeter and Chart will appear in the Name box on the Formula bar. To deselect, click outside this area. Practise selecting and deselecting the chart area. If you want to copy the chart to another sheet, you should ensure that the entire chart area is selected first.

Selecting, moving and sizing the plot area

The plot area is the area immediately surrounding the chart itself and should be selected if you wish to format it, move it to another part of the sheet or change its size. Try and select the plot area by positioning the pointer just outside the circle of the pie and clicking. You'll know it's been selected when a square box with 'handles' at the corners appears round the chart and Plot will appear in the Name box on the Formula bar. It's not easy at first – you may need a few attempts. If you click the pointer too far away from the pie, the Chart Area will be selected, and if the pointer is 'inside' the pie, the chart itself will be selected (handles will appear round the chart). If you click on a data label they will be selected.

Once the plot area has been selected, you can move the chart to a different position on the sheet. Locate the pointer in one of the four areas which are inside the plot area but outside the chart itself. When the pointer is located in one of these areas you should be able to click and drag the pointer to relocate the plot area. If you make any mistakes while trying this remember **Edit/Undo**.

The chart can also be sized using the square handles located at each corner of the plot area. Position the pointer over one of the handles. It will change to a double-headed arrow when correctly located and you can then click and drag the pointer to re-size the chart.

Practise moving the chart to different positions on the sheet and altering its size. To deselect the plot area, click anywhere outside it.

Moving, sizing and formatting the legend

♦ Click on the legend and the square 'handles' will appear round the perimeter. To move the legend locate the pointer inside the perimeter of the legend and click and drag to a new position.

◆ If you locate the pointer directly over one of the 'handles', it will change to a double-headed arrow allowing you to resize the legend by clicking and dragging.

◆ Make sure the legend is selected (handles round the border) and open the **Format** menu on the Menu bar. From the **Format** menu choose the option, **Selected Legend**.

◆ When the **Format Legend** dialogue box opens, select the **Font** tab button at the top and the Font 'page' will be displayed. Select the **Font Style** as **Italic** and the **Size** as **12** then click the **OK** button. When you return to the chart sheet, the legend text should appear in italic style. You may have to increase the size of the legend box to accommodate the increased font size.

◆ Now select the data labels and increase the font size to 12.

Note: You can use the **Font Size** button on the formatting Toolbar if it is displayed.

Modifying and formatting the title

◆ Select the title by pointing and clicking and the 'handles' will appear round the border. Locate the pointer inside the border and click again. The vertical bar insertion cursor will now start flashing allowing you to edit and insert text. Change the title to AREA INCOME – JAN and click anywhere in the chart area.

◆ Select the title again, change the font size to 14 and underline it.

Exploding pie slices

◆ Locate the pointer on the chart itself and click. The chart will be activated and 'handles' will appear round the circular perimeter. Point to the small South area segment (value, £500) and click again. The handles should now surround this segment only. Position the pointer over this segment and click and drag the slice slightly away from the pie chart. This facility can be used to emphasise a particularly good or bad result.

Text and arrows can also be added to the chart area (e.g. to explain the poor result in this instance) using the facilities on the drawing Toolbar.

If you've had problems with the last few operations on the PieChart sheet remember you can always 'abandon' the workbook by **Closing** without saving changes and revert back to the previously saved version. If you have encountered no difficulties your chart should now be similar to the following:

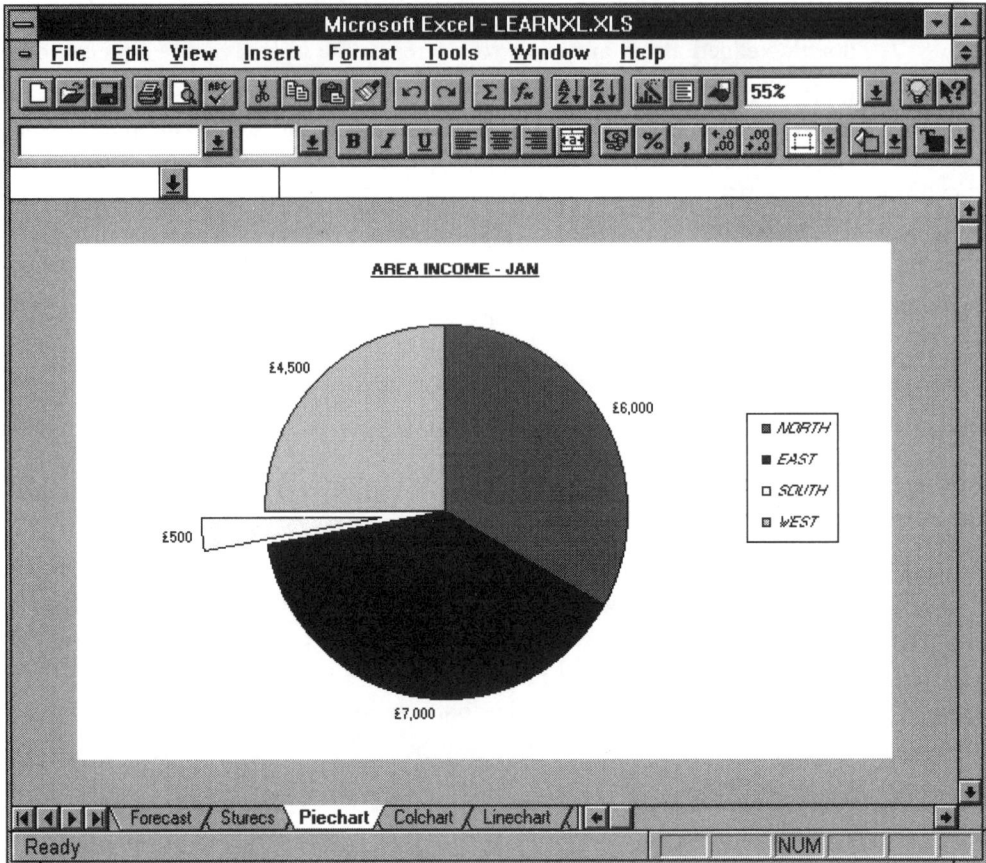

♦ We won't do any more to this particular chart so **Save** the workbook.

Formatting axis labels

♦ Activate the chart sheet, ColChart.

♦ Point to either JAN or FEB or MAR, the labels on the *x*-axis, and click. This will select the *x*-axis and a small 'handle' should appear at each end.

♦ When the *x*-axis has been selected, choose **Format** from the Menu bar and **Selected Axis** from the **Format** menu.

The **Format Axis** dialogue box should now open giving you access to five 'pages' of formatting options – **Patterns, Scale, Font, Number** and **Alignment**.

♦ Select the **Font** tab button at the top of the box and the Font 'page' will come to the forefront.

♦ Select **Bold** as the **Font Style** and **14** as the **Size**.

♦ Click the **OK** button and you will be returned to the chart sheet where your formatting selections will have been effected.

♦ Now select the *y*-axis by pointing and clicking on the axis itself or one of the values.

♦ When the 'handles' appear on the *y*-axis, select **Format** from the Menu bar and **Selected Axis** from the **Format** menu.

♦ Select the **Scale** tab button at the top of the **Format Axis** dialogue box and the **Scale** 'page' will come to the forefront.

♦ Click in the **Major Unit** box and change this from 1000 to 500.

♦ Select the **OK** button and you will be returned to the chart sheet. The *y*-axis will now be calibrated at intervals of 500. It looks a bit cluttered, so change the interval back to 1000. With the *y*-axis still selected, choose **14** from the **Font Size** drop-down list on the formatting Toolbar and click the **Bold** button. If the formatting Toolbar is not displayed, you can perform the same operations using the **Format** menu.

♦ **Save** the workbook.

Adding a data series

When we created the chart sheet, Linechart, we used cost data for the North and South areas only. We'll now complete that chart with the data for the other two areas, East and West.

♦ Activate the worksheet, PROFITS.

♦ Select the ranges A14:D14 and A16:D16 (hold down the **[Ctrl]** key while selecting the second range).

♦ When both ranges have been selected, choose **Edit** from the Menu bar then **Copy** from the **Edit** menu.

♦ Activate the chart sheet, LineChart.

♦ Select **Edit** from the Menu bar then **Paste** from the **Edit** menu and the two new data series will be inserted to the chart.

♦ Press **[Esc]** to remove the flowing border surrounding the selections in the worksheet PROFITS.

Deleting items from a chart

♦ Activate the chart sheet, LineChart.

♦ Point to the line which represents the costs for the East area and click. This should select the East area data series and small square handles will appear along the line confirming that it has been selected.

♦ Press the **[Delete]** key and this data series will be removed from the chart. The same operation can be carried out using the menu commands (**Edit** then **Clear** then **Series**) instead of the **[Delete]** key.

♦ Since this was only a demonstration and we wish the East area data series to appear on the chart, select **Edit** from the Menu bar and **Undo Clear** from the **Edit** menu.

The data series should be replaced on the chart.

Other chart items such as titles, axis labels, legends, etc can be deleted in similar fashion once they have been selected.

♦ **Save** the workbook.

COPYING A CHART SHEET

The chart can be copied quite easily and quickly to another sheet.

♦ Activate the chart sheet ColChart and select **Edit** from the Menu bar.

♦ Select **Move or Copy Sheet** from the **Edit** menu and the **Move or Copy** dialogue box should open allowing you to move or copy the selected sheet to another workbook or to another location within the same workbook.

♦ From the dialogue box, select PROFITS in the **Before Sheet** section (this will insert the copy of the chart sheet before the worksheet, PROFITS) and select the **Create a Copy** check box at the bottom.

♦ Click the **OK** button.

ColChart(2), a copy of ColChart, should now be displayed.

♦ Select **Format** from the Menu bar then **Chart Type** from the **Format** menu.

♦ When the **Chart Type** dialogue box opens, ensure that the **Column** box is selected (darkened) and click the **Options** button.

♦ When the **Format Column Group** dialogue box opens, ensure that the **Subtype** 'page' tab button at the top of the box has been selected allowing you to choose a different format for your column chart.

♦ Select the second **Subtype** (stacked column chart) and watch the sample format change. The third **Subtype** is a percentage stacked column chart.

♦ Click the **OK** button and you will be returned to the chart sheet ColChart (2) now showing the data displayed in stacked column format.

You now have two charts of different format based on the same data.

♦ **Save** the workbook.

PRINTING A CHART SHEET

The procedure for printing a chart sheet is very similar to that for printing a worksheet. Select the chart sheet (i.e. display it on the screen), access **Page Setup** from the **File** menu and set up the print page, preview if you wish, then print. The scaling of the chart sheet can be adjusted using the **Chart** tab button in the **Page Setup** dialogue box.

You have now been introduced to some of the main chart formatting facilities offered by the program. You may wish to investigate others using the existing charts as models. Alternatively, you could create new charts based on the data contained in the worksheet PROFITS.

LINK BETWEEN WORKSHEET AND CHART

The charts and the related worksheet are on separate 'pages' of the same workbook but they are still linked. Any changes made to the data in the worksheet will be reflected automatically in the chart. This relationship can be demonstrated by displaying the chart and the worksheet on the screen at the same time.

Displaying worksheet and chart sheet simultaneously

♦ Activate the worksheet PROFITS by clicking the sheet name tab at the bottom of the screen.

♦ Select **Window** from the Menu bar and **New Window** from the **Window** menu. A new window will open but it will not be immediately apparent since the same worksheet will be displayed. However, the workbook name in the Title bar at the top of the screen should now be LEARNXL.XLS:2.

♦ Select **Window** again from the Menu bar and **Arrange** from the **Window** menu.

♦ When the **Arrange Windows** dialogue box opens select the **Vertical** option button, click the **Windows of Active Workbook** check box then click **OK**.

♦ Two windows should now appear side by side on the screen, both displaying the same worksheet. The Title bar on one should display LEARNXL.XLS:1 and the other Title bar should show LEARNXL.XLS:2. To display a different worksheet in one of the windows, you must first activate that window by clicking anywhere in the window area (the Title bar is darkened when the window is active), then select a sheet from the sheet name tab bar at the bottom.

♦ Activate one of the windows (it doesn't matter which one) and select the sheet PieChart from the sheet name tab bar at the bottom of the *same window* (you may have to scroll the bar to bring the sheet name into view).

You should now have the chart displayed in one window and the related worksheet in the other. If the chart is not completely visible, you can resize the window to bring it all into view although this will obviously reduce the size of the worksheet window.

♦ To resize a window you must first make it active. Then locate the pointer on the vertical border between the two windows (there's actually two borders there, one for each window). When the pointer is located correctly it will change to a double-headed arrow ⇔. You can then click and drag the border to the left or right to alter the size.

♦ The chart relates to the area income for January, so reduce the width of your *worksheet* window so that it displays January data only. This should then allow you to increase the size of the chart window, bringing more of it into view.

Once you have done this, you can have a visual demonstration of the link between the worksheet data and the chart.

♦ Activate the worksheet window and then select cell B8 (South Area Income for January).

♦ Change the entry in the cell to 3500 and observe the immediate effect on the chart.

♦ Select cell B8 again and change the entry back to 500.

The chart also should return to its original state.

♦ To close the second window, activate the window whose Title bar displays LEARNXL.XLS:2. To the left of the Title bar there is a control button, ⊟. Click the control button and select **Close** from the drop-down list of options.

♦ The second window will be closed and you'll be returned to normal. Well almost normal – your worksheet or chart sheet will now have to be resized to full screen size. You can do this by dragging the window's border or by opening the **Window** menu and selecting **Arrange**, then click **OK** when the **Arrange Windows** dialogue box opens.

Opening more than one window on the screen and resizing is not an easy operation, particularly if you're doing it for the first time. If you have made any mistakes, don't worry, simply **Close** the file, *do not save changes*, and reopen the previously saved file.

CHAPTER 19

Embedded Charts and Practice Exercises

Embedded Charts · Selecting, Moving and Sizing an Embedded Chart · Activating and Modifying an Embedded Chart · Link between Worksheet and Chart · Adding a Data Series to an Embedded Chart · Deletion · Printing a Worksheet with an Embedded Chart · Practice Exercises

EMBEDDED CHARTS

A chart can be embedded as an object in a worksheet so that the worksheet and the related chart can be printed as one document. We'll produce a column chart showing area income for each month and embed it beneath the worksheet data. To allow us to view the chart and related data on the one screen, we'll create a new worksheet containing the income data only.

♦ Open the workbook, LearnXL, and activate the worksheet PROFITS.

♦ Select the range A1:F10.

♦ Select **Edit** from the Menu bar and **Copy** from the **Edit** menu.

♦ Activate Sheet4 (the next blank worksheet) by clicking the name tab button at the bottom of the screen and a blank worksheet should be displayed.

♦ Select cell A1 in the blank worksheet.

♦ Select **Edit** from the Menu bar then **Paste** from the **Edit** menu.

♦ The selected cells representing area income should now be pasted into the new worksheet. Press the [Esc] key to remove the flowing border round the selected cells in the worksheet PROFITS.

♦ Rename the Sheet4 worksheet to INCOME.

♦ Change the title from AREA PROFIT STATEMENT to AREA INCOME STATEMENT. You may also have to widen column A.

♦ **Save** the workbook.

♦ To allow us to see more cells in the worksheet, select **View** from the Menu bar and **Full Screen** from the **View** menu.

Creating an embedded chart

♦ First select the data ranges to be used for the chart – A5:D7 and A9:D9 (hold down the [**Ctrl**] key for second range selection). We'll add the data for South area later.

♦ Now select **Insert** from the Menu bar then **Chart** from the **Insert** menu then **On This Sheet** from the **Chart** sub-menu.

The mouse pointer should have changed to a cross hair with a chart symbol (when located on the worksheet) and you can use this to mark out the area on the worksheet where the chart will be placed. You don't have to be particularly accurate at this point since the chart area can be moved and resized later.

♦ Place the cross hair at the position you want the top left corner of the chart area to be; somewhere in column A just under the data.

♦ Hold the mouse button down and drag the pointer downwards and to the right. You should be producing a box or rectangular shape which will hold your chart. When you have achieved a suitable shape and size, release the mouse button and the first **ChartWizard** dialogue box should appear displaying your selected data ranges.

♦ Click the **Next** button in the Step 1 dialogue box.

♦ Select the chart type **Column** from the Step 2 box and click **Next**.

♦ Select format **1** from the Step 3 box and click **Next**.

♦ A **Sample Chart** will be displayed in the Step 4 box; click the **Next** button.

♦ When the Step 5 dialogue box opens, select the **Yes** check box for **Add a Legend** and enter the **Chart Title** as Area Income (Jan–Mar). These entries will be reflected in the **Sample Chart**.

♦ Select the **Finish** button. You will be returned to the worksheet and the chart should appear in the area you marked for it.

♦ **Save** the workbook.

ChartWizard tool

An embedded chart can be created without the aid of the menu commands. First select the data you wish to plot and then click the **ChartWizard** button on the standard Toolbar. This will change the mouse pointer to a cross hair and the procedure from then on is exactly the same as that described in the previous section.

SELECTING, MOVING AND SIZING AN EMBEDDED CHART

At the moment, the chart area should be *selected*, i.e. small square 'handles' should be positioned round the perimeter.

♦ Click on the worksheet outside the chart area and the handles will disappear (the chart has been deselected).

If you wish to move or resize the chart area, you must first of all *select* it.

♦ Click anywhere in the chart area, this will select it and the 'handles' will appear. Position the mouse pointer anywhere within the selected chart area. Press and hold down the mouse button and drag the pointer slightly to the right or downwards. When you release the mouse button the chart area will be repositioned.

♦ If you feel the chart area is too large or too small, you can resize it using the perimeter handles. Locate the mouse pointer over one of the handles; when correctly located, the pointer will change to a double-headed arrow. Press and hold down the mouse button and drag the pointer to resize the chart area. Practise this with each of the handles in turn and you should appreciate that the chart area can be resized vertically and/or horizontally depending on which handle you use. Use the corner handles to resize proportionally.

ACTIVATING AND MODIFYING AN EMBEDDED CHART

Before any changes can be made to a chart or items within the chart area (legend, title, etc.) it must first of all be *activated*. To activate the chart double-click anywhere in the chart area. This will cause the perimeter of the chart area to change from a thin line to a thicker cross-hatch border. To deactivate the chart, click on the worksheet outside the chart area. When the chart area has been activated, the chart commands from the **Insert** and **Format** menus become available and any item within the chart area can be selected. This means that all the modifying and formatting operations carried out in the previous chapter on chart sheets can also be performed on the embedded chart. Operations such as moving, sizing and formatting can be carried out on the legend, the title and the chart itself once the item concerned has been selected.

For example, ensure that the chart area is *activated* then *select* the legend. When the handles appear round the perimeter of the legend it can be resized and moved in the normal way and formatted using the **Format** menu. Other items in the chart area such as the title and the chart itself can be similarly modified once they have been selected, but remember, *the chart area must be active before an item can be selected.*

Your worksheet should now be similar to the following:

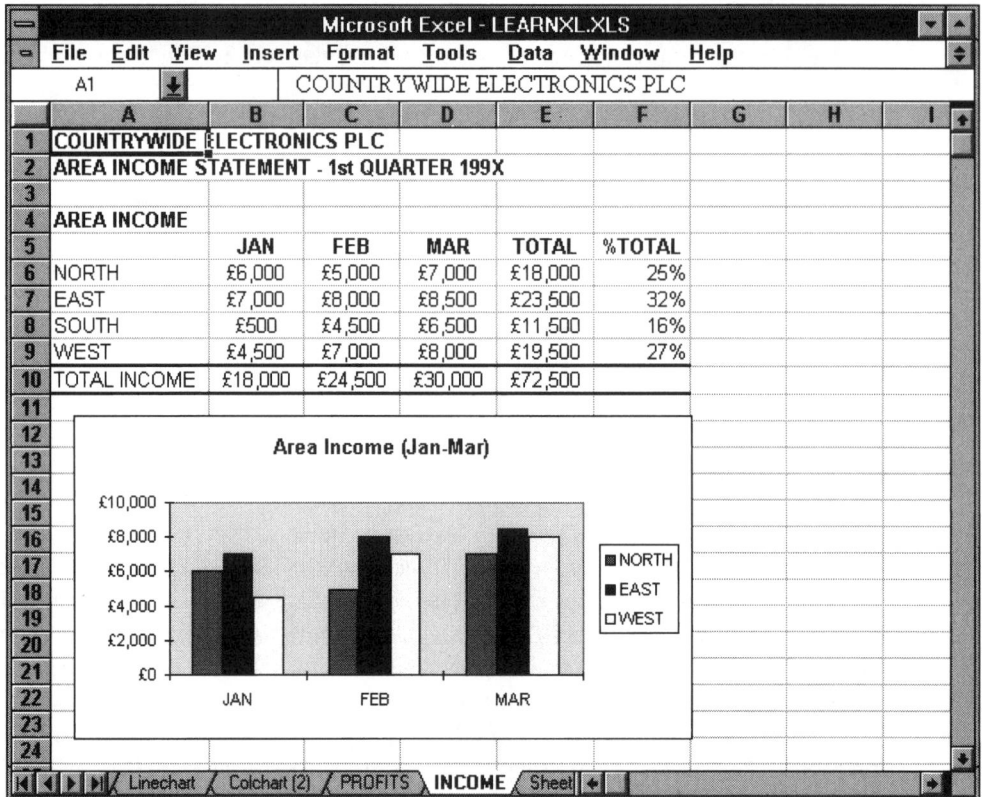

LINK BETWEEN WORKSHEET AND CHART

◆ Ensure that the chart area is deactivated.

◆ Select cell B9 (West area income for January), change the entry to 9,000 and observe the effect on the chart.

◆ Select cell B9 again and change the entry back to 4,500.

Any changes made to the worksheet data will be immediately reflected on the chart.

ADDING A DATA SERIES TO AN EMBEDDED CHART

We'll now insert the South area's data to the chart.

◆ Activate the chart area.

◆ Select **Insert** from the Menu bar and **New Data** from the **Insert** menu.

◆ When the **New Data** dialogue box opens, enter the **Range** A8:D8 and click the **OK** button.

Your chart should now contain the data for the four areas.

◆ **Save** the workbook.

There is a quicker way to add a new data series to an embedded chart. To demonstrate this we'll delete the series we have just inserted then reinsert using the new method.

◆ Ensure that the chart area is activated.

◆ Point to one of the columns on the chart representing the South area's income and click. Small square 'handles' should appear on each of the three columns indicating that the data series has been selected.

◆ Press the [**Delete**] key and the data series will be removed from the chart.

◆ Deactivate the chart area.

◆ Select the cell range A8:D8.

◆ Locate the mouse pointer on one of the borders of the selected range (the pointer will change to an arrow shape when correctly located).

◆ Press and hold down the mouse button and drag the pointer down to the chart area. Release the mouse button when the pointer is anywhere in the chart area and the new data series will be inserted to the chart.

◆ If you haven't been successful with this operation, don't worry, you can **Close** the workbook, *do not save changes*, **Open** the previously saved workbook and try again.

When your chart is complete with the four data series your worksheet, complete with chart, should be similar to the following:

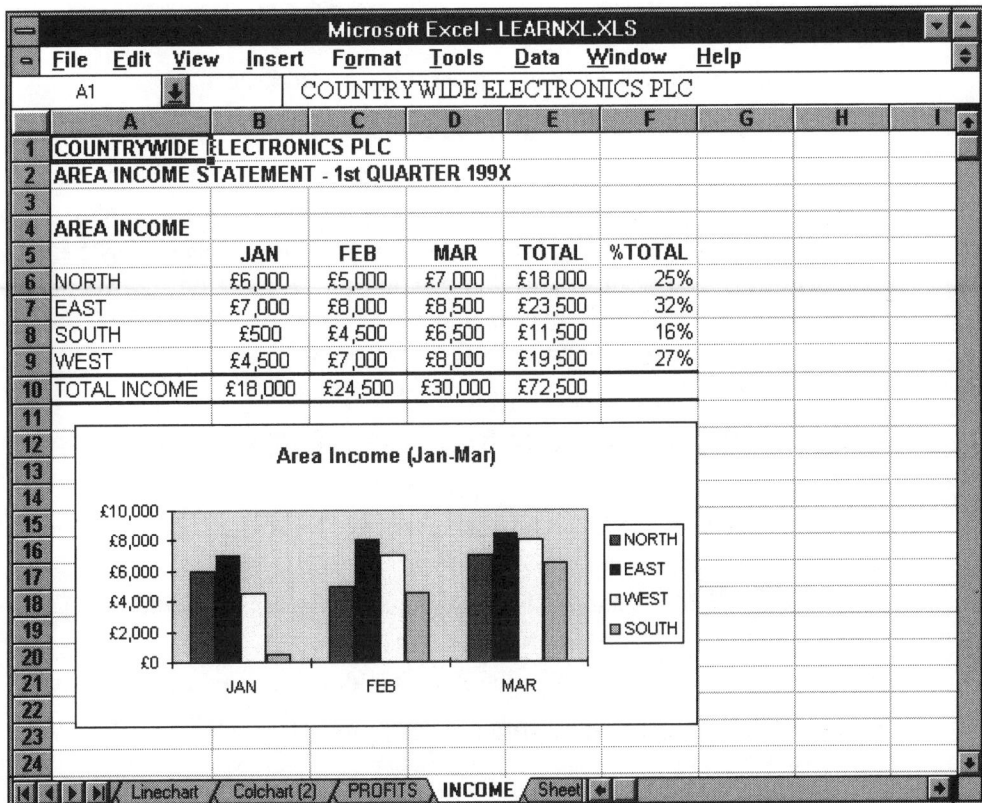

♦ You should now return the screen view to normal by selecting **View** from the Menu bar and then **Full Screen**.

♦ **Save** the workbook.

DELETION

Deleting an item from an embedded chart

The procedure is as follows:

♦ *Activate* the chart area.

♦ *Select* the item for deletion.

♦ Press the [**Delete**] key or choose **Edit** from the Menu bar then **Clear** then **All**.

Deleting an embedded chart from the worksheet

The procedure is as follows:

♦ *Select* the chart area (do not activate).

♦ Press the [**Delete**] key or use the menus, **Edit/Clear/All**.

PRINTING A WORKSHEET WITH AN EMBEDDED CHART

An embedded chart will print as it appears on the worksheet.

♦ Activate (i.e. display) the worksheet, INCOME.

♦ Select **File** from the Menu bar and **Print Preview** from the **File** menu.

♦ A preview of the printed worksheet should now be displayed. The full worksheet (including chart) can be scaled and repositioned on the page using the **Setup** option. However, if you wish to alter the position of the chart on the worksheet or adjust any of the chart items, you should **Close** the Preview window and make these alterations when you are returned to the worksheet.

♦ From the **Print Preview** window select **Setup**.

♦ When the **Page Setup** dialogue box is displayed, select the **Page** tab from the top.

♦ Adjust the **Scaling** to 125% of normal size.

♦ Click the **Margins** tab button and select the **Centre on Page Horizontally** check box from the Margins 'page'.

♦ Select the **Header/Footer** tab and remove the header and footer by choosing **(none)** from the drop-down list in each case.

♦ Select the **Sheet** tab and click the **Print Gridlines** check box (to remove the cross).

♦ Select **OK** from the **Page Setup** dialogue box and you will be returned to the **Print Preview** screen.

♦ Select **Print** and the **Print** dialogue box will appear.

♦ Ensure that the **Selected Sheets** check box has been selected and click **OK**.

The worksheet should now be printed.

PRACTICE EXERCISES

1   Based on the data in the worksheet PROFITS, produce a line graph on a separate chart sheet, showing total income, total costs and total profit for each of the three months. The chart should have a title (COUNTRYWIDE ELECTRONICS PLC) and a legend. Format the chart and print it.

2   (a) Select a new blank sheet in your workbook and produce the following worksheet. Parts of it can be copied over from your existing worksheet, PROFITS.

	A	B	C	D	E	F
1	COUNTRYWIDE ELECTRONICS PLC					
2	AREA COST STATEMENT – 1st QUARTER 199X					
3						
4		JAN	FEB	MAR	TOTAL	
5	NORTH	£4500	£3000	£4500	£12000	
6	EAST	£3500	£6000	£6000	£15500	
7	SOUTH	£1000	£3500	£5000	£9500	
8	WEST	£5000	£4500	£4500	£14000	
9	TOTAL COSTS	£14000	£17000	£20000	£51000	

You may have to widen some of the columns.
Rename the new worksheet, COSTS.

(b) Create a piechart below the data on the worksheet showing total costs for each area for the three-month period. The chart should have a title, legend and data labels. Format the chart, size and position it and print the worksheet.

CHAPTER 20

Worksheet and Workbook Linking

3-D Spreadsheets and Worksheet Linking · **Workbook Linking** · **Working with Linked Workbooks** · **Saving Linked Workbooks** · **Workspace Files** · **Practice Exercise**

3-D SPREADSHEETS AND WORKSHEET LINKING

Worksheets are based on two dimensions – rows and columns. A company could record its monthly product sales using this format by listing months across the top (as column headings) and product types down the side (as row headings). However, if the company maintains this data on a regional basis, this would be a third dimension requiring another worksheet for each region. In addition, it would be necessary to have a summary worksheet containing total monthly sales for the company as a whole. The summary worksheet would be based on data contained in the regional worksheets.

The program's workbook structure with tabbed worksheets lends itself ideally to the three-dimensional situation just described. Formulae in the summary worksheet can be linked to cells in the regional worksheets and formulae, formatting and data can be added to all the linked sheets in one operation.

To demonstrate this facility we will use the example of a wine merchant who has a chain of retail shops throughout the country which he divides into three areas: North, Central and South. We will set up a worksheet for each area which will show quarterly wine sales analysed by country of origin and a summary worksheet to collate the regional figures.

Our workbook LearnXL now contains quite a lot of data and the more it contains the longer it takes to **Open** and **Save**. So we will open a new workbook to record the wine sales.

♦ Open the **File** menu and select **Close**.

The worksheet part of the screen should now be blank since no workbook is open.

♦ Open the **File** menu again and select **New**.

A new workbook should now open and Sheet1 will be displayed.

The four worksheets we are about to create will have identical layouts so we will use Microsoft® Excel's worksheet linking facility to set them up simultaneously.

♦ Click on the Sheet1 name tab.

♦ Hold down the [**Shift**] key and click on the Sheet4 name tab.

The four sheets should now be selected with their name tabs highlighted. This means that anything entered to one sheet – data, formulae or formatting – will be replicated in the others.

♦ Select Sheet1 and create the following worksheet:

	A	B	C	D	E	F
1	WINE SALES ANALYSIS 199X					
2						
3	COUNTRY OF ORIGIN	QTR1	QTR2	QTR3	QTR4	TOTAL
4		£	£	£	£	£
5	AUSTRALIA					
6	FRANCE					
7	ITALY					
8	CALIFORNIA					
9	E. EUROPE					
10						

♦ Embolden all entries and centre the column headings.

♦ Widen the columns as necessary.

♦ Insert the formula =SUM(B5:E5) in cell F5 and copy this to the range F6:F9.

♦ Insert the formula =SUM(F5:F9) in cell F10.

♦ Deselect the four worksheets by holding down the **[Shift]** key and clicking on the Sheet1 name tab. Anything entered to the sheets now will not be replicated in the others.

♦ Examine Sheets 2, 3 and 4 and you should find them identical to Sheet1.

♦ Rename the Sheets as follows:

Sheet1   –   SUMMARY
Sheet2   –   NORTH
Sheet3   –   CENTRAL
Sheet4   –   SOUTH

The worksheet SUMMARY will be used to collate the data from the other three worksheets so we will now enter the linking formulae.

♦ Activate (display) the worksheet SUMMARY.

♦ Select cell B5 and enter the formula =SUM(NORTH:SOUTH!B5). This formula adds the values contained in cell B5 in each of the sheets between and including NORTH and SOUTH, i.e. the three area worksheets.

Note: Any reference to another sheet must have an exclamation mark between the sheet name and cell address. For example:

(a) to replicate the contents of cell A1, Sheet1 in cell A1, Sheet2 the following entry would be made to cell A1, Sheet2: =Sheet1!A1.

(b) to add the values contained in the range A1:D1 in each of the sheets from Sheet2 to Sheet5 the following formula would be used: =SUM(Sheet2:Sheet5!A1:D1).

◆ Copy the formula in cell B5 to the range B6:B9.

◆ Now copy the range B5:B9 to the range C5:E9.

The three area worksheets have now been set up and the appropriate linking formulae entered in the SUMMARY worksheet.

◆ Check your formulae in the SUMMARY worksheet before proceeding.

◆ **Save** the workbook. Remember to save to the floppy drive and give the workbook the filename UKSALES.

◆ Enter the following sales data to the three area worksheets:

NORTH	QTR 1 £	QTR 2 £	QTR 3 £	QTR 4 £
Australia	10000	10500	10400	10300
France	25000	26000	25600	25500
Italy	15000	14800	14800	15200
California	12000	11600	11800	12100
E. Europe	5000	5400	5200	5300

CENTRAL	QTR 1 £	QTR 2 £	QTR 3 £	QTR 4 £
Australia	12000	12300	12400	12500
France	27000	27500	27400	27600
Italy	17000	16800	16900	17200
California	14000	14400	14500	14300
E. Europe	7000	6500	6500	6800

SOUTH	QTR 1 £	QTR 2 £	QTR 3 £	QTR 4 £
Australia	14000	14400	14300	14500
France	29000	28800	28800	28600
Italy	19000	19200	19400	19000
California	16000	16300	16500	16100
E. Europe	9000	9200	9100	8900

◆ Check the worksheet SUMMARY and note that it has been completed automatically, based on the linking formulae. Your worksheet should be similar to the following:

	A	B	C	D	E	F
1	WINE SALES ANALYSIS 199X					
2						
3	COUNTRY OF ORIGIN	QTR1	QTR2	QTR3	QTR4	TOTAL
4		£	£	£	£	£
5	AUSTRALIA	36000	37200	37100	37300	147600
6	FRANCE	81000	82300	81800	81700	326800
7	ITALY	51000	50800	51100	51400	204300
8	CALIFORNIA	42000	42300	42800	42500	169600
9	E. EUROPE	21000	21100	20800	21000	83900
10						932200

♦ **Save** the workbook.

We'll now create an embedded chart on the worksheet SUMMARY.

♦ Select the data ranges A3:E3 and A5:E9.

♦ Select **Insert** from the Menu bar then **Chart** from the **Insert** menu then **On This Sheet** from the **Chart** sub-menu.

♦ The mouse pointer should now be a cross hair with a chart symbol (when located on the worksheet). Use the pointer to map out the area on the worksheet where you want the chart to appear.

The first **ChartWizard** dialogue box should now open displaying the selected cell ranges.

♦ Click the **Next** button in the Step 1 box.

♦ Select the chart type **3-D Column** from the Step 2 dialogue box and click the **Next** button.

♦ Select format **6** from the Step 3 box and click the **Next** button.

♦ In the Step 4 dialogue box, select the **Data Series in Rows** button and click **Next**.

♦ Select **Finish** from the Step 5 box and you will be returned to the worksheet where the chart will be embedded.

If you made the chart area too small, the chart will not be displayed completely. To correct this, simply adjust the size of the chart area.

We'll now rearrange the columns on the chart so that all are visible.

♦ Activate the chart area by double clicking and the thick cross hatch border should appear round it.

♦ Select **Format** from the Menu bar and **Chart Type** from the **Format** menu.

♦ When the **Chart Type** dialogue box opens select the **Options** button and the **Format 3-D Column Group** dialogue box should now open, similar to the following:

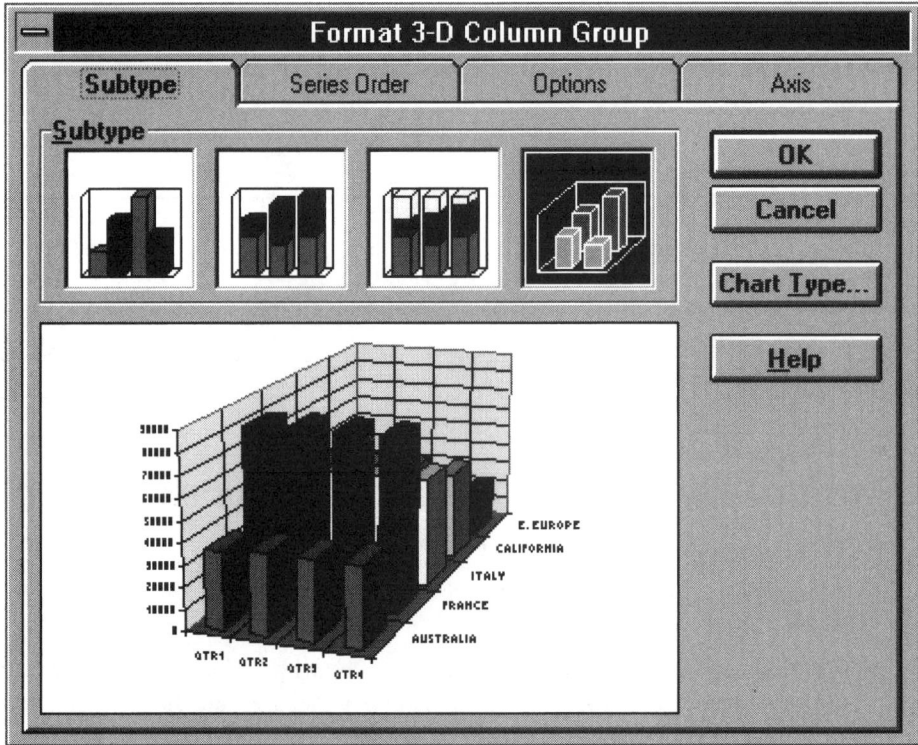

This dialogue box allows you to alter the display order of the columns. We'll put the smallest columns at the front and the largest at the back of the chart.

♦ Select the **Series Order** tab button at the top of the dialogue box and the following **Series Order** 'page' should be displayed:

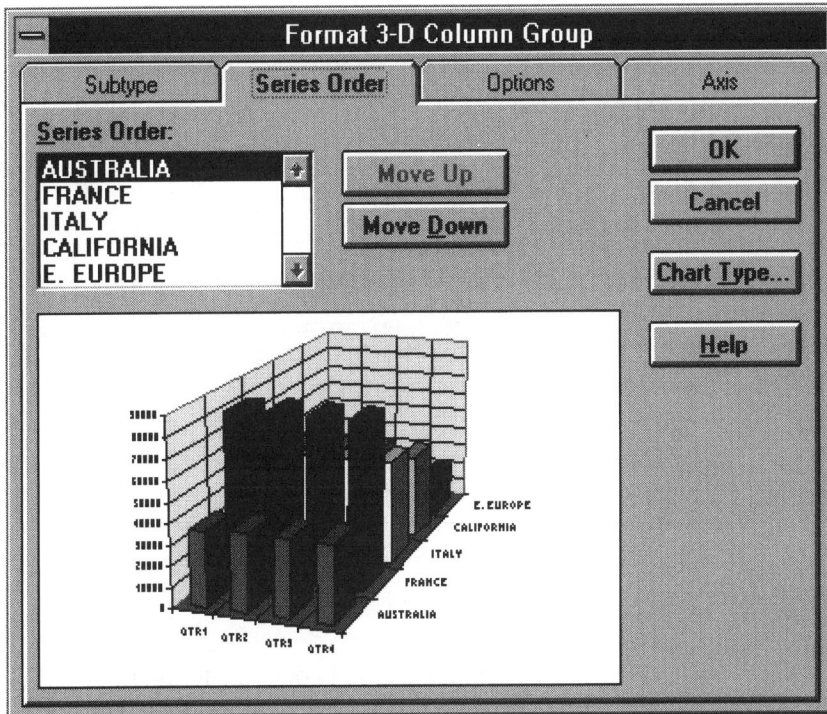

◆ Select E. EUROPE in the **Series Order** list and click the **Move Up** button. Keep clicking the **Move Up** button until the E. EUROPE columns are at the front of the display.

◆ Now select CALIFORNIA in the **Series Order** list and click the **Move Up** button until the CALIFORNIA columns are third in the display.

◆ Finally, select ITALY and move it to fourth position. It should now be much easier to read the values for each column.

◆ Click the **OK** button and you will be returned to the worksheet where the columns will now be displayed in the new order.

◆ **Save** the workbook.

WORKBOOK LINKING

Let's say our wine merchant also has a chain of shops in Ireland. They are responsible for maintaining their own records and at the end of each year they send a workbook file to head office in the UK. Amongst other things, the workbook contains an identical SUMMARY worksheet analysing wine sales in Ireland by country of origin. The figures in the worksheet have already been converted to £ sterling. Head office combine information from both SUMMARY worksheets to produce a world wine sales analysis.

We'll open two new workbooks – one for Irish sales and one for World sales.

♦ **Close** down any workbook which is open at the moment. When all workbooks have been closed, the worksheet part of the screen should be blank.

♦ Select **New** from the **File** menu and a new workbook will open. Set up the following worksheet:

	A	B	C	D	E	F
1	WINE SALES ANALYSIS 199X					
2						
3	COUNTRY OF ORIGIN	QTR1	QTR2	QTR3	QTR4	TOTAL
4		£STERLING	£STERLING	£STERLING	£STERLING	£STERLING
5	AUSTRALIA					
6	FRANCE					
7	ITALY					
8	CALIFORNIA					
9	E. EUROPE					
10						

♦ Embolden all entries and centre the column headings. Widen the columns as necessary.

♦ Insert the formula =SUM(B5:E5) in cell F5 and copy this to the range F6:F9.

♦ Insert the formula =SUM(F5:F9) in cell F10.

♦ Rename Sheet1 to SUMMARY.

♦ **Save** the workbook to the floppy drive and give the workbook the filename IRLSALES. This workbook will hold the summary data for Irish sales.

We'll now open a workbook for World Sales:

♦ Select **New** from the **File** menu and a new workbook will open. Two workbooks should now be open with the new one overlaying IRLSALES.

♦ It will be easier to refer to the workbooks by name so you should save your new workbook now even though it is empty and this will allow you to give it a name. **Save** to the floppy drive and give the workbook the filename WORLDSLS.

♦ The name WORLDSLS.XLS should now appear in the Title bar at the top of the screen.

Two workbooks are now open but only one is visible – WORLDSLS in the foreground is overlaying IRLSALES in the background. Although two workbooks are open, only one can be active at a time and allow you to enter data. At the moment WORLDSLS is in the foreground and is therefore active.

♦ To bring IRLSALES to the foreground, select **Window** from the Menu bar and choose IRLSALES.XLS from the bottom of the **Window** menu.

Note that the Title bar now displays the name IRLSALES.XLS.

WORLDSLS is still open (but not active) in the background.

Since the WORLDSLS workbook will contain an identical SUMMARY worksheet to the one we have just set up in IRLSALES, we'll copy the sheet from one workbook to the other:

♦ Ensure that the IRLSALES workbook is active and the SUMMARY worksheet is displayed on the screen.

♦ Select **Edit** from the Menu bar then **Move or Copy Sheet** from the **Edit** menu.

The following **Move or Copy** dialogue box should now open:

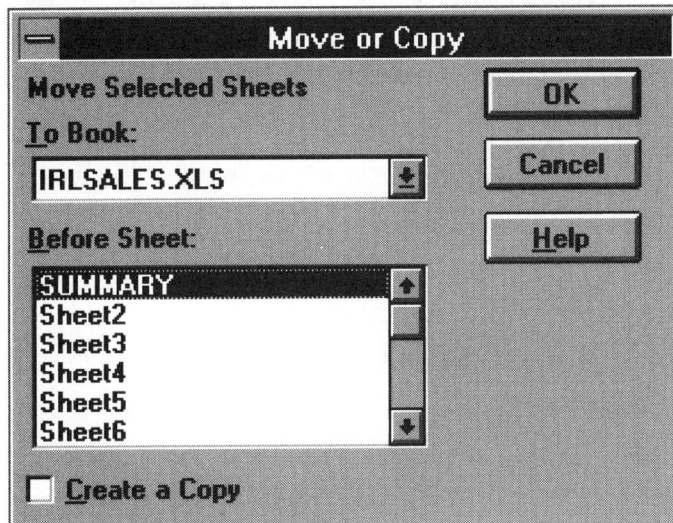

```
┌─────────────────────────────────────────────────┐
│ ─      │         Move or Copy                    │
│ Move Selected Sheets        ┌───────────────┐    │
│                             │      OK       │    │
│ To Book:                    └───────────────┘    │
│ ┌──────────────────────┬─┐  ┌───────────────┐    │
│ │ IRLSALES.XLS         │±│  │    Cancel     │    │
│ └──────────────────────┴─┘  └───────────────┘    │
│ Before Sheet:               ┌───────────────┐    │
│ ┌──────────────────────┬─┐  │     Help      │    │
│ │ SUMMARY            │↑│  └───────────────┘    │
│ │ Sheet2             │ │                         │
│ │ Sheet3             │ │                         │
│ │ Sheet4             │ │                         │
│ │ Sheet5             │ │                         │
│ │ Sheet6             │↓│                         │
│ └──────────────────────┴─┘                       │
│ □ Create a Copy                                   │
└─────────────────────────────────────────────────┘
```

♦ Click the ⊡ button at the end of the **To Book** box and select WORLDSLS.XLS from the drop-down list.

♦ Select the **Create a Copy** check box at the bottom of the dialogue box and click **OK**.

The WORLDSLS workbook should now be active (in the foreground) with a SUMMARY worksheet displayed identical to the one in the IRLSALES workbook.

♦ **Save** the WORLDSLS workbook in the normal way.

We'll now enter the sales data to the SUMMARY sheet in the IRLSALES workbook:

♦ Select **Window** from the Menu bar and choose IRLSALES.XLS from the bottom of the **Window** menu. IRLSALES should now be active so enter the following data to its SUMMARY worksheet:

	QTR 1	QTR 2	QTR 3	QTR 4
Australia	12000	12600	12500	12300
France	27000	27200	26600	26800
Italy	17000	16800	17400	17200
California	14000	14500	14400	14100
E. Europe	7000	7200	6800	7000

♦ **Save** the workbook.

♦ Select **File** from the Menu bar then **Open** from the **File** menu and open the third wine sales workbook, UKSALES.

The three wine sales workbooks should now be open with UKSALES in the foreground.

♦ Select **Window** from the Menu bar. Note that the three workbook names are listed at the bottom of the **Window** menu. Select WORLDSLS.

We'll now enter the workbook linking formulae to the SUMMARY worksheet in the WORLDSLS workbook:

♦ Select cell B5 and enter the following formula:

=[UKSALES.XLS]SUMMARY!B5+[IRLSALES.XLS]SUMMARY!B5

The linking reference to each workbook in this case contains three parts:

(a) the name of the workbook, enclosed in square brackets;

(b) the name of the worksheet followed by an exclamation mark;

(c) the cell reference in the worksheet.

♦ Copy the formula to cell range B6:B9.

♦ Copy the range B5:B9 to C5:E9.

The SUMMARY worksheet in the WORLDSLS workbook should now display total world sales figures based on the data in the other two workbooks.

♦ **Save** the workbook.

Note: If source and dependent workbooks are in different directories the linking formulae would have to contain a reference to the path. For example, if the WORLDSLS workbook was stored on the hard disc and the other two were on a floppy disc in drive a:, the previous linking formula would become:

='a:\[UKSALES.XLS]SUMMARY'!B5+'a:\[IRLSALES.XLS]SUMMARY'!B5

When the path is included, the path, filename and sheet name must be enclosed in single quotes.

WORKING WITH LINKED WORKBOOKS

You can display all three workbooks on the screen at once making it easier to demonstrate the link between source and dependent books.

♦ Select **Window** from the Menu bar then **Arrange** from the **Window** menu.

♦ When the **Arrange Windows** dialogue box opens, click the **Tiled** button and select **OK**.

The three workbooks should now be displayed on the screen in a tiled arrangement.

♦ Select cell B5 in the workbook IRLSALES, change the entry from 12000 to 18000 and observe the immediate effect in cell B5 in the workbook WORLDSLS.

♦ Select cell B5 in IRLSALES again and change the entry back to 12000.

♦ Select **Window** from the Menu bar then **Arrange** from the **Window** menu.

♦ When the **Arrange Windows** dialogue box opens this time select **Cascade** and click **OK**. The workbooks should now be displayed on the screen in cascade format with the Title bar of each visible.

♦ To return to full screen display, click the maximise button, ⬛, at the extreme right of the Title bar of the active workbook (the one in the foreground).

SAVING LINKED WORKBOOKS

The *source* workbook(s) should be saved first followed by the *dependent* workbook which is linked to it or them. In our case, this would mean saving UKSALES and IRLSALES followed by WORLDSLS.

♦ **Activate, Save** and **Close** the workbooks in the following order:
UKSALES
IRLSALES
WORLDSLS

It is not necessary that all linked workbooks are open for the links to operate. You can open a source workbook on its own, amend it and resave. Next time the dependent workbook is opened a dialogue box will prompt you to re-establish links and the workbook will be updated.

WORKSPACE FILES

A number of workbook files can be grouped together and saved as one workspace file. All the workbooks can then be opened in one step by opening the workspace file.

The workspace file does not contain the actual workbooks themselves. The individual workbooks remain as separate files and the workspace file contains information relating to their location, size and position on the screen. Each individual workbook can therefore still be opened separately.

The procedure for creating and saving a workspace file is as follows:

♦ Open all the workbook files you want included in the workspace.

♦ Arrange them on the screen in the style you require.

♦ Open the **File** menu and select **Save Workspace**.

♦ When the **Save Workspace** dialogue box opens give the file a name.

A workspace file is opened in the normal way using the **Open** command on the **File** menu. When it is opened all the individual workbooks will be opened and arranged on the screen as they were when the workspace file was saved.

PRACTICE EXERCISE

1 Open the workbook WORLDSLS.

2 Create an embedded 3-D piechart in percentage format on the SUMMARY worksheet showing total world sales for the year analysed by country of origin.

3 When complete, print the worksheet then **Save** and **Close** the workbook.

CHAPTER 21

Databases and Lists

Databases · Worksheet Lists · Building a List · Sorting a List · Maintaining a List using a Data Form · Filtering a List · Filtering a List using AutoFilter · Filtering a List using Advanced Filter · Entering Subtotals to a List

DATABASES

A computerised database could be described as an electronic filing system consisting of a collection of records of related information. For example, a company could maintain an employee database containing the name, address, telephone no., age, job description and salary of each employee. Each record in the database would contain the details of one employee. For example:

	SURNAME	INITS	ADDR1	ADDR2	TELNO	AGE	JOBTITLE	SALARY
RECORD 1	Adams	J	23 High Street	Carlisle	063-224-1234	52	Painter	15000
RECORD 2	Brown	A	6 White Street	Kendal	073-322-1433	46	Joiner	15000
RECORD 3	Jones	T	15 Doon Avenue	Carlisle	063-421-5667	29	Electrician	16000
RECORD 4								

Each record in the database has an identical structure consisting of several fields with each field having a name, e.g. SURNAME, ADDR1, JOBTITLE.

Once the database has been built in this manner and stored on computer, it makes the job of finding, adding, editing, deleting and sorting records very quick and simple. It also becomes very easy to search for and list records from the database which meet a particular criterion, e.g. SALARY < 10000, AGE > 55. Imagine how long it would take you to search manually through a telephone directory to locate everyone with a particular area code. This information could be retrieved in seconds if the contents of the directory were held in a database on computer.

WORKSHEET LISTS

The Microsoft® Excel worksheet, with its row and column format, lends itself well to the construction of a database. Data can be stored on the worksheet in the form of a *list* which is a series of rows containing similar data and column labels immediately above the first row. The *list* can then be regarded as a simple database, where rows are records and columns are fields.

Guidelines for creating a list

Certain guidelines should be followed when constructing a list which will be used as a database:

List

- One list per worksheet.
- At least one blank column and one blank row between the list and other data on the worksheet.
- Top row of list should contain field names.
- There should be no blank rows or dashed lines between field names and data. If you wish to separate field names from the rest of the data, use a cell border to insert lines below the column labels (field names).
- The list can be given a name using the **Name** command on the **Insert** menu. If you use the name Database, Microsoft® Excel will automatically identify the first row of the list as the field names.

Records

- Every record must have same fields although fields can be left blank.

Field names

- Field names can be up to 256 characters long and each field must have a unique name.
- Format of field names should be different to data in list, e.g. use a different font, data type, alignment, format or capitalisation style.

Fields

- Use same format for all cells in a column.
- Uppercase or lowercase characters can be used when entering data to the list.
- Do not insert extra spaces at the beginning of fields.
- The list may contain calculated fields, i.e. fields which contain a formula.

With these guidelines in mind, we'll draw up a product stock list for a retailer, Derwent Tiles Ltd, who sells a variety of wall, floor and ceiling tiles. The retailer has coded his stock in the following way:

Stock code	Description	Stock code	Description
FT-L-V	Floor tile, large, vinyl	WT-L-C	Wall tile, large, ceramic
FT-L-C	Floor tile, large, ceramic	WT-L-G	Wall tile, large, granite
FT-L-G	Floor tile, large, granite	WT-M-C	Wall tile, medium, ceramic
FT-M-V	Floor tile, medium, vinyl	WT-M-G	Wall tile, medium, granite
FT-M-C	Floor tile, medium, ceramic	WT-S-C	Wall tile, small, ceramic
FT-M-G	Floor tile, medium, granite	WT-S-G	Wall tile, small, granite
FT-S-V	Floor tile, small, vinyl		
FT-S-C	Floor tile, small, ceramic	CT-L-P	Ceiling tile, large, polystyrene
FT-S-G	Floor tile, small, granite	CT-M-P	Ceiling tile, medium, polystyrene
		CT-S-P	Ceiling tile, small, polystyrene

A good coding structure can greatly facilitate reporting from a database designed to hold product records.

When building a database, thoughtful consideration should be given to the type of information you may wish to extract from the data. This will determine the record structure, i.e. field contents. It should also be remembered that the database can be interrogated using only part of a field's contents with the help of 'wildcard' characters. So our tile retailer could produce a report on all wall tiles (WT*) or all granite tiles (*G) or all small tiles (??-S-?).

BUILDING A LIST

If you follow the previous guidelines, creating the list is just like building any other worksheet.

♦ **Close** down any workbook(s) which are open and **Open** the workbook LearnXL.

♦ Select the first blank sheet in the workbook and create the following LIST:

	A	B	C	D	E	F	G	H	I
1	**DERWENT TILES LTD – Product Records**								
2									
3	CODE	DESCRIPTION	SUPPLIER	COST	MARKUP	TAX	PRICE	INSTOCK	REORDER
4	FT-L-V	Floor, large, vinyl	Hanson Vinyls	1.10				1100	1000
5	WT-S-C	Wall, small, ceramic	Ascot Ceramics	0.50				2500	2000
6	FT-L-C	Floor, large, ceramic	Ascot Ceramics	1.80				3700	3000
7	CT-S-P	Ceiling, small, poly.	UTile	0.60					1000
8	FT-S-C	Floor, small, ceramic	Ascot Ceramics	1.30				3100	3000
9	WT-S-G	Wall, small, granite	Glen Tiles	0.90				600	500
10	FT-L-G	Floor, large, granite	Glen Tiles	2.20				1800	1500
11	CT-L-P	Ceiling, large, poly.	UTile	1.20				1700	2000
12	WT-M-G	Wall, medium, granite	Glen Tiles	1.10				900	500
13	FT-S-G	Floor, small, granite	Glen Tiles	1.60				1400	1000
14	WT-L-G	Wall, large, granite	Glen Tiles	1.50				800	1000
15	WT-M-C	Wall, medium, ceramic	Ascot Ceramics	0.75				3200	3000
16	FT-M-C	Floor, medium, ceramic	Ascot Ceramics	1.50				3500	3000
17	FT-M-G	Floor, medium, granite	Glen Tiles	2.00					1500
18	CT-M-P	Ceiling, medium, poly.	UTile	0.80				1500	1000
19	FT-S-V	Floor, small, vinyl	Hanson Vinyls	0.80				900	500
20	WT-L-C	Wall, large, ceramic	Ascot Ceramics	0.90				2900	2500
21	FT-M-V	Floor, medium, vinyl	Hanson Vinyls	1.00				800	500

♦ Building a list of this nature is a laborious task so **Save** the workbook before you do any more.

Now carry out the following tasks:

(a) Embolden the title and underline.

(b) Capitalise, embolden and centre the column headings – cell range A3:I3.
Do not underline these headings, they will become the field names.

(c) Widen the columns as necessary.

(d) Select cell range D4:D21 and format to currency style with two decimal places.

(e) Select cell E4 and enter the formula =D4*0.4. Format the cell to currency style with two decimal places and then copy the formula and formatting to the range E5:E21.

(f) Select cell F4 and enter the formula =(D4+E4)*0.175.
Format the cell to currency style with two decimal places and then copy the formula and formatting to the range F5:F21.

(g) Select cell G4 and enter the formula =SUM(D4.F4).
The cell should be formatted correctly so all you need do is copy to the range G5:G21.

♦ Your list of product records is now complete, you don't have to do anything special to it to make it a database. It should be similar to the following:

	A	B	C	D	E	F	G	H	I
1	**DERWENT TILES LTD – Product Records**								
2									
3	**CODE**	**DESCRIPTION**	**SUPPLIER**	**COST**	**MARKUP**	**TAX**	**PRICE**	**INSTOCK**	**REORDER**
4	FT-L-V	Floor, large, vinyl	Hanson Vinyls	£1.10	£0.44	£0.27	£1.81	1100	1000
5	WT-S-C	Wall, small, ceramic	Ascot Ceramics	£0.50	£0.20	£0.12	£0.82	2500	2000
6	FT-L-C	Floor, large, ceramic	Ascot Ceramics	£1.80	£0.72	£0.44	£2.96	3700	3000
7	CT-S-P	Ceiling, small, poly.	UTile	£0.60	£0.24	£0.15	£0.99		1000
8	FT-S-C	Floor, small, ceramic	Ascot Ceramics	£1.30	£0.52	£0.32	£2.14	3100	3000
9	WT-S-G	Wall, small, granite	Glen Tiles	£0.90	£0.36	£0.22	£1.48	600	500
10	FT-L-G	Floor, large, granite	Glen Tiles	£2.20	£0.88	£0.54	£3.62	1800	1500
11	CT-L-P	Ceiling, large, poly.	UTile	£1.20	£0.48	£0.29	£1.97	1700	2000
12	WT-M-G	Wall, medium, granite	Glen Tiles	£1.10	£0.44	£0.27	£1.81	900	500
13	FT-S-G	Floor, small, granite	Glen Tiles	£1.60	£0.64	£0.39	£2.63	1400	1000
14	WT-L-G	Wall, large, granite	Glen Tiles	£1.50	£0.60	£0.37	£2.47	800	1000
15	WT-M-C	Wall, medium, ceramic	Ascot Ceramics	£0.75	£0.30	£0.18	£1.23	3200	3000
16	FT-M-C	Floor, medium, ceramic	Ascot Ceramics	£1.50	£0.60	£0.37	£2.47	3500	3000
17	FT-M-G	Floor, medium, granite	Glen Tiles	£2.00	£0.80	£0.49	£3.29		1500
18	CT-M-P	Ceiling, medium, poly.	UTile	£0.80	£0.32	£0.20	£1.32	1500	1000
19	FT-S-V	Floor, small, vinyl	Hanson Vinyls	£0.80	£0.32	£0.20	£1.32	900	500
20	WT-L-C	Wall, large, ceramic	Ascot Ceramics	£0.90	£0.36	£0.22	£1.48	2900	2500
21	FT-M-V	Floor, medium, vinyl	Hanson Vinyls	£1.00	£0.40	£0.25	£1.65	800	500

♦ Rename the sheet Database and **Save** the workbook.

SORTING A LIST

A list can be sorted alphabetically, numerically or chronologically according to the contents of a specified column or columns. It is only necessary to select one cell from the entire list before invoking the **Sort** command.

Our list covers the range A3:I21 (first two rows in worksheet are *not* part of list).

♦ We will perform a sort based on the product code so select any cell in column A from A3 to A21. It is not necessary to select a column A cell but it makes it easier when the **Sort** dialogue box opens.

♦ When you have selected a cell, choose **Data** from the Menu bar then **Sort** from the **Data** menu.

The **Sort** dialogue box should now open and in the background notice that the entire list has been selected (darkened). Microsoft® Excel has recognised the first row in the list as the field names and excluded them from the selection since they will obviously not be sorted.

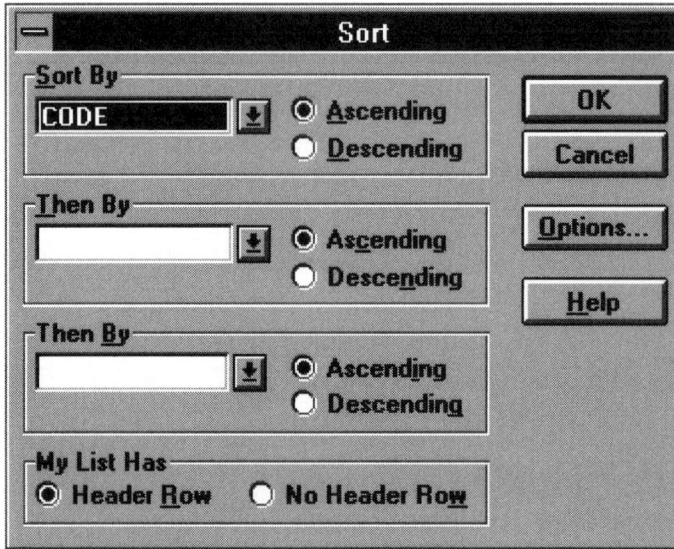

The dialogue box allows you to choose sort fields and whether the sort should be carried out in ascending (A–Z, 1–9) or descending (Z–A, 9–1) order. Up to three levels of sort can be specified in case there are duplicate entries in the first or second fields.

♦ The field name CODE should be displayed in the **Sort By** box, if not, click on the ⬇ button and select it from the drop-down list.

♦ Select the **Ascending** button in the **Sort By** section and, since we are performing only one level of sort, click **OK**.

You will be returned to the worksheet where the list should have been sorted alphabetically by CODE as follows:

	A	B	C	D	E	F	G	H	I
1	**DERWENT TILES LTD – Product Records**								
2									
3	**CODE**	**DESCRIPTION**	**SUPPLIER**	**COST**	**MARKUP**	**TAX**	**PRICE**	**INSTOCK**	**REORDER**
4	CT-L-P	Ceiling, large, poly.	UTile	£1.20	£0.48	£0.29	£1.97	1700	2000
5	CT-M-P	Ceiling, medium, poly.	UTile	£0.80	£0.32	£0.20	£1.32	1500	1000
6	CT-S-P	Ceiling, small, poly.	UTile	£0.60	£0.24	£0.15	£0.99		1000
7	FT-L-C	Floor, large, ceramic	Ascot Ceramics	£1.80	£0.72	£0.44	£2.96	3700	3000
8	FT-L-G	Floor, large, granite	Glen Tiles	£2.20	£0.88	£0.54	£3.62	1800	1500
9	FT-L-V	Floor, large, vinyl	Hanson Vinyls	£1.10	£0.44	£0.27	£1.81	1100	1000
10	FT-M-C	Floor, medium, ceramic	Ascot Ceramics	£1.50	£0.60	£0.37	£2.47	3500	3000
11	FT-M-G	Floor, medium, granite	Glen Tiles	£2.00	£0.80	£0.49	£3.29		1500
12	FT-M-V	Floor, medium, vinyl	Hanson Vinyls	£1.00	£0.40	£0.25	£1.65	800	500
13	FT-S-C	Floor, small, ceramic	Ascot Ceramics	£1.30	£0.52	£0.32	£2.14	3100	3000
14	FT-S-G	Floor, small, granite	Glen Tiles	£1.60	£0.64	£0.39	£2.63	1400	1000
15	FT-S-V	Floor, small, vinyl	Hanson Vinyls	£0.80	£0.32	£0.20	£1.32	900	500
16	WT-L-C	Wall, large, ceramic	Ascot Ceramics	£0.90	£0.36	£0.22	£1.48	2900	2500
17	WT-L-G	Wall, large, granite	Glen Tiles	£1.50	£0.60	£0.37	£2.47	800	1000
18	WT-M-C	Wall, medium, ceramic	Ascot Ceramics	£0.75	£0.30	£0.18	£1.23	3200	3000
19	WT-M-G	Wall, medium, granite	Glen Tiles	£1.10	£0.44	£0.27	£1.81	900	500
20	WT-S-C	Wall, small, ceramic	Ascot Ceramics	£0.50	£0.20	£0.12	£0.82	2500	2000
21	WT-S-G	Wall, small, granite	Glen Tiles	£0.90	£0.36	£0.22	£1.48	600	500

♦ **Save** the workbook.

Quick sort

If you wish to sort a list by one column only, you can simply select one of the cells in that column and then click the **Sort Ascending** or the **Sort Descending** button on the standard Toolbar.

Field names/column labels

A list usually has column labels in the first row. To allow Microsoft® Excel to identify them as column labels, they must be different to the other rows in one of the following respects: font, capitalisation, alignment, data type or pattern. However, the **Sort** dialogue box does allow you to specify whether or not the list has a Header row containing column labels.

Sorting columns

If your list consists of records laid out in columns instead of rows, it can still be sorted using the **Sort** command. In this case you would choose the **Options** button from the **Sort** dialogue box and the **Sort Left to Right** button from the **Sort Options** dialogue box. Then return to the **Sort** dialogue box and specify the row(s) you wish to sort by.

Sorting part of the list

To sort part of a list only, select the rows or columns for sorting before invoking the **Sort** command.

MAINTAINING A LIST USING A DATA FORM

Once a list has been built, it will be necessary to update it from time to time, e.g. records will need to be added, deleted and amended. These operations can be carried out using a data form. Note, however, that before a data form can be used, the list must have column labels.

The data form

♦ Select any cell in the list and choose the **Form** command from the **Data** menu. The following dialogue box/data form should open:

The list's field names (column labels) are shown down the left-hand side of the box and the field contents for the first record should be displayed. Some field contents can be edited on the data form, others contain the results of formulae and cannot be amended on the form. In our case, the **MARKUP**, **TAX** and **PRICE** fields cannot be altered.

♦ Clicking the **Find Next** and **Find Prev** buttons will move you through the list one record at a time in a forwards or backwards direction. Try this and watch how the record indicator at the top right of the form shows the current record being displayed, e.g. 3 of 18.

♦ The scroll bar to the right of the field contents enables you to move through the list more quickly.

Deleting a record

Due to lack of demand, we have decided not to stock small polystyrene ceiling tiles any longer and we wish to remove the record from our list.

♦ Ensure that the Data Form dialogue box is open and display the appropriate record (should be No. 3) using one of the **Find** buttons or the scroll bar.

♦ When the record is displayed, click the **Delete** button. You will be advised that the record will be permanently deleted. At this point you can cancel or continue. Check that the displayed record is the correct one for deletion and select **OK**. You should be able to note from the list in the background that this record has been removed.

Adding a new record

Due to popular demand, we have decided to stock cork floor tiles in two sizes – medium and large.

♦ Select the **New** button in the Data Form dialogue box and enter the details of the following two records. Use the **[Tab]** key to move between fields and press the **[Enter]** key once you have entered the details of the first record.

	(a)	(b)
CODE:	FT-M-K	FT-L-K
DESCRIPTION:	Floor, medium, cork	Floor, large, cork
SUPPLIER:	Fine Tiles	Fine Tiles
COST:	0.85	1.15
INSTOCK:	2500	3000
REORDER:	1500	2000

♦ When you have entered the details for the second record, press the **[Enter]** key then select the **Close** button and you will be returned to the list. The two new records should have been added to the bottom of the list. Note that the entries have been made to the calculated fields and that the currency fields are all formatted correctly.

♦ Resort the list by CODE and the two new records will be slotted into their correct alphabetic locations.

Editing a record

Let's say you made a mistake when entering the details for large cork floor tiles. The cost should have been 1.25 and not 1.15.

♦ Open the Data Form, find the correct record, select the **COST** field and make the alteration.

♦ Click the **Close** button in the Data Form and you will be returned to the list where your alteration should have been effected.

Note: It is not necessary to use the Data Form for changes of this nature. You can edit cells directly in the list.

♦ **Save** the workbook.

Restore button

The **Restore** button on the Data Form can be used to cancel changes which have been made to a displayed record provided you use it before you move on to the next record or select the **Close** button. Moving on to another record or selecting the **Close** button would automatically save the changes.

Finding records using the criteria button

The **Criteria** button in the Data Form enables you to find records which conform to specified criteria.

♦ Select any cell in the list, open the Data Form and click the **Criteria** button.

The form will now change and you'll be allowed to enter a search condition to any field. The program will then check the list for records which conform to that search condition.

To demonstrate, let's search the list for all products supplied by Fine Tiles.

♦ Click in the **SUPPLIER** field, type in Fine Tiles and press the **[Enter]** key.

The Data Form should now display the first record which meets the specified criterion.

♦ Select the **Find Next** button and the next matching record will be displayed. There should be only two matching records in this case.

When search criteria have been specified, the **Find Next** and **Find Prev** buttons move you only between records which conform to the criteria.

♦ Click the **Criteria** button again and select **Clear**.

♦ Now click in the **COST** field, type in >1.50 and press **[Enter]**.

♦ The record displayed should have a cost price which is greater than £1.50. You can view all records which conform to this criterion using the **Find Next** and **Find Prev** buttons.

♦ To switch off the search condition, click the **Criteria** button and select **Clear**.

Note: You can specify more than one search condition using **Criteria**. Try searching the list for all records where the **SUPPLIER** is Glen Tiles *and* the **COST** is >1.50.

♦ **Close** the Data Form.

FILTERING A LIST

The **Filter** command enables you to display a subset of your list, i.e. only those records which meet specified criteria. The other records are temporarily hidden. You can then edit, print, format or delete all records in the subset at the same time.

FILTERING A LIST USING AUTOFILTER

Filtering using one criterion

♦ Select any cell in your list then choose the **Filter** command from the **Data** menu.

♦ Select **AutoFilter** from the **Filter** sub-menu and note that drop-down arrow buttons have been placed on each column label in the list.

♦ Click the arrow button for the column label **SUPPLIER** and select **Hanson Vinyls** from the drop-down display.

Your list will have been filtered and should now display only those records where the supplier is Hanson Vinyls, all other records being temporarily hidden.

♦ To remove the filter from the column, click the down arrow button once again and select **[All]** from the drop-down display (you may have to scroll the display to bring **[All]** into view).

The full list should now be restored.

♦ Click the down arrow button for the column label **COST** and select **£1.10** from the drop-down display.

Your list should now show only those records where the cost is £1.10.

♦ Remove the filter from the **COST** column and return to full list display.

Filtering using more than one criterion

♦ Select **Hanson Vinyls** from the **SUPPLIER** drop-down display then **£1.10** from the **COST** display.

Your list should have been filtered twice and display one record only which conforms to the specified criteria: **SUPPLIER**, Hanson Vinyls *and* **COST**, £1.10.

♦ Select **Data** from the Menu bar then **Filter** then **Show All** and your list will be returned to full display once again.

Custom filter

AutoFilter allows you to specify **Custom Criteria** for each column. You can use this facility to:

(a) Filter the list to display only records which contain *either* of two items in a field, e.g. records where the **SUPPLIER** is *either* UTile *or* Fine Tiles.

(b) Display only records where a value falls within a specified range, e.g. **COST**>£1.00 *and* <£1.50.

♦ To demonstrate this facility, click the down arrow button for the column label **SUPPLIER** then select [**Custom . . .**] from the drop-down display.

The following **Custom AutoFilter** dialogue box should now appear:

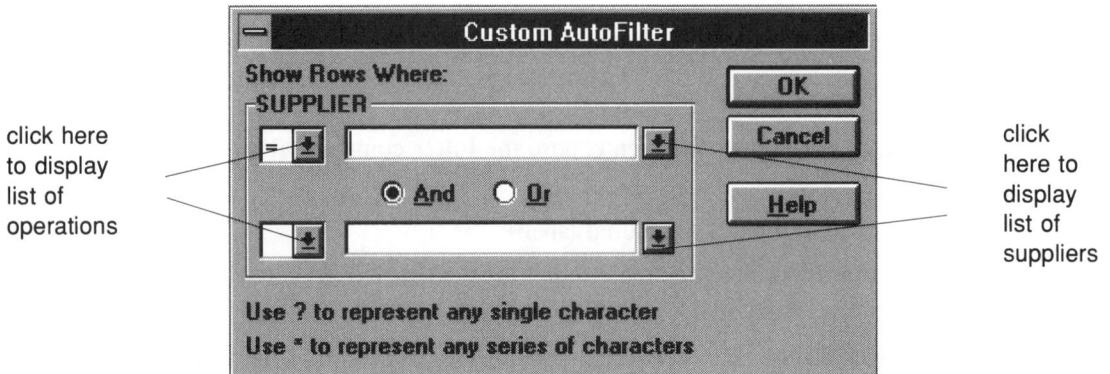

click here to display list of operations

click here to display list of suppliers

```
┌──────────────────────────────────────────────────────────┐
│ ─              Custom AutoFilter                           │
│ Show Rows Where:                          ┌──────────┐     │
│ ┌SUPPLIER──────────────────────────────┐  │   OK     │     │
│ │ ┌─┬─┐ ┌────────────────────────┬─┬─┐ │  └──────────┘     │
│ │ │=│▼│ │                        │ ▼│ │  ┌──────────┐     │
│ │ └─┴─┘ └────────────────────────┴─┴─┘ │  │  Cancel  │     │
│ │        ◉ And    ○ Or                  │  └──────────┘     │
│ │ ┌─┬─┐ ┌────────────────────────┬─┬─┐ │  ┌──────────┐     │
│ │ │ │▼│ │                        │ ▼│ │  │   Help   │     │
│ │ └─┴─┘ └────────────────────────┴─┴─┘ │  └──────────┘     │
│ └──────────────────────────────────────┘                  │
│ Use ? to represent any single character                    │
│ Use * to represent any series of characters                │
└──────────────────────────────────────────────────────────┘
```

♦ Complete the dialogue box as follows:

Show Rows Where:
SUPPLIER

=		Glen Tiles	(Select = and Glen Tiles from the drop-down lists)
And	**Or**		Select the **Or** option button
=		UTile	(Select = and UTile from the drop-down lists)

♦ When your entries are accurate and complete, click the **OK** button and your list should now display only those records where the **SUPPLIER** is Glen Tiles *or* UTile.

♦ Remove the filter from the **SUPPLIER** column and return to full list display.

♦ This time click the down arrow button for the column label **PRICE** then select [**Custom . . .**] from the drop-down display.

♦ Complete the **Custom AutoFilter** dialogue box as follows:

Show Rows Where:
PRICE

<		1.00	(Select < from the drop-down list and enter 1.00 manually
And	**Or**		Select the **And** option button
—		—	(Leave these two fields blank)

♦ Click the **OK** button in the dialogue box and your list should now display only those records whose **PRICE** is less than £1.00.

♦ Remove the filter from the **PRICE** column.

Comparison operators

The comparison operators which are available to you in the **Custom AutoFilter** dialogue box are the following:

Operator	Meaning
=	Equal to
>	Greater than
<	Less than
> =	Greater than or equal to
< =	Less than or equal to
< >	Not equal to

♦ Click the down arrow button for **PRICE** again then select [**Custom ...**] from the drop-down display.

♦ Complete the **Custom AutoFilter** dialogue box as follows:

Show Rows Where:
PRICE

<		1.00	(Select < from the drop-down list, enter 1.00 manually)
	And	**Or**	Select the **Or** option button
>		2.00	(Select > from the drop-down list, enter 2.00 manually)

♦ Click the **OK** button in the dialogue box and your list should display only those records whose price is less than £1.00 or greater than £2.00.

♦ *Do not* remove the filter from the **PRICE** column.

♦ Click the down arrow button for **SUPPLIER** then select [**Custom ...**] and complete the dialogue box as follows:

Show Rows Where:
SUPPLIER

=		Fine Tiles	(Select = and Fine Tiles from the drop-down lists)
	And	**Or**	Select the **Or** option button
=		Ascot Ceramics	(Select = and Ascot Ceramics from the drop-down lists)

♦ Select **OK** from the dialogue box. The following criteria have now been applied to the records in your list:

> **SUPPLIER** must be Fine Tiles *or* Ascot Ceramics
> *and*
> **PRICE** must be <£1.00 *or* >£2.00

♦ Select **Data** from the Menu bar then **Filter** then **Show All** and you should be returned to full list display.

Let's say we now wish to display only the records for floor tiles. We can do this by applying a filter criterion to either the **CODE** field or the **DESCRIPTION** field. We'll do it using the **CODE** field first which means we'll have to use *wildcard characters*.

♦ Click the down arrow button for **CODE** and select **[Custom ...]** from the drop-down display.

♦ Complete the dialogue box as follows:

Show Rows Where:
CODE

=	FT*	(Enter FT* manually using upper case or lower case)
And	**Or**	Select the **And** option button
—	—	(Leave these fields blank)

♦ Select **OK** from the dialogue box and your list should now display only records for floor tiles.

♦ Remove the filter from the **CODE** column.

Wildcard characters

Wildcard characters such as * (asterisk) and ? (question mark) can be used to represent one or more unspecified characters in a comparison search.

• The ? (question mark)   can be used to represent any single character in the same position as the question mark.

• The * (asterisk)   can be used to represent any number of characters in the same position as the asterisk.

Example

FT*	would find all *floor* tiles;
*g	would find all *granite* tiles;
??-S-?	would find all *small* tiles;
S	would also find all *small* tiles.

Carry out a few trial searches using these characters.

We'll now display the floor tile records using a filter criterion in the **DESCRIPTION** column.

♦ Remove any filters to display the full list.

♦ Click the down arrow button for **DESCRIPTION** then select **[Custom ...]** from the drop-down display. Complete the dialogue box as follows:

Show Rows Where:
DESCRIPTION

=	Floor*	(Enter Floor* manually using upper or lower case)
And	**Or**	Select the **And** option button
—	—	(Leave these fields blank)

♦ Select **OK** from the dialogue box and once again your list should display only the floor tile records.

♦ Remove the filter from the **DESCRIPTION** column.

Exercise

♦ Filter the list so that it displays only records for floor tiles whose price is less than £1.50.

Removing AutoFilter

♦ When you have completed your exercise, remove **AutoFilter** by selecting **Data** from the menu bar then **Filter** then **AutoFilter**.

FILTERING A LIST USING ADVANCED FILTER

The list can be filtered on the basis of more complex comparison criteria using the **Advanced Filter** option. This option does not place drop-down lists on each column, instead you must set up a criteria range on the worksheet.

Setting up the criteria range

It's best to place the criteria range above the list so that it is visible after the list has been filtered. We'll use rows 3, 4 and 5 for our criteria range so first of all it will be necessary to move the list down four rows (to allow us one blank row above and below the range).

♦ Select row headings 3, 4, 5 and 6 (located to the left of cells A3, A4, A5 and A6).

♦ When the four rows have been selected (darkened) open the **Insert** menu and select **Rows**. The list should have now moved down by four rows and appear as follows:

	A	B	C	D	E	F	G	H	I
1	DERWENT TILES LTD – Product Records								
2									
3									
4									
5									
6									
7	CODE	DESCRIPTION	SUPPLIER	COST	MARKUP	TAX	PRICE	INSTOCK	REORDER
8	CT-L-P	Ceiling, large, poly.	Utile	£1.20	£0.48	£0.29	£1.97	1700	2000
9	CT-M-P	Ceiling, medium, poly.	UTile	£0.80	£0.32	£0.20	£1.32	1500	1000
10	FT-L-C	Floor, large, ceramic	Ascot Ceramics	£1.80	£0.72	£0.44	£2.96	3700	3000
11	FT-L-G	Floor, large, granite	Glen Tiles	£2.20	£0.88	£0.54	£3.62	1800	1500
12	FT-L-K	Floor, large, cork	Fine Tiles	£1.25	£0.50	£0.31	£2.06	3000	2000
13	FT-L-V	Floor, large, vinyl	Hanson Vinyls	£1.10	£0.44	£0.27	£1.81	1100	1000
14	FT-M-C	Floor, medium, ceramic	Ascot Ceramics	£1.50	£0.60	£0.37	£2.47	3500	3000
15	FT-M-G	Floor, medium, granite	Glen Tiles	£2.00	£0.80	£0.49	£3.29		1500
16	FT-M-K	Floor, medium, cork	Fine Tiles	£0.85	£0.34	£0.21	£1.40	2500	1500
17	FT-M-V	Floor, medium, vinyl	Hanson Vinyls	£1.00	£0.40	£0.25	£1.65	800	500
18	FT-S-C	Floor, small, ceramic	Ascot Ceramics	£1.30	£0.52	£0.32	£2.14	3100	3000
19	FT-S-G	Floor, small, granite	Glen Tiles	£1.60	£0.64	£0.39	£2.63	1400	1000
20	FT-S-V	Floor, small, vinyl	Hanson Vinyls	£0.80	£0.32	£0.20	£1.32	900	500
21	WT-L-C	Wall, large, ceramic	Ascot Ceramics	£0.90	£0.36	£0.22	£1.48	2900	2500
22	WT-L-G	Wall, large, granite	Glen Tiles	£1.50	£0.60	£0.37	£2.47	800	1000
23	WT-M-C	Wall, medium, ceramic	Ascot Ceramics	£0.75	£0.30	£0.18	£1.23	3200	3000
24	WT-M-G	Wall, medium, granite	Glen Tiles	£1.10	£0.44	£0.27	£1.81	900	500
25	WT-S-C	Wall, small, ceramic	Ascot Ceramics	£0.50	£0.20	£0.12	£0.82	2500	2000
26	WT-S-G	Wall, small, granite	Glen Tiles	£0.90	£0.36	£0.22	£1.48	600	500

Using comparison criteria in a criteria range

This will enable you to filter the list on the basis of criteria specified in the criteria range. In this case the first row of the criteria range should contain an exact copy of the column labels. The best way to ensure that the criteria labels in the criteria range match exactly the column labels in the list is to **Copy** and **Paste** the column labels.

♦ Select cell C7 (containing the column label, **SUPPLIER**).

♦ Select **Edit** from the Menu bar then **Copy** from the **Edit** menu.

♦ Select cell C3, open the **Edit** menu again and choose **Paste**.

An exact duplicate of the column label, **SUPPLIER**, should now appear in cell C3.

♦ Press the **[Esc]** key to remove the flowing border round cell C7.

♦ Select cell C4 and enter Glen Tiles (you can use upper or lower case).

♦ Select any cell in the list then open the **Data** menu and choose **Filter** then **Advanced Filter**.

The **Advanced Filter** dialogue box should now open similar to the following:

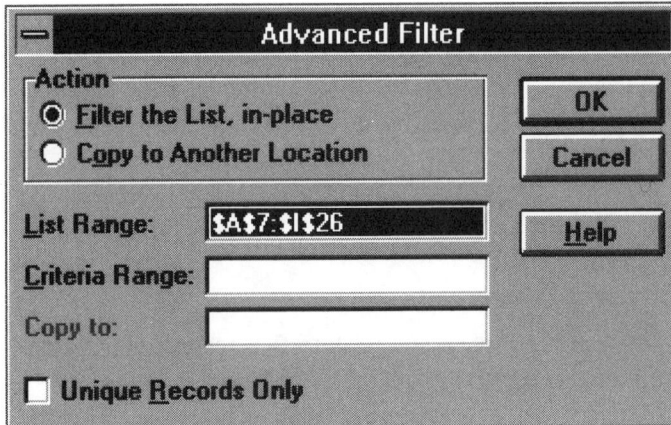

Advanced Filter dialogue box

- The **List Range** box should display the data range for the full list (if not, enter the range as A7:I26).

- Enter the **Criteria Range** as C3:C4.

- Ensure that the **Filter the List, in-place** option button has been selected.

- Click **OK** in the dialogue box and your list should now display only those records where the **SUPPLIER** is Glen Tiles.

- To remove the filter, open the **Data** menu, select **Filter** then **Show All**.

Guidelines for using comparison criteria

1   When copying column labels to the criteria range, they need not be entered in the same column.

	A	B
1	DERWENT TILES LTD	
2		
3	**SUPPLIER**	
4	Fine Tiles	
5		

In this example the criteria range is A3:A4 and the filtered list would display only those records where the **SUPPLIER** is Fine Tiles. Wildcard characters can be used when specifying criteria; F* in this case would produce the same result.

2   Enter all your criteria in the same row to find records that match all criteria in that row.

	A	B
1	DERWENT TILES LTD	
2		
3	**SUPPLIER**	PRICE
4	UTile	<1.50
5		

In this example the criteria range is A3:B4 and the filtered list would display only those records where the **SUPPLIER** is UTile *and* the **PRICE** is less than £1.50.

3 You can use a column label more than once in the criteria range if you wish to find records which meet more than one criterion for the same column.

	A	B
1	DERWENT TILES LTD	
2		
3	**PRICE**	**PRICE**
4	>2.00	<3.00
5		

In this example the criteria range is A3:B4 and the filtered list would display only those records where the price is greater than £2.00 *and* less than £3.00.

4 Enter criteria to different rows when you wish to find records that match all criteria in the first row *or* the second row.

	A	B
1	DERWENT TILES LTD	
2		
3	**SUPPLIER**	COST
4	Hanson Vinyls	<1.00
5	Ascot Ceramics	>1.50

In this example the criteria range is A3:B5. The filtered list would display only those records which meet *either* of the following two conditions:

Condition 1: **SUPPLIER**, Hanson Vinyls *and* **COST**, <£1.00

Condition 2: **SUPPLIER**, Ascot Ceramics *and* **COST**, >£1.50

5 The criteria range need not be restricted to three rows and two columns.

Using computed criteria in a criteria range

A worksheet formula can be specified in a criteria range and used to match records.

Guidelines for using computed criteria in a criteria range

1 The formula entered as a criterion must produce the logical value **TRUE** or **FALSE** when used to match records and only those records containing values which produce **TRUE** are displayed in the filtered list.

2 The formula must refer to at least one column in the list.

3 If you label the computed formula in the criteria range the label must not be the same as any column label in the list otherwise the formula will be used as comparison criteria.

We will use a computed criterion formula to filter the list and display only those records where the quantity in stock is less than the re-order quantity.

♦ Ensure that the full list is displayed. Remove any filters using **Data/Filter/Show All**.

♦ Clear all cell entries in the criteria range using **Edit/Clear/All**.

♦ Select cell A3 and enter the text LowStock. (Note that this is not a column label, merely a means of identifying the formula which will be entered in cell A4.)

- ♦ Select cell A4 and enter the formula =H8<I8. Note that **TRUE** now appears in cell A4 since the formula is true for the first record (row 8).
- ♦ When the **Advanced Filter** option is invoked, the program will check each record in the list and those whose **INSTOCK** quantity (column H) is less than the **REORDER** quantity (column I) will be displayed in the filtered list.
- ♦ Select any cell in the list, open the **Data** menu and select **Filter** then **Advanced Filter**.

When the **Advanced Filter** dialogue box opens, the **List Range** should be displayed as $A$7:$I$26.

- ♦ Enter the **Criteria Range** as A3:A4. The cell immediately above the formula must be included in the range even though you have not given the formula a label.
- ♦ Ensure that the **Filter the List, in-place** button is selected and click **OK**.

The list should now display only those records which match the specified computed criterion.

- ♦ Remove the filter using **Data/Filter/Show All**.

Relative or absolute cell references

The cell references used in the criterion formula in the previous example were relative, i.e. H8 and I8. When the **Advanced Filter** option is invoked, the program checks each record in the list and adjusts the formula while doing so. By the time the last record is being checked, the formula will be =H26<I26. Each record for which the formula evaluates to **TRUE** is then displayed in the filtered list.

Absolute cell referencing can also be used if you wish to compare a value in each record with a fixed value.

- ♦ To demonstrate this, select cell B3 and enter the value 1000.
- ♦ Select cell A4 and enter the formula =H8<$B$3.
- ♦ Select any cell in the list, open the **Data** menu and choose **Filter** then **Advanced Filter**. In the **Advanced Filter** dialogue box, the **List Range** should be $A$7:$I$26.
- ♦ Enter the **Criteria Range** as A3:A4.
- ♦ Check that the **Filter the List, in-place** button is selected and click **OK**.

The list should be filtered and display only those records whose **INSTOCK** quantity is less than 1000.

This time, the program has checked each record in the list but has only adjusted the first part of the formula while doing so. This means that each record's **INSTOCK** quantity is compared with the contents of cell B3.

- ♦ Remove the filter using **Data/Filter/Show All**.
- ♦ Clear the contents of cell B3 using **Edit/Clear/All**.

Using a mixture of computed and comparison criteria

Computed and comparison criteria can be combined in the same criteria range. We will use this facility to filter the list and display only those records where the quantity in stock is less than the reorder quantity *and* the supplier is Glen Tiles.

♦ **Copy** the column label **SUPPLIER** to cell B3 (remember to press the **[Esc]** key when you are finished to remove the flowing border).

♦ Select cell B4 and enter Glen Tiles.

♦ Select cell A4 and enter the formula =H8<I8.

Your criteria range should now appear as follows:

	A	B
1	**DERWENT TILES LTD**	
2		
3	Low Stock	**SUPPLIER**
4	TRUE	Glen Tiles
5		

Criteria range is A3:B4.

♦ Select any cell in the list, open the **Data** menu, choose **Filter** then **Advanced Filter**. The **List Range** in the dialogue box should be $A$7:$I$26.

♦ Enter the **Criteria Range** as A3:B4.

♦ Ensure that the **Filter the List, in-place** button is selected and click **OK**.

The filtered list should display only those records where the supplier is Glen Tiles and the instock quantity is less than the reorder quantity.

♦ Remove the filter using **Data/Filter/Show All**.

Copying complete filtered records to another location

The **Advanced Filter** option can be used to copy filtered data to another part of the worksheet.

♦ Select any cell in the list, open the **Data** menu, choose **Filter** then **Advanced Filter**. In the dialogue box the **List Range** should be $A$7:$I$26 and the **Criteria Range** should be $A$3:$B$4.

♦ Select the **Copy to Another Location** button.

♦ Enter the cell reference A30 to the **Copy to** box and click **OK**.

You will be returned to the full list, and the filtered data will be in a different location.

♦ Scroll the window until rows 30–32 come into view and you'll see your filtered records complete with column labels.

♦ Select the cell range A30:I32 and clear the entries using **Edit/Clear/All**.

Copying specified columns of filtered records to another location

♦ Copy the column labels **CODE, DESCRIPTION, SUPPLIER, INSTOCK** and **REORDER** to the cells A30, B30, C30, D30 and E30 respectively.

♦ Select any cell in the list, open the **Data** menu, choose **Filter** then **Advanced Filter**. In the **Advanced Filter** dialogue box the **List Range** should be $A$7:$I$26 and the **Criteria Range** should be $A$3:$B$4.

♦ Select the **Copy to Another Location** button.

♦ Enter the cell range A30:E30 to the **Copy to** box and click **OK**.

When you are returned to the full list scroll the window until rows 30–32 come into view and the specified column contents for the matching records should be displayed.

♦ Select the cell range A30:E32 and clear the entries using **Edit/Clear/All**.

Benefits of filtering

Filtering enables you to view, edit, print, sort and create charts from only those records in your list which conform to specified criteria. When you are in **Filter** mode many of the commands and features operate only on the displayed records.

ENTERING SUBTOTALS TO A LIST

A Microsoft® Excel list can be easily summarised using subtotals. Let's say we want our list to show the total number of tiles we have in stock *from each supplier*.
First of all we'll resort our list so that it displays the records alphabetically by supplier name (this will obviously group all records with the same supplier name together).

♦ Select any cell in the list, open the **Data** menu and choose **Sort**.

♦ When the **Sort** dialogue box opens, select **SUPPLIER** from the drop-down list in the **Sort By** section.

♦ Ensure that the **Ascending** button is selected and click **OK**.

You will be returned to your list where the records should be displayed in alphabetic order by supplier name.

♦ Select any cell in the list, open the **Data** menu again and choose **Subtotals**.

The **Subtotal** dialogue box should now appear as follows:

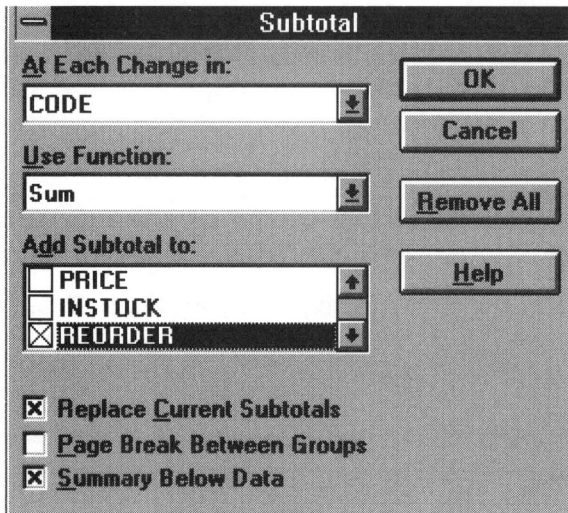

♦ Select **SUPPLIER** from the drop-down list in the **At Each Change in** box.

♦ Ensure that **Sum** is displayed in the **Use Function** box, otherwise select it from the drop-down list.

♦ Select the **INSTOCK** check box in the **Add Subtotal to** section and ensure that none of the other data check boxes in this section are selected.

♦ Click the **OK** button and you will be returned to the list where total stock subtotals should have been entered for each supplier.

You can also produce a summary report using the outline buttons, ⊟, which have been placed on the extreme left of the screen against each supplier's total. Click each button in turn and observe the effect. Clicking the buttons again will return you to the original display. The same effects can be achieved using the three number buttons, ①②③, located above the outline buttons.

♦ To remove the subtotals from the list, open the **Data** menu, choose **Subtotals** and select the **Remove All** button in the **Subtotal** dialogue box.

The **Subtotal** command can also be used on a filtered list. The command will produce subtotals for the filtered records only. As with an unfiltered list, you should **Sort** the records before using the **Subtotals** command.

CHAPTER 22

Introduction to Pivot Tables

An Introduction to Pivot Tables · Creating a Pivot Table from a Single Worksheet List · Deleting a Pivot Table · Creating a Pivot Table with Several Pages · Pivot Table Functions · Updating a Pivot Table · Creating a Pivot Table from Multiple Worksheet Ranges · Creating a Chart from a Pivot Table

AN INTRODUCTION TO PIVOT TABLES

A Pivot Table allows you to summarise large amounts of data from a list, a worksheet or several worksheets. You can rotate the row and column headings to enable you to examine and analyse the source data from different viewpoints. For example, if you have a record of your sales by region, by month, by product and by salesperson, the Pivot Table enables you to produce different 'views' of this data based on format and calculation methods which you specify. You could produce a table showing sales by product by region for a specific time period or sales by a particular salesperson analysed by product over several time periods.

To help understand the basics of Pivot Table use and construction, we will produce one for a wholesaler, Solent Systems, who distributes TVs, hi-fis and video equipment to retail establishments throughout the country. For the purpose of analysis reporting, the company has divided the country into three sales regions: North, Central and South, and allocated two salesmen to cover each area.

♦ Open the workbook, LearnXL, and select the first blank worksheet.

The following list is a sales report for Solent Systems for the first three months of 199X which analyses sales by region, product type and salesperson. There is little structure to the report as it stands but the Pivot Table we produce later will display the data in an organised format which we specify.

♦ Set up this list on the worksheet.

	A	B	C	D	E
1	**SOLENT SYSTEMS Sales Report 199X**				
2					
3	**MONTH**	**REGION**	**PRODUCT**	**SALESPERSON**	**SALES**
4	JAN	NORTH	TV	JIM	30000
5	JAN	NORTH	HI-FI	JOHN	32000
6	JAN	SOUTH	VIDEO	AHMED	25000
7	JAN	CENTRAL	HI-FI	DAVE	44000
8	JAN	SOUTH	VIDEO	MARY	27000
9	JAN	SOUTH	TV	AHMED	50000
10	JAN	NORTH	VIDEO	JIM	15000
11	JAN	CENTRAL	VIDEO	DAVE	20000
12	JAN	CENTRAL	VIDEO	ALICE	21000
13	JAN	NORTH	HI-FI	JIM	33000
14	JAN	SOUTH	TV	MARY	60000
15	JAN	CENTRAL	TV	ALICE	40000
16	JAN	NORTH	VIDEO	JOHN	17000
17	JAN	NORTH	TV	JOHN	25000
18	JAN	CENTRAL	TV	DAVE	44000
19	JAN	SOUTH	HI-FI	MARY	54000
20	JAN	SOUTH	HI-FI	AHMED	51000
21	JAN	CENTRAL	HI-FI	ALICE	48000
22	FEB	NORTH	TV	JIM	33000
23	FEB	CENTRAL	TV	DAVE	41000
24	FEB	CENTRAL	TV	ALICE	46000
25	FEB	NORTH	TV	JOHN	26000
26	FEB	SOUTH	VIDEO	MARY	27000
27	FEB	SOUTH	VIDEO	AHMED	28000
28	FEB	NORTH	HI-FI	JIM	38000
29	FEB	NORTH	HI-FI	JOHN	36000
30	FEB	NORTH	VIDEO	JIM	18000
31	FEB	CENTRAL	HI-FI	DAVE	46000
32	FEB	SOUTH	HI-FI	AHMED	55000
33	FEB	NORTH	VIDEO	JOHN	19000
34	FEB	SOUTH	TV	MARY	62000
35	FEB	CENTRAL	HI-FI	ALICE	49000
36	FEB	CENTRAL	VIDEO	DAVE	22000
37	FEB	SOUTH	TV	AHMED	51000
38	FEB	SOUTH	HI-FI	MARY	56000
39	FEB	CENTRAL	VIDEO	ALICE	23000
40	MAR	NORTH	TV	JIM	32000
41	MAR	SOUTH	TV	MARY	60000
42	MAR	NORTH	HI-FI	JIM	28000

	A	B	C	D	E
43	MAR	CENTRAL	VIDEO	ALICE	19000
44	MAR	SOUTH	HI-FI	AHMED	59000
45	MAR	SOUTH	VIDEO	AHMED	29000
46	MAR	NORTH	VIDEO	JIM	17000
47	MAR	NORTH	TV	JOHN	24000
48	MAR	SOUTH	HI-FI	MARY	60000
49	MAR	NORTH	HI-FI	JOHN	32000
50	MAR	CENTRAL	TV	DAVE	45000
51	MAR	CENTRAL	HI-FI	DAVE	41000
52	MAR	NORTH	VIDEO	JOHN	18000
53	MAR	SOUTH	VIDEO	MARY	31000
54	MAR	CENTRAL	VIDEO	DAVE	24000
55	MAR	CENTRAL	TV	ALICE	47000
56	MAR	SOUTH	TV	AHMED	55000
57	MAR	CENTRAL	HI-FI	ALICE	40000

♦ Embolden and centre the column headings (MONTH, REGION, etc.).

♦ **Save** the workbook.

CREATING A PIVOT TABLE FROM A SINGLE WORKSHEET LIST

♦ Select any cell in the Sales Report list (A3:E57), open the **Data** menu and choose the **PivotTable** command.

The **PivotTable Wizard** tool will now be activated. This is a series of dialogue boxes which lead you through the design of your Pivot Table in four steps with instructions at each stage.

♦ *Step 1.* The Step 1 dialogue box, which should be displayed at the moment, allows you to choose the type of source data to be used in the Pivot Table. Our data is contained in a list so ensure that the **Microsoft Excel List** button is selected and click the **Next** button.

Note: The list must have labelled columns.

♦ *Step 2.* The Step 2 dialogue box allows you to specify the location of the source data to be used for the Table. The range displayed should be $A$3:$E$57 since you selected a cell in the list before invoking **PivotTable Wizard**. If this range is not displayed, you should enter it now.

♦ Click the **Next** button.

♦ *Step 3.* The Step 3 dialogue box which should appear as follows, will allow you to design a layout for your Pivot Table.

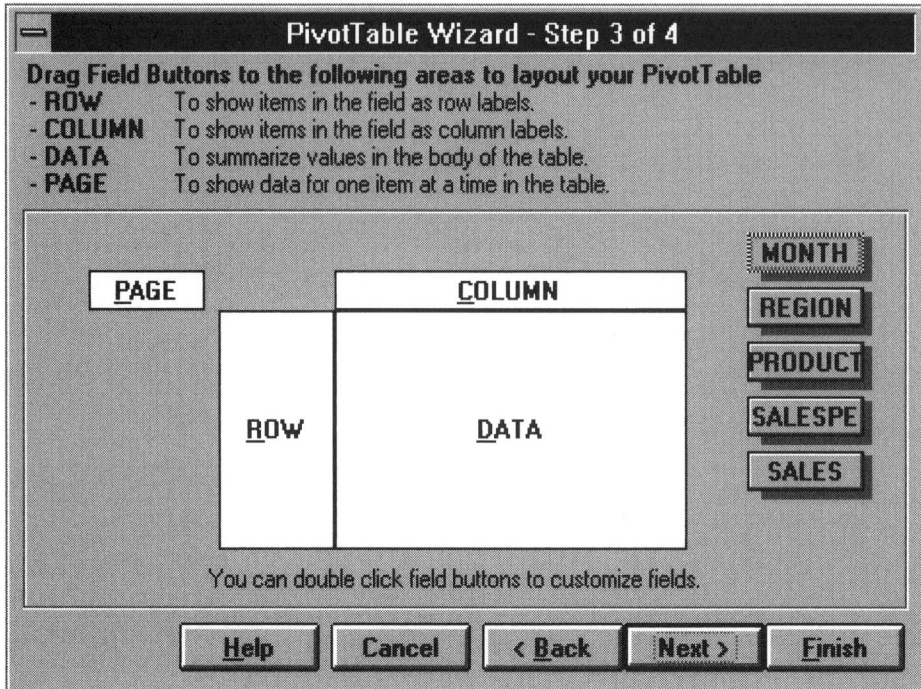

Note that the column labels (field names) from the source list (**MONTH, REGION, PRODUCT, SALESPERSON, SALES**) have been placed down the right side of the box. The layout design section of the dialogue box consists of four areas: **ROW**, **COLUMN**, **DATA** and **PAGE**. The Pivot Table is designed quite simply by moving fields into one of these areas.

Let's say we want to produce a report showing total sales of each product per month over the three month period. The report will have the following format:

	JAN	FEB	MAR	TOTAL
HI-FI	XX	XX	XX	XXX
TV	XX	XX	XX	XXX
VIDEO	XX	XX	XX	XXX
	XXX	XXX	XXX	XXX

♦ Point to the field name **MONTH** and click and hold down the mouse button. Move the pointer into the **COLUMN** area (the field will move with the pointer) and release the mouse button. The field **MONTH** should now be located in the **COLUMN** area. This means that the unique items in the **MONTH** column in the source list (JAN, FEB, MAR) will be placed as column labels in the Pivot Table.

If you drop the field in the wrong area by mistake, move it using the same procedure. You can also move it back to 'base' if you pick up the wrong field.

♦ In a similar manner, move the field **PRODUCT** into the **ROW** area. The result will be that the unique items in the **PRODUCT** column in the source list (HI-FI, TV, VIDEO) will be placed as row headings in the Pivot Table.

♦ We must now identify the column which contains the data on which the calculations will be based. Move the **SALES** field into the **DATA** area. The appropriate figures from the **SALES** column in the source list will be extracted and summed to produce the data for the report.

The completed dialogue box should be similar to the following:

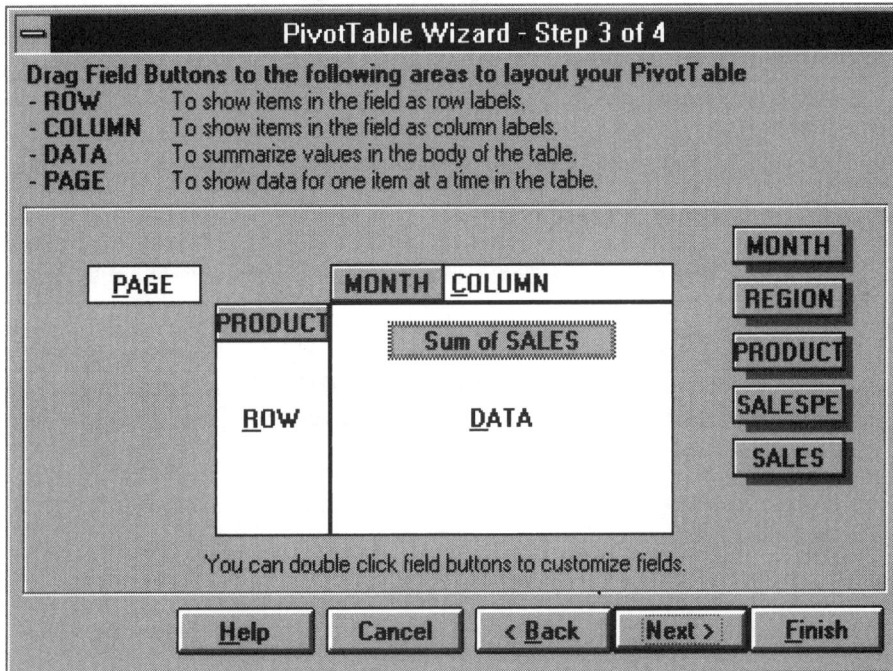

♦ Click the **Next** button.

♦ *Step 4.* The final dialogue box (No. 4) allows you to specify where you want the Pivot Table placed. This can be on the existing worksheet beside the list or another worksheet in the same or a different workbook. We'll locate the Table at the side of our list, so type the reference G3 in the **PivotTable Starting Cell** box. Ensure that all the **PivotTable Options** check boxes have been selected and click the **Finish** button.

You will be returned to the list where the Pivot Table should have been inserted. Bring it into view and examine its contents. The Table should be similar to the following:

	G	H	I	J	K
1					
2					
3	Sum of SALES	MONTH			
4	PRODUCT	JAN	FEB	MAR	Grand Total
5	HI-FI	262000	280000	260000	802000
6	TV	249000	259000	263000	771000
7	VIDEO	125000	137000	138000	400000
8	Grand Total	636000	676000	661000	1973000

♦ If the Query and Pivot Toolbar is also displayed, remove it by clicking its **Close** button, ⊟, on the left of its Title bar.

♦ If you wish to alter the Table, you can recall the **PivotTable Wizard** dialogue boxes by selecting any cell in the Table and then choosing the **PivotTable** command from the **Data** menu.

♦ The layout of the Pivot Table can also be modified without the aid of the Wizard. Note that the field names, **MONTH** and **PRODUCT**, are highlighted. These can be dragged and dropped in a different location (within the table area) to give a different view of the data.

We'll now produce another Pivot Table showing the same data as the first one but this time analysed by region.

♦ Select any cell in the list, open the **Data** menu and choose **PivotTable**.

♦ Complete the **PivotTable Wizard** dialogue boxes in the following way:

♦ *Step 1*. Ensure that the **Microsoft Excel List** option button is selected then click the **Next** button.

♦ *Step 2*. Ensure that the range $A$3:$E$57 is displayed then click the **Next** button.

♦ *Step 3*:
  – Move the **MONTH** field into the **COLUMN** area.
  – Move the **PRODUCT** field into the **ROW** area.
  – Move the **REGION** field into the **ROW** area.
  – Move the **SALES** field into the **DATA** area.
  – Select the **Next** button.

♦ *Step 4*. Enter the **PivotTable Starting Cell** reference as G10. Ensure that all the **PivotTable Options** check boxes have been selected and click the **Finish** button.

The second Pivot Table should now be inserted to the side of your list below the first one. Bring it into view and note that by placing two fields in the **ROW** area in the Step 3 dialogue box, you get two row fields in the Pivot Table. The Table should be similar to the following:

	G	H	I	J	K	L
9						
10	Sum of SALES		MONTH			
11	PRODUCT	REGION	JAN	FEB	MAR	Grand Total
12	HI-FI	CENTRAL	92000	95000	81000	268000
13		NORTH	65000	74000	60000	199000
14		SOUTH	105000	111000	119000	335000
15	HI-FI Total		262000	280000	260000	802000
16	TV	CENTRAL	84000	87000	92000	263000
17		NORTH	55000	59000	56000	170000
18		SOUTH	110000	113000	115000	338000
19	TV Total		249000	259000	263000	771000
20	VIDEO	CENTRAL	41000	45000	43000	129000
21		NORTH	32000	37000	35000	104000
22		SOUTH	52000	55000	60000	167000
23	VIDEO Total		125000	137000	138000	400000
24	Grand Total		636000	676000	661000	1973000

DELETING A PIVOT TABLE

Delete the existing Pivot Tables from your worksheet in the same way as you would clear any other range of cells, i.e. select (highlight) the range of cells then choose **Edit**/**Clear**/**All** from the menus.

CREATING A PIVOT TABLE WITH SEVERAL PAGES

It is possible to produce a Pivot Table with a third dimension, i.e. with several 'pages'. This time we'll produce a Table to show monthly product sales for each region but we'll put each region's data on a separate 'page' of the Table.

♦ Select any cell in the list, open the **Data** menu and choose **PivotTable**.

♦ Complete the dialogue boxes as follows:

♦ *Step 1*. Ensure that the **Microsoft Excel List** option button is selected then click the **Next** button.

♦ *Step 2*. Ensure that the range $A$3:$E$57 is displayed then click the **Next** button.

♦ *Step 3*:
  – Move the **MONTH** field into the **COLUMN** area.
  – Move the **PRODUCT** field into the **ROW** area.
  – Move the **SALES** field into the **DATA** area.
  – Move the **REGION** field into the **PAGE** area.
  – Note that the **PAGE** area has increased in size to accommodate more fields if required.
  – Click the **Next** button.

♦ *Step 4*. Enter the **PivotTable Starting Cell** reference as G3.

♦ Ensure that all the **Option** check boxes have been selected and click the **Finish** button.

The Pivot Table should now appear beside the list as follows:

	G	H	I	J	K
1					
2					
3	REGION	(All) ↓			
4					
5	Sum of SALES	MONTH			
6	PRODUCT	JAN	FEB	MAR	Grand Total
7	HI-FI	262000	280000	260000	802000
8	TV	249000	259000	263000	771000
9	VIDEO	125000	137000	138000	400000
10	Grand Total	636000	676000	661000	1973000

Note that the **REGION** field has been placed immediately above the Table enabling you to access separate 'pages' which will display the figures for each region. At the moment the word **All** should appear to the right of the field name meaning that the existing figures are the totals for all regions. To display the figures for a particular region, click the ⬇ button to the right of the **REGION** field name, select a region from the drop-down list and that region's 'page' of figures will be displayed.

PIVOT TABLE FUNCTIONS

So far the data in the Pivot Table has been produced by summing figures from the source list using the program's SUM function. However, there are other functions which can be used to carry out operations on Pivot Table data. To demonstrate this we'll create one more Pivot Table from our list to show product sales by salesperson.

♦ Delete the existing Pivot Table by selecting the range G2:K10 (slightly more than the Table range) and then choose **Edit/Clear/All**.

♦ Select any cell in the list, open the **Data** menu and choose **PivotTable**.

♦ Complete the dialogue boxes as follows:

♦ *Step 1*. Ensure that the **Microsoft Excel List** option button is selected then click the **Next** button.

♦ *Step 2*. Ensure that the range $A$3:$E$57 is displayed then click the **Next** button.

♦ *Step 3*:
  – Move the **PRODUCT** field into the **COLUMN** area.
  – Move the **SALESPERSON** field (the full name may not be displayed) into the **ROW** area.

– Move the **SALES** field into the **DATA** area.
– Click the **Next** button.

♦ *Step 4.* Enter the **PivotTable Starting Cell** reference as G3. Deselect the **Grand Totals for Columns** and **Grand Totals for Rows** check boxes and click the **Finish** button.

The Pivot Table should display the total sales of each product by salesperson for the three-month period similar to the following:

	G	H	I	J
1				
2				
3	Sum of SALES	PRODUCT		
4	SALESPERSON	HI-FI	TV	VIDEO
5	AHMED	165000	156000	82000
6	ALICE	137000	133000	63000
7	DAVE	131000	130000	66000
8	JIM	99000	95000	50000
9	JOHN	100000	75000	54000
10	MARY	170000	182000	85000

♦ Select any numeric cell in the Pivot Table.

♦ Open the **Data** menu and select **PivotTable Field**.

The following **PivotTable Field** dialogue box should now open allowing you to specify a function to be used on the data, e.g. **Sum, Average, Count, Product**, etc.

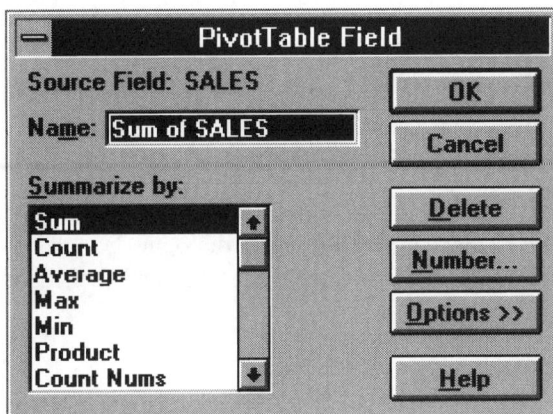

♦ Select the function, **Average**, from the **Summarize by** section of the dialogue box then click the **Number** button.

The **Format Cells** dialogue box should now open.

♦ Select **Number** from the **Category** section and select the format for zero decimal places (**0**) in the **Format Codes** section.

♦ Click the **OK** button in the **Format Cells** dialogue box then **OK** in the **PivotTable Field** dialogue box.

The Pivot Table should now be displayed as follows showing monthly averages instead of period totals:

	G	H	I	J
1				
2				
3	Average of SALES	PRODUCT		
4	SALESPERSON	HI-FI	TV	VIDEO
5	AHMED	55000	52000	27333
6	ALICE	45667	44333	21000
7	DAVE	43667	43333	22000
8	JIM	33000	31667	16667
9	JOHN	33333	25000	18000
10	MARY	56667	60667	28333

♦ Rename the worksheet, PivotTable and **Save** the workbook.

UPDATING A PIVOT TABLE

Changes to data in the source list will not be automatically reflected in the Pivot Table. If you alter the data in the source list you must use the **Refresh Data** command from the **Data** menu.

♦ Bring the Pivot Table into view and select cell E4 in the source list – Jim's TV sales for January.

♦ Change the sales figure from 30000 to 130000.

♦ Select any cell in the Pivot Table, open the **Data** menu and choose the **Refresh Data** command. The change should now be reflected in the Pivot Table.

♦ Change the sales figure in the list back to 30000 then refresh the Pivot Table again.

If you insert additional rows or columns in the source list, the new list range would need to be specified in the **PivotTable Wizard** Step 2 dialogue box. The dialogue boxes can be accessed by selecting any cell in the Pivot Table and then choosing the **PivotTable** command from the **Data** menu.

CREATING A PIVOT TABLE FROM MULTIPLE WORKSHEET RANGES

It is possible to create a Pivot Table using ranges from one or more worksheets. Each range must have row and column labels, and data with identical labels will be summarised.

Let's say Solent Systems keep the sales figures for each region on separate worksheets and they wish to consolidate them into one table.

♦ **Close** any workbooks which are open at the moment.

♦ Select **File** from the Menu bar and choose the **New** command.

A new workbook should open and the first worksheet (Sheet1) should be displayed.

♦ We'll keep Sheet1 blank at the moment and use it for our Pivot Table later.

♦ Select Sheet2 and set up the following worksheet:

	A	B	C	D
1	*Sales Report – North Region 1996*			
2				
3		JAN	FEB	MAR
4	HI-FI	65000	74000	60000
5	TV	55000	59000	56000
6	VIDEO	32000	37000	35000

♦ Rename the worksheet NORTH96.

♦ Select Sheet3 and set up the following worksheet:

	A	B	C	D
1	*Sales Report – South Region 1996*			
2				
3		JAN	FEB	MAR
4	TV	110000	113000	115000
5	VIDEO	52000	55000	60000
6	HI-FI	105000	111000	119000

Note: The products have been listed in a different order deliberately.

♦ Rename the worksheet SOUTH96.

♦ Select Sheet4 and set up the following worksheet:

	A	B	C	D
1	*Sales Report – Central Region 1996*			
2				
3		JAN	FEB	MAR
4	VIDEO	41000	45000	43000
5	HI-FI	92000	95000	81000
6	TV	84000	87000	92000

♦ Rename the worksheet CENTRAL96.

♦ **Save** the workbook as SOLENT.

We'll now produce a Pivot Table which will consolidate the results of the three regions and also provide a separate 'page' for each region's results.

♦ Open the **Data** menu and select the **PivotTable** command.

♦ The **PivotTable Wizard** tool will be activated and the Step 1 dialogue box should open.

♦ *Step 1.* Select the **Multiple Consolidation Ranges** option button and click the **Next** button.

♦ *Step 2a.* Select the **Create a single page field for me** option button and click the **Next** button.

♦ *Step 2b.* This step allows you to enter the data ranges you wish consolidated; these ranges must include the row and column labels.

♦ In the **Range** box enter NORTH96!A3:D6 (a reference to the worksheet and the cell range) and click the **Add** button. This reference should now appear in the **All Ranges** section.

♦ Enter the second reference in the **Range** box as SOUTH96!A3:D6 and click the **Add** button. The second worksheet reference should now appear in the **All Ranges** section.

♦ Enter the third reference as CENTRAL96!A3:D6 and click **Add**. The three references should now appear in the **All Ranges** section.

♦ Click the **Next** button.

♦ *Step 3.* In the Step 3 box a layout should have already been established, although it can be altered by moving fields in the usual way. Click the **Next** button.

♦ *Step 4.* Type the reference Sheet1!A1 in the **PivotTable Starting Cell** box.

♦ Ensure that all the **Options** check boxes have been selected and click the **Finish** button.

The Pivot Table should now be displayed on Sheet1 of the workbook showing the total monthly sales for each product for **All** regions. The ⬇ button on the right of the **Page1** field will enable you to select other pages showing the data for each region. The Table should be similar to the following:

	A	B	C	D	E
1	Page1	(All) ↓			
2					
3	Sum of Value	Column			
4	Row	JAN	FEB	MAR	Grand Total
5	HI-FI	262000	280000	260000	802000
6	TV	249000	259000	263000	771000
7	VIDEO	125000	137000	138000	400000
8	Grand Total	636000	676000	661000	1973000

Note: Field labels are **Page1**, **Column** and **Row** (cells A1, B3 and A4 respectively). Page Items are displayed by clicking the ⬇ button to the right of the **Page1** field.

We can make the Table a bit more meaningful by renaming the field labels and page items.

♦ Select the field label **Page1** (i.e. point to cell A1 and click).

♦ Type REGION and press [**Enter**].

♦ In a similar manner, change the field labels **Column** and **Row** to MONTH and PRODUCT respectively.

♦ Click the ⬇ button to the right of the **REGION** field and select **Item1** from the drop-down list.

♦ Now select the cell containing the **Item1** label (B1), type as Central and press [**Enter**].

You should now be 'asked' if you wish to rename Item1 Central; select **OK**.

♦ In a similar manner, rename Items 2 and 3 as North and South respectively.

♦ **Save** the workbook.

We'll now create a Pivot Table which can display the total results for the three regions for 1995 and 1996. Firstly, set up the following worksheets on Sheets 5, 6 and 7 of the Solent workbook and rename them NORTH95, SOUTH95 and CENTRAL95:

	A	B	C	D
1	Sales Report – North Region 1995			
2				
3		JAN	FEB	MAR
4	HI-FI	59000	66000	56000
5	TV	49000	55000	51000
6	VIDEO	28000	34000	32000

	A	B	C	D
1	Sales Report – South Region 1995			
2				
3		JAN	FEB	MAR
4	TV	98000	105000	106000
5	VIDEO	48000	50000	54000
6	HI-FI	97000	101000	110000

	A	B	C	D
1	Sales Report – Central Region 1995			
2				
3		JAN	FEB	MAR
4	VIDEO	36000	40000	38000
5	HI-FI	85000	89000	76000
6	TV	80000	82000	86000

- Open the **Data** menu and select the **PivotTable** command.
- Complete the **PivotTable Wizard** dialogue boxes in the following way:

- *Step 1*. Select the **Multiple Consolidation Ranges** option button and click the **Next** button.

- *Step 2a*. Select the **I will create the page fields** option button and click the **Next** button.

- *Step 2b*. The Step 2b dialogue box should appear as follows:

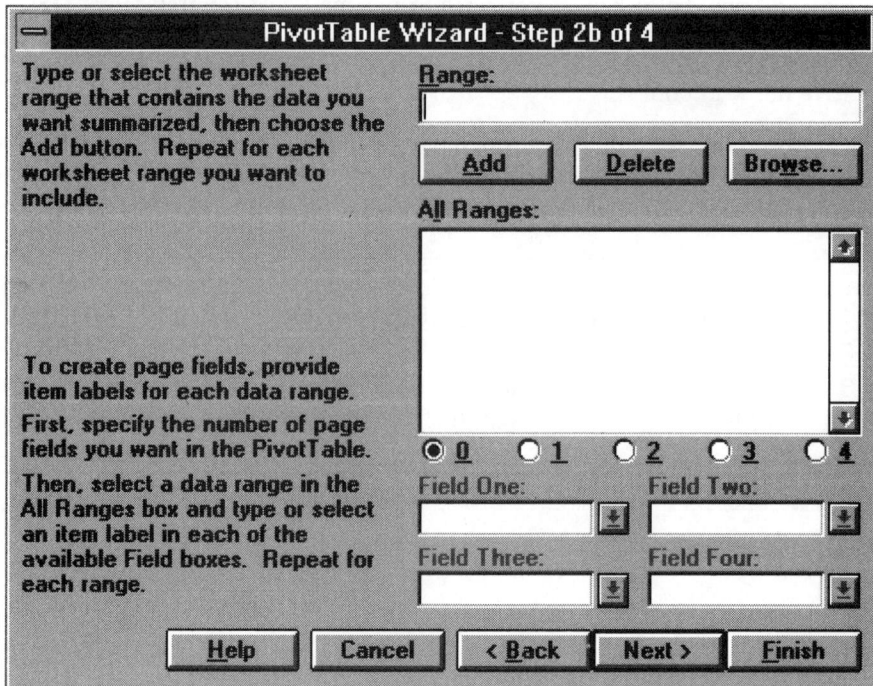

◆ *Step 2b contd.* Enter the following references to the **Range** box clicking the **Add** button after each entry:
NORTH96!A3:D6
SOUTH96!A3:D6
CENTRAL96!A3:D6
NORTH95!A3:D6
SOUTH95!A3:D6
CENTRAL95!A3:D6

These references should now appear in the **All Ranges** section of the dialogue box.

◆ Select the number **1** button below the **All Ranges** section to indicate that we want one Page Field. The **Field One** box should now be active, ready to accept an entry.

◆ We must now enter the two item labels, 1995 and 1996, to the **Field One** box and assign the appropriate references to them.

◆ Highlight the reference, **CENTRAL95!$A$3:$D$6** in the **All Ranges** section. Click in the **Field One** box and type the item label, 1995. (*Don't press the* **[Enter]** *key.*)

◆ Highlight the reference **CENTRAL96!$A$3:$D$6** in the **All Ranges** section; 1995 will disappear from the box but the item will have been stored. Click in the **Field One** box and type the item label, 1996.

◆ Highlight the reference **NORTH95!$A$3:$D$6** in the **All Ranges** section, click the ⬇ button in the **Field One** box and select **1995** from the drop-down list.

◆ Highlight the reference **NORTH96!$A$3:$D$6**, click the ⬇ button in the **Field One** box and select **1996** from the drop-down list.

◆ Highlight the reference **SOUTH95!$A$3:$D$6**, click the ⬇ button in the **Field One** box and select **1995** from the drop-down list.

◆ Highlight the reference **SOUTH96!$A$3:$D$6**, click the ⬇ button in the **Field One** box and select **1996** from the drop-down list.

◆ Each region's 1995 results should now be linked to the item label **1995** and the 1996 results to the label **1996**.

◆ Before you leave the Step 2b dialogue box, select each reference in the **All Ranges** section in turn and the corresponding item label will appear in the **Field One** box. Check that you have linked the references and the item labels accurately.

◆ Select the **Next** button.

◆ *Step 3.* The Step 3 dialogue box should display your layout. The row, column and page labels can all be given names in this dialogue box. Point to the field **Column** and double click.

◆ The **PivotTable Field** dialogue box should now open. Enter the **Name** as MONTH and click **OK**. You'll be returned to the Step 3 dialogue box and the new column label will be shown in the layout.

◆ In similar manner, change the field labels, **Row** and **Page1**, to PRODUCT and YEAR respectively.

♦ The Step 3 dialogue box should now be similar to the following:

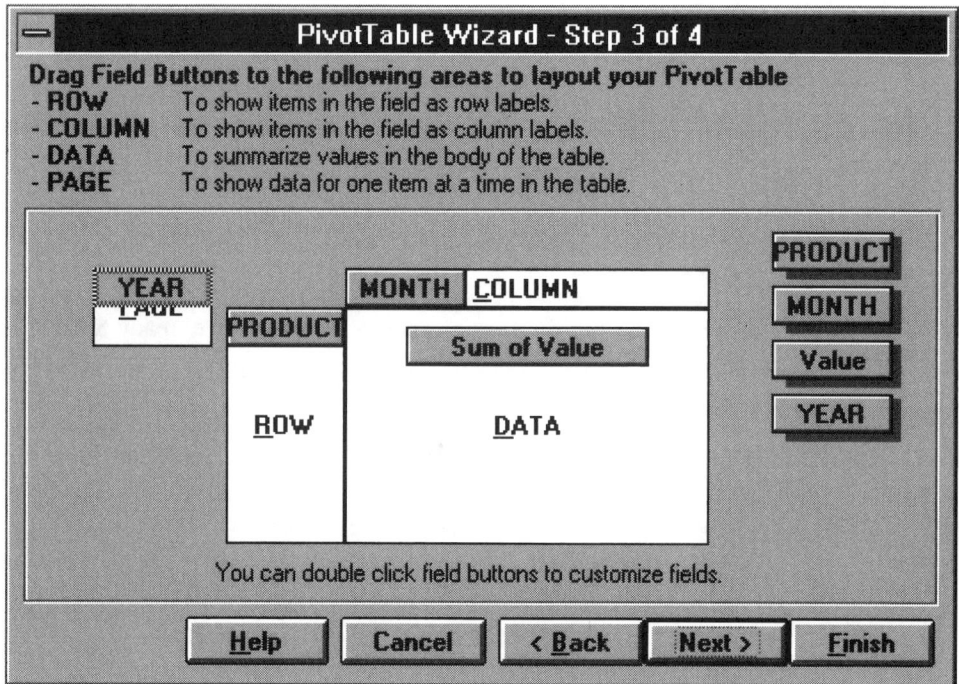

♦ Select the **Next** button.

♦ *Step 4.* Type the reference Sheet1!A10 in the **PivotTable Starting Cell** box.

♦ Ensure that all the **Options** check boxes have been selected and click the **Finish** button.

The Pivot Table should now appear on Sheet1, similar to the following, displaying the total results for both years combined:

	A	B	C	D	E
10	YEAR	(All) ↓			
11					
12	Sum of Value	MONTH			
13	PRODUCT	JAN	FEB	MAR	Grand Total
14	HI-FI	503000	536000	502000	1541000
15	TV	476000	501000	506000	1483000
16	VIDEO	237000	261000	262000	760000
17	Grand Total	1216000	1298000	1270000	3784000

♦ The 1995 and 1996 results can be displayed separately by selecting from the drop-down list in the **YEAR** field.

♦ **Save** the workbook.

CREATING A CHART FROM A PIVOT TABLE

Charting from a Pivot Table is a straightforward matter of selecting the data (including row and column headings) and creating a chart sheet or embedded chart in the normal way.

CHAPTER 23

Useful tools

Goal Seek · Data Tables · Scenario Manager · Problem Solving by Iteration · 'Lookup' Functions · Recording a Macro · Templates · Opening a Text File from Sage Sterling for Windows

GOAL SEEK

It is sometimes the case that you know the result you wish a formula to produce and you want to determine the input value of one of the formula's variables necessary to reach that result. For example, the level of sales required to produce a profit of £x.

This is the type of problem which is suitable for the Microsoft® Excel goal-seeking tool.

♦ To demonstrate, **Close** down any workbooks which are open at the moment and open the file LearnXL.

♦ Select the first blank sheet in the LearnXL workbook and set up the following worksheet:

	A	B
1	GOAL SEEK DEMO	
2		
3	Selling Price (per unit)	
4	Cost (per unit)	
5	Sales (units)	
6		
7	PROFIT	
8		

♦ Enter the Selling Price in cell B3 as 26.

♦ Enter the Cost in cell B4 as 18.

♦ Enter the Sales in cell B5 as 50000.

♦ Enter the formula =(B5*B3)–(B5*B4) in cell B7.

This formula should produce a profit figure of 400000 in cell B7.

To find the level of sales required to produce a profit of 500000 proceed as follows:

♦ Select Cell B7, open the **Tools** menu and select the **Goal Seek** command.

The following **Goal Seek** dialogue box should now open:

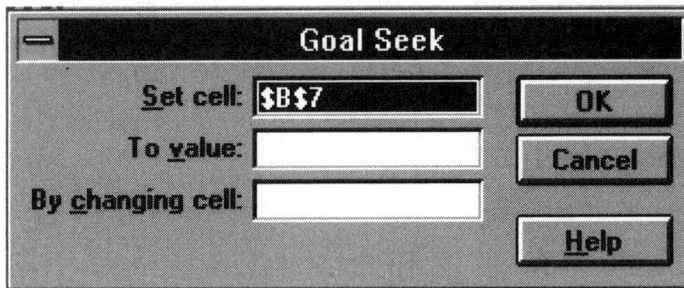

♦ Make the following entries to the dialogue box:

Set cell   : $B$7   (reference should be displayed already)
To value   : 500000
By changing cell   :   B5

♦ Click the **OK** button.
♦ Click **OK** again in the **Goal Seek Status** dialogue box and you will be returned to the worksheet.

The required profit of 500000 will have been entered to cell B7 and the level of sales necessary to achieve that profit (62500) to cell B5.

The **Goal Seek** tool enables you to produce a specific value in a particular cell by adjusting the value of *one other cell* to which it is linked by formula.

Practice exercise

1   Activate the worksheet, FORECAST, in the workbook, LearnXL.
2   Use **Goal Seek** to answer the following question:

By how much can we afford the labour cost per unit to rise without allowing the profit margin for the *year* to fall below 20 per cent?

DATA TABLES

Data tables enable you to perform 'what if' analyses on worksheet data and record the results in a table. For example, *what* will the effect on total costs be *if* wage rates increase by *x* per cent, *y* per cent, *z* per cent, etc.?

One-input tables allow you to examine the effect of altering one variable, e.g. the effect on profit of varying price.

Two-input tables enable you to alter two variables simultaneously and observe the result, e.g. the effect on profit of varying price and sales growth rate.

One-input table

An airline company operates a daily return service between London and the south of Spain and it wishes to estimate profit figures for the four summer months,

June–September. In June and September there is one return flight per day and in August, the peak month, two daily return flights. In July there is one return flight on weekdays and two at the weekend. Although the plane can carry a maximum of 300 passengers the average payload for each of these four months is normally 80 per cent.

♦ Select the first blank sheet in the workbook, LearnXL, and set up the following worksheet:

	A	B	C	D	E	F
1	**DATA TABLES DEMO**					
2						
3	**KEY VARIABLES**					
4	Ticket price per journey	105				
5	Variable costs %age	65%				
6	Fixed costs per month	260000				
7	Maximum No. of passengers	300				
8	Average payload	80%				
9						
10		**JUNE**	**JULY**	**AUG**	**SEPT**	**TOTAL**
11	No. of journeys	60	78	124	60	
12	Passenger revenue					
13	Variable costs					
14	Fixed costs					
15	Profit/Loss					

♦ Format the ticket price in cell B4 to currency style with two decimal places.

♦ Format cell B6 to currency style with no decimal places.

♦ Enter the following formulae to the appropriate cells:

Cell	Formula
B12	=B11*($B$4*$B$7*$B$8)
B13	=B12*$B$5
B14	=$B$6
B15	=B12–(B13+B14)

♦ Copy these formulae across to the columns for July, August and September.

♦ Enter the formula =SUM(B11:E11) to cell F11 and then copy this formula to the cell range F12:F15.

♦ Format the range B12:F15 to currency style with no decimal places.

♦ If you now get hash signs (###) in some of the cells simply widen the columns slightly.

♦ **Save** the workbook.

We'll now create a data table which will show the effect on profit of varying the average payload.

♦ Extend your worksheet in the following way:

	A	B	C	D	E
17	**PROFITS DATA TABLE 1**				
18		**PROFITS**			
19	**PAYLOAD**	**JUNE**	**JULY**	**AUG**	**SEPT**
20					
21	85%				
22	75%				
23	70%				
24	65%				

As far as the program is concerned the data table will cover the range A20:E24. We have merely added labels at the top for our benefit.

♦ Enter the cell reference =B15 to cell B20.

♦ Copy this reference across to cells C20, D20 and E20.

The values in cells B20–E20 are now the same as those in B15–E15 and are based on an average payload of 80 per cent. Any change to the payload figure would affect all of these cells.

♦ To complete the data table, select the range A20:E24, open the **Data** menu and choose the **Table** command.

♦ When the **Table** dialogue box opens, enter B8 to the **Column Input Cell** box and click **OK**. You'll be returned to the worksheet where the data table should have been completed.

♦ Format the range B21:E24 to currency style with no decimal places.

♦ **Save** the workbook.

Two-input table

We'll now produce a table to show the effect on profit of varying two input variables – average payload and ticket price. However, you can only use one formula in a two-input table so we'll show the effect of those variations on total profit (cell F15).

♦ Set up the structure of the second data table in your worksheet as follows:

	A	B	C	D	E
26	**PROFITS DATA TABLE 2**				
27					
28		100	110	115	120
29	85%				
30	75%				
31	70%				
32	65%				

This time the data table occupies the range A28:E32.

Four possible payload figures have been entered in the cells A29:A32, and four alternative ticket price figures are shown in the cells B28:E28.

♦ Format the range B28:E28 to currency style with no decimal places.

The data table will show the effect on total profit for the four-month period of the various combinations of price and payload.

♦ Enter the cell reference =F15 to cell A28.

♦ To complete the data table, select the range A28:E32, open the **Data** menu and choose the **Table** command.

♦ When the **Table** dialogue box opens, make the following entries:

Row Input Cell: B4
Column Input Cell: B8

♦ Click the **OK** button.

♦ The data table should now have been completed. Format the range B29:E32 to currency style with no decimal places. Widen the columns if necessary.

♦ **Save** the workbook.

Data tables – further example

♦ Set up the following details on a blank worksheet:

	A	B
1	**MORTGAGE LOAN REPAYMENT TABLE**	
2		
3	Sum borrowed	40000
4	Annual interest rate	7.00%
5	Repayment term (years)	25
6		
7	**Interest Rate**	**Monthly Repayment**
8		
9	6.00%	
10	6.50%	
11	7.50%	
12	8.00%	
13	8.50%	
14	9.00%	
15	9.50%	
16	10.00%	

♦ Format cell B3 to currency style with no decimal places.

♦ Produce a data table in the range A8:B16 which will calculate the monthly repayment at the various interest rates shown. The formula required to calculate the monthly repayment is =PMT(B4/12,B5*12,–B3).

♦ When the table is complete, format the range B8:B16 in currency style with two decimal places.

The data table should be similar to the following:

	A	B
1	**MORTGAGE LOAN REPAYMENT TABLE**	
2		
3	Sum borrowed	£40000
4	Annual interest rate	7.00%
5	Repayment term (years)	25
6		
7	**Interest Rate**	**Monthly Repayment**
8		£282.71
9	**6.00%**	£257.72
10	**6.50%**	£270.08
11	**7.50%**	£295.60
12	**8.00%**	£308.73
13	**8.50%**	£322.09
14	**9.00%**	£335.68
15	**9.50%**	£349.48
16	**10.00%**	£363.48

Cell B8 contains the formula =PMT(B4/12,B5*12,–B3). Cell B4 is the Column Input Cell.

If you alter either the sum borrowed or the repayment term, the figures in the data table will be recalculated automatically.

Let's say you would also like the data table to show the total interest paid over the duration of the loan. To do this, you'll need another column in the data table.

♦ Select cell C7 and enter the heading Total Interest Paid.

♦ Enter the appropriate formula to cell C8 and complete the data table.

The table should be similar to the following:

	A	B	C
1	**MORTGAGE LOAN REPAYMENT TABLE**		
2			
3	Sum borrowed	£40000	
4	Annual interest rate	7.00%	
5	Repayment term (years)	25	
6			
7	**Interest Rate**	**Monthly Repayment**	**Total Interest Paid**
8		£282.71	£44813.50
9	**6.00%**	£257.72	£37316.17
10	**6.50%**	£270.08	£41024.86
11	**7.50%**	£295.60	£48678.94
12	**8.00%**	£308.73	£52617.95
13	**8.50%**	£322.09	£56627.25
14	**9.00%**	£335.68	£60703.56
15	**9.50%**	£349.48	£64843.60
16	**10.00%**	£363.48	£69044.09

Cell C8 contains the formula =(B8*12*B5)–B3. Note that this formula refers to cell B8 which in turn refers to the Column Input Cell B4.

We'll now extend the worksheet and produce a second data table which will show the monthly repayment at different interest rate and repayment term combinations.

♦ Enter the following details to the worksheet below the Mortgage Loan Repayment Table:

	A	B	C	D
18	MONTHLY PAYMENTS TABLE			
19		Repayment term (yrs)	Repayment term (yrs)	Repayment term (yrs)
20		20	30	35
21	**6.00%**			
22	**6.50%**			
23	**7.00%**			
24	**7.50%**			
25	**8.00%**			
26	**8.50%**			
27	**9.00%**			
28	**9.50%**			
29	**10.00%**			

♦ Produce a data table in the range A20:D29 which will calculate the monthly repayment for the combinations of interest rate and repayment terms shown.

When complete, and after formatting, the table should be similar to the following:

	A	B	C	D
18	**MONTHLY PAYMENTS TABLE**			
19		**Repayment term (yrs)**	**Repayment term (yrs)**	**Repayment term (yrs)**
20	**£282.71**	**20**	**30**	**35**
21	**6.00%**	£286.57	£239.82	£228.08
22	**6.50%**	£298.23	£252.83	£241.66
23	**7.00%**	£310.12	£266.12	£255.54
24	**7.50%**	£322.24	£279.69	£269.70
25	**8.00%**	£334.58	£293.51	£284.10
26	**8.50%**	£347.13	£307.57	£298.74
27	**9.00%**	£359.89	£321.85	£313.60
28	**9.50%**	£372.85	£336.34	£328.64
29	**10.00%**	£386.01	£351.03	£343.87

The formula in cell A20 is =PMT(B4/12,B5*12,–B3).

The Column Input Cell is B4 and the Row Input Cell is B5.

SCENARIO MANAGER

It is often the case that complex spreadsheet models are built based on values assigned to a few key variables, e.g. a monthly profits projection for three years based on an assumed sales growth rate of three per cent each quarter and a ten per cent annual increase in price. If the values of the key variables are altered, the data in the spreadsheet model which is linked by formula to those variables will change automatically.

The values attached to the key variables are referred to as 'what-if' assumptions. Different combinations of these what-if assumptions can be recorded and applied separately to the spreadsheet data to produce different *scenarios*. For example, a finance manager might wish to produce a budget for next year but he is not certain what the revenue or certain costs will be.

To demonstrate the application of Scenario Manager, assume that three business partners, Dave, Robert and Wilma, have decided to produce a new product and each has drawn up a set of cost and revenue assumptions for the first year's operations.

♦ Select the first blank sheet in the workbook LearnXL and set up the following worksheet:

	A	B
1	**NEW PRODUCT PROJECTIONS**	
2		
3	**Key variables**	
4	Price (per unit)	
5	Labour cost (per unit)	
6	Material cost (per unit)	
7	Overheads (per unit)	
8	Sales (units)	
9		
10	Sales revenue	
11	Total costs	
12	Profit/Loss	

♦ Enter the following formulae in the cells indicated:

Cell	Formula
B10	=B4*B8
B11	=(B5+B6+B7)*B8
B12	=B10–B11

Each partner has a different opinion on the price the market will bear, the level of sales achievable and the type and quality of input resources required in production. This has led to three different sets of values being produced for the following variables: price, sales and labour, material and overhead costs.

Although not really necessary, we'll first of all define a name for each cell which contains variable data.

♦ Select the cell B4.

♦ Select **Insert** from the Menu bar, then **Name** from the **Insert** menu, then **Define** from the sub-menu.

♦ Enter the name, Price, and click the **OK** button.

♦ In similar manner, define the following names for the cells indicated:

Cell	Name
B5	Labour_cost
B6	Material_cost
B7	Overhead_cost
B8	Sales

♦ Once the cell names have been defined, open the **Tools** menu and select the **Scenarios** command.

The following **Scenario Manager** dialogue box should now appear:

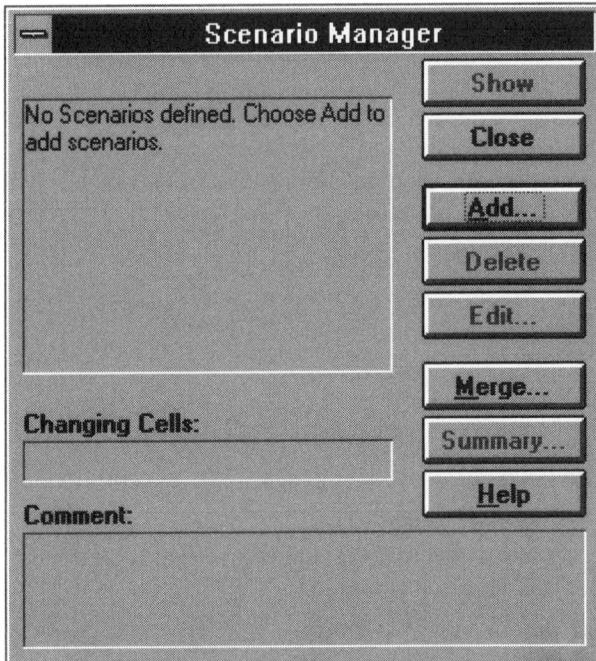

♦ Select the **Add** button and the following **Add Scenario** dialogue box should open:

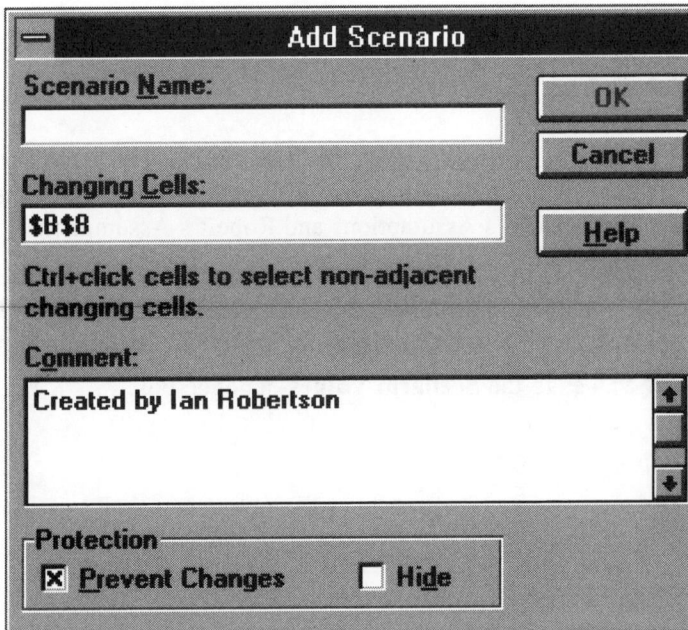

♦ Enter the **Scenario Name** as Dave's Assumptions and press the [**Tab**] key.

♦ Delete any entries from the **Changing Cells** box and enter the following cell references, separating each reference with a comma: B4,B5,B6,B7,B8.

♦ Click the **OK** button.

♦ The **Scenario Values** dialogue box should now appear. Enter the following values (press the [**Tab**] key to move from one box to the next).

Price	:	20
Labour_cost	:	6
Material_cost	:	5
Overhead_cost	:	4
Sales	:	5000

♦ When the values have been entered, click the **OK** button and you will be returned to the **Scenario Manager** dialogue box where the scenario name, Dave's Assumptions, will appear in the **Scenarios** section.

♦ Select the **Add** button and when the **Add Scenario** dialogue box opens, enter the **Scenario Name** this time as Robert's Assumptions.

♦ The **Changing Cells** box should already display the cell references $B$4,$B$5,$B$6,$B$7 and $B$8, so click the **OK** button.

♦ When the **Scenario Values** dialogue box opens, enter the following values:

Price	:	25
Labour_cost	:	7
Material_cost	:	5.5
Overhead_cost	:	5
Sales	:	4000

♦ When you have entered these values, click the **OK** button and again you will be returned to the **Scenario Manager** dialogue box which should now display the names of two scenarios – Dave's Assumptions and Robert's Assumptions.

♦ Select the **Add** button and in the **Add Scenario** dialogue box enter the **Scenario Name** as Wilma's Assumptions. Check that the cell references $B$4,$B$5,$B$6,$B$7 and $B$8 are displayed in the **Changing Cells** box and click the **OK** button.

♦ Enter the following values to the **Scenario Values** dialogue box:

Price	:	23
Labour_cost	:	6.5
Material_cost	:	5
Overhead_cost	:	4.5
Sales	:	4500

♦ Click the **OK** button.

The **Scenario Manager** dialogue box should now display the names for three **Scenarios** (sets of assumptions).

♦ To view the results of a particular scenario on the worksheet, simply select the scenario name (e.g. Dave's Assumptions) and click the **Show** button.

♦ Dave's values should now be inserted to the worksheet and the effect on Sales revenue, Total costs and Profit/Loss calculated and displayed.

♦ If the **Scenario Manager** dialogue box is obscuring your view of the worksheet you can move it slightly to the right. To do this, point to the dialogue box Title bar, click and hold down the mouse button and drag it to the right.

♦ To view a different scenario, select a different set of assumptions (e.g. Robert's) and click the **Show** button. The worksheet figures should now display the results of the new scenario.

As you can see, it is a simple matter to switch between scenarios and observe the effect on other parts of the worksheet. The larger the worksheet model, the more useful this facility becomes.

♦ Close the **Scenario Manager** dialogue box by clicking the **Close** button.

Scenario summary report

The summary report allows you to compare the various scenarios and their effect on a *result* cell or cells. A result cell normally contains a formula which links it to one of the key variables and the value is therefore recalculated when the scenario changes. In our example, a result cell could be either Sales revenue in B10, Total costs in B11 or Profit/Loss in B12.

We'll produce a summary report which shows the effect of the different scenarios on the result cell B12 (Profit/Loss).

♦ First of all define the name, Profit, for this cell using **Insert/Name/Define**.

♦ Open the **Tools** menu, select the **Scenarios** command and when the **Scenario Manager** dialogue box opens, click the **Summary** button.

♦ The **Scenario Summary** dialogue box should now appear. Ensure that the **Report Type** selected is **Scenario Summary**. Enter B12 to the **Result Cells** box and click the **OK** button.

♦ In a few seconds the Scenario Summary should be displayed on screen comparing the different sets of assumptions and their effect on Profit.

Note: The Scenario Summary Report is created on a new sheet in the workbook.

♦ **Save** the workbook.

PROBLEM SOLVING BY ITERATION

It is sometimes the case in worksheets that two formulae depend on each other for their results. This means that each formula will contain a reference to the other. This is known as circular referencing and you will get an error message when you insert such formulae.

For example, examine the following worksheet statement:

	A	B
1	GROSS PROFIT	10000
2	EXPENSES	4000
3	COMMISSION	=B4*10%
4	NET PROFIT	=B1–(B2+B3)

In this example, assume that the commission is payable to the sales manager and that it should represent 10% of the net profit. At the same time, the net profit is dependent on the size of the commission, i.e. Net profit = Gross profit – (Expenses + Commission). This results in the formula in cell B4 referencing cell B3 and the formula in cell B3 referencing cell B4. This is called circular referencing and cannot be solved in the normal way. It must be solved by *iteration*, i.e. repeated calculation until the required condition is achieved.

♦ Set up the statement shown above on a blank worksheet in LearnXL. When you enter the second formula you will receive an error message: 'Cannot resolve circular references'.

♦ Click the **OK** button.

The value zero should now be displayed in each of the formula cells.

♦ Open the **Tools** menu and select the **Options** command.

♦ When the **Options** dialogue box opens, select the **Calculation** tab button at the top to display the Calculation 'page'.

♦ Click the **Iteration** check box and select **OK**.

When you return to the worksheet the problem should have been solved and the results displayed.

♦ **Save** the workbook.

'LOOKUP' FUNCTIONS

'Lookup' functions are designed to search lists or tables to find an item of data which is associated with another item of data, e.g. given the product name, find the price or stock level; or given the value of an order, find the appropriate discount.

We will examine the operation of three related functions in this area: VLOOKUP, LOOKUP and HLOOKUP.

VLOOKUP

This function searches the *first* (leftmost) column in a table for a specified value and returns an associated value from the same row of another column in the table.

The syntax is as follows:

=VLOOKUP (lookup_value, table_range, col_index, range_lookup)

Lookup_value This is the value to be found in the first column of the table. This can be a numeric value, a cell reference or a text string.

Table_range This is the cell range which the table covers. The values in the first column of this range must be placed in *ascending* order (1, 2, 3 ..., a, b, c ...) if range_lookup is **True** or omitted. If range_lookup is **False**, these values do not have to be sorted.

Col_index This is the column number which contains the value you want returned.

Range_lookup This is a logical value (**True** or **False**) which indicates whether you wish to find an exact or an approximate match for lookup_value. It does not have to be entered as one of the arguments. If this value is **True** or omitted, then an approximate match is used, i.e. if an exact match is not found, the next largest value that is less than lookup_value is used. If range_lookup is **False**, an exact match will be found or an error value returned.

♦ To demonstrate the operation of VLOOKUP set up the following simple stock table on a blank worksheet in the workbook LearnXL:

	A	B	C	D
1	**LOOKUP TABLE DEMO**			
2				
3	CODE	DESCRIPTION	STOCK	PRICE
4	9	Bolt	20000	0.5
5	10	Nut	35000	0.05
6	8	Screw	30000	0.09
7	4	Washer	40000	0.04
8	3	Nail	50000	0.06
9	6	Hammer	100	12
10	7	Screwdriver	120	9
11	5	Saw	50	15
12	2	Pliers	80	4
13	1	Plane	30	21

♦ Format the range D4:D13 to currency style with two decimal places.

♦ Sort the table so that the first column (CODE) is arranged in ascending order.

♦ **Save** the workbook.

♦ Enter the following formula to cell A15: =VLOOKUP(5,A4:D13,3).

The result should be 50.

The VLOOKUP function has searched for lookup_value 5 in the *first* column of table_range A4:D13 and returned the value which appears in the same row of column 3. So in this case you have used the code to find the stock level of an item.

Note: There was no need to enter a value for range_lookup.

We'll now enter a formula which will return the price of an item from its description.

♦ Select cell A15 and edit the formula to the following:
=VLOOKUP ("Screwdriver",B4:D13,3,FALSE).

The result should be 9 (i.e. £9.00).

Notes:
(a) When the search is for a piece of text, as it was here, it must be enclosed with double quotes.
(b) VLOOKUP will always search the first column of a table for lookup_value so this time the table_range was entered as B4:D13.
(c) Price is in the third column of the range stated.
(d) There was no need to re-sort the table on the basis of description since we entered **False** for range_lookup. This does mean, however, that an exact match will be searched for.

We'll now enter an incorrect code and see what happens.

♦ Select cell A15 and edit the formula to the following:
=VLOOKUP (12,A4:D13,2,FALSE).

The error message #N/A should have appeared in cell A15 because the function was searching for a code number (12) which does not exist. Since we also entered **False** for range_lookup, the absence of an exact match resulted in an error message being returned.

♦ Select cell A15 again and edit the formula to: =VLOOKUP(12,A4:D13,2,TRUE).

The result should be Nut which is the description for code 10.

If range_lookup is **True** or omitted and an exact match cannot be found, the next largest value that is less than lookup_value is used. In this case the next largest value to 12 is 10 and since we asked for the description (col_index 2) the result returned is Nut.

LOOKUP

The vector form of this function allows you to search for a value in one row or column and return the corresponding figure from a second row or column. This should be used when lookup_value is not contained in the first column or row of a table.

The syntax is as follows:

=LOOKUP (lookup_value, lookup_range, result_range)

Lookup_value   This is the value to be found in lookup_range (a column or row). This can be a number, a piece of text, a logical value or a cell reference.

Lookup_range   This is a one-column or one-row range where lookup_value is searched for. This range can contain numbers, text or logical values and they must be sorted in *ascending* order.

If lookup_value cannot be found in lookup_range, the next largest value that is less than lookup_value is used.

Result_range   This is a one-column or one-row range which should be the same size as lookup_range. The value in this range which corresponds to the value in lookup_range is the result which will be returned.

♦ Select cell A15 and alter the formula to: =LOOKUP(9,A4:A13,D4:D13).

The result should be 0.5 (i.e. £0.50).

The LOOKUP function has searched for lookup_value 9 in the lookup_range A4:A13 and returned the corresponding value from result_range D4:D13. So you have used the code to find the price of an item.

This time we'll use the description to find the code.

♦ Sort the table so that the second column (DESCRIPTION) is arranged in ascending order.

♦ Select cell A15 and alter the formula to: =LOOKUP("Hammer",B4:B13,A4:A13).

The result should be 6, the code for hammer.

So with this form of LOOKUP there is no need for lookup_value to be in the first column or row of a table. You actually specify the range to be searched (lookup_range).

HLOOKUP

This function searches the first row in a table for a specified value and returns an associated value from the same column of another row in the table.

The syntax is:

=HLOOKUP (lookup_value, table_range, row_index, range_lookup)

As you can see, the syntax is similar to VLOOKUP and should be used when the data is arranged in rows instead of columns.

Lookup functions – example 1

The operatives in a factory are paid a basic wage of £240 per week. In addition they receive a bonus which depends on their weekly output. The bonus is calculated as a percentage of basic pay and the rates are as follows:

Output (units)	Bonus rate
Under 1000	Nil
1000 –1244	10%
1250 –1499	15%
1500 –1744	25%
1750 and over	35%

♦ Move to column G in your 'lookup' worksheet and enter the following data as shown:

	G	H	I	J	K
1	**BONUS TABLE**				
2	**Output (units)**	**Bonus Rate**			
3	0	0%			
4	1000	10%			
5	1250	15%			
6	1500	25%			
7	1750	35%			
8					
9	**EMPLOYEE**	**BASIC**	**OUTPUT**	**BONUS**	**GROSS**
10	**NAME**	**PAY**	**(units)**		**PAY**
11		**£**		**£**	**£**
12	Jim	240	965		
13	Wendy	240	1232		
14	Francis	240	1319		
15	Jack	240	1051		
16	Fauzia	240	1510		
17	Dave	240	1844		
18	Fred	240	1624		
19	Rashid	240	1500		
20	Linda	240	1470		
21	Anne	240	984		

♦ Enter the following formulae to the cells indicated:

Cell	Formula
J12	=H12*VLOOKUP(I12,$G$3:$H$7,2)
K12	=H12+J12

♦ Copy the formula in cell J12 to the cell range J13:J21.

♦ Copy the formula in cell K12 to the cell range K13:K21.

♦ **Save** the workbook.

Lookup functions – Example 2

A car parts wholesaler sells to the motor trade and also to the public. The level of discount offered on orders depends on the order size and the order category; cash sale to the public, cash sale to the trade or credit sale to the trade.

The following discount table shows the discount applicable to each order size and category.

♦ Set this up on the 'lookup' worksheet beginning at row 20.

	A	B	C	D
20	DISCOUNT TABLE			
21		CATEGORY A	CATEGORY B	CATEGORY C
22		PUBLIC CASH	TRADE CASH	TRADE CREDIT
23	ORDER SIZE	DISCOUNT	DISCOUNT	DISCOUNT
24	0	0.00%	2.50%	2.50%
25	750	2.50%	6.00%	4.00%
26	1500	4.00%	12.00%	8.00%
27	2500	8.00%	15.00%	10.00%
28	5000	15.00%	25.00%	20.00%
29				
30	ORDER SIZE		ORDER SIZE	
31	ORDER CATEGORY		DISCOUNT	
32			NET	
33			VAT	
34			AMOUNT DUE	

♦ Format cell B30 to currency style with two decimal places.

♦ Enter the following formula to cell D31:

=IF(B31="A",VLOOKUP(B30,A24:D28,2),IF(B31="B",VLOOKUP(B30,A24:D28,3), IF(B31="C",VLOOKUP(B30,A24:D28,4),"ERROR")))

Don't worry if the word ERROR now appears in cell D31.

The formula looks complicated because of its length. It's combining the 'VLOOKUP' function with nested 'IF' functions. The formula searches the table, A24:D28, to find the appropriate level of discount based on the order category (B31) and the order size (B30). If any character besides A, B or C is entered to cell B31 the formula will insert the word ERROR to cell D31. That's why ERROR should appear in D31 now.

♦ Format cell D31 to percentage style with two decimal places.

♦ Enter the following formulae to the cells shown:

Cell   Formula
D30   =B30
D32   =D30–(D30*D31)   (ignore the #VALUE! error message)
D33   =D32*0.175   (ignore the #VALUE! error message)
D34   =D32+D33   (ignore the #VALUE! error message)

♦ Format the three cells D32, D33 and D34 to currency style with two decimal places.

♦ The worksheet should now be similar to the following:

	A	B	C	D
20	**DISCOUNT TABLE**			
21		**CATEGORY A**	**CATEGORY B**	**CATEGORY C**
22		**PUBLIC CASH**	**TRADE CASH**	**TRADE CREDIT**
23	**ORDER SIZE**	**DISCOUNT**	**DISCOUNT**	**DISCOUNT**
24	0	0.00%	2.50%	2.50%
25	750	2.50%	6.00%	4.00%
26	1500	4.00%	12.00%	8.00%
27	2500	8.00%	15.00%	10.00%
28	5000	15.00%	25.00%	20.00%
29				
30	**ORDER SIZE**		**ORDER SIZE**	£0.00
31	**ORDER CATEGORY**		**DISCOUNT**	**ERROR**
32			**NET**	**#VALUE!**
33			**VAT**	**#VALUE!**
34			**AMOUNT DUE**	**#VALUE!**

♦ If you enter the order size and the order category to cells B30 and B31 respectively, the figures in the cell range D30:D34 will be calculated automatically.

♦ Practise this and check that the results are accurate.

Note: If an exact match cannot be found for the order size in the discount table, the VLOOKUP function will take the next largest value that is less than the order size (since range_lookup has been omitted). So if you insert an order size of 3500 vlookup will return the discount applicable to 2500. This is exactly how we want the table to work since the discount figures for 2500 apply to the range 2500–4999.

♦ **Save** the workbook.

RECORDING A MACRO

Macros are powerful tools which can be used to automate the spreadsheet. A simple macro might enter the current date to a cell or place some formatted text in a particular location on the worksheet. A more complex one could place dialogue boxes on the screen, prompt the user to enter values and then perform calculations using these values.

One way to create a macro is to record the keystrokes and/or mouse actions necessary to carry out a particular task. These commands can then be run automatically whenever you want to repeat the task. To demonstrate this we'll create a macro which will insert a formatted heading to a worksheet.

♦ **Close** any workbook which is open at the moment.

♦ Open the **File** menu and select **New**.

♦ Open the **Tools** menu, select **Record Macro** then choose **Record New Macro** from the sub-menu.

The following **Record New Macro** dialogue box should now open:

```
┌─────────────────────────────────────────────────────┐
│ ─            Record New Macro                         │
├─────────────────────────────────────────────────────┤
│  Macro Name:                         ┌──────────────┐ │
│  ┌─────────────────────────────────┐ │      OK      │ │
│  │Macro1                           │ └──────────────┘ │
│  └─────────────────────────────────┘ ┌──────────────┐ │
│  Description:                        │    Cancel    │ │
│  ┌─────────────────────────────┐ ▲  └──────────────┘ │
│  │Macro recorded by Ian Robertson│    ┌──────────────┐ │
│  │                             │    │  Options >>  │ │
│  │                             │ ▼  └──────────────┘ │
│  └─────────────────────────────┘    ┌──────────────┐ │
│                                      │     Help     │ │
│                                      └──────────────┘ │
└─────────────────────────────────────────────────────┘
```

♦ Enter the **Macro Name** as Heading.

♦ Click in the **Description** box, delete any entries which are already there and type the description: Insert a formatted heading.

♦ Click the **Options** button and the dialogue box will extend as follows:

```
┌─────────────────────────────────────────────────────┐
│ ─            Record New Macro                         │
├─────────────────────────────────────────────────────┤
│  Macro Name:                         ┌──────────────┐ │
│  ┌─────────────────────────────────┐ │      OK      │ │
│  │Heading                          │ └──────────────┘ │
│  └─────────────────────────────────┘ ┌──────────────┐ │
│  Description:                        │    Cancel    │ │
│  ┌─────────────────────────────┐ ▲  └──────────────┘ │
│  │Insert a formatted heading   │    ┌──────────────┐ │
│  │                             │    │  Options >>  │ │
│  │                             │ ▼  └──────────────┘ │
│  └─────────────────────────────┘    ┌──────────────┐ │
│  ┌─Assign to──────────────────────┐ │     Help     │ │
│  │ ☐ Menu Item on Tools Menu:     │ └──────────────┘ │
│  │  ┌─────────────────────────┐   │                   │
│  │  │                         │   │                   │
│  │  └─────────────────────────┘   │                   │
│  │ ☐ Shortcut Key:                │                   │
│  │       Ctrl+ │e│                │                   │
│  └────────────────────────────────┘                   │
│  ┌─Store in──────────────┐ ┌─Language─────────────┐   │
│  │ ○ Personal Macro Workbook│ ● Visual Basic       │   │
│  │ ● This Workbook       │ │ ○ MS Excel 4.0 Macro │   │
│  │ ○ New Workbook        │ │                      │   │
│  └───────────────────────┘ └──────────────────────┘   │
└─────────────────────────────────────────────────────┘
```

♦ In the **Assign to** section select the **Shortcut Key** check box. Click in the **Ctrl+** box, delete any entry which appears there and type in the letter e (if this letter is already shown in the box do not make any changes). Once you have created the macro the key combination **[Ctrl] + e** will run it.

♦ In the **Store in** section of the dialogue box select **This Workbook** option button. This means that you will be able to use the macro on any worksheet in the current workbook. Selecting the **Personal Macro Workbook** button would have placed the macro on a workbook file called Personal.XLS. This file would then be opened automatically whenever Microsoft® Excel is run allowing you to use the macro on any workbook.

♦ Click the **OK** button in the dialogue box and you will be returned to the worksheet where the macro **Stop** (stop recording) button should appear at the top right and the 'Recording' message should be displayed in the Status bar.

Every action you carry out from now on (with mouse or keyboard) will be recorded until you click the **Stop** button so *be careful.*

Before you do anything you should read through the following instructions to familiarise yourself with the task you are about to carry out and the actions involved.

If you make a mistake during the recording process click the **Stop** button, delete the macro and begin again. Instructions on how to delete a macro are given later.

♦ Open the **Edit** menu and select **Go To**.

♦ When the **Go To** dialogue box opens type the **Reference** as A1 and click the **OK** button. This means that the first job the macro does is to activate cell A1 so that the heading always begins there.

♦ Type the heading NEWSOUNDS RECORDING PLC and click the ☑ button.

♦ Click the ⬇ button in the **Font Size** box on the formatting Toolbar and select **12** from the drop-down list.

♦ Click the **Bold** button on the formatting Toolbar.

♦ Click the **Italic** button on the formatting Toolbar.

♦ Click the macro **Stop** button.

Your macro has now been recorded and can be 'played back' on any sheet of the current workbook using the key combination **[Crtl] + e** or by selecting and running it from the **Macro** dialogue box.

♦ Click on the **Sheet2** name tab at the bottom of the screen to display the second worksheet in your workbook.

♦ Hold down the **[Ctrl]** key and press the letter **e**.

♦ A correctly formatted heading should now be inserted to cell A1 on **Sheet2**.

♦ Click on the **Sheet3** name tab and when the third worksheet appears activate cell D5.

♦ Open the **Tools** menu and select **Macro**.

♦ When the **Macro** dialogue box opens select your macro name, Heading, from the panel below the **Macro Name/Reference** box and click the **Run** button.

♦ Once again a correctly formatted heading should have been inserted to A1.

Deleting a macro

The procedure for deleting a macro is as follows:

♦ Open the **Tools** menu and select **Macro**.

♦ When the **Macro** dialogue box opens select your macro name from the panel below the **Macro Name/Reference** box and click the **Delete** button.

The macro will be deleted and you will be returned to the worksheet.

You should now close your workbook file. Since this was only a demonstration on simple macro recording there is no need to save changes to the file.

TEMPLATES

A template is basically a pattern for a type of workbook which you use regularly. The template contains the standard data which is common to every workbook. For example, if you are required to prepare a monthly Profit and Loss Account for your company the items in the account will be more or less the same each month, the only things that will change will be the actual figures. It would save you a lot of time, therefore, if you were to design and save a standard Profit and Loss Account layout and use this template as a pattern to produce each month's Profit and Loss Account complete with figures.

♦ **Close** any workbook which is open at the moment and open a new workbook using **File/New**.

♦ Design the following worksheet on Sheet1 of the new workbook:

	A	B	C	D	E	F
1	**COMIS TRADERS**					
2	**Profit & Loss Account for the period:**					
3						
4					£	£
5	Turnover					
6						
7	Cost of goods sold:					
8	Opening stock					
9	add net Purchases					
10	less Closing stock					
11						
12	Gross profit					
13						
14	Expenses:					
15	Rent and rates					
16	Heat and light					
17	Wages and salaries					
18	Telephone					
19	Printing and stationery					
20	Insurance					
21	Repairs and maintenance					
22	Depreciation					
23						
24	Net profit					
25						
26	Gross profit %age					
27	Net profit %age					
28						

♦ Insert the following formulae in the appropriate cells:

Cell   Formula
F11   =(E8+E9)−E10
F12   =F5−F11
F23   =SUM(E15:E22)
F24   =F12−F23
F26   =F12/F5
F27   =F24/F5

♦ Format cells F26 and F27 to display in percentage style with two decimal places.

This worksheet complete with text, formatting and formulae can be used as a template for the preparation of monthly Profit and Loss Accounts but first of all the workbook must be saved as a template.

♦ Open the **File** menu and select **Save As**.

♦ When the **Save As** dialogue box opens enter the **File Name** as P&L and select the correct floppy drive (a: or b:) from the drop-down list in the **Drives** box. Click the ⬇ button in the **Save File as Type** box and select **Template** from the drop-down list. Note that the **File Name** is now P&L.XLT (.XLT is the extension for a template file). Check your settings and if they are accurate click the **OK** button.

Your template file, P&L.XLT, should have now been saved to the floppy drive and you will be returned to the worksheet.

♦ Open the **File** menu and select **Close**.

You are now given the following figures for the month of February 199X and asked to prepare the Profit and Loss Account:

Turnover	52000
Opening stock	18000
Net purchases	22000
Closing stock	10000
Rent and rates	1800
Heat and light	600
Wages and salaries	4500
Telephone	200
Printing and stationery	150
Insurance	850
Repairs and maintenance	1000
Depreciation	1500

♦ Open the **File** menu and select **Open**.

♦ When the **Open** dialogue box appears select the correct floppy drive (a: or b:) from the **Drives** box. Click the ⬇ button in the **List Files of Type** box and select **Templates (*.xlt)** from the drop-down list. Your template file, P&L.XLT, should now be listed in the panel below the **File Name** box. Select this file and click the **OK** button.

A copy of the Profit & Loss Account template should now appear on screen.

♦ Complete the worksheet using the figures supplied.

♦ When the Profit and Loss Account is complete open the **File** menu and select **Save**.

♦ When the **Save As** dialogue box opens ensure that the correct floppy drive (a: or b:) is displayed in the **Drives** box and that **Microsoft Excel Workbook** is displayed in the **Save File as Type** box. Enter the **File Name** as P&L_Feb and click the **OK** button.

♦ The Profit and Loss Account for February (P&L_Feb.XLS) will now be saved as a normal workbook file. The Profit and Loss Account template (P&L.XLT) will remain intact on the floppy disc and can be used as a pattern for future monthly Profit and Loss Accounts.

♦ Open the **File** menu and select **Close**.

Editing the original template

If you wish to make changes to the original template open it in the following way:

♦ Open the **File** menu and select **Open**.

♦ When the **Open** dialogue box appears select the correct drive in the **Drives** box and select **Templates** in the **List Files of Type** box.

♦ Select the template file from the panel below the **File Name** box.

♦ *Hold down the [Shift] key* and click the **OK** button.

♦ Once you have made the changes and are ready to save, open the **File** menu and select **Save**. The updated template will be saved using the template format.

Alternatively, open the template file in the normal way and when you are ready to save the changes open the **Save As** dialogue box. Select the **File Type** as **Template** and enter the existing file name (say P&L.XLT) to the **File Name** box. You will be asked to confirm that you wish to replace the original template with the updated file. Select **Yes** to confirm.

OPENING A TEXT FILE FROM SAGE STERLING FOR WINDOWS

You can import data from Sage Sterling for Windows to Microsoft® Excel if you wish to analyse the data using the facilities of the spreadsheet. A fairly straightforward way to do this is to save and import the data as a text file. For example, the procedure for importing a Sage Sterling for Windows Trial Balance to Microsoft® Excel is as follows:

♦ Run the program Sage Sterling for Windows.

♦ Select the **Financials** option in the **Desktop** window and when the **Financials** window opens click the **Trial Balance** button.

♦ When the **Trial Balance Report** dialogue box opens select the **Output** medium as **File** and click the **Run** button.

♦ When the **Save As** dialogue box appears click the 🔽 button in the **Save File as Type** box and select **Text Files** from the drop-down list.

♦ Enter a name for the file in the **File Name** box (e.g. TrialBal).

♦ The **Directories** box will indicate the name of the directory the file will be saved to. You can change this if you wish. Make a note of this location.

♦ Click the **OK** button and the file will be saved.

♦ **Exit** the Sage Sterling for Windows program and open Microsoft® Excel or switch to Microsoft® Excel if both programs are running at the moment.

♦ When the spreadsheet screen appears, open the **File** menu and select **Open**.

♦ When the **Open** dialogue box appears use the **Drives** and **Directories** boxes to select the location of your Trial Balance file (as specified in the Sage Sterling for Windows **Save As** dialogue box).

♦ Click the ⬇ button in the **List Files of Type** box and select **Text Files** from the drop-down list.

♦ Your file should now be listed below the **File Name** box. Select the file and the name will appear in the **File Name** box.

♦ Click the **OK** button in the **Open** dialogue box and the **Text Import Wizard** tool should be activated. This is a series of dialogue boxes which guide you through the steps necessary to convert the text. 'Step' through the dialogue boxes using the **Next** button making the appropriate selections in each. When complete click the **Finish** button in the Step 3 dialogue box.

♦ The Trial Balance should now appear on the worksheet. You may have to widen the columns to view it fully.

This procedure can be used for any Sage Sterling for Windows report file whether it is pre-designed or user-designed.

CHAPTER 24

Spreadsheet Exercises

EXERCISE 1: OPERATING STATEMENT (1)

The newly formed printing firm of Weber & Villiers has been set up specifically to print a safety information leaflet for use in the engineering industry. The two partners have estimated that the cost of printing 1000 leaflets would be as follows:

Machine set-up	:	6 hours at £12.50 per hour
Design work	:	£60
Paper	:	£25
Other printing materials	:	£6
Direct labour	:	0.5 hours at £9.00 per hour
Fixed overhead	:	£30

The partners also estimate that the following costs will remain the same irrespective of how many leaflets are printed:

- machine set-up costs;
- design work costs;
- fixed overheads.

All other costs will vary proportionally according to the number of leaflets printed. The profit mark-up on total costs is 40 per cent.

As the firm's accountant, you are required to carry out the following tasks:

1   Using a spreadsheet prepare an operating statement for output levels of 10000, 20000, 30000 and 40000 leaflets which will show the following:

   (a) total cost;

   (b) total profit;

   (c) selling price per 1000 leaflets.

2   Investigate the effects of the following:

   (a) an increase in the direct labour rate to £9.75 per hour;

   (b) an increase in paper costs to £45.

3   When the firm was set up they agreed to share profits and losses in the ratio 2:3, Weber receiving more since he works at weekends. Calculate how much profit each partner would receive at each of the four output levels.

EXERCISE 2: OPERATING STATEMENT (2)*

The Eyeseeye Chemical Company Ltd have developed a new product called AB Mix and they have set up a small branch plant to manufacture this product only. They have been asked by one of their customers to quote for varying amounts of this product. The firm's accountant has estimated that the costs to produce 1000 kg of the product are as follows:

Material A	:	250 kg @ £15.60 per kg
Material B	:	750 kg @ £16.20 per kg
Labour – Grade 1	:	200 hours @ £8 per hour
Labour – Grade 2	:	150 hours @ £6 per hour
Variable overheads	:	£4000
Fixed overheads	:	£15000

All costs, apart from fixed overheads, vary directly with production.
  Normal profit mark-up on total costs is 30 per cent.

Required:

1 Using a spreadsheet prepare an operating statement for output levels of 5000, 10000, 15000 and 20000 kg. which will show the following:

  (a) total cost;

  (b) total profit;

  (c) selling price per 1000 kg.

2 Investigate the effects of the following:

  (a) an increase in the grade 1 labour rate from £8.00 per hour to £8.50 per hour;

  (b) a reduction in material B cost from £16.20 per kg to £15.80 per kg.

3 If the company wished to expand production beyond 20000 kg it would involve building an extension to their new premises and increasing fixed overheads to £30000. Extend your worksheet to show the total cost, total profit and selling price per 1000 kg associated with an output of 25000 kg.

EXERCISE 3: DEPRECIATION

The firm with whom you are employed, Saleemi Systems, have just purchased a new machine for £30000 which they expect to last five years. You are asked to produce a table which will compare the depreciation charge using the straight line method to the depreciation method using the reducing balance method for each of the next five years. The depreciation rate used should be 20 per cent per annum in both cases.
  You decide to build a model using a spreadsheet package and to make it versatile enough to permit easy alteration of initial cost and depreciation rate.

EXERCISE 4: STOCK VALUATION

The accountant for an electronics company produces the following closing stock figures at the end of the financial year for one of the departments:

Stock item	Qty	Unit cost £	Unit market value £
1	80	215	205
2	170	380	410
3	39	110	130
4	145	95	75

Required:

1 Produce a spreadsheet model which will determine the total value of the stock on an *item-by-item basis*:

(a) at cost;

(b) at market value;

(c) at the lower of cost or market value.

2 Test the model using the following figures:

Stock item	Qty	Unit cost £	Unit market value £
5	110	15	17
6	45	18	21
7	230	12	9
8	160	14	11

EXERCISE 5: EXTENDED TRIAL BALANCE (1)

You are employed in the accounts department of Crinan Controls Plc. You are given the task of producing the Extended Trial Balance at the end of the financial year to 30 June 19X1. You decide to build the model on a spreadsheet in order to simplify the task in future years.

The following are the ledger account balances at 30 June 19X1:

	£
Sales	280000
Purchases	173000
Carriage inwards	5900
Drawings	15000
Rent and rates	12000
Postage and stationery	6500
Advertising and promotion	2500
Wages and salaries	51000
Bad debts	1800
Provision for bad debts	250
Debtors	25000
Creditors	13000
Cash	400
Bank	1800
Stock (at 1 July 19X0)	24000
Equipment at cost	120000
Provision for depreciation on equipment (at 1 July 19X0)	40000
Capital	105650

The following details should be taken into consideration in the construction of the ETB:

1   A rates instalment of £1800 made on 20 June 19X1 represents rates for July to September 19X1.

2   Equipment should be depreciated by 15 per cent per annum on the straight line basis.

3   Rent due, but unpaid at 30 June 19X1, is £460.

4   It is decided to increase the provision for bad debts by £90.

5   Stock at 30 June 19X1 was valued at £26000.

Required:

(a) Prepare the Extended Trial Balance using a spreadsheet.

(b) After having prepared the ETB you are informed by your supervisor that the closing stock at 30 June had been grossly overvalued. The correct figure is £13200. In addition he wishes the provision for bad debts to be increased by £75 rather than £90. Make the necessary alterations to the spreadsheet ETB.

(c) Save your file as ETB_19X1.

EXERCISE 6: EXTENDED TRIAL BALANCE (2)*

This is a follow-on from the previous exercise. One year later, on 30 June 19X2, you are still employed by Crinan Controls and you are asked to produce the Extended Trial Balance. The following are the ledger account balances on this date:

	£
Sales	340000
Purchases	240000
Carriage inwards	6100
Drawings	14000
Rent and rates	13600
Postage and stationery	6200
Advertising and promotion	3100
Wages and salaries	55800
Bad debts	1700
Provision for bad debts	325
Debtors	32000
Creditors	10200
Cash	350
Bank	2400
Stock (at 1 July 19X1)	13200
Equipment at cost	120000
Provision for depreciation on equipment (at 1 July 19X1)	58000
Capital	99925

The following details should be taken into consideration in the construction of the ETB:

1   During the year, the owner had withdrawn stock worth £510 from the business for his own use and made no payment for it.

2   A rates payment of £1900 made on 20 June 19X2 represents rates for July to September 19X2.

3   Rent due but unpaid at 30 June 19X2 is £600.

4   Equipment should be depreciated by 15 per cent per annum on the straight line basis.

5   The provision for bad debts is to be increased to 1½ per cent of debtors.

6   Stock at 30 June 19X2 was valued at £29000.

Required:

(a) Prepare the Extended Trial Balance using last year's file (ETB_19X1) as a model.

(b) Save your file as ETB_19X2.

*Solutions to those exercises marked with an asterisk (*) can be found in the Instructor's Manual which accompanies this text.

EXERCISE 7: OVERHEAD ALLOCATION (1)

Overhead costs – allocation and apportionment (excluding service departments)

Do-re-mee Ltd, a music shop, has three departments, one selling CDs and cassettes, one selling hi-fi equipment and one selling musical instruments. Information regarding year ended 30 April 19X1 is:

	CDs £000	Hi-Fi £000	Instruments £000	Total £000
Purchases	75	210	55	340
Sales	150	350	100	600
Wages	30	50	20	100
Overheads				
Heating and lighting				15
First Aid and welfare				4
Advertising and promotion				9
Insurance of buildings				8
Pension contributions (earnings related)				6
Depreciation of fittings				12

Other information	CD	Hi-Fi	Instruments
Floor Area (sq m)	100	200	100
Number of employees	6	9	5
Book value of fittings (£000)	20	30	10

Required:

1   Prepare a spreadsheet model which will apportion the overheads to each department. The model should show clearly the basis of apportionment chosen for each cost.

2   Use the model to investigate the effect which the following changes would have:

   (a) An extension is built to the musical instruments department increasing its floor area and that of the whole shop by 50 square metres.

   (b) The shop hires two additional members of staff to work in the CD and cassettes department.

   (c) The following increases in costs occur:

   (i)   buildings insurance by 50 per cent;

   (ii) heating and lighting by £3000;

   (iii) wages in the CD and cassettes department by £20000;

   (iv) pension contributions by £3000.

EXERCISE 8: OVERHEAD ALLOCATION (2)*

Overhead allocation and apportionment (including Service Departments)

Ascot Holdings manufacture electric motors for air conditioning units. The factory has three production departments (press shop, welding and fabrication) and two service departments (stores and maintenance). The budgeted annual overhead costs for the factory are as follows:

	Total £000	Press shop £000	Welding £000	Fabrication £000	Stores £000	Maintenance £000
Indirect wages	724	200	199	185	20	120
Indirect materials	506	200	200	80	8	18
Rent and rates	200					
Heat and light	100					
Buildings insurance	50					
Insurance of machinery	30					
Depreciation of machinery	300					
Salaries of production management	160					

The following details are relevant:

	Net book value of machinery £000	Floor area (000 sq. m.)	Number of employees
Press shop	400	5.0	15
Welding	250	2.5	10
Fabrication	50	7.5	15
Stores	25	7.5	5
Maintenance	25	2.5	5
	750	25.0	50

Maintenance department personnel spend the bulk of their time working in the three production departments. Their records have revealed the following details regarding time spent in these departments:

Press shop	6000 hours
Welding	4000 hours
Fabrication	2500 hours
	12500 hours

The value of material issues by stores to the production departments are as follows:

	£000
Press shop	800
Welding	600
Fabrication	200
	1600

Required:

1 Using a spreadsheet prepare an overhead analysis model to show:

(a) apportionment of overheads to production and service departments;

(b) reapportionment of service department costs to production departments.

2   Given the following information:

Budgeted machine hours: Press shop   –   120000

Welding   –   60000

Budgeted direct labour hours: Fabrication   –   240000

Calculate overhead absorption rates for each department.

3   Investigate the effects of the following:

(a) An extension is added to the Fabrication Department increasing its area by 66⅔ per cent.

(b) The total charge for rent and rates increases by 50 per cent.

(c) The number of employees in Stores increases to 8 and in Fabrication to 20.

(d) Indirect wages in Stores increases to £32000 and in Fabrication to £250000.

EXERCISE 9: JOB COST SHEET

You are asked to produce a job cost model on a spreadsheet which can be used by your company when making bids for orders. The following data relates to a job presently under consideration:

Department	Direct material cost per unit	Direct labour hours per unit	Direct labour hourly rate	Machine hours per unit
Press shop	£2.50	0.02	£5.00	0.125
Welding	£0.50	0.015	£6.00	0.115
Assembly and packing	£0.40	0.25	£4.50	—

Factory overhead is applied at the rate of 60 per cent of direct labour cost in the Assembly and Packing department and £12.00 per machine hour in the Press Shop and Welding departments.

Non-factory overheads are applied at the rate of 20 per cent of total production cost. The company uses a 35 per cent mark-up on total cost to determine its bid price.

Required:

1   Assuming that the order is for 1,000 units of the product, use the previous data to develop the model and produce a bid price for the job.

2   Test your model using the following data which represent the costings for another job your company has been asked to quote for. Assume the order size in this case is 800 units:

Department	Direct material cost per unit	Direct labour hours per unit	Direct labour hourly rate	Machine hours per unit
Press shop	£4.50	0.03	£5.00	0.25
Welding	£1.25	0.015	£6.00	0.20
Assembly and packing	£1.00	0.75	£4.50	—

EXERCISE 10: PROCESS COSTING

For the moulding department of a steel foundry, the following information was available for the month of October:

1 Opening work in progress (WIP) stood at 90 tons with the following costs and completion levels:

	Cost £	% Complete
Materials	1800	100
Labour	1350	50
Overheads	900	50
	4050	

2 Tonnage added to the department during the month was 610, incurring costs as follows:

	Cost £
Materials	12900
Labour	17355
Overheads	12645
	42900

3 Completed tonnage for October totalled 590 tons, leaving 110 tons in closing WIP which had identical completion factors to the opening WIP at the beginning of the month.

Required:

(a) Using a spreadsheet, build a process costing model which can be used to calculate the cost per ton, the value of closing WIP and the value of tonnage completed during the period. The model should be capable of producing these results using the weighted average method *and* the FIFO method.

(b) Test your model using the following figures which relate to a process carried out in April:

Opening work in progress stood at 180 tons with the following costs:

	Cost £	% Complete
Materials	7200	100
Labour	5400	50
Overheads	3600	25
	16200	

Tonnage added to the process in April was 1,280 tons incurring costs as follows:

	£
Materials	51600
Labour	69420
Overheads	50740
	171760

Completed tonnage for April totalled 1180 tons, leaving 280 tons closing work in progress which had identical completion factors to the opening WIP at the beginning of April.

EXERCISE 11: STANDARD COSTING AND VARIANCE ANALYSIS

Design a spreadsheet model which will compute the following variances:

1 material price variance;

2 material usage variance;

3 labour rate variance;

4 labour efficiency variance.

The model should indicate whether the variance is favourable or adverse.

Use the following input data to design the model:

Materials	– actual usage and price	– 1800 kg @ £1.10 per kg
	– standard usage and price	– 1500 kg @ £1.20 per kg
Labour	– actual hours and rate	– 3600 hours @ £6.70 per hour
	– standard hours and rate	– 4000 hours @ £6.50 per hour

Assume that the actual material purchases are identical to the material used.

EXERCISE 12: CASH BUDGET

The accountant of a small company, MacRoberts Ltd, wishes to computerise his cash flow projections using a spreadsheet. The projection is to provide a monthly cash flow analysis over a six-month period.
    The following data is relevant:

1 Credit sales (units):

19X1		*19X2*						
Nov.	*Dec.*	*Jan.*	*Feb.*	*Mar.*	*Apr.*	*May*	*Jun.*	*Jul.*
1800	1850	2000	2000	2000	2100	2100	2200	2200

2 Selling price per unit is £15.00 and not expected to increase over the period.

3 On average, payment is received from customers as follows:

(i) 60 per cent one month after sale;

(ii) 39 per cent two months after sale.

The balance is not normally received (i.e. it is a bad debt).

4 The company buys stock one month in advance of sales and pays cash. The stock costs 55 per cent of sales value.

5 It is expected that £20000 will be spent on a new delivery vehicle during March 19X2.

6 VAT is paid in February, May, August and November for the previous three-month period in each case (i.e. VAT for Feb.–Apr. is paid in May). As an estimate for VAT payable you should use the sales and purchase figures for the relevant three-month period and take 17½ per cent of the *difference*.

7 It is expected that one dividend payment will be made during the period: £2000 in April.

8 Details of overhead payments are as follows:

(i) Production overheads are 15 per cent of each month's cost of sales (purchases) figure and are paid for in the month incurred.

(ii) Administration overheads are eight per cent of each month's sales figure and are paid for in the month incurred.

(iii) Selling and distribution overheads are 10 per cent of each month's sales and are paid for in the month incurred.

9 Bank interest is charged for a three-month period (end March, June, September and December) on any negative balances at the end of each month. A negative balance is charged interest at the appropriate rate for the full month. The current rate is 9.5 per cent *per annum*.

10 The opening cash balance at 1 January 19X2 is £12000.

Required:

(a) Prepare a cash budget for MacRoberts for the period January–June 19X2.

(b) Test the consequences of an increase in purchasing costs from 55–60 per cent of sales value.

(c) Test the result of an increase in price from £15–£17.50 per unit.

(d) Attempt to remove any negative closing cash balances by manipulating the key variables.

EXERCISE 13: INVESTMENT APPRAISAL

Hi-Flyers Airlines is considering setting up a trans-Atlantic service beginning in the summer of 199X. For this purpose the company will shortly acquire a new aircraft which is expected to cost £450000. The aircraft will be used exclusively on this route for six years after which time it will be sold off for a nominal sum. Although this plane can carry a maximum of 400 passengers the company expects that the average payload will be only 60 per cent of this figure and that only 200 crossings each year will be made.

The price of a single ticket is £200 and it has been estimated that the operating costs per passenger will be around £180. The company will have to meet fixed costs including insurances and landing fees which are expected to amount to £750000 per annum. Money to finance the venture has been provided by a consortium of banks who would normally expect a rate of return of 20 per cent on any of their investments.

Required:

1   Design a spreadsheet model which will:

   (a) calculate the payback period for this investment;

   (b) Calculate the NPV of this investment;

   (c) Calculate the IRR for this investment.

2   Use the model to examine the effect of the following changes on the investment's NPV. Reset the key variables to their original values between each change:

   (a) ticket prices rise/fall by five per cent maximum;

   (b) passenger numbers increase/decrease by five per cent per annum;

   (c) landing fees rise by £75000 per annum;

   (d) interest rates rise by 5 percentage points;

   (e) cost of an aircraft rises to £500000;

   (f) useful life changes by +2/–1 years.

You should use the functions NPV and IRR explained below in this question.

NPV

This function returns the net present value of an investment based on a series of periodic cash flows and a discount rate. The net present value of an investment is the value today of a series of future payments (negative) and income (positive).

   The syntax is:

=NPV (rate, value 1, value 2, . . .)

- *Rate* is the rate of discount over the length of one period.

- *Value 1, value 2, etc.* represent the payments and income (payments are negative and income is positive). These values must be equally spaced in time and occur at the *end* of each period.

The NPV function uses the order of value 1, value 2, etc. to interpret the order of cash flows. Make sure your payment and income values are entered in the correct sequence.

Note: The NPV investment begins one period before the date of the value 1 cash flow and ends with the last cash flow in the list. The NPV calculation is based on future cash flows. If your first cash flow occurs at the beginning of the first period, the first value must be added to the NPV result, *not* included in the values in parenthesis.

Example 1

The following payments and income relate to an investment you are considering:

End year	Payments	Income
1	20000	
2		1800
3		1900
4		2100

If the annual discount rate is eight per cent the net present value of the investment would be calculated using the function:

= NPV (8%, –20000, 1800, 1900, 2100)

Note: The initial payment of 20,000 is included as one of the values in parenthesis since it is made at the *end* of the first period.

Example 2

An investment you are considering involves the following payments and income:

	A	B	C	D
1	YEAR	PAYMENTS	INCOME	NET
2	0	50000		–50000
3	1	5000	15000	10000
4	2	5000	17000	12000
5	3	6000	16000	10000
6	4	6000	18000	12000
7	5	6000	18000	12000

Notes:

(a) Year 0 means the beginning of the first year. These payments or income obviously do not have to be discounted since they are already at present value. Year 1, 2, 3, etc. means the *end* of these years.

b) If both income is received and a payment made at the end of a year they should be netted off so that there is only one *value* for the period (positive or negative).

If the annual discount rate is 12 per cent the net present value of the previous investment could be calculated as follows:

= NPV (12%,10000,12000,10000,12000,12000)–50000

However, a neater and more elegant way of stating the values would be:

= NPV (12%,D3:D7)+D2

IRR

The internal rate of return is the interest rate received for an investment which consists of payment(s) and income which occur at regular intervals.

The syntax is:

=IRR (values, guess)

- *Values*. This is usually a reference to the cells containing the payment and income values for which you want to calculate the IRR. There must be at least one positive value (income) and one negative value (payment) in the range of cells.

  The IRR function uses the order in which the values are listed to interpret the order of cash flows. Make sure your payment and income values are entered in the correct sequence.

- *Guess*. This is your estimate for the value of IRR and will be used as a starting point for the calculation. It is an optional entry in the function and in most cases does not have to be entered. If it is omitted it is assumed to be 10 per cent. If IRR can't find a result that works after 20 attempts the #NUM error value is displayed in the cell. If this happens change the value for guess or enter one if it has been omitted. The closer guess is to the actual IRR the quicker will be the calculation.

Example

Using the payment and income figures from Example 2 in the section on NPV, the internal rate of return on the investment after five years would be calculated using the function:

=IRR(D2:D7,6%)

The guess of six per cent could be omitted and the result would be the same.

EXERCISE 14: COST–VOLUME–PROFIT ANALYSIS (1)

A manufacturing company, Swale Engineering, makes a single product with a total output capacity of 40000 units and a budgeted output of 30000 units.

Data relating to costs and sales are as follows:

Selling price	£8.00 per unit
Variable costs	£4.00 per unit
Fixed costs	£55000

Required:

1 Construct a spreadsheet model which will calculate:

   (a) the contribution;

   (b) the number of unit sales required to break even;

   (c) the sales value at breakeven level;

   (d) profit at the budgeted level of activity;

(e) the number of units that need to be sold to make a target profit of £70000;

(f) sales value required to make a target profit of £70000.

2 Using the same model construct a table of information containing the data required to produce a break-even chart and design the chart for an output range of 0–40000 units.

EXERCISE 15: COST–VOLUME–PROFIT ANALYSIS (2)*

The Woodylea Trading Co. manufactures chairs which it sells to hotels and retailers for £20 each. Variable costs of manufacture are £10 and fixed overheads are £800000.

Design a spreadsheet model which will carry out the following tasks:

1 Using the above figures calculate the number of chairs which the manufacturer needs to produce in order to break even. Produce a break-even chart assuming that maximum production is 120000 chairs.

2 The company is currently manufacturing and selling 90000 chairs. The marketing manager has stated that a price reduction of 20 per cent would increase sales by 33⅓ per cent and thereby allow the factory to operate at 100 per cent capacity. Would this be worthwhile?

3 Again, assume that the company is manufacturing and selling 90000 chairs at £20 each. Woodylea Trading has been trying to break into the export market for some time. It receives an order for 10000 chairs at £12 each from an overseas company. Should the company accept this offer?

4 How many chairs at £20 each would have to be sold to produce a target profit of £120000?

EXERCISE 16: COST/REVENUE BUDGET

Consumer Gadgets Plc has recently been set up to manufacture food processors. It is anticipated that the costs for each processor will be as follows:

Material	:	£15
Labour	:	£10
Variable overhead	:	£2.50

In addition fixed costs of £50000 per month will be incurred.

The sales manager is looking at several price/output combinations for the period January–June and has produced the following budgets:

	Jan.	Feb.	Mar.	Apr.	May	Jun.
Price £50						
Sales (units)	4000	4000	4000	4500	4500	4500
Price £45						
Sales (units)	5000	5000	5000	6500	6500	6500
Price £40						
Sales (units)	5500	5500	5500	6750	6750	6750

He has been advised that if profits for the six-month period exceed £250000 he will receive a bonus according to the following table:

Profit (£)	Bonus
Under 250000	0%
250000 –299000	5% of excess above 250000
300000 –399000	7½% of excess above 250000
400000 and above	10% of excess above 250000

Produce a spreadsheet model for the sales manager which will allow him to vary the input data to arrive at the price/output combination which will maximise his bonus. The bonus earned should be shown in the model.

EXERCISE 17: STUDENT GRADES

The Department of Accounting in Graystones College wishes to design a spreadsheet to record student marks. Assessment for all subjects in the department consists of a combination of class tests and final examination. There is a class test in December and one in March and *together* they contribute 30 per cent to the overall results for the subject concerned. The final examination contributes 70 per cent to the overall result.

1 Design the spreadsheet, enter the following results and calculate the overall result for the year for each student. The overall results should be rounded to the nearest whole number.

Student name	Class test December %	Class test March %	Final examination %
Hennessy, I	43	48	52
Ashdown, H	72	76	65
Kirkton, J	82	78	70
Ridley, J	34	40	48
Stevenson, L	45	55	62
Wells, F	89	81	82
Ashquar, M	67	73	69
Dawson, G	21	16	42
Davidson, B	38	42	36
Hassan, T	54	56	48
Evans, A	52	67	78
Lipton, M	54	61	74
Davidson, C	79	85	90
Peterson, S	74	72	80
Johnson, A	51	59	58

2   (a) For each of the class tests, the final examination and the overall result, calculate the average mark, highest mark and lowest mark.

(b) Arrange the names and results in alphabetical order.

3   Add a further column to the spreadsheet which will allocate a grade to each student based on the following grading table:

Mark	Grade
85 and above	A
70–84	B
50–69	C
40–49	D
Below 40	E

You should insert a grading table at the top of the worksheet and use it in conjunction with a 'LOOKUP' function to carry out this task.

EXERCISE 18: COUNCIL TAX

You are employed in the Finance Department of a local authority and you are asked to prepare a spreadsheet model which will calculate the council tax payable by local residents.

The council tax consists of three elements: a regional tax, a district tax and a water charge. These taxes vary and are dependent on the resident's tax band which in turn depends on the value of his/her house.

The following are the figures which relate to the current year and you should use these as a basis to build the model:

House value £	Tax band	Regional council tax £	District council tax £	Water charge £
Up to 27000	A	271	226	58
27001–35000	B	316	251	65
35001–45000	C	362	277	74
45001–58000	D	404	302	86
58001–80000	E	497	351	101
80001–106000	F	581	403	115
106001–212000	G	673	447	130
Over 212000	H	801	526	160

The previous data should be set up as a 'lookup' table and the following spreadsheet designed and completed using formulae based on this data:

Name	House Value £	Discount	Tax Band	Regional Tax £	District Tax £	Water Charge £	Amount Payable £
Resident 1	39000	YES					
Resident 2	78000	YES					
Resident 3	49000	NO					
Resident 4	260000	NO					
Resident 5	55000	NO					
Resident 6	72000	YES					
Resident 7	44000	NO					
Resident 8	98000	NO					
Resident 9	25500	YES					
Resident 10	31000	NO					

If a resident is the sole occupier of the house he/she is entitled to a discount of 25 per cent on the total amount payable.

EXERCISE 19: MORTGAGE PAYMENTS

You are employed by Anyold Building Society and you are asked to construct a spreadsheet model which will produce repayment quotations for customers who apply for a mortgage loan.

The two main types of mortgage loan offered to customers are the repayment and the endowment. With the former the repayment is made on the basis of a monthly payment for the duration of the loan. During the early stages of the repayment period the bulk of the payment is interest with only a small amount representing repayment of capital. As progress is made through the repayment term, the interest element of the payment gradually reduces and the capital element increases until finally, towards the end of the period, the bulk of the payment represents repayment of capital.

With an endowment loan the borrower takes out an endowment insurance policy which will mature at the end of the loan repayment term. During the repayment period the borrower makes payments to the lender to cover interest only. In addition, premiums on the insurance policy must be paid. When the policy matures the proceeds are used to repay the capital to the lender.

1   Design a spreadsheet model suitable for the repayment type of mortgage. The format of the spreadsheet should be as follows:-

	A	B	C	D
1	**ANYOLD BUILDING SOCIETY**			
2				
3	**Mortgage Loan Quotation**			
4				
5	**Mortgage Details**			
6	Annual interest rate	XX		
7	Repayment term (years)	XX		
8	Sum borrowed	XX		
9				
10				
11	Monthly repayment (gross)	XX		

Your model should be easy to modify so that different quotations can be produced using different input variables.

To calculate the monthly repayment you should use the function PMT. PMT (rate, nper, pv) returns the periodic payment for an annuity based on constant payments and a constant interest rate:

- *rate* is the interest rate per period;

- *nper* is the total number of payment periods;

- *pv* is the present value, i.e. the total amount that a series of future payments is worth now.

Example 1. The following function would produce the *yearly* payment on a *£25,000* loan which had to be repaid over *20 years* at an annual interest rate of *10 per cent:*

= PMT (10%,20,–25000)

Notes:
(a) The units used to express 'rate' and 'nper' must be consistent. In the previous example 10 per cent represents a *yearly* rate and 20 relates to *years.*

(b) The negative sign in front of pv avoids the result being negative.

Example 2. The following function would produce the *monthly* payment on a £25,000 loan which had to be repaid over *20 years* at an annual interest rate of *10 per cent:*

= PMT (10%/12, 20*12, –25000)

This time the number of payment periods has been expressed in months, i.e. 20×12 and the annual interest rate of 10 per cent has been converted to a monthly figure by dividing by 12. Converting an annual interest rate to a monthly one by dividing by 12 is not strictly accurate but it is often used in this function as an approximation.

Use your model to calculate the *monthly* payment (gross) on a £30,000 mortgage at seven per cent interest over 25 years.

SAVE YOUR WORK.

2   The total interest paid throughout the lifetime of the loan should be a part of the quotation and this should now be inserted using the following worksheet as a guide.

	A	B	C	D
1	**ANYOLD BUILDING SOCIETY**			
2				
3	**Mortgage Loan Quotation**			
4				
5	**Mortgage Details**			
6	Annual interest rate	XX		
7	Repayment term (years)	XX		
8	Sum borrowed	XX		
9				
10				
11	Monthly repayment (gross)	XX	Total interest payment (gross)	XX

SAVE YOUR WORK.

3   Income tax relief is normally allowed on mortgage *interest* payments. You should now insert the following additional information to your quotation so that tax relief and net payments can be shown.

(a) tax relief rate;

(b) tax relief on monthly repayments (gross);

(c) net monthly repayment;

(d) tax relief on total interest payment (gross);

(e) total interest payment (net).

The format of your worksheet should be as follows:

	A	B	C	D
1	**ANYOLD BUILDING SOCIETY**			
2				
3	**Mortgage Loan Quotation**			
4				
5	**Mortgage Details**			
6	Annual interest rate	XX		
7	Repayment term (years)	XX		
8	Sum borrowed	XX		
9	Tax relief rate	XX		
10				
11	Monthly repayment (gross)	XX	Total interest payment (gross)	XX
12	Tax relief	XX	Tax relief	XX
13	Monthly repayment (net)	XX	Total interest payment (net)	XX

Assume a tax relief rate of 15 per cent and that tax relief is calculated on the total interest paid throughout the loan period and then allocated evenly to monthly repayments so that tax relief is the same each month. However, there is a further complication in that tax relief is allowed on loans up to a maximum of £30,000 only. The 'IF' function will be useful to you in this part of the calculation.

Remember, the formulae you use in the quotation should be as general as you can make them to allow the same model to be used for different input variables.

SAVE YOUR WORK.

4 You can now complete the quotation by adding the following two pieces of information:

(a) total capital repayment;

(b) total payment (capital and interest).

The format of the relevant part of the worksheet should be as follows:

	A	B	C	D
10				
11	Monthly repayment (gross)	XX	Total interest payment (gross)	XX
12	Tax relief	XX	Tax relief	XX
13	Monthly repayment (net)	XX	Total interest payment (net)	XX
14			Total capital repayment	XX
15			Total payment	XX
16				

SAVE YOUR WORK.

5 Copy the entire worksheet to a new blank sheet in the workbook using the **Move or Copy Sheet** command from the **Edit** menu.

Expand the new worksheet so that it can be used to give comparison costings for the repayment and the endowment type mortgages. The following details should be added for an endowment loan quotation:

(a) monthly interest payment (gross);

(b) tax relief;

(c) monthly interest payment (net);

(d) monthly insurance premium (assume £50);

(e) total monthly payment;

(f) total payment (over lifetime of loan).

The format of your worksheet should be similar to the following:

	A	B	C	D
1	**ANYOLD BUILDING SOCIETY**			
2				
3	**Mortgage Loan Quotation**			
4				
5	**Mortgage Details**			
6	Annual interest rate	XX		
7	Repayment term (years)	XX		
8	Sum borrowed	XX		
9	Tax relief rate	XX		
10	Monthly insurance premium	XX		
11				
12	**REPAYMENT LOAN**			
13	Monthly repayment (gross)	XX	Total interest payment (gross)	XX
14	Tax relief	XX	Tax relief	XX
15	Monthly repayment (net)	XX	Total interest payment (net)	XX
16			Total capital repayment	XX
17			Total payment	XX
18				
19	**ENDOWMENT LOAN**			
20	Monthly interest payment (gross)	XX		
21	Tax relief			
22	Monthly interest payment (net)	XX		
23	Total monthly payment	XX		
24	Total payment	XX		

The quotations for both types of mortgage – repayment and endowment – are based on the key variables entered in the cell range B6:B10. New quotations can now be provided almost instantaneously by altering one or more of these input variables.

EXERCISE 20: REGIONAL EXPENSES BUDGET

An office equipment retailer who sells throughout the UK maintains a regional network of sales staff. He has divided the country into four regions, England, Scotland, Ireland and Wales – and appointed a regional sales manager for each. At the beginning of each six-month period each sales manager submits a selling expenses budget to head office in Manchester. The following four budgets represent the figures produced by each region for the period January–June 199X. Set up these budgets in a workbook, using a separate sheet for each region and rename each worksheet appropriately (England, Ireland, etc.).

1 ENGLAND:

	A	B	C	D	E	F	G
1	SELLING EXPENSES BUDGET JAN–JUNE 199X						
2							
3		JAN	FEB	MAR	APR	MAY	JUN
4		£	£	£	£	£	£
5	SALARIES	12500	12500	12500	13000	13000	13000
6	COMMISSION	10000	10000	11000	12000	14000	14000
7	CAR EXPENSES	2000	2000	2500	2500	2000	2500
8	ADVERTISING	3000	3000	4000	4000	4500	4500
9	TOTAL	27500	27500	30000	31500	33500	34000

2 IRELAND:

	A	B	C	D	E	F	G
1	SELLING EXPENSES BUDGET JAN–JUNE 199X						
2							
3		JAN	FEB	MAR	APR	MAY	JUN
4		£	£	£	£	£	£
5	SALARIES	4000	4000	4000	4500	4500	4500
6	COMMISSION	3000	3000	3500	3500	4000	4000
7	CAR EXPENSES	1000	1000	1500	1800	2000	1500
8	ADVERTISING	1500	1500	1800	1800	1600	1600
9	TOTAL	9500	9500	10800	11600	12100	11600

3   SCOTLAND:

	A	B	C	D	E	F	G
1	**SELLING EXPENSES BUDGET JAN–JUNE 199X**						
2							
3		JAN	FEB	MAR	APR	MAY	JUN
4		£	£	£	£	£	£
5	SALARIES	5000	5000	5500	5500	6000	6000
6	COMMISSION	4000	4000	4500	4500	5000	5000
7	CAR EXPENSES	1000	1200	1200	1000	1200	1200
8	ADVERTISING	1200	1400	1500	1500	1500	1600
9	TOTAL	11200	11600	12700	12500	13700	13800

4   WALES:

	A	B	C	D	E	F	G
1	**SELLING EXPENSES BUDGET JAN–JUNE 199X**						
2							
3		JAN	FEB	MAR	APR	MAY	JUN
4		£	£	£	£	£	£
5	SALARIES	2500	2500	2700	2700	2700	2700
6	COMMISSION	2000	2000	2500	2500	2500	2500
7	CAR EXPENSES	500	600	600	500	500	600
8	ADVERTISING	1000	1000	1200	1200	1400	1200
9	TOTAL	6000	6100	7000	6900	7100	7000

Set up a fifth worksheet which has the same format as the four regional sheets and rename it SUMMARY. Enter appropriate formulae to the worksheet, SUMMARY, which will total the results from the four regional sheets.

Note: You should only need to enter a formula to one cell and copy it to all the others.

Create an embedded line chart on the SUMMARY worksheet showing the figures for all four expenses for each of the six months January–June.

Suggested Solutions for Spreadsheet Exercises

EXERCISE 1: OPERATING STATEMENT (1)

Worksheet for Exercise 1, question 1

	A	B	C	D	E	F	G
1	**WEBER & VILLIERS**						
2							
3	**OPERATING STATEMENT FOR SAFETY LEAFLET**						
4							
5			INPUT DATA				
6	**Production (leaflets)**		**1000**	10000	20000	30000	40000
7							
8	Direct labour - hours		**0.5**				
9	Direct labour - rate per hour		**£9.00**				
10	**Total direct labour costs**		**£4.50**	£45.00	£90.00	£135.00	£180.00
11	Paper		**£25.00**				
12	Other printing matls.		**£6.00**				
13	**Total material costs**		**£31.00**	£310.00	£620.00	£930.00	£1,240.00
14	Machine set up costs - hours		**6**				
15	Machine set up costs - rate per hour		**£12.50**				
16	Design work		**£60.00**				
17	Fixed overheads		**£30.00**				
18	**Total fixed costs**		**£165.00**	£165.00	£165.00	£165.00	£165.00
19	**Total costs**		**£200.50**	£520.00	£875.00	£1,230.00	£1,585.00
20							
21	Profit mark-up	40%	**£80.20**	£208.00	£350.00	£492.00	£634.00
22							
23	Selling price (per 1000 leaflets)		**£280.70**	£72.80	£61.25	£57.40	£55.48
24							

OPERATING STATEMENT (1)

Worksheet formulae for Exercise 1, question 1

	A	B	C	D	E	F	G
1	WEBER & VILLIERS						
2							
3	OPERATING STATEMENT FOR SAFETY LEAFLET						
4							
5		INPUT DATA					
6	Production (leaflets)		1000	10000	20000	30000	40000
7							
8	Direct labour - hours		0.5				
9	Direct labour - rate per hour		9				
10	Total direct labour costs		=C8*C9	=$C$10*(D6/$C$6)	=$C$10*(E6/$C$6)	=$C$10*(F6/$C$6)	=$C$10*(G6/$C$6)
11	Paper		25				
12	Other printing matls.		6				
13	Total material costs		=C11+C12	=$C$13*(D6/$C$6)	=$C$13*(E6/$C$6)	=$C$13*(F6/$C$6)	=$C$13*(G6/$C$6)
14	Machine set up costs - hours		6				
15	Machine set up costs - rate per hour		12.5				
16	Design work		60				
17	Fixed overheads		30				
18	Total fixed costs		=(C14*C15)+C16+C17	=$C$18	=$C$18	=$C$18	=$C$18
19	Total costs		=C10+C13+C18	=D10+D13+D18	=E10+E13+E18	=F10+F13+F18	=G10+G13+G18
20							
21	Profit mark-up	0.4	=C19*$B$21	=D19*$B$21	=E19*$B$21	=F19*$B$21	=G19*$B$21
22							
23	Selling price (per 1000 leaflets)		=C19+C21	=(D19+D21)/(D6/$C$6)	=(E19+E21)/(E6/$C$6)	=(F19+F21)/(F6/$C$6)	=(G19+G21)/(G6/$C$6)
24							

OPERATING STATEMENT (1)

Worksheet for Exercise 1, questions 2 and 3

	A	B	C	D	E	F	G
1	**WEBER & VILLIERS**						
2							
3	**OPERATING STATEMENT FOR SAFETY LEAFLET**						
4							
5			**INPUT DATA**				
6	**Production (leaflets)**		**1000**	10000	20000	30000	40000
7							
8	Direct labour - hours		**0.5**				
9	Direct labour - rate per hour		**£9.75**				
10	**Total direct labour costs**		**£4.88**	£48.75	£97.50	£146.25	£195.00
11	Paper		**£45.00**				
12	Other printing matls.		**£6.00**				
13	**Total material costs**		**£51.00**	£510.00	£1,020.00	£1,530.00	£2,040.00
14	Machine set up costs - hours		**6**				
15	Machine set up costs - rate per hour		**£12.50**				
16	Design work		**£60.00**				
17	Fixed overheads		**£30.00**				
18	**Total fixed costs**		**£165.00**	£165.00	£165.00	£165.00	£165.00
19	**Total costs**		**£220.88**	£723.75	£1,282.50	£1,841.25	£2,400.00
20							
21	**Profit mark-up**	40%	**£88.35**	£289.50	£513.00	£736.50	£960.00
22							
23	**Selling price (per 1000 leaflets)**		**£309.23**	£101.33	£89.78	£85.93	£84.00
24							
25	**Share of profit : Weber**	0.6		£173.70	£307.80	£441.90	£576.00
26	**Share of profit : Villiers**	0.4		£115.80	£205.20	£294.60	£384.00
27							

OPERATING STATEMENT (1)

Worksheet formulae for Exercise 1, questions 2 and 3

	A	B	C	D	E	F	G
1	WEBER & VILLIERS						
2							
3	OPERATING STATEMENT FOR SAFETY LEAFLET						
4							
5		INPUT DATA					
6	Production (leaflets)		1000	10000	20000	30000	40000
7							
8	Direct labour - hours	0.5					
9	Direct labour - rate per hour	9.75					
10	Total direct labour costs		=C8*C9	=$C$10*(D6/$C$6)	=$C$10*(E6/$C$6)	=$C$10*(F6/$C$6)	=$C$10*(G6/$C$6)
11	Paper	45					
12	Other printing matls.	6					
13	Total material costs		=C11+C12	=$C$13*(D6/$C$6)	=$C$13*(E6/$C$6)	=$C$13*(F6/$C$6)	=$C$13*(G6/$C$6)
14	Machine set up costs - hours	6					
15	Machine set up costs - rate per hour	12.5					
16	Design work	60					
17	Fixed overheads	30					
18	Total fixed costs		=(C14*C15)+C16+C17	=$C$18	=$C$18	=$C$18	=$C$18
19	Total costs		=C10+C13+C18	=D10+D13+D18	=E10+E13+E18	=F10+F13+F18	=G10+G13+G18
20							
21	Profit mark-up	0.4	=C19*$B$21	=D19*$B$21	=E19*$B$21	=F19*$B$21	=G19*$B$21
22							
23	Selling price (per 1000 leaflets)		=C19+C21	=(D19+D21)/(D6/$C$6)	=(E19+E21)/(E6/$C$6)	=(F19+F21)/(F6/$C$6)	=(G19+G21)/(G6/$C$6)
24							
25	Share of profit : Weber	0.6		=D21*$B$25	=E21*$B$25	=F21*$B$25	=G21*$B$25
26	Share of profit : Villiers	0.4		=D21*$B$26	=E21*$B$26	=F21*$B$26	=G21*$B$26
27							

OPERATING STATEMENT (1)

EXERCISE 3: DEPRECIATION

Worksheet for Exercise 3

	A	B	C	D	E
1	SALEEMI SYSTEMS				
2					
3	DEPRECIATION TABLE				
4					
5	KEY VARIABLES				
6	Initial cost of asset	£30,000			
7	Depreciation rate	20.00%			
8					
9	STRAIGHT LINE METHOD			REDUCING BALANCE METHOD	
10					
11	Initial cost	£30,000		Initial cost	£30,000
12	Depreciation Year 1	£6,000		Depreciation Year 1	£6,000
13	NBV at end of year 1	£24,000		NBV at end of year 1	£24,000
14	Depreciation Year 2	£6,000		Depreciation Year 2	£4,800
15	NBV at end of year 2	£18,000		NBV at end of year 2	£19,200
16	Depreciation Year 3	£6,000		Depreciation Year 3	£3,840
17	NBV at end of year 3	£12,000		NBV at end of year 3	£15,360
18	Depreciation Year 4	£6,000		Depreciation Year 4	£3,072
19	NBV at end of year 4	£6,000		NBV at end of year 4	£12,288
20	Depreciation Year 5	£6,000		Depreciation Year 5	£2,458
21	NBV at end of year 5	£0		NBV at end of year 5	£9,830
22					

Worksheet formulae for Exercise 3

	A	B	C	D	E
1	SALEEMI SYSTEMS				
2					
3	DEPRECIATION TABLE				
4					
5	KEY VARIABLES				
6	Initial cost of asset	30000			
7	Depreciation rate	0.2			
8					
9	STRAIGHT LINE METHOD			REDUCING BALANCE METHOD	
10					
11	Initial cost	=B6		Initial cost	=B6
12	Depreciation Year 1	=$B$11*$B$7		Depreciation Year 1	=E11*$B$7
13	NBV at end of year 1	=B11-B12		NBV at end of year 1	=E11-E12
14	Depreciation Year 2	=$B$11*$B$7		Depreciation Year 2	=E13*$B$7
15	NBV at end of year 2	=B13-B14		NBV at end of year 2	=E13-E14
16	Depreciation Year 3	=$B$11*$B$7		Depreciation Year 3	=E15*$B$7
17	NBV at end of year 3	=B15-B16		NBV at end of year 3	=E15-E16
18	Depreciation Year 4	=$B$11*$B$7		Depreciation Year 4	=E17*$B$7
19	NBV at end of year 4	=B17-B18		NBV at end of year 4	=E17-E18
20	Depreciation Year 5	=$B$11*$B$7		Depreciation Year 5	=E19*$B$7
21	NBV at end of year 5	=B19-B20		NBV at end of year 5	=E19-E20
22					

DEPRECIATION

EXERCISE 4: STOCK VALUATION

Worksheet for Exercise 4, question 1

	A	B	C	D	E	F	G
1	STOCK VALUATION			DEPARTMENT			
2							
3				DATE			
4							
5							
6	STOCK ITEM	QTY	UNIT COST	UNIT	VALUATION	VALUATION	VALUATION
7				MARKET VALUE	AT COST	AT MARKET	AT LOWER OF
8			(£)	(£)	(£)	(£)	COST OR MARKET
9	Item 1	80	215	205	17200	16400	16400
10	Item 2	170	380	410	64600	69700	64600
11	Item 3	39	110	130	4290	5070	4290
12	Item 4	145	95	75	13775	10875	10875
13							
14	TOTAL				99865	102045	£96,165
15							

STOCK VALUATION

Worksheet formulae for Exercise 4, question 1

	A	B	C	D	E	F	G
1	STOCK VALUATION			DEPARTMENT			
2							
3				DATE			
4							
5							
6	STOCK ITEM	QTY	UNIT COST	UNIT	VALUATION	VALUATION	VALUATION
7				MARKET VALUE	AT COST	AT MARKET	AT LOWER OF
8			(£)	(£)	(£)	(£)	COST OR MARKET
9	Item 1	80	215	205	=B9*C9	=B9*D9	=MIN(E9,F9)
10	Item 2	170	380	410	=B10*C10	=B10*D10	=MIN(E10,F10)
11	Item 3	39	110	130	=B11*C11	=B11*D11	=MIN(E11,F11)
12	Item 4	145	95	75	=B12*C12	=B12*D12	=MIN(E12,F12)
13							
14	TOTAL				=SUM(E9:E12)	=SUM(F9:F12)	=SUM(G9:G12)
15							

STOCK VALUATION

Worksheet for Exercise 4, question 2

	A	B	C	D	E	F	G
1	STOCK VALUATION			DEPARTMENT			
2							
3				DATE			
4							
5							
6	STOCK ITEM	QTY	UNIT COST	UNIT	VALUATION	VALUATION	VALUATION
7				MARKET VALUE	AT COST	AT MARKET	AT LOWER OF
8			(£)	(£)	(£)	(£)	COST OR MARKET
9	Item 5	110	15	17	1650	1870	1650
10	Item 6	45	18	21	810	945	810
11	Item 7	230	12	9	2760	2070	2070
12	Item 8	160	14	11	2240	1760	1760
13							
14	TOTAL				7460	6645	£6,290
15							

STOCK VALUATION

EXERCISE 5: EXTENDED TRIAL BALANCE (1)

Worksheet for Exercise 5, question 1

CRINAN CONTROLS PLC

EXTENDED TRIAL BALANCE AS AT 30/06/19X1

Account Name	Original Balance		Adjustments		Adjusted Trial Balance		Profit & Loss		Balance Sheet	
	Dr	Cr	Dr	Cr	Dr	Cr	Dr	Cr	Assets	Liabilities
P & L a/c ENTRIES :										
Sales		280000			0	280000	0	280000		
Purchases	173000				173000	0	173000	0		
Carriage inwards	5900				5900	0	5900	0		
Stock (01/07/19X0)	24000				24000	0	24000	0		
Rent & rates	12000		460	1800	10660	0	10660	0		
Postage & stationery	6500				6500	0	6500	0		
Advertising & promotion	2500				2500	0	2500	0		
Wages & salaries	51000				51000	0	51000	0		
Bad debt expense	1800		90		1890	0	1890	0		
Depreciation expense			18000		18000	0	18000	0		
Closing stock (P & L a/c)				26000	0	26000	0	26000		
					0	0	0	0	0	0
BALANCE SHEET ENTRIES :										
Prov. for bad debts		250		90	0	340			0	340
Debtors	25000				25000	0			25000	0
Creditors		13000			0	13000			0	13000
Cash	400				400	0			400	0
Bank	1800				1800	0			1800	0
Drawings	15000				15000	0			15000	0
Equipment : cost	120000				120000	0			120000	0
Equipment : prov. for depr.(01/07/19X0)		40000		18000	0	58000			0	58000
Capital		105650			0	105650			0	105650
Closing stock (Balance Sheet)			26000		26000	0			26000	0
Prepayments			1800		1800	0			1800	0
Accruals				460	0	460			0	460
					0	0			0	0
	438900	438900	46350	46350	483450	483450	293450	306000	190000	177450
PROFIT/LOSS							12550	0	0	12550
							306000	306000	190000	190000

EXTENDED TRIAL BALANCE (1)

Worksheet formulae for Exercise 5, question 1

Row	Original Balance		Adjustments		Adjusted Trial Balance		Profit & Loss		Balance Sheet	
	Dr (B)	Cr (C)	Dr (D)	Cr (E)	Dr (F)	Cr (G)	Dr (H)	Cr (I)	Assets (J)	Liabilities (K)
7					** formula below	** formula below				
8		280000					=F8	=G8		
9	173000						=F9	=G9		
10	5900						=F10	=G10		
11	24000						=F11	=G11		
12	12000		460				=F12	=G12		
13	6500			1800			=F13	=G13		
14	2500						=F14	=G14		
15	51000						=F15	=G15		
16	1800		90				=F16	=G16		
17							=F17	=G17		
18			18000	26000			=F18	=G18		
19							=F19	=G19		
20										
21	250			90					=F21	=G21
22	25000								=F22	=G22
23	13000								=F23	=G23
24	400								=F24	=G24
25	1800								=F25	=G25
26	15000								=F26	=G26
27	120000								=F27	=G27
28				18000					=F28	=G28
29	40000								=F29	=G29
30	105650		26000						=F30	=G30
31			1800						=F31	=G31
32			460	460					=F32	=G32
33									=F33	=G33
34	=SUM(B8:B33)	=SUM(C8:C33)	=SUM(D8:D33)	=SUM(E8:E33)	=SUM(F8:F33)	=SUM(G8:G33)	=SUM(H8:H19)	=SUM(I8:I19)	=SUM(J21:J33)	=SUM(K21:K33)
35							=IF(I34>H34,I34-H34,0)	=IF(H34>I34,H34-I34,0)	=IF(K34>J34,K34-J34,0)	=IF(J34>K34,J34-K34,0)
36							=SUM(H34:H35)	=SUM(I34:I35)	=SUM(J34:J35)	=SUM(K34:K35)

```
*   Formula in cell F8 :   =IF(B8+D8-C8-E8<=0,0,B8+D8-C8-E8)
                           This formula is copied to cell range F9:F33

**  Formula in cell G8 :   =IF(C8+E8-B8-D8<=0,0,C8+E8-B8-D8)
                           This formula is copied to cell range G9:G33
```

EXTENDED TRIAL BALANCE (1)

Worksheet for Exercise 5, question 2

	A	B	C	D	E	F	G	H	I	J	K
	Account Name	Original Balance		Adjustments		Adjusted Trial Balance		Profit & Loss		Balance Sheet	
		Dr	Cr	Dr	Cr	Dr	Cr	Dr	Cr	Assets	Liabilities
1	CRINAN CONTROLS PLC										
2											
3	EXTENDED TRIAL BALANCE AS AT 30/06/19X1										
4											
5	Account Name										
6											
7	P & L a/c ENTRIES :										
8	Sales		280000			0	280000	0	280000		
9	Purchases	173000				173000	0	173000	0		
10	Carriage inwards	5900				5900	0	5900	0		
11	Stock (01/07/19X0)	24000				24000	0	24000	0		
12	Rent & rates	12000		460	1800	10660	0	10660	0		
13	Postage & stationery	6500				6500	0	6500	0		
14	Advertising & promotion	2500				2500	0	2500	0		
15	Wages & salaries	51000				51000	0	51000	0		
16	Bad debt expense	1800		75		1875	0	1875	0		
17	Depreciation expense			18000		18000	0	18000	0		
18	Closing stock (P & L a/c)				13200	0	13200	0	13200		
19						0	0	0	0		
20	BALANCE SHEET ENTRIES :										
21	Prov. for bad debts		250		75	0	325			0	325
22	Debtors	25000				25000	0			25000	0
23	Creditors		13000			0	13000			0	13000
24	Cash	400				400	0			400	0
25	Bank	1800				1800	0			1800	0
26	Drawings	15000				15000	0			15000	0
27	Equipment : cost	120000				120000	0			120000	0
28	Equipment : prov. for depr.(01/07/19X0)		40000		18000	0	58000			0	58000
29	Capital		105650			0	105650			0	105650
30	Closing stock (Balance Sheet)			13200		13200	0			13200	0
31	Prepayments			1800		1800	0			1800	0
32	Accruals				460	0	460			0	460
33						0	0			0	0
34		438900	438900	33535	33535	470635	470635	293435	293200	177200	177435
35	PROFIT/LOSS							0	235	235	0
36								293435	293435	177435	177435
37											

EXTENDED TRIAL BALANCE (1)

EXERCISE 7: OVERHEAD ALLOCATION (1)

Worksheet for Exercise 7, question 1

	A	B	C	D	E	F
1	DO-RE-MEE					
2						
3	OVERHEAD COST ALLLOCATION & APPORTIONMENT					
4						
5	APPORTIONMENT BASES					
6						
7	DESCRIPTION	CATEGORY	CD's	HI-FI	INSTRUMENTS	TOTAL
8	Floor Area (sq.m.)	1	100	200	100	400
9	No of Employees	2	6	9	5	20
10	Value of Fittings (£000)	3	20	30	10	60
11	Sales (£000)	4	150	350	100	600
12	Wages (£000)	5	30	50	20	100
13						
14						
15	OVERHEAD APPORTIONMENT					
16						
17	DESCRIPTION	CATEGORY	CD's	HI-FI	INSTRUMENTS	TOTAL O/HEAD
18			£'000	£'000	£'000	£'000
19	Heat & Light	1	3.75	7.50	3.75	15.00
20	First Aid & Welfare	2	1.20	1.80	1.00	4.00
21	Adv. & Promotion	4	2.25	5.25	1.50	9.00
22	Insurance of Buildings	1	2.00	4.00	2.00	8.00
23	Pension conts.	5	1.80	3.00	1.20	6.00
24	Deprn. of Fittings	3	4.00	6.00	2.00	12.00
25			15.00	27.55	11.45	54.00
26						

OVERHEAD ALLOCATION (1)

Worksheet formulae (a) for Exercise 7, question 1

	A	B	C	D	E	F
1	DO-RE-MEE					
2						
3	OVERHEAD COST ALLOCATION & APPORTIONMENT					
4						
5	APPORTIONMENT BASES					
6						
7	DESCRIPTION	CATEGORY	CD's	HI-FI	INSTRUMENTS	TOTAL
8	Floor Area (sq.m.)	1	100	200	100	=SUM(C8:E8)
9	No of Employees	2	6	9	5	=SUM(C9:E9)
10	Value of Fittings (£000)	3	20	30	10	=SUM(C10:E10)
11	Sales (£000)	4	150	350	100	=SUM(C11:E11)
12	Wages (£000)	5	30	50	20	=SUM(C12:E12)
13						
14						
15	OVERHEAD APPORTIONMENT					
16						
17	DESCRIPTION	CATEGORY	CD's	HI-FI	INSTRUMENTS	TOTAL O/HEAD
18			£'000	£'000	£'000	£'000
19	Heat & Light	1	=(C8/$F$8)*$F$19	=(D8/$F$8)*$F$19	=(E8/$F$8)*$F$19	15
20	First Aid & Welfare	2	=(C9/$F$9)*$F$20	=(D9/$F$9)*$F$20	=(E9/$F$9)*$F$20	4
21	Adv. & Promotion	4	=(C11/$F$11)*$F$21	=(D11/$F$11)*$F$21	=(E11/$F$11)*$F$21	9
22	Insurance of Buildings	1	=(C8/$F$8)*$F$22	=(D8/$F$8)*$F$22	=(E8/$F$8)*$F$22	8
23	Pension conts.	5	=(C12/$F$12)*$F$23	=(D12/$F$12)*$F$23	=(E12/$F$12)*$F$23	6
24	Depn. of Fittings	3	=(C10/$F$10)*$F$24	=(D10/$F$10)*$F$24	=(E10/$F$10)*$F$24	12
25			=SUM(C19:C24)	=SUM(D19:D24)	=SUM(E19:E24)	=SUM(F19:F24)
26						
27						
28	This model could be improved by using a "LOOKUP" function. See Worksheet Formulae (b).					
29						

OVERHEAD ALLOCATION (1)

Worksheet formulae (b) for Exercise 7, question 1

	A	B	C	D	E	F
1	DO-RE-MEE					
2						
3	OVERHEAD COST ALLOCATION & APPORTIONMENT					
4						
5	APPORTIONMENT BASES					
6						
7	DESCRIPTION	CATEGORY	CD's	HI-FI	INSTRUMENTS	TOTAL
8	Floor Area (sq.m.)	1	100	200	100	=SUM(C8:E8)
9	No of Employees	2	6	9	5	=SUM(C9:E9)
10	Value of Fittings (£000)	3	20	30	10	=SUM(C10:E10)
11	Sales (£000)	4	150	350	100	=SUM(C11:E11)
12	Wages (£000)	5	30	50	20	=SUM(C12:E12)
13						
14						
15	OVERHEAD APPORTIONMENT					
16						
17	DESCRIPTION	CATEGORY	CD's	HI-FI	INSTRUMENTS	TOTAL O/HEAD
18			£'000	£'000	£'000	£'000
19	Heat & Light	1	** formula below	** formula below	** formula below	15
20	First Aid & Welfare	2				4
21	Adv. & Promotion	4				9
22	Insurance of Buildings	1				8
23	Pension conts.	5				6
24	Depm. of Fittings	3				12
25			=SUM(C19:C24)	=SUM(D19:D24)	=SUM(E19:E24)	=SUM(F19:F24)
26						
27	** Formula in cell C19					
28	=(VLOOKUP(B19,$B$8:$F$12,2,false)/VLOOKUP(B19,$B$8:$F$12,5,false))*F19					
29	This formula is copied to the range C20:C24.					
30						
31	** Formula in cell D19					
32	=(VLOOKUP(B19,$B$8:$F$12,3,false)/VLOOKUP(B19,$B$8:$F$12,5,false))*F19					
33	This formula is copied to the range D20:D24.					
34						
35	** Formula in cell E19					
36	=(VLOOKUP(B19,$B$8:$F$12,4,false)/VLOOKUP(B19,$B$8:$F$12,5,false))*F19					
37	This formula is copied to the range E20:E24.					
38						

OVERHEAD ALLOCATION (1)

Worksheet for Exercise 7, question 2

	A	B	C	D	E	F
1	DO-RE-MEE					
2						
3	OVERHEAD COST ALLLOCATION & APPORTIONMENT					
4						
5	APPORTIONMENT BASES					
6						
7	DESCRIPTION	CATEGORY	CD's	HI-FI	INSTRUMENTS	TOTAL
8	Floor Area (sq.m.)	1	100	200	150	450
9	No of Employees	2	8	9	5	22
10	Value of Fittings (£000)	3	20	30	10	60
11	Sales (£000)	4	150	350	100	600
12	Wages (£000)	5	50	50	20	120
13						
14						
15	OVERHEAD APPORTIONMENT					
16						
17	DESCRIPTION	CATEGORY	CD's	HI-FI	INSTRUMENTS	TOTAL O/HEAD
18			£'000	£'000	£'000	£'000
19	Heat & Light	1	4.00	8.00	6.00	18.00
20	First Aid & Welfare	2	1.45	1.64	0.91	4.00
21	Adv. & Promotion	4	2.25	5.25	1.50	9.00
22	Insurance of Buildings	1	2.67	5.33	4.00	12.00
23	Pension conts.	5	3.75	3.75	1.50	9.00
24	Deprn. of Fittings	3	4.00	6.00	2.00	12.00
25			18.12	29.97	15.91	64.00
26						

OVERHEAD ALLOCATION (1)

EXERCISE 9: JOB COST SHEET

Worksheet for Exercise 9, question 1

	A	B	C	D	E	F
1	JOB COST SHEET					
2						
3	Job No.					
4	Product					
5						
6	KEY VARIABLES					
7			PRESS SHOP	WELDING	ASSEMBLY &	
8					PACKING	
9	Production quantity	1000				
10	Direct material cost per unit		£2.50	£0.50	£0.40	
11	Direct labour hours per unit		0.02	0.015	0.25	
12	Direct labour rate (per hour)		£5.00	£6.00	£4.50	
13	Machine hours per unit		0.125	0.115		
14	Factory overhead absorption :					
15	Direct labour cost rate				60%	
16	Machine hour rate		£12	£12		
17	Non-factory overhead abs. rate	20%				
18	Mark-up	35%				
19						
20	COST & PRICE CALCULATION					
21			PRESS SHOP	WELDING	ASSEMBLY &	TOTAL
22					PACKING	
23			£	£	£	£
24	Direct material		2,500.00	500.00	400.00	3,400.00
25	Direct labour		100.00	90.00	1,125.00	1,315.00
26	Factory overhead		1,500.00	1,380.00	675.00	3,555.00
27	TOTAL PRODUCTION COST					8,270.00
28	Non-factory overhead					1,654.00
29	TOTAL COST					9,924.00
30	Mark-up					3,473.40
31	BID PRICE					13,397.40
32						

JOB COST SHEET

Worksheet formulae for Exercise 9, question 1

	A	B	C	D	E	F
1	JOB COST SHEET					
2						
3	Job No.					
4	Product					
5						
6	KEY VARIABLES					
7			PRESS SHOP	WELDING	ASSEMBLY &	
8					PACKING	
9	Production quantity	1000				
10	Direct material cost per unit		2.5	0.5	0.4	
11	Direct labour hours per unit		0.02	0.015	0.25	
12	Direct labour rate (per hour)		5	6	4.5	
13	Machine hours per unit		0.125	0.115		
14	Factory overhead absorption :					
15	Direct labour cost rate				0.6	
16	Machine hour rate		12	12		
17	Non-factory overhead abs. rate	0.2				
18	Mark-up	0.35				
19						
20	COST & PRICE CALCULATION					
21			PRESS SHOP	WELDING	ASSEMBLY &	TOTAL
22					PACKING	
23			£	£	£	£
24	Direct material		=$B$9*C10	=$B$9*D10	=$B$9*E10	=SUM(C24:E24)
25	Direct labour		=$B$9*C11*C12	=$B$9*D11*D12	=$B$9*E11*E12	=SUM(C25:E25)
26	Factory overhead		=$B$9*C13*C16	=$B$9*D13*D16	=E25*E15	=SUM(C26:E26)
27	TOTAL PRODUCTION COST					=SUM(F24:F26)
28	Non-factory overhead					=F27*B17
29	TOTAL COST					=SUM(F27:F28)
30	Mark-up					=F29*B18
31	BID PRICE					=SUM(F29:F30)
32						

JOB COST SHEET

Worksheet for Exercise 9, question 2

	A	B	C	D	E	F
1	JOB COST SHEET					
2						
3	Job No.					
4	Product					
5						
6	KEY VARIABLES					
7			PRESS SHOP	WELDING	ASSEMBLY &	
8					PACKING	
9	Production quantity	800				
10	Direct material cost per unit		£4.50	£1.25	£1.00	
11	Direct labour hours per unit		0.03	0.015	0.75	
12	Direct labour rate (per hour)		£5.00	£6.00	£4.50	
13	Machine hours per unit		0.25	0.2		
14	Factory overhead absorption :					
15	Direct labour cost rate				60%	
16	Machine hour rate		£12	£12		
17	Non-factory overhead abs. rate	20%				
18	Mark-up	35%				
19						
20	COST & PRICE CALCULATION					
21			PRESS SHOP	WELDING	ASSEMBLY &	TOTAL
22					PACKING	
23			£	£	£	£
24	Direct material		3,600.00	1,000.00	800.00	5,400.00
25	Direct labour		120.00	72.00	2,700.00	2,892.00
26	Factory overhead		2,400.00	1,920.00	1,620.00	5,940.00
27	TOTAL PRODUCTION COST					14,232.00
28	Non-factory overhead					2,846.40
29	TOTAL COST					17,078.40
30	Mark-up					5,977.44
31	BID PRICE					23,055.84
32						

JOB COST SHEET

EXERCISE 10: PROCESS COSTING

Worksheet for Exercise 10, question 1

	A	B	C	D	E	F	G	H
1	PROCESS COSTING							
2								
3	KEY VARIABLES							
4								
5	WORK IN PROGRESS DETAILS			CURRENT PERIOD DETAILS				
6		OPENING	CLOSING					
7		WIP	WIP					
8	No. of units	90	110	Units completed	590			
9	% complete - matl.	100.00%	100.00%	Material cost	£12,900			
10	% complete - labour	50.00%	50.00%	Labour cost	£17,355			
11	% complete - o/head	50.00%	50.00%	Overhead cost	£12,645			
12	Matl. cost	£1,800						
13	Labour cost	£1,350						
14	Overhead cost	£900						
15								
16								
17	WEIGHTED AVERAGE METHOD							
18								
19	COST	OPENING	CURRENT	TOTAL	COMPLETED	CLOSING	TOTAL	COST/
20	ELEMENT	WIP	PERIOD	COST	UNITS	WIP EQUIV.	EQUIV.	UNIT
21		COST	COST			UNITS	UNITS	
22								
23	Materials	£1,800	£12,900	£14,700	590	110	700	£21.00
24	Labour	£1,350	£17,355	£18,705	590	55	645	£29.00
25	Overhead	£900	£12,645	£13,545	590	55	645	£21.00
26				£46,950				£71.00
27								
28						Cost of completed production		£41,890
29						Cost of closing WIP		£5,060
30								£46,950
31	FIFO METHOD							
32								
33	COST	CURRENT	COMPLETED UNITS		CLOSING	CURRENT	COST/	
34	ELEMENT	PERIOD	LESS OPENING WIP		WIP EQUIV.	TOTAL	UNIT	
35		COSTS	EQUIV. UNITS		UNITS	EQUIV. UNITS		
36								
37	Materials	£12,900	500		110	610	£21.15	
38	Labour	£17,355	545		55	600	£28.93	
39	Overhead	£12,645	545		55	600	£21.08	
40		£42,900					£71.15	
41								
42					Cost of completed production		£41,874	
43					Cost of closing WIP		£5,076	
44							£46,950	
45								

PROCESS COSTING

Worksheet formulae for Exercise 10, question 1

	A	B	C	D	E	F	G	H
1	PROCESS COSTING							
2								
3	KEY VARIABLES							
4								
5		WORK IN PROGRESS DETAILS			CURRENT PERIOD DETAILS			
6		OPENING	CLOSING					
7		WIP	WIP					
8	No. of units	90	110	Units completed	590			
9	% complete - matl.	1	1	Material cost	12900			
10	% complete - labour	0.5	0.5	Labour cost	17355			
11	% complete - o/head	0.5	0.5	Overhead cost	12845			
12	Matl. cost	1800						
13	Labour cost	1350						
14	Overhead cost	900						
15								
16								
17	WEIGHTED AVERAGE METHOD							
18	COST	OPENING	CURRENT	TOTAL	COMPLETED	CLOSING	TOTAL	COST/
19		WIP	PERIOD	COST	UNITS	WIP EQUIV.	EQUIV.	UNIT
20	ELEMENT		COST				UNITS	
21						UNITS		
22								
23	Materials	=B12	=E9	=B23+C23	=E8	=C8*C9	=E23+F23	=D23/G23
24	Labour	=B13	=E10	=B24+C24	=E8	=C8*C10	=E24+F24	=D24/G24
25	Overhead	=B14	=E11	=B25+C25	=E8	=C8*C11	=E25+F25	=D25/G25
26				=SUM(D23:D25)				=SUM(H23:H25)
27								
28						Cost of completed production		=E8*H26
29						Cost of closing WIP		=(F23*H23)+(F24*H24)+(F25*H25)
30								=SUM(H28:H29)
31	FIFO METHOD							
32								
33	COST	CURRENT	COMPLET ED UNITS		CLOSING	CURRENT	COST/	
34		PERIOD	LESS OPE NING WIP		WIP EQUIV.	TOTAL	UNIT	
35	ELEMENT	COSTS	EQUIV. UNITS		UNITS	EQUIV. UNITS		
36								
37	Materials	=E9	=E8-(B8*B9)		=C8*C9	=C37+E37	=B37/F37	
38	Labour	=E10	=E8-(B8*B10)		=C8*C10	=C38+E38	=B38/F38	
39	Overhead	=E11	=E8-(B8*B11)		=C8*C11	=C39+E39	=B39/F39	
40		=SUM(B37:B39)				=SUM(G37:G39)		
41								
42					Cost of completed production	=(B12+B13+B14)+(C37*G37)+(C38*G38)+(C39*G39)		
43					Cost of closing WIP	=(E37*G37)+(E38*G38)+(E39*G39)		
44						=SUM(G42:G43)		
45								

PROCESS COSTING

Worksheet for Exercise 10, question 2

	A	B	C	D	E	F	G	H
1	PROCESS COSTING							
2								
3	KEY VARIABLES							
4								
5	WORK IN PROGRESS DETAILS			CURRENT PERIOD DETAILS				
6		OPENING	CLOSING					
7		WIP	WIP					
8	No. of units	180	280	Units completed	1180			
9	% complete - matl.	100.00%	100.00%	Material cost	£51,600			
10	% complete - labour	50.00%	50.00%	Labour cost	£69,420			
11	% complete - o/head	25.00%	25.00%	Overhead cost	£50,740			
12	Matl. cost	£7,200						
13	Labour cost	£5,400						
14	Overhead cost	£3,600						
15								
16								
17	WEIGHTED AVERAGE METHOD							
18								
19	COST	OPENING	CURRENT	TOTAL	COMPLETED	CLOSING	TOTAL	COST/
20	ELEMENT	WIP	PERIOD	COST	UNITS	WIP EQUIV.	EQUIV.	UNIT
21		COST	COST			UNITS	UNITS	
22								
23	Materials	£7,200	£51,600	£58,800	1180	280	1460	£40.27
24	Labour	£5,400	£69,420	£74,820	1180	140	1320	£56.68
25	Overhead	£3,600	£50,740	£54,340	1180	70	1250	£43.47
26				£187,960				£140.43
27								
28						Cost of completed production		£165,705
29						Cost of closing WIP		£22,255
30								£187,960
31	FIFO METHOD							
32								
33	COST	CURRENT	COMPLETED UNITS		CLOSING	CURRENT	COST/	
34	ELEMENT	PERIOD	LESS OPENING WIP		WIP EQUIV.	TOTAL	UNIT	
35		COSTS	EQUIV. UNITS		UNITS	EQUIV. UNITS		
36								
37	Materials	£51,600	1000		280	1280	£40.31	
38	Labour	£69,420	1090		140	1230	£56.44	
39	Overhead	£50,740	1135		70	1205	£42.11	
40		£171,760					£138.86	
41								
42					Cost of completed production		£165,823	
43					Cost of closing WIP		£22,137	
44							£187,960	
45								

PROCESS COSTING

EXERCISE 11: STANDARD COSTING AND VARIANCE ANALYSIS

Worksheet for Exercise 11

	A	B	C	D	E	F
1	STANDARD COSTING & VARIANCE ANALYSIS					
2						
3						
4		STANDARD		ACTUAL	VARIANCE	
5						
6	Material usage	1500	Kgs	1800	£360.00	ADVERSE
7	Material price	£1.20	per kg.	£1.10	£180.00	FAVOURABLE
8	Labour efficiency	4000	hours	3600	£2,600.00	FAVOURABLE
9	Labour rate	£6.50	per hour	£6.70	£720.00	ADVERSE
10						

STANDARD COSTING

Worksheet formulae for Exercise 11

	A	B	C	D	E	F
1	STANDARD COSTING & VARIANCE ANALYSIS					
2						
3						
4		STANDARD		ACTUAL	VARIANCE	
5						
6	Material usage	1500	Kgs	1800	=ABS((B6-D6)*B7)	=IF(B6>D6,"FAVOURABLE","ADVERSE")
7	Material price	1.2	per kg.	1.1	=ABS((B7-D7)*D6)	=IF(B7>D7,"FAVOURABLE","ADVERSE")
8	Labour efficiency	4000	hours	3600	=ABS((B8-D8)*B9)	=IF(B8>D8,"FAVOURABLE","ADVERSE")
9	Labour rate	6.5	per hour	6.7	=ABS((B9-D9)*D8)	=IF(B9>D9,"FAVOURABLE","ADVERSE")
10						

STANDARD COSTING

EXERCISE 12: CASH BUDGET

Worksheet for Exercise 12

	A	B	C	D	E	F	G	H	I	J
1	MacROBERTS LTD.									
2										
3	CASH BUDGET									
4										
5	KEY VARIABLES									
6										
7	Sales (units) :	19X1		19X2						
8		NOV	DEC	JAN	FEB	MAR	APR	MAY	JUN	JULY
9		1800	1850	2000	2000	2000	2100	2100	2200	2200
10										
11	Selling Price (per unit)	£15.00								
12	Income from debtors - 1 month in arrears	60%								
13	Income from debtors - 2 months in arrears	39%								
14	Purchases as %age of sales	55%								
15	VAT rate	17.50%								
16	Bank interest rate	9.50%								
17	Prod. O/heads as %age of Purchases	15%								
18	Admin. O/heads as %age of Sales	8%								
19	Distribution O/heads as %age of Sales	10%								
20	Opening cash balance	£12,000								
21										
22										
23	CASH BUDGET FOR PERIOD JAN. - JUNE 19X2									
24										
25		JAN	FEB	MAR	APR	MAY	JUN	TOTAL		
26	RECEIPTS	£	£	£	£	£	£	£		
27	Sales receipts	27,180.00	28,822.50	29,700.00	29,700.00	30,600.00	31,185.00	177,187.50		
28	Other							0.00		
29	TOTAL RECEIPTS	27,180.00	28,822.50	29,700.00	29,700.00	30,600.00	31,185.00	177,187.50		
30										
31	PAYMENTS									
32	Purchase of stock	16,500.00	16,500.00	17,325.00	17,325.00	18,150.00	18,150.00	103,950.00		
33	Delivery vehicle			20,000.00				20,000.00		
34	VAT		6,385.31			7,061.25		13,446.56		
35	Dividends				2,000.00			2,000.00		
36	Prod. O/heads	2,475.00	2,475.00	2,598.75	2,598.75	2,722.50	2,722.50	15,592.50		
37	Admin. O/heads	2,400.00	2,400.00	2,400.00	2,520.00	2,520.00	2,640.00	14,880.00		
38	Distribution O/heads	3,000.00	3,000.00	3,000.00	3,150.00	3,150.00	3,300.00	18,600.00		
39	Other							0.00		
40	TOTAL PAYMENTS	24,375.00	30,760.31	45,323.75	27,593.75	33,603.75	26,812.50	188,469.06		
41										
42	NET CASH FLOW	2,805.00	(1,937.81)	(15,623.75)	2,106.25	(3,003.75)	4,372.50	(11,281.56)		
43	BALANCE b/fwd	12,000.00	14,805.00	12,867.19	(2,778.39)	(672.14)	(3,675.89)			
44	END BALANCE	14,805.00	12,867.19	(2,756.56)	(672.14)	(3,675.89)	696.61			
45	Bank Interest payable			21.82			34.42			
46	BALANCE c/fwd	14,805.00	12,867.19	(2,778.39)	(672.14)	(3,675.89)	662.19			
47										

CASH BUDGET

Worksheet formulae for Exercise 12

Row	A	B	C	D	E	F	G	H
1	MacROBERTS LTD.							
2								
3	CASH BUDGET							
4								
5	KEY VARIABLES							
6								
7	Sales (units) :	19X1		19X2				
8		NOV	DEC	JAN	FEB	MAR	APR	MAY
9		1800	1850	2000	2000	2000	2100	2100
10								
11	Selling Price (per unit)	15						
12	Income from debtors - 1 month in arrears	0.6						
13	Income from debtors - 2 months in arrears	0.39						
14	Purchases as %age of sales	0.55						
15	VAT rate	0.175						
16	Bank interest rate	0.095						
17	Prod . O/heads as %age of Purchases	0.15						
18	Admin. O/heads as %age of Sales	0.08						
19	Distribution O/heads as %age of Sales	0.1						
20	Opening cash balance	12000						
21								
22								
23	CASH BUDGET FOR PERIOD JAN. - JUNE 19X2							
24								
25		JAN	FEB	MAR	APR	MAY	JUN	TOTAL
26	RECEIPTS	£	£	£	£	£	£	£
27	Sales receipts	=(($B$13*B9)+($B$12*C9))*$B$11	copied from B27	copied from B27	copied from B27	copied from B27	copied from B27	=SUM(B27:G27)
28	Other							=SUM(B28:G28)
29	TOTAL RECEIPTS	=SUM(B27:B28)	=SUM(C27:C28)	=SUM(D27:D28)	=SUM(E27:E28)	=SUM(F27:F28)	=SUM(G27:G28)	=SUM(B29:G29)
30								
31	PAYMENTS							
32	Purchase of stock	=(E9*$B$11)*$B$14	=(F9*$B$11)*$B$14	=(G9*$B$11)*$B$14	=(H9*$B$11)*$B$14	=(I9*$B$11)*$B$14	=(J9*$B$11)*$B$14	=SUM(B32:G32)
33	Delivery vehicle			20000				=SUM(B33:G33)
34	VAT		** formula below	copied from C34		copied from C34		=SUM(B34:G34)
35	Dividends				2000			=SUM(B35:G35)
36	Prod. O/heads	=B32*$B$17	=C32*$B$17	=D32*$B$17	=E32*$B$17	=F32*$B$17	=G32*$B$17	=SUM(B36:G36)
37	Admin. O/heads	=(D9*$B$11)*$B$18	=(E9*$B$11)*$B$18	=(F9*$B$11)*$B$18	=(G9*$B$11)*$B$18	=(H9*$B$11)*$B$18	=(I9*$B$11)*$B$18	=SUM(B37:G37)
38	Distribution O/heads	=(D9*$B$11)*$B$19	=(E9*$B$11)*$B$19	=(F9*$B$11)*$B$19	=(G9*$B$11)*$B$19	=(H9*$B$11)*$B$19	=(I9*$B$11)*$B$19	=SUM(B38:G38)
39	Other							=SUM(B39:G39)
40	TOTAL PAYMENTS	=SUM(B32:B39)	=SUM(C32:C39)	=SUM(D32:D39)	=SUM(E32:E39)	=SUM(F32:F39)	=SUM(G32:G39)	=SUM(H32:H39)
41								
42	NET CASH FLOW	=B29-B40	=C29-C40	=D29-D40	=E29-E40	=F29-F40	=G29-G40	=H29-H40
43	BALANCE b/fwd	=B20	=B46	=C46	=D46	=E46	=F46	
44	END BALANCE	=SUM(B42:B43)	=SUM(C42:C43)	=SUM(D42:D43)	=SUM(E42:E43)	=SUM(F42:F43)	=SUM(G42:G43)	
45	Bank interest payable			** formula below			copied from D45	
46	BALANCE c/fwd	=B44-B45	=C44-C45	=D44-D45	=E44-E45	=F44-F45	=G44-G45	
47								
48	** FORMULA IN CELL C34 : =(((B9+C9+D9)*$B$11)-((C9+D9+E9)*($B$11*$B$14)))*$B$15							
49								
50	** FORMULA IN CELL D45 : =ABS((((IF(B44<0,B44,0)+IF(C44<0,C44,0)+IF(D44<0,D44,0))*$B$16)/12)							
51								

CASH BUDGET

EXERCISE 13: INVESTMENT APPRAISAL

Worksheet for Exercise 13

	A	B	C	D	E
1	HI-FLYERS AIRLINES				
2					
3	INVESTMENT APPRAISAL FOR TRANS-ATLANTIC SERVICE				
4					
5	BUDGETED VALUES				
6					
7	Initial Investment	£450,000			
8	Initial Income	£0			
9	Max. no. of passengers	400			
10	Average payload	60%			
11	No. of crossings (per year)	200			
12	Single ticket price	£200			
13	Operating costs (per passenger)	£180			
14	Fixed costs (per annum)	£750,000			
15	Expected rate of return	20%			
16					
17					
18	YEAR	CASH	CASH	NET	CUMULATIVE
19		INFLOW	OUTFLOW	CASH FLOW	RETURN
20		£	£	£	£
21	0	0	450,000	(450,000)	0
22	1	9,600,000	9,390,000	210,000	210,000
23	2	9,600,000	9,390,000	210,000	420,000
24	3	9,600,000	9,390,000	210,000	630,000
25	4	9,600,000	9,390,000	210,000	840,000
26	5	9,600,000	9,390,000	210,000	1,050,000
27	6	9,600,000	9,390,000	210,000	1,260,000
28					
29					
30	PAYBACK PERIOD	2 years	and	52 days	
31					
32	NET PRESENT VALUE (NPV)	£248,357.12			
33					
34	INTERNAL RATE OF RETURN (IRR)	41%			
35					

INVESTMENT APPRAISAL

Worksheet formulae for Exercise 13

	A	B	C	D	E
1	HI-FLYERS AIRLINES				
2					
3	INVESTMENT APPRAISAL FOR TRANS-ATLANTIC SERVICE				
4					
5	BUDGETED VALUES				
6					
7	Initial Investment	450000			
8	Initial Income	0			
9	Max. no. of passengers	400			
10	Average payload	0.6			
11	No. of crossings (per year)	200			
12	Single ticket price	200			
13	Operating costs (per passenger)	180			
14	Fixed costs (per annum)	750000			
15	Expected rate of return	0.2			
16					
17					
18	YEAR	CASH INFLOW	CASH OUTFLOW	NET CASH FLOW	CUMULATIVE RETURN
19		£	£	£	£
20					
21	0	=B8	=B7	=B21-C21	=B21
22	1	=$B$9*$B$10*$B$11*$B$12	=($B$9*$B$10*$B$11*$B$13)+$B$14	=B22-C22	=E21+D22
23	2	=$B$9*$B$10*$B$11*$B$12	=($B$9*$B$10*$B$11*$B$13)+$B$14	=B23-C23	=E22+D23
24	3	=$B$9*$B$10*$B$11*$B$12	=($B$9*$B$10*$B$11*$B$13)+$B$14	=B24-C24	=E23+D24
25	4	=$B$9*$B$10*$B$11*$B$12	=($B$9*$B$10*$B$11*$B$13)+$B$14	=B25-C25	=E24+D25
26	5	=$B$9*$B$10*$B$11*$B$12	=($B$9*$B$10*$B$11*$B$13)+$B$14	=B26-C26	=E25+D26
27	6	=$B$9*$B$10*$B$11*$B$12	=($B$9*$B$10*$B$11*$B$13)+$B$14	=B27-C27	=E26+D27
28					
29					
30	PAYBACK PERIOD	=LOOKUP(B7,E21:E27,A21:A27)	years and	** formula below	days
31					
32	NET PRESENT VALUE (NPV)	=NPV(B15,D22:D27)+D21			
33					
34	INTERNAL RATE OF RETURN (IRR)	=IRR(D21:D27)			
35					
36	** FORMULA IN CELL D30 : =((B7-VLOOKUP(B30,A21:E27,5))/((VLOOKUP(B30+1,A21:E27,5))-(VLOOKUP(B30,A21:E27,5))))*365				
37					
38	The formulae in cells B30 and D30 assume that the initial investment is paid back within the life of the project. If this is not the case an error message will appear in cell D30.				
39					

INVESTMENT APPRAISAL

EXERCISE 14: COST-VOLUME-PROFIT ANALYSIS (1)

Worksheet for Exercise 14

	A	B	C	D	E	F
1	**SWALE ENGINEERING**					
2						
3	**COST-VOLUME-PROFIT ANALYSIS**					
4						
5	**KEY VARIABLES**					
6						
7	Selling Price	£8.00				
8	Fixed costs	£55,000				
9	Variable cost (per unit)	£4.00				
10	Output range : Min. units	0				
11	Output range : Max. units	40000				
12	Budgeted level of activity (units)	30000				
13	Target profit	£70,000				
14						
15						
16	**OUTPUT DATA**					
17						
18	Contribution	£4.00				
19	Break-even point : sales units	13750				
20	Break-even point : sales value	£110,000				
21	Profit at budgeted level of activity	£65,000				
22	Sales to produce target profit : units	31250				
23	Sales to produce target profit : value	£250,000				
24						
25	**CHART DATA**					
26						
27	OUTPUT	VAR. COST	FIXED COST	TOTAL COST	TOTAL REV.	PROFIT/LOSS
28		£	£	£	£	£
29	0	0	55,000	55,000	0	(55,000)
30	4000	16,000	55,000	71,000	32,000	(39,000)
31	8000	32,000	55,000	87,000	64,000	(23,000)
32	12000	48,000	55,000	103,000	96,000	(7,000)
33	16000	64,000	55,000	119,000	128,000	9,000
34	20000	80,000	55,000	135,000	160,000	25,000
35	24000	96,000	55,000	151,000	192,000	41,000
36	28000	112,000	55,000	167,000	224,000	57,000
37	32000	128,000	55,000	183,000	256,000	73,000
38	36000	144,000	55,000	199,000	288,000	89,000
39	40000	160,000	55,000	215,000	320,000	105,000
40						

CVP (1)

Worksheet formulae for Exercise 14

	A	B	C	D	E	F
1	SWALE ENGINEERING					
2						
3	COST-VOLUME-PROFIT ANALYSIS					
4						
5	KEY VARIABLES					
6						
7	Selling Price	8				
8	Fixed costs	55000				
9	Variable cost (per unit)	4				
10	Output range : Min. units	0				
11	Output range : Max. units	40000				
12	Budgeted level of activity (units)	30000				
13	Target profit	70000				
14						
15						
16	OUTPUT DATA					
17						
18	Contribution	=B7-B9				
19	Break-even point : sales units	=B8/B18				
20	Break-even point : sales value	=B19*B7				
21	Profit at budgeted level of activity	=(B12-B19)*B18				
22	Sales to produce target profit : units	=(B13+B8)/B18				
23	Sales to produce target profit : value	=B7*B22				
24						
25	CHART DATA					
26						
27	OUTPUT	VAR. COST £	FIXED COST £	TOTAL COST £	TOTAL REV. £	PROFIT/LOSS £
28						
29	=B10	=A29*$B$9	=$B$8	=B29+C29	=A29*$B$7	=E29-D29
30	=A29+(($B$11-$B$10)/10)	=A30*$B$9	=$B$8	=B30+C30	=A30*$B$7	=E30-D30
31	=A30+(($B$11-$B$10)/10)	=A31*$B$9	=$B$8	=B31+C31	=A31*$B$7	=E31-D31
32	=A31+(($B$11-$B$10)/10)	=A32*$B$9	=$B$8	=B32+C32	=A32*$B$7	=E32-D32
33	=A32+(($B$11-$B$10)/10)	=A33*$B$9	=$B$8	=B33+C33	=A33*$B$7	=E33-D33
34	=A33+(($B$11-$B$10)/10)	=A34*$B$9	=$B$8	=B34+C34	=A34*$B$7	=E34-D34
35	=A34+(($B$11-$B$10)/10)	=A35*$B$9	=$B$8	=B35+C35	=A35*$B$7	=E35-D35
36	=A35+(($B$11-$B$10)/10)	=A36*$B$9	=$B$8	=B36+C36	=A36*$B$7	=E36-D36
37	=A36+(($B$11-$B$10)/10)'	=A37*$B$9	=$B$8	=B37+C37	=A37*$B$7	=E37-D37
38	=A37+(($B$11-$B$10)/10)	=A38*$B$9	=$B$8	=B38+C38	=A38*$B$7	=E38-D38
39	=A38+(($B$11-$B$10)/10)	=A39*$B$9	=$B$8	=B39+C39	=A39*$B$7	=E39-D39
40						

CVP (1)

Chartsheet for Exercise 14

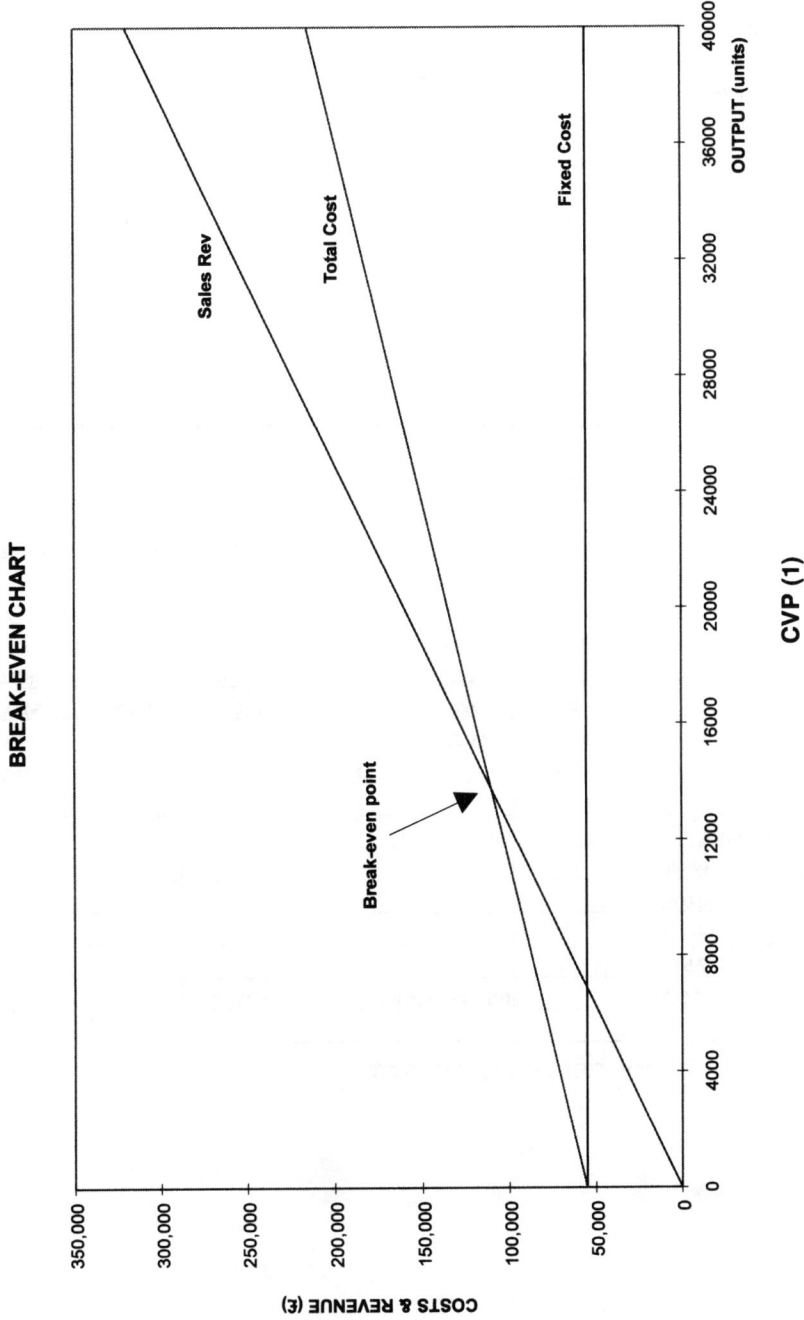

BREAK-EVEN CHART

Sales Rev

Total Cost

Break-even point

Fixed Cost

COSTS & REVENUE (£)

350,000
300,000
250,000
200,000
150,000
100,000
50,000
0

0
4000
8000
12000
16000
20000
24000
28000
32000
36000
40000

OUTPUT (units)

CVP (1)

EXERCISE 16: COST/REVENUE BUDGET

Worksheet for Exercise 16

	A	B	C	D	E	F	G	H
1	CONSUMER GADGETS PLC							
2								
3	COST/REVENUE BUDGET JAN - JUNE							
4								
5	KEY VARIABLES							
6	Price	£45						
7			JAN	FEB	MAR	APR	MAY	JUN
8	Budget sales (units)		5000	5000	5000	6500	6500	6500
9	Material costs (per unit)	£15.00						
10	Direct labour costs (per unit)	£10.00						
11	Variable overheads (per unit)	£2.50						
12	Fixed overheads (per month)	£50,000						
13								
14	FORECAST							
15			JAN	FEB	MAR	APR	MAY	JUN
16			£	£	£	£	£	£
17	Sales Income		225000	225000	225000	292500	292500	292500
18	Costs :							
19	Material		75000	75000	75000	97500	97500	97500
20	Labour		50000	50000	50000	65000	65000	65000
21	Var. O/heads		12500	12500	12500	16250	16250	16250
22	Fixed O/heads		50000	50000	50000	50000	50000	50000
23	Total costs		187500	187500	187500	228750	228750	228750
24	Profit		37500	37500	37500	63750	63750	63750
25								
26	BONUS CALCULATION TABLE							
27	PROFIT	BONUS						
28	0	0.00%						
29	250000	5.00%						
30	300000	7.50%						
31	400000	10.00%		BONUS EARNED		£4,031.25		
32								

COST/REVENUE BUDGET

Worksheet formulae for Exercise 16

	A	B	C	D	E	F	G	H
1	CONSUMER GADGETS PLC							
2								
3	COST/REVENUE BUDGET JAN - JUNE							
4								
5	KEY VARIABLES							
6	Price	45						
7								
8	Budget sales (units)		5000	5000	5000	6500	6500	6500
9	Material costs (per unit)	15						
10	Direct labour costs (per unit)	10						
11	Variable overheads (per unit)	2.5						
12	Fixed overheads (per month)	50000						
13								
14	FORECAST							
15			JAN	FEB	MAR	APR	MAY	JUN
16			£	£	£	£	£	£
17	Sales Income		=$B$6*C8	=$B$6*D8	=$B$6*E8	=$B$6*F8	=$B$6*G8	=$B$6*H8
18	Costs :							
19	Material		=C8*$B$9	=D8*$B$9	=E8*$B$9	=F8*$B$9	=G8*$B$9	=H8*$B$9
20	Labour		=C8*$B$10	=D8*$B$10	=E8*$B$10	=F8*$B$10	=G8*$B$10	=H8*$B$10
21	Var. O/heads		=C8*$B$11	=D8*$B$11	=E8*$B$11	=F8*$B$11	=G8*$B$11	=H8*$B$11
22	Fixed O/heads		=$B$12	=$B$12	=$B$12	=$B$12	=$B$12	=$B$12
23	Total costs		=SUM(C19:C22)	=SUM(D19:D22)	=SUM(E19:E22)	=SUM(F19:F22)	=SUM(G19:G22)	=SUM(H19:H22)
24	Profit		=C17-C23	=D17-D23	=E17-E23	=F17-F23	=G17-G23	=H17-H23
25								
26	BONUS CALCULATION TABLE							
27	PROFIT	BONUS						
28	0	0						
29	250000	0.05						
30	300000	0.075						
31	400000	0.1			BONUS EARNED	** formula below		
32								

** FORMULA IN CELL F31 : =IF(SUM(C24:H24)>250000,LOOKUP(SUM(C24:H24),A28:A31,B28:B31)*(SUM(C24:H24)-250000),0)

NOTE: Once the worksheet has been designed the price/output combinations can be altered manually and the effect on the bonus noted. Alternatively the three sets of price/output combinations can be set up as different scenarios using the Scenario Manager tool. The effect on bonus earned can then be noted by activating each scenario in turn.

COST/REVENUE BUDGET

EXERCISE 17: STUDENT GRADES

Worksheet for Exercise 17, question 1

	A	B	C	D	E	F
1	GRAYSTONES COLLEGE					
2						
3	DEPARTMENT OF ACCOUNTING				CLASS	
4						
5	SURNAME	INITS	CLASS TEST	CLASS TEST	FINAL	OVERALL
6			DECEMBER	MARCH	EXAM	RESULT
7			%	%	%	%
8	Hennessy	I	43	48	52	50
9	Ashdown	H	72	76	65	68
10	Kirkton	J	82	78	70	73
11	Ridley	J	34	40	48	45
12	Stevenson	L	45	55	62	58
13	Wells	F	89	81	82	83
14	Ashquar	M	67	73	69	69
15	Dawson	G	21	16	42	35
16	Davidson	B	38	42	36	37
17	Hassan	T	54	56	48	50
18	Evans	A	52	67	78	72
19	Lipton	M	54	61	74	69
20	Davidson	C	79	85	90	88
21	Peterson	S	74	72	80	78
22	Johnson	A	51	59	58	57
23						

Worksheet formulae for Exercise 17, question 1

	A	B	C	D	E	F
1	GRAYSTONES COLLEGE					
2						
3	DEPARTMENT OF ACCOUNTING				CLASS	
4						
5	SURNAME	INITS	CLASS TEST	CLASS TEST	FINAL	OVERALL
6			DECEMBER	MARCH	EXAM	RESULT
7			%	%	%	%
8	Hennessy	I	43	48	52	=(((C8+D8)/2)*0.3)+(E8*0.7)
9	Ashdown	H	72	76	65	=(((C9+D9)/2)*0.3)+(E9*0.7)
10	Kirkton	J	82	78	70	=(((C10+D10)/2)*0.3)+(E10*0.7)
11	Ridley	J	34	40	48	=(((C11+D11)/2)*0.3)+(E11*0.7)
12	Stevenson	L	45	55	62	=(((C12+D12)/2)*0.3)+(E12*0.7)
13	Wells	F	89	81	82	=(((C13+D13)/2)*0.3)+(E13*0.7)
14	Ashquar	M	67	73	69	=(((C14+D14)/2)*0.3)+(E14*0.7)
15	Dawson	G	21	16	42	=(((C15+D15)/2)*0.3)+(E15*0.7)
16	Davidson	B	38	42	36	=(((C16+D16)/2)*0.3)+(E16*0.7)
17	Hassan	T	54	56	48	=(((C17+D17)/2)*0.3)+(E17*0.7)
18	Evans	A	52	67	78	=(((C18+D18)/2)*0.3)+(E18*0.7)
19	Lipton	M	54	61	74	=(((C19+D19)/2)*0.3)+(E19*0.7)
20	Davidson	C	79	85	90	=(((C20+D20)/2)*0.3)+(E20*0.7)
21	Peterson	S	74	72	80	=(((C21+D21)/2)*0.3)+(E21*0.7)
22	Johnson	A	51	59	58	=(((C22+D22)/2)*0.3)+(E22*0.7)
23						

STUDENT GRADES

Worksheet for Exercise 17, question 2

	A	B	C	D	E	F
1	GRAYSTONES COLLEGE					
2						
3	DEPARTMENT OF ACCOUNTING				CLASS	
4						
5	SURNAME	INITS	CLASS TEST	CLASS TEST	FINAL	OVERALL
6			DECEMBER	MARCH	EXAM	RESULT
7			%	%	%	%
8	Ashdown	H	72	76	65	68
9	Ashquar	M	67	73	69	69
10	Davidson	B	38	42	36	37
11	Davidson	C	79	85	90	88
12	Dawson	G	21	16	42	35
13	Evans	A	52	67	78	72
14	Hassan	T	54	56	48	50
15	Hennessy	I	43	48	52	50
16	Johnson	A	51	59	58	57
17	Kirkton	J	82	78	70	73
18	Lipton	M	54	61	74	69
19	Peterson	S	74	72	80	78
20	Ridley	J	34	40	48	45
21	Stevenson	L	45	55	62	58
22	Wells	F	89	81	82	83
23						
24	AVERAGE		57.00	60.60	63.60	62.16
25	HIGHEST		89	85	90	88
26	LOWEST		21	16	36	35
27						

Worksheet formulae for Exercise 17, question 2

	A	B	C	D	E	F
1	GRAYSTONES COLLEGE					
2						
3	DEPARTMENT OF ACCOUNTING				CLASS	
4						
5	SURNAME	INITS	CLASS TEST	CLASS TEST	FINAL	OVERALL
6			DECEMBER	MARCH	EXAM	RESULT
7			%	%	%	%
8	Ashdown	H	72	76	65	=(((C8+D8)/2)*0.3)+(E8*0.7)
9	Ashquar	M	67	73	69	=(((C9+D9)/2)*0.3)+(E9*0.7)
10	Davidson	B	38	42	36	=(((C10+D10)/2)*0.3)+(E10*0.7)
11	Davidson	C	79	85	90	=(((C11+D11)/2)*0.3)+(E11*0.7)
12	Dawson	G	21	16	42	=(((C12+D12)/2)*0.3)+(E12*0.7)
13	Evans	A	52	67	78	=(((C13+D13)/2)*0.3)+(E13*0.7)
14	Hassan	T	54	56	48	=(((C14+D14)/2)*0.3)+(E14*0.7)
15	Hennessy	I	43	48	52	=(((C15+D15)/2)*0.3)+(E15*0.7)
16	Johnson	A	51	59	58	=(((C16+D16)/2)*0.3)+(E16*0.7)
17	Kirkton	J	82	78	70	=(((C17+D17)/2)*0.3)+(E17*0.7)
18	Lipton	M	54	61	74	=(((C18+D18)/2)*0.3)+(E18*0.7)
19	Peterson	S	74	72	80	=(((C19+D19)/2)*0.3)+(E19*0.7)
20	Ridley	J	34	40	48	=(((C20+D20)/2)*0.3)+(E20*0.7)
21	Stevenson	L	45	55	62	=(((C21+D21)/2)*0.3)+(E21*0.7)
22	Wells	F	89	81	82	=(((C22+D22)/2)*0.3)+(E22*0.7)
23						
24	AVERAGE		=AVERAGE(C8:C22)	=AVERAGE(D8:D22)	=AVERAGE(E8:E22)	=AVERAGE(F8:F22)
25	HIGHEST		=MAX(C8:C22)	=MAX(D8:D22)	=MAX(E8:E22)	=MAX(F8:F22)
26	LOWEST		=MIN(C8:C22)	=MIN(D8:D22)	=MIN(E8:E22)	=MIN(F8:F22)
27						

STUDENT GRADES

Worksheet for Exercise 17, question 3

	A	B	C	D	E	F	G
1	GRAYSTONES COLLEGE						
2							
3	DEPARTMENT OF ACCOUNTING				CLASS		
4							
5	GRADING TABLE						
6	0	E					
7	40	D					
8	50	C					
9	70	B					
10	85	A					
11							
12	SURNAME	INITS	CLASS TEST	CLASS TEST	FINAL	OVERALL	GRADE
13			DECEMBER	MARCH	EXAM	RESULT	
14			%	%	%	%	
15	Ashdown	H	72	76	65	68	C
16	Ashquar	M	67	73	69	69	C
17	Davidson	B	38	42	36	37	E
18	Davidson	C	79	85	90	88	A
19	Dawson	G	21	16	42	35	E
20	Evans	A	52	67	78	72	B
21	Hassan	T	54	56	48	50	C
22	Hennessy	I	43	48	52	50	C
23	Johnson	A	51	59	58	57	C
24	Kirkton	J	82	78	70	73	B
25	Lipton	M	54	61	74	69	C
26	Peterson	S	74	72	80	78	B
27	Ridley	J	34	40	48	45	D
28	Stevenson	L	45	55	62	58	C
29	Wells	F	89	81	82	83	B
30							
31	AVERAGE		57.00	60.60	63.60	62.16	
32	HIGHEST		89	85	90	88	
33	LOWEST		21	16	36	35	
34							

STUDENT GRADES

Worksheet formulae for Exercise 17, question 3

	A	B	C	D	E	F	G
1	GRAYSTONES COLLEGE						
2							
3	DEPARTMENT OF ACCOUNTING				CLASS		
4							
5	GRADING TABLE						
6	0	E					
7	40	D					
8	50	C					
9	70	B					
10	85	A					
11							
12	SURNAME	INITS	CLASS TEST	CLASS TEST	FINAL EXAM	OVERALL RESULT	GRADE
13			DECEMBER	MARCH			
14			%	%	%	%	
15	Ashdown	H	72	76	65	=(((C15+D15)/2)*0.3)+(E15*0.7)	=VLOOKUP(F15,$A$6:$B$10,2)
16	Ashquar	M	67	73	69	=(((C16+D16)/2)*0.3)+(E16*0.7)	=VLOOKUP(F16,$A$6:$B$10,2)
17	Davidson	B	38	42	36	=(((C17+D17)/2)*0.3)+(E17*0.7)	=VLOOKUP(F17,$A$6:$B$10,2)
18	Davidson	C	79	85	90	=(((C18+D18)/2)*0.3)+(E18*0.7)	=VLOOKUP(F18,$A$6:$B$10,2)
19	Dawson	G	21	16	42	=(((C19+D19)/2)*0.3)+(E19*0.7)	=VLOOKUP(F19,$A$6:$B$10,2)
20	Evans	A	52	67	78	=(((C20+D20)/2)*0.3)+(E20*0.7)	=VLOOKUP(F20,$A$6:$B$10,2)
21	Hassan	T	54	56	48	=(((C21+D21)/2)*0.3)+(E21*0.7)	=VLOOKUP(F21,$A$6:$B$10,2)
22	Hennessy	I	43	48	52	=(((C22+D22)/2)*0.3)+(E22*0.7)	=VLOOKUP(F22,$A$6:$B$10,2)
23	Johnson	A	51	59	58	=(((C23+D23)/2)*0.3)+(E23*0.7)	=VLOOKUP(F23,$A$6:$B$10,2)
24	Kirkton	J	82	78	70	=(((C24+D24)/2)*0.3)+(E24*0.7)	=VLOOKUP(F24,$A$6:$B$10,2)
25	Lipton	M	54	61	74	=(((C25+D25)/2)*0.3)+(E25*0.7)	=VLOOKUP(F25,$A$6:$B$10,2)
26	Peterson	S	74	72	80	=(((C26+D26)/2)*0.3)+(E26*0.7)	=VLOOKUP(F26,$A$6:$B$10,2)
27	Ridley	J	34	40	48	=(((C27+D27)/2)*0.3)+(E27*0.7)	=VLOOKUP(F27,$A$6:$B$10,2)
28	Stevenson	L	45	55	62	=(((C28+D28)/2)*0.3)+(E28*0.7)	=VLOOKUP(F28,$A$6:$B$10,2)
29	Wells	F	89	81	82	=(((C29+D29)/2)*0.3)+(E29*0.7)	=VLOOKUP(F29,$A$6:$B$10,2)
30							
31	AVERAGE		=AVERAGE(C15:C29)	=AVERAGE(D15:D29)	=AVERAGE(E15:E29)	=AVERAGE(F15:F29)	
32	HIGHEST		=MAX(C15:C29)	=MAX(D15:D29)	=MAX(E15:E29)	=MAX(F15:F29)	
33	LOWEST		=MIN(C15:C29)	=MIN(D15:D29)	=MIN(E15:E29)	=MIN(F15:F29)	
34							

STUDENT GRADES

EXERCISE 18: COUNCIL TAX

Worksheet for Exercise 18

	A	B	C	D	E	F	G	H
1	LOCAL GOVERNMENT COUNCIL TAX							
2								
3	TAX BANDS & RATES							
4								
5	HOUSE	TAX	REGIONAL	DISTRICT	WATER			
6	VALUE	BAND	COUNCIL TAX	COUNCIL TAX	CHARGE			
7	£		£	£	£			
8	1	A	271	226	58			
9	27001	B	316	251	65			
10	35001	C	362	277	74			
11	45001	D	404	302	86			
12	58001	E	497	351	101			
13	80001	F	581	403	115			
14	106001	G	673	447	130			
15	212001	H	801	526	160			
16								
17								
18	NAME	HOUSE	DISCOUNT	TAX	REGIONAL	DISTRICT	WATER	AMOUNT
19		VALUE		BAND	TAX	TAX	CHARGE	PAYABLE
20		£			£	£	£	£
21	Resident 1	39000	yes	C	362	277	74	534.75
22	Resident 2	78000	yes	E	497	351	101	711.75
23	Resident 3	49000	no	D	404	302	86	792.00
24	Resident 4	260000	no	H	801	526	160	1487.00
25	Resident 5	55000	no	D	404	302	86	792.00
26	Resident 6	72000	yes	E	497	351	101	711.75
27	Resident 7	44000	no	C	362	277	74	713.00
28	Resident 8	98000	no	F	581	403	115	1099.00
29	Resident 9	25500	yes	A	271	226	58	416.25
30	Resident 10	31000	no	B	316	251	65	632.00
31								

COUNCIL TAX

Worksheet formulae for Exercise 18

	A	B	C	D	E	F	G	H
1	LOCAL GOVERNMENT COUNCIL TAX							
2								
3	TAX BANDS & RATES							
4								
5	HOUSE	TAX	REGIONAL	DISTRICT	WATER			
6	VALUE	BAND	COUNCIL TAX	COUNCIL TAX	CHARGE			
7	£		£	£	£			
8	1	A	271	226	58			
9	27001	B	316	251	65			
10	35001	C	362	277	74			
11	45001	D	404	302	86			
12	56001	E	497	351	101			
13	80001	F	581	403	115			
14	106001	G	673	447	130			
15	212001	H	801	526	160			
16								
17								
18	NAME	HOUSE	DISCOUNT	TAX	REGIONAL	DISTRICT	WATER	AMOUNT
19		VALUE		BAND	TAX	TAX	CHARGE	PAYABLE
20		£			£	£	£	£
21	Resident 1	39000	yes	=VLOOKUP(B21,$A$8:$E$15,2)	=VLOOKUP(B21,$A$8:$E$15,3)	=VLOOKUP(B21,$A$8:$E$15,4)	=VLOOKUP(B21,$A$8:$E$15,5)	=IF(C21="YES",(SUM(E21:G21)*0.75),SUM(E21:G21))
22	Resident 2	78000	yes	=VLOOKUP(B22,$A$8:$E$15,2)	=VLOOKUP(B22,$A$8:$E$15,3)	=VLOOKUP(B22,$A$8:$E$15,4)	=VLOOKUP(B22,$A$8:$E$15,5)	=IF(C22="YES",(SUM(E22:G22)*0.75),SUM(E22:G22))
23	Resident 3	49000	no	=VLOOKUP(B23,$A$8:$E$15,2)	=VLOOKUP(B23,$A$8:$E$15,3)	=VLOOKUP(B23,$A$8:$E$15,4)	=VLOOKUP(B23,$A$8:$E$15,5)	=IF(C23="YES",(SUM(E23:G23)*0.75),SUM(E23:G23))
24	Resident 4	260000	no	=VLOOKUP(B24,$A$8:$E$15,2)	=VLOOKUP(B24,$A$8:$E$15,3)	=VLOOKUP(B24,$A$8:$E$15,4)	=VLOOKUP(B24,$A$8:$E$15,5)	=IF(C24="YES",(SUM(E24:G24)*0.75),SUM(E24:G24))
25	Resident 5	55000	no	=VLOOKUP(B25,$A$8:$E$15,2)	=VLOOKUP(B25,$A$8:$E$15,3)	=VLOOKUP(B25,$A$8:$E$15,4)	=VLOOKUP(B25,$A$8:$E$15,5)	=IF(C25="YES",(SUM(E25:G25)*0.75),SUM(E25:G25))
26	Resident 6	72000	yes	=VLOOKUP(B26,$A$8:$E$15,2)	=VLOOKUP(B26,$A$8:$E$15,3)	=VLOOKUP(B26,$A$8:$E$15,4)	=VLOOKUP(B26,$A$8:$E$15,5)	=IF(C26="YES",(SUM(E26:G26)*0.75),SUM(E26:G26))
27	Resident 7	44000	no	=VLOOKUP(B27,$A$8:$E$15,2)	=VLOOKUP(B27,$A$8:$E$15,3)	=VLOOKUP(B27,$A$8:$E$15,4)	=VLOOKUP(B27,$A$8:$E$15,5)	=IF(C27="YES",(SUM(E27:G27)*0.75),SUM(E27:G27))
28	Resident 8	98000	no	=VLOOKUP(B28,$A$8:$E$15,2)	=VLOOKUP(B28,$A$8:$E$15,3)	=VLOOKUP(B28,$A$8:$E$15,4)	=VLOOKUP(B28,$A$8:$E$15,5)	=IF(C28="YES",(SUM(E28:G28)*0.75),SUM(E28:G28))
29	Resident 9	25500	yes	=VLOOKUP(B29,$A$8:$E$15,2)	=VLOOKUP(B29,$A$8:$E$15,3)	=VLOOKUP(B29,$A$8:$E$15,4)	=VLOOKUP(B29,$A$8:$E$15,5)	=IF(C29="YES",(SUM(E29:G29)*0.75),SUM(E29:G29))
30	Resident 10	31000	no	=VLOOKUP(B30,$A$8:$E$15,2)	=VLOOKUP(B30,$A$8:$E$15,3)	=VLOOKUP(B30,$A$8:$E$15,4)	=VLOOKUP(B30,$A$8:$E$15,5)	=IF(C30="YES",(SUM(E30:G30)*0.75),SUM(E30:G30))
31								

COUNCIL TAX

EXERCISE 19: MORTGAGE PAYMENTS

Worksheet for Exercise 19, question 1

	A	B
1	**ANYOLD BUILDING SOCIETY**	
2		
3	**Mortgage Loan Quotation**	
4		
5	**Mortgage Details**	
6	Annual interest rate	7.00%
7	Repayment term (years)	25
8	Sum borrowed	£30,000
9		
10		
11	Monthly repayment (gross)	£212.03
12		

MORTGAGE PAYMENTS

Worksheet formulae for Exercise 19, question 1

	A	B
1	**ANYOLD BUILDING SOCIETY**	
2		
3	**Mortgage Loan Quotation**	
4		
5	**Mortgage Details**	
6	Annual interest rate	0.07
7	Repayment term (years)	25
8	Sum borrowed	30000
9		
10		
11	Monthly repayment (gross)	=PMT(B6/12,B7*12,-B8)
12		

MORTGAGE PAYMENTS

Worksheet for Exercise 19, question 2

	A	B	C	D
1	**ANYOLD BUILDING SOCIETY**			
2				
3	**Mortgage Loan Quotation**			
4				
5	**Mortgage Details**			
6	Annual interest rate	7.00%		
7	Repayment term (years)	25		
8	Sum borrowed	£30,000		
9				
10				
11	Monthly repayment (gross)	£212.03	Total interest payment (gross)	£33,610.13
12				

MORTGAGE PAYMENTS

Worksheet formulae for Exercise 19, question 2

	A	B	C	D
1	**ANYOLD BUILDING SOCIETY**			
2				
3	**Mortgage Loan Quotation**			
4				
5	**Mortgage Details**			
6	Annual interest rate	0.07		
7	Repayment term (years)	25		
8	Sum borrowed	30000		
9				
10				
11	Monthly repayment (gross)	=PMT(B6/12,B7*12,-B8)	Total interest payment (gross)	=(B11*B7*12)-B8
12				

MORTGAGE PAYMENTS

Worksheet for Exercise 19, question 3

	A	B	C	D
1	**ANYOLD BUILDING SOCIETY**			
2				
3	**Mortgage Loan Quotation**			
4				
5	**Mortgage Details**			
6	Annual interest rate	7.00%		
7	Repayment term (years)	25		
8	Sum borrowed	£30,000		
9	Tax relief rate	15%		
10				
11	Monthly repayment (gross)	£212.03	Total interest payment (gross)	£33,610.13
12	Tax relief	£16.81	Tax relief	£5,041.52
13	Monthly repayment (net)	£195.23	Total interest payment (net)	£28,568.61
14				

MORTGAGE PAYMENTS

Worksheet formulae for Exercise 19, question 3

	A	B	C	D
1	**ANYOLD BUILDING SOCIETY**			
2				
3	**Mortgage Loan Quotation**			
4				
5	**Mortgage Details**			
6	Annual interest rate	0.07		
7	Repayment term (years)	25		
8	Sum borrowed	30000		
9	Tax relief rate	0.15		
10				
11	Monthly repayment (gross)	=PMT(B6/12,B7*12,-B8)	Total interest payment (gross)	=(B11*B7*12)-B8
12	Tax relief	=D12/(B7*12)	Tax relief	** formula below
13	Monthly repayment (net)	=B11-B12	Total interest payment (net)	=D11-D12
14	** FORMULA IN CELL D12 : =IF(B8<=30000,D11*B9,(((PMT(B6/12,B7*12,-30000)*(B7*12))-30000)*B9))			
15				
16				

MORTGAGE PAYMENTS

Worksheet for Exercise 19, question 4

	A	B	C	D
1	ANYOLD BUILDING SOCIETY			
2				
3	Mortgage Loan Quotation			
4				
5	Mortgage Details			
6	Annual interest rate	7.00%		
7	Repayment term (years)	25		
8	Sum borrowed	£30,000		
9	Tax relief rate	15%		
10				
11	Monthly repayment (gross)	£212.03	Total interest payment (gross)	£33,610.13
12	Tax relief	£16.81	Tax relief	£5,041.52
13	Monthly repayment (net)	£195.23	Total interest payment (net)	£28,568.61
14			Total capital repayment	£30,000
15			Total payment	£58,568.61
16				

MORTGAGE PAYMENTS

Worksheet formulae for Exercise 19, question 4

	A	B	C	D
1	ANYOLD BUILDING SOCIETY			
2				
3	Mortgage Loan Quotation			
4				
5	Mortgage Details			
6	Annual interest rate	0.07		
7	Repayment term (years)	25		
8	Sum borrowed	30000		
9	Tax relief rate	0.15		
10				
11	Monthly repayment (gross)	=PMT(B6/12,B7*12,-B8)	Total interest payment (gross)	=(B11*B7*12)-B8
12	Tax relief	=D12/(B7*12)	Tax relief	** formula below
13	Monthly repayment (net)	=B11-B12	Total interest payment (net)	=D11-D12
14			Total capital repayment	=B8
15			Total payment	=D13+D14
16	** FORMULA IN CELL D12 : =IF(B8<=30000,D11*B9,(((PMT(B6/12,B7*12,-30000)*(B7*12))-30000)*B9))			
17				
18				

MORTGAGE PAYMENTS

Worksheet for Exercise 19, question 5

	A	B	C	D
1	**ANYOLD BUILDING SOCIETY**			
2				
3	**Mortgage Loan Quotation**			
4				
5	**Mortgage Details**			
6	Annual interest rate	7.00%		
7	Repayment term (years)	25		
8	Sum borrowed	£30,000		
9	Tax relief rate	15%		
10	Monthly insurance premium	£50.00		
11				
12	**REPAYMENT LOAN**			
13	Monthly repayment (gross)	£212.03	Total interest payment (gross)	£33,610.13
14	Tax relief	£16.81	Tax relief	£5,041.52
15	Monthly repayment (net)	£195.23	Total interest payment (net)	£28,568.61
16			Total capital repayment	£30,000
17			Total payment	£58,568.61
18				
19	**ENDOWMENT LOAN**			
20	Monthly interest payment (gross)	£175.00		
21	Tax relief	£26.25		
22	Monthly interest payment (net)	£148.75		
23	Total monthly payment	£198.75		
24	Total payment	£59,625.00		
25				

MORTGAGE PAYMENTS

Worksheet formulae for Exercise 19, question 5

	A	B	C	D
1	ANYOLD BUILDING SOCIETY			
2				
3	Mortgage Loan Quotation			
4				
5	Mortgage Details			
6	Annual interest rate	0.07		
7	Repayment term (years)	25		
8	Sum borrowed	30000		
9	Tax relief rate	0.15		
10	Monthly insurance premium	50		
11				
12	REPAYMENT LOAN			
13	Monthly repayment (gross)	=PMT(B6/12,B7*12,-B8)	Total interest payment (gross)	=(B13*B7*12)-B8
14	Tax relief	=D14/(B7*12)	Tax relief	=IF(B8<=30000,D13*B9,(((PMT(B6/12,B7*12,-30000)*(B7*12))-30000)*B9))
15	Monthly repayment (net)	=B13-B14	Total interest payment (net)	=D13-D14
16			Total capital repayment	=B8
17			Total payment	=D15+D16
18				
19	ENDOWMENT LOAN			
20	Monthly interest payment (gross)	=(B8*B6)/12		
21	Tax relief	=IF(B8<=30000,B20*B9,((30000*B6)*B9)/12)		
22	Monthly interest payment (net)	=B20-B21		
23	Total monthly payment	=B22+B10		
24	Total payment	=B23*12*B7		
25				

MORTGAGE PAYMENTS

EXERCISE 20 REGIONAL EXPENSES BUDGET

Summary worksheet for Exercise 20

	A	B	C	D	E	F	G
1	SELLING EXPENSES BUDGET JAN - JUNE 199X						
2							
3		JAN	FEB	MAR	APR	MAY	JUN
4		£	£	£	£	£	£
5	SALARIES	24000	24000	24700	25700	26200	26200
6	COMMISSION	19000	19000	21500	22500	25500	25500
7	CAR EXPENSES	4500	4800	5800	5800	5700	5800
8	ADVERTISING	6700	6900	8500	8500	9000	8900
9	TOTAL	54200	54700	60500	62500	66400	66400

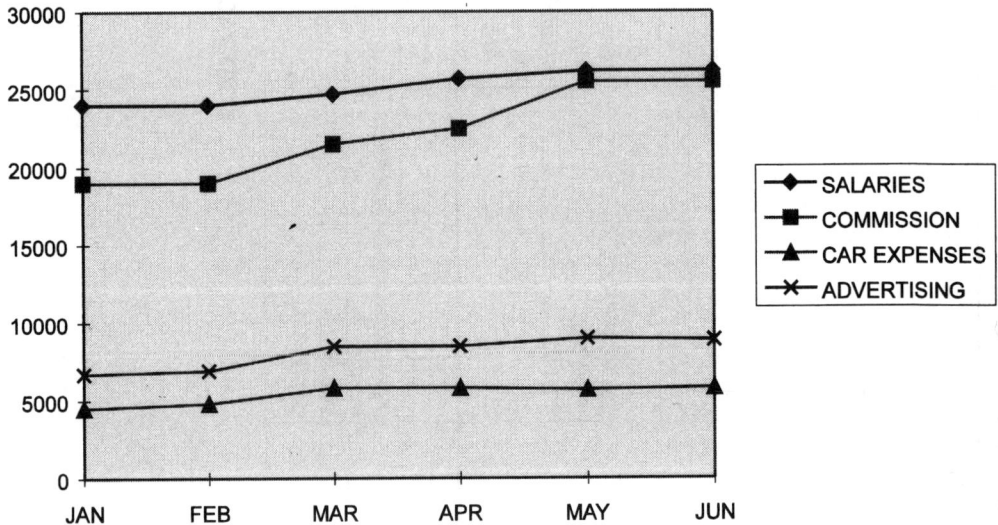

FORMULA IN CELL B5 :
=SUM(ENGLAND:WALES!B5)
This formula is then copied to other relevant cells.

REGIONAL EXPENSES BUDGET

INDEX

NB   Emboldened numbers indicate an illustration on the page.